Progress in Behavior Modification

Volume 30

Progress in Behavior Modification

Volume 30

Edited by

Michel Hersen
NOVA UNIVERSITY

Richard M. Eisler
VIRGINIA POLYTECHNIC INSTITUTE
AND STATE UNIVERSITY

Peter M. Miller
HILTON HEAD HEALTH INSTITUTE

Brooks/Cole Publishing Company

I**T**P™An International Thomson Publishing Company

Pacific Grove • Albany • Bonn • Boston • Cincinnati • Detroit • London • Madrid • Melbourne
Mexico City • New York • Paris • San Francisco • Singapore • Tokyo • Toronto • Washington

Sponsoring Editor: *Vicki Knight*
Marketing Team: *Carolyn Crockett and Jean Vevers Thompson*
Editorial Associate: *Lauri Banks Ataide*
Production Editor: *Laurel Jackson*
Production Assistant: *Dorothy Bell*
Manuscript Editor: *Kay Mikel*
Permissions Editor: *Cathleen S. Collins*

Interior Design: *Vernon T. Boes*
Cover Design: *Laurie Albrecht*
Art Editor: *Lisa Torri*
Indexer: *James Minkin*
Typesetting: *Joan Mueller Cochrane*
Cover Printing: *Phoenix Color Corporation, Inc.*
Printing and Binding: *Quebecor Printing Fairfield*

For more information, contact:

BROOKS/COLE PUBLISHING COMPANY
511 Forest Lodge Road
Pacific Grove, CA 93950
USA

International Thomson Publishing Europe
Berkshire House 168–173
High Holborn
London WC1V 7AA
England

Thomas Nelson Australia
102 Dodds Street
South Melbourne, 3205
Victoria, Australia

Nelson Canada
1120 Birchmount Road
Scarborough, Ontario
Canada M1K 5G4

International Thomson Editores
Campos Eliseos 385, Piso 7
Col. Polanco
11560 México D. F. México

International Thomson Publishing GmbH
Königswinterer Strasse 418
53227 Bonn
Germany

International Thomson Publishing Asia
221 Henderson Road
#05–10 Henderson Building
Singapore 0315

International Thomson Publishing Japan
Hirakawacho Kyowa Building, 3F
2-2-1 Hirakawacho
Chiyoda-ku, Tokyo 102
Japan

Printed in the United States of America

10   9   8   7   6   5   4   3   2   1

ISBN: 0-534-26304-6

ISSN: 0099-037X

THIS BOOK IS PRINTED ON ACID-FREE RECYCLED PAPER

CONTRIBUTORS

STEVEN R. H. BEACH is currently Associate Professor and Director of the Psychology Clinic at the University of Georgia. His current research interests include marital discord, depression, and self-protective processes in marriage.

GAIL S. BERNSTEIN (Ph.D.), a licensed psychologist in private practice, has a clinical faculty appointment at the University of Denver School of Professional Psychology. Her clinical and academic interests include the unique mental health needs of lesbians and gay men, women's issues, and adult survivors of child abuse.

PATRICK A. BOUDEWYNS (Ph.D.) is Professor in the Department of Psychiatry and Health Behavior at the Medical College of Georgia and the Chief, Psychology Service, at the Augusta VA Medical Center. He is past president of Division 18 (Psychologists in Public Service) of the APA. His current research is focused on psychotherapy outcome studies in combat-related posttraumatic stress disorder.

AMY E. BROOKS is a doctoral candidate at the University of Georgia. Her research interests include the role of aggressive and depressive behaviors in marital interaction, HIV knowledge and risk behaviors, and the neuropsychological aspects of AIDS and of aging.

GREGORY N. CLARKE (Ph.D.) is an assistant professor in the Department of Psychiatry at the Oregon Health Sciences University and Associate Director of the Western Mental Health Research Center. His clinical and research interests include prevention, treatment, and epidemiology of adolescent and adult unipolar depression; anabolic steroid abuse prevention; and the costs and utilization of mental health services for persons with severe mental illness. He is the principal author of the *Adolescent Coping with Depression Course.*

RICHARD G. HEIMBERG (Ph.D.) is Professor of Psychology at the University at Albany, State University of New York, and director of the Social Phobia Program at the University at Albany's Center for Stress and Anxiety Disorders. He is currently conducting research on a variety of topics related to social phobia, including the relative efficacy of cognitive behavioral and pharmacological treatment methods, information processing biases among social phobics, the relationship of social phobia to depression and Axis II disorders, and methods for the assessment of social phobia. Dr. Heimberg is the author of two forthcoming books

(both from Guilford Press), *Treatment of Social Fears and Phobias* (with Robert Becker) and *Social Phobia: Diagnosis, Assessment, and Treatment* (with Michael Liebowitz, Debra Hope, and Franklin Schneier).

HARRY M. HOBERMAN (Ph.D.) is an assistant professor of psychiatry at the Division of Child and Adolescent Psychiatry. He is the co-director of clinics for youth with mood disorders and with eating disorders. His varied research interests include psychiatric epidemiology, particularly regarding disadvantaged populations; psychotherapy outcome studies emphasizing the relationship between process and outcome; and mental health services for youth.

CRAIG S. HOLT (Ph.D.) is Assistant Professor, Departments of Psychology and Psychiatry, University of Iowa, and staff psychologist, VA Medical Center, Iowa City. His current research interests include assessment and treatment of anxiety disorders and the relation of psychopathology to quality of life and the social environment.

HARLAN R. JUSTER (Ph.D.) is a postdoctoral associate with the Social Phobia Program at the University at Albany's Center for Stress and Anxiety Disorders. His clinical and research interests include the assessment and treatment of anxiety disorders and the impact of childhood abuse on adult functioning.

BARBARA S. KOHLENBERG is a graduate student in clinical psychology at the University of Nevada–Reno and works for the VA psychology service in the addictive disorders treatment program. Her research interests are in stimulus equivalence and radical behavioral views of psychotherapy. She also is interested in the scientific analysis of psychotherapy supervision.

ROBERT J. KOHLENBERG (Ph.D.) is an associate professor of psychology at the University of Washington. In-depth psychotherapy and its integration with cognitive behavior therapy are his primary research and clinical interests.

ANDREW W. MEYERS (Ph.D.) is Professor of Psychology and Chairman of the Department of Psychology at Memphis State University. Dr. Meyers has published extensively in the areas of sport psychology, behavioral medicine, and children's problem solving. He is a Fellow of both the Association for the Advancement of Applied Sport Psychology and the American Psychological Association's Division

47. Dr. Meyers is currently on the editorial boards of *The Sport Psychologist, Journal of Exercise and Sport Psychology, and Journal of Applied Sport Psychology.*

MEGAN E. MILLER (Ph.D.) is a psychotherapist in private practice. Her clinical, political, and academic interests include women's issues, deafness, and psychotherapy with lesbians and gay men.

SHANE M. MURPHY (Ph.D.), a native of Australia, has been with the U.S. Olympic Committee for six years, first as head of the Department of Sport Psychology and currently as chair of the Athlete Performance Division. He is vitally concerned with helping athletes reach peak performance levels, educating coaches, and helping athletes at all levels to enjoy sport participation. Dr. Murphy has published numerous articles on sport psychology, serves on the editorial board of *The Sport Psychologist,* and is currently completing a book entitled *Clinical Sport Psychology.*

STEPHEN M. SAUNDERS (Ph.D.) is a clinical psychologist at the University of Minnesota Department of Psychiatry. His clinical and research interests are in the areas of mental health help-seeking, health psychology, and processes and outcomes of psychotherapy.

MAVIS TSAI (Ph.D.) is a psychologist in private practice and a clinical supervisor of graduate students at the University of Washington. Her clinical and research interests include intensive psychotherapy, adult survivors of childhood sexual abuse, and ethnic minority mental health.

JAMES P. WHELAN (Ph.D.) is an assistant professor and Director of the Psychological Services Center in the Department of Psychology at Memphis State University. Dr. Whelan's sport psychology interests include athletic performance enhancement and the role of sport and exercise involvement in psychological well-being. His primary clinical research area is psychotherapy outcome research, and he has published in the areas of treatment of child abuse and neglect, children's adjustment to disabilities, and pediatric health psychology. Dr. Whelan is also actively involved with legal and professional practice standards for psychologists.

KATHERINE R. WRIGHT is a doctoral candidate at the University of Georgia. Her research interests are marital interaction and the relationship of physical and mental illness to long-term family functioning.

PREFACE

Number 30 is the second volume of *Progress in Behavior Modification* published by Brooks/Cole Publishing Company. It contains seven chapters that deal with a variety of issues.

In Chapter 1, "Functional Analysis in Behavior Therapy," Robert J. Kohlenberg, Mavis Tsai, and Barbara S. Kohlenberg review the important underpinnings of the functional analysis in behavior therapy. With a clear historical context as a basis, the authors carefully consider the therapist-client relationship, particularly as it applies to reciprocal inhibition, social skills training, and cognitive therapy. The authors also present a revised formulation of cognitive therapy, its clinical implications, and the new directions it might take in the future.

In Chapter 2, "Psychological Interventions for Adolescent Depression: Issues, Evidence, and Future Directions," Harry M. Hoberman, Gregory N. Clarke, and Stephen M. Saunders consider in detail a much-neglected issue in psychotherapeutics: psychosocial interactions with depressed adolescents. Not only do the authors examine the definition, phenomenology, epidemiology, associated clinical characteristics, antecedents, and developmental factors of adolescent depression, but they also describe all the extant psychosocial strategies. The strategies reviewed are cognitive behavior therapy, interpersonal psychotherapy, psychodynamic therapy, and family therapy. The authors carefully review the literature with respect to pharmacotherapy, case studies, uncontrolled psychotherapy evaluations, and controlled outcome studies. The critical issues of the suicidal adolescent and preventive strategies also are presented in detail.

In Chapter 3, "Social Phobia: Diagnostic Issues and Review of Cognitive Behavioral Treatment Strategies," Harlan R. Juster, Richard G. Heimberg, and Craig S. Holt review the diagnostic and cognitive behavioral treatment strategies carried out with social phobia. In an incisive critique of the existing studies in this area, Juster and his colleagues point out the methodological problems with the studies conducted to date. Some of these problems relate to subclassifi-cations of social phobias as they are matched to specific treatments, whereas the more critical methodological issue relates to the absence of no-treatment comparison groups.

In Chapter 4, "Behavioral Treatment of Depression in the Context of Marital Discord," Steven R. H. Beach, Amy E. Brooks, and Katherine R. Wright evaluate the use of behavioral approaches to treating depression in the context of marital discord. In so doing, the authors first consider various aspects of depressed persons and their spouses, such as the magnitude of the relationship, its temporal patterning, and its behavioral manifestations. The authors identify and describe the components of marital therapy in depression, including the final phase of therapy: enhancing maintenance. Beach and his colleagues then examine the empirical literature documenting efficacy of this strategy and follow this discussion with a section on prevention.

In Chapter 5, "Behavior Therapy with Lesbian and Gay Individuals," Gail S. Bernstein and Megan E. Miller survey the growing body of literature on behavior therapy strategies with lesbian and gay individuals. After they describe the historical issues, the authors examine cultural and institutional contextual variables, assessment and case formulation, and extant treatment. The chapter ends with recommendations for research, training, and professional development in this area.

In Chapter 6, "Cognitive Behavioral Strategies in Athletic Performance Enhancement," Andrew W. Meyers, James P. Whelan, and Shane M. Murphy present the reader with a look at how cognitive behavioral strategies can enhance athletic performance. The chapter begins with the scope and history of sport psychology, followed by a description of currently applied cognitive behavioral interventions. The chapter also includes sections on treatment effectiveness, design issues, generalizability, and how these strategies might be applied to elite athletes.

Finally, in Chapter 7, "Posttraumatic Stress Disorder: Conceptualization and Treatment," Patrick A.

Boudewyns considers the behavioral conceptualization and treatment of PTSD (posttraumatic stress disorder). Not only does Boudewyns outline the behavioral approach, but he also looks at the problem from psychodynamic and information processing theory, Foa's behavioral cognitive model, and the biological perspective. In the review on treatment strategies, the author presents case demonstrations, uncontrolled outcome studies, and controlled outcome studies. Additional issues discussed include PTSD in children and the use of pharmacotherapy for PTSD.

Many individuals have, of course, contributed to the fruition of Volume 30. First of all, we thank our eminent contributors for sharing their expertise with us. Second, we thank Burt G. Bolton for his technical expertise. And third, but hardly least of all, we appreciate the efforts of Vicki Knight and her colleagues at Brooks/Cole.

Michel Hersen
Richard M. Eisler
Peter M. Miller

BRIEF CONTENTS

Chapter 1   1
Functional Analysis in Behavior Therapy
Robert J. Kohlenberg, Mavis Tsai, Barbara S. Kohlenberg

Chapter 2   25
Psychological Interventions for Adolescent Depression: Issues, Evidence, and Future Directions
Harry M. Hoberman, Gregory N. Clarke, Stephen M. Saunders

Chapter 3   74
Social Phobia: Diagnostic Issues and Review of Cognitive Behavioral Treatment Strategies
Harlan R. Juster, Richard G. Heimberg, Craig S. Holt

Chapter 4   99
Behavioral Treatment of Depression in the Context of Marital Discord
Steven R. H. Beach, Amy E. Brooks, Katherine R. Wright

Chapter 5   123
Behavior Therapy with Lesbian and Gay Individuals
Gail S. Bernstein, Megan E. Miller

Chapter 6   137
Cognitive Behavioral Strategies in Athletic Performance Enhancement
Andrew W. Meyers, James P. Whelan, Shane M. Murphy

Chapter 7   165
Posttraumatic Stress Disorder: Conceptualization and Treatment
Patrick A. Boudewyns

CONTENTS

Chapter 1   1
Functional Analysis in Behavior Therapy
  Robert J. Kohlenberg, Mavis Tsai,
  Barbara S. Kohlenberg

I. Introduction   2
II. The Functional Definition of Functional Analysis   2
A. *Reinforcement   3*
B. *Contextualism   3*
III. A Functional Analysis of Behavior Therapy   4
A. *What the Therapist and the Client Do   4*
B. *The Therapeutic Relationship in Behavior Therapy   5*
IV. Historical Factors   7
A. *The Animal Model   7*
B. *Empiricism   7*
V. The Adult Outpatient Within-Session Behavior
Conundrum   9
A. *Psychotherapy by Reciprocal Inhibition   9*
B. *Social Skills Training   9*
C. *Cognitive Therapy   10*
VI. A Functional Analysis of Cognitive Therapy   10
A. *Problems with Cognitive Therapy and the* ABC
Paradigm   10
B. *Revised Formulation of Cognitive Therapy   12*
C. *A Functional Analytic Revision   13*
VII. New Directions   20
References   21

Chapter 2   25
Psychological Interventions for Adolescent Depression:
  Issues, Evidence, and Future Directions
  Harry M. Hoberman, Gregory N. Clarke,
  Stephen M. Saunders

I. Introduction   26
II. Adolescent Psychotherapy Research   26
III. The Nature of Depressive Disorders among
Adolescents   28
A. *Definition   28*
B. *Phenomenology of Adolescent Depression   29*
C. *Epidemiology of Adolescent Depression   30*
D. *Associated Clinical Characteristics of Depressive
Episodes during Adolescence   30*
E. *Psychosocial Correlates and Antecedents of
Adolescent Depression   33*
F. *Developmental Factors in Increased Risk for
Depressive Episodes during Adolescence   33*
G. *Mental Health Services Utilization among
Depressed Youth   34*
IV. Etiological Theories and Models of Psychosocial
Treatment of Depressive Episodes   34
V. Efficacy of Psychotherapy of Depressive
Episodes among Adults   37
VI. Theories and Issues in the Psychosocial
Treatment of Depressed Adolescents   38
A. *Etiological and Maintenance Factors in Adole-
scent Depression: Common Targets in the Treat-
ment of Depressed Adolescents   38*
B. *Models of Treatment of Depressive Disorders in
Adolescents   39*
VII. Treatment Outcome Research for Depressive
Disorders among Adolescents   44
A. *Pharmacologic Treatment of Adolescent
Depression   44*
B. *Psychotherapy Case Studies   45*
C. *Uncontrolled Psychotherapy Studies   45*
D. *Controlled Psychotherapy Outcome Studies   52*
E. *Comparative Psychotherapy Outcome Studies   52*
VIII. Psychosocial Treatments of Suicidal
Adolescents   55
IX. Prevention of Adolescent Depression   57
X. Common Tactics and Developmental Considera-
tions in Psychosocial Treatments for Depressed
Adolescents   58
XI. Critique and Future Direction of Psychosocial
Treatments for Adolescent Depression   60
XII. Conclusion   65
References   65

Chapter 3   74
Social Phobia: Diagnostic Issues and Review of
  Cognitive Behavioral Treatment Strategies
  Harlan R. Juster, Richard G. Heimberg, Craig S. Holt

I. Introduction   75
II. Diagnostic Issues   75
A. *Diagnostic Criteria for Social Phobia   76*
B. *Empirical Support for Subtypes of Social Phobia   76*
C. *Generalized Social Phobia and Avoidant
Personality Disorder   78*

D. Situationist Perspective   *79*
E. DSM-IV   *80*
III. Treatment Review   81
A. Social Skills Training   *81*
B. Exposure   *85*
C. Cognitive Interventions   *88*
IV. Conclusions and Recommendations   95
References   96

Chapter 4   99
Behavioral Treatment of Depression in the Context of Marital Discord
Steven R. H. Beach, Amy E. Brooks,
Katherine R. Wright

I. Introduction   100
II. Depressed Persons and Their Spouses   100
A. Magnitude of the Relationship between Marital
Discord and Depression   *100*
B. Temporal Patterning of the Relationship between
Marital Discord and Depression   *101*
C. Observation of Depressed Persons Interacting with
Their Spouses   *101*
III. The Marital Discord Model and Basic Points of
Intervention   104
A. Overview of the Marital Discord Model   *104*
IV. Marital Therapy for Depression in the Context of
Marital Discord   105
A. First Phase of Therapy: Identifying and Eliminating
Stressors   *106*
B. Second Phase of Therapy: Enhancing Communication
and Interaction   *108*
C. Third Phase of Therapy: Enhancing
Maintenance   *110*
V. Individual Approaches with Maritally Discordant
and Depressed Persons   111
A. Social Skills Training   *112*
B. Cognitive Therapy   *112*
VI. Outcome of Marital Interventions for
Depression   113
A. Early Investigations of Dyadic Treatment with
Heterogeneous Populations   *113*
B. Outcome Work with Depressed Outpatients   *114*
C. Outcome Work with Depressed Inpatients   *117*
VII. Can Depression Be Prevented?   117
VIII. Conclusion   118
References   118

Chapter 5   123
Behavior Therapy with Lesbian and Gay Individuals
Gail S. Bernstein, Megan E. Miller

I. Introduction   124
II. History of Behavior Therapy with Lesbians and Gay
Men   124
A. Articles and Papers   *125*
B. Clinical Practice   *126*
C. Books   *126*
D. Professional Organizations   *127*
E. Summary   *127*
III. Case Formulation and Treatment   127
A. Cultural and Institutional Contextual Variables   *128*
B. Assessment and Case Formulation   *129*
C. Treatment   *131*
IV. Recommendations   132
A. Research   *132*
B. Training   *133*
C. Professional Development   *133*
V. Conclusion   134
References   134

Chapter 6   137
Cognitive Behavioral Strategies in Athletic Performance
Enhancement
Andrew W. Meyers, James P. Whelan,
Shane M. Murphy

I. Introduction   138
II. Scope and History   138
A. Scope of Sport Psychology   *138*
B. History of Sport Psychology   *138*
III. Cognitive Behavioral Interventions   140
A. A Cautionary Note on Adopting a Model   *140*
B. Goal Setting   *140*
C. Imagery and Mental Rehearsal   *142*
D. Arousal Management   *143*
E. Cognitive Self-Regulation   *144*
F. Multicomponent Interventions   *145*
IV. Quantitative Review   146
A. Existing Reviews   *146*
B. Execution of the Meta-Analysis   *146*
C. The Database   *147*
D. Overall Effectiveness of Psychological
Interventions   *148*
E. Reliability of Treatment Effectiveness   *149*

F. Design Issues   153
G. Generalizability   155
V. Applications to Elite Athletes   157
VI. Summary and Conclusions   158
References   159

Chapter 7   165

Posttraumatic Stress Disorder: Conceptualization and
Treatment
Patrick A. Boudewyns

I. Historical Overview: What's in a Name?   166
II. PTSD: Definition, Epidemiology, and
Codiagnoses   167
III. Conceptual Models of PTSD and the Sequelae of
Trauma   171
*A. Horowitz's Psychodynamic and Information
Processing Theory   171*
B. Conditioning and Learning Models   172
C. Foa's Behavioral Cognitive Model   174
D. Biological Approaches   174
E. A Comprehensive Model of PTSD   175
IV. Treatment Strategies   176
A. Behavioral Strategies   176
*B. Case Demonstrations and Uncontrolled Outcome
Studies   177*
C. Controlled Outcome Studies   178
V. PTSD in Children   183
VI. Conclusions Regarding Treatment of PTSD   183
VII. A Word about Pharmacotherapy for PTSD   184
VIII. Summary and Conclusions   184
References   185

Name Index   191
Subject Index   199

CHAPTER 1

Functional Analysis in Behavior Therapy

Robert J. Kohlenberg
Mavis Tsai
Barbara S. Kohlenberg

I. Introduction
II. The Functional Definition of Functional Analysis
   A. Reinforcement
   B. Contextualism
III. A Functional Analysis of Behavior Therapy
   A. What the Therapist and the Client Do
   B. The Therapeutic Relationship in Behavior Therapy
IV. Historical Factors
   A. The Animal Model
   B. Empiricism
V. The Adult Outpatient Within-Session Behavior Conundrum
   A. Psychotherapy by Reciprocal Inhibition
   B. Social Skills Training
   C. Cognitive Therapy
VI. A Functional Analysis of Cognitive Therapy
   A. Problems with Cognitive Therapy and the *ABC* Paradigm
   B. Revised Formulation of Cognitive Therapy
   C. A Functional Analytic Revision
      1. Contingency-Shaped Behavior
      2. Tacts and Mands: Two Types of Verbal Behavior
      3. Rule-Governed Behavior
      4. Cognitive Structures and Contingency-Shaped Behavior
      5. Clinical Implications
VII. New Directions
References

I. Introduction

In his 1991 presidential address to the Association for the Advancement of Behavior Therapy, Neil Jacobson chided the audience for ignoring functional analysis. As a result of this inattention, he stated, "behavior therapy is not very behavioral." Haynes and O'Brien (1990) found that only 20% of a sample of behavior therapy studies employed a functional analysis. How is it possible that "behavior therapy" is "not very behavioral," and what is this "functional analysis" that behavior therapists do not do? Cognitive behavior therapists who are knowledgeable about functional analysis but who do not do it may ask: "So what—why would anyone want to be 'more behavioral' when just the opposite, 'being more cognitive,' has proven to be so useful?"

The purpose of this chapter is to answer these questions and to show how a reintroduction of functional analysis into behavior therapy, and even into cognitive therapy, can expand our horizons both in terms of treatment methods and in the range of clinical problems deemed suitable for behavior therapists to treat. Our discussion will focus on cognitive behavior therapy for adults who typically are seen in an office setting. We will begin by defining functional analysis and then show how a functional analysis can be applied to behavior therapy. Next, we examine the historical factors leading to a deemphasis on functional analysis and the derivation of current behavior therapies: psychotherapy by reciprocal inhibition, social skills training, and cognitive therapy. Since cognitive therapy is the most prevalent treatment used by behavior therapists, we devote the bulk of our analysis to the problems in cognitive therapy and to some functional analytic solutions. We end with a look at the exciting new therapeutic directions functional analysis has opened for us.

II. The Functional Definition of Functional Analysis

Since a functional analysis is a type of analysis, it is a process performed by a person. For the purposes of this chapter, that person is the behavior therapist. The most accurate way to define a process is to specify the results obtained as a consequence of engaging in that process, in other words, a functional definition. According to Skinner (1953), the results of a functional analysis yield "the external variables of which behavior is a function" (p. 35). Thus, any process that yields the external variables is a functional analysis.

Since functional analysis is nearly synonymous with a radical behavioral approach, it is important to understand radical behaviorism to properly assess the role of functional analysis in behavior therapy. Radical behaviorism (Skinner, 1953, 1969, 1974), however, is the "most widely misunderstood term in psychology" (Branch, 1987, p. 80).

The misunderstanding of functional analysis and radical behaviorism has a long history (see Catania, 1991; Morris, 1990), and the tenets of radical behaviorism have been explained many times with seemingly limited success (for example, see Branch, 1987; Day, 1969; Hayes, 1987; Kohlenberg & Tsai, 1991). As a means of increasing understanding, this chapter will emphasize the application of (or lack of) functional analysis in cognitive behavior therapy. With the exception of the section on reinforcement and contextualism, radical behavioral concepts will be clarified along the way as needed.

Let us now return to the aim of a functional analysis. According to the definition, you will know you have done a functional analysis if you are able to specify (a) the causes[1] of the client's problem behavior and (b) the changes in terms of external variables as a result of therapy. Simplistic as it appears, this goal of functional analysis has profound and far-reaching implications for the practice of behavior therapy that are more relevant today than ever before (Glenn, 1983; Hayes, 1987; Kohlenberg & Tsai, 1991). For one, using a functional analysis would lead the

---

[1] According to Skinner (1953), "The terms cause and effect are no longer widely used in science. The terms which replace them, however, refer to the same factual core. A 'cause' becomes a 'change in an independent variable' and an 'effect' a 'change in a dependent variable.' The old 'cause and effect' connection becomes a 'functional relation.' Any condition or event which can be shown to have an effect on behavior must be taken into account" (p. 23).

"We undertake to predict and control the behavior of the individual organism. This is our 'dependent variable'—the effect for which we are to find the cause" (1953, p. 35).

behavior[2] therapist into a more complete consideration of the therapist-client relationship—a relatively neglected factor in the field. For another, it would provide a unifying theoretical background that can accommodate the traditional methods used by behavior therapists as well as the highly effective procedures of cognitive therapy.

A sophisticated use of functional analysis by behavior therapists would also lead to new avenues of treatment such as acceptance (as opposed to behavior change) and nondidactic, in-depth, emotionally based methods. Additionally, functional analysis can expand the types of client problems that are suitable for behavior therapy. Through the use of functional analysis, problems of the self such as multiple personality, narcissistic personality disorder, and self-identity problems that have traditionally been difficult to describe in cognitive behavioral terms can be included.

A. Reinforcement

The definition of functional analysis refers only to external variables and does not make any reference to contingencies of reinforcement. In this spirit, any external "condition or event must be taken into account" (Skinner, 1953, p. 23). What is most important here is the emphasis on "external." External refers to something from the outside applied to clients that affects their behavior. Therapy done by one person with another is *always* external.

To assure that the causes we discover are external ones (which can then be used by therapists), Hayes and Brownstein (1986) have argued that causal explanations ultimately should be given in terms of contingencies. We say *ultimately* because intermediate external causes, such as the interventions of cognitive therapy, are often useful and sufficient. As discussed later, however, cognitive interventions can potentially be even more effective if their connection to reinforcement is delineated. The requirement that explanations ultimately refer to reinforcement does not preclude the importance of cognition or feeling in therapeutic work. These points are discussed in more detail later in our discussion of cognitive therapy.

We use the term *reinforcement* in its technical, generic sense, referring to all consequences or contingencies that affect (increase or decrease) the strength of behavior. The definition of reinforcement is a functional one; that is, something can be defined as a reinforcer only after it has shown an effect in increasing or decreasing the strength of a behavior.

The requirement of ultimately identifying contingencies has an important implication. Functional analytic explanations always go back into the past and are known as reinforcement history. For example, a client may say he yelled at his spouse because he was angry. This explanation, given in terms of current variables, can be useful for many purposes. It is not satisfactory, however, as a functional analytic explanation; this would require information about the past contingencies[3] that account for (1) the getting angry and (2) the yelling. That is, not all spouses get angry under those circumstances nor, even if they are angry, do all spouses yell. The functional analytic explanation addresses these issues.

B. Contextualism

Early in his career, the first author was having a discussion with Bob Pagano, a colleague who rejected the functional analytic approach and its emphasis on explaining everything ultimately in terms of reinforcement. He said to me, "So you think that nearly all behavior occurs because you have been reinforced for emitting it?" "Yes," I emphatically replied, "That's right." "Does that include your verbal behavior right now?" he asked. Somewhat hesitantly, since I was wary of where this was going, I said, "Sure, since my talking is behaving, and behavior is the result of reinforcement, then what I am saying now comes from my reinforcement history." "Well, then," he said, "how can you be sure that your beliefs about reinforcement are really true or, alternatively, that they merely reflect what you have been reinforced for believing and saying about such matters?" I was stymied and sputtered something about him not understanding, and the discussion ended. In my heart,

---

[2]We use the term *behavior therapy* (and *behavior therapist*) generically, which also includes cognitive therapy.

[3]Keep in mind that past contingencies include contingencies of survival that could implicate genetic predispositions in a functional analytic explanation of getting angry.

however, I was deeply troubled by the logical problems of my position.

What I did not realize back then was that reinforcement theory is, at its core, a contextualist theory (Hayes, 1987; Hayes, Hayes, & Reese, 1988; Pepper, 1957). There are two significant implications of this approach. First, there is no such thing as ultimate truth.[4] Second, and most important, a complete functional analysis of a person's actions by a functional analyst must include an analysis of why we say what we do and, hence, an analysis of the functional analyst's behavior as well. Thus, the role of functional analysis in behavior therapy requires, so to speak, that we take one step back from the behavior therapy we are doing and examine the actions and verbal behavior of the behavior therapist as well as the client. Our review of functional analysis in behavior therapy begins with an overview of a functional analysis *of* behavior therapy.

III. A Functional Analysis of Behavior Therapy

Two people sitting in an office are talking to each other. One is a client who has problems that occur in daily life. The client is an outpatient who voluntarily comes to the session and pays for the time of the therapist. The other person, the therapist, does not observe the client outside of the session and has no control over the contingencies present in the client's daily life. The therapist's task is to help the client by acting in ways that favorably affect daily life behavior. This situation is known as adult outpatient behavior therapy.

A functional analysis of behavior therapy requires that we account for the client and the therapist doing what they do during the session as well as how these activities help the client in her or his daily life.

A. What the Therapist and the Client Do

A typical behavior therapy consists of the client asking for help with some type of problem, the thera-

pist doing an assessment and treatment, and the client reacting to what the therapist does. A lot of give and take occurs in the process, and the whole endeavor is known as the client-therapist interaction.

A behavior therapy for adult outpatients begins with the client initiating treatment, which includes deciding to seek therapy, selecting a therapist, presenting a problem, and asking for help. We will focus our analysis on "asking for help," but it could equally apply to any other aspect of the client initiating treatment. Our analysis of "asking for help" will also serve to illustrate some of the general implications of a functional analysis.

A functional analysis first leads to a focus on the reinforcement history that brings a client to ask for help. That is, "asking for help" itself is seen as a behavior that needs to be accounted for. There are probably as many different kinds of reinforcement histories relevant to "asking for help" as there are clients. We will describe several types that serve to illustrate the implications of our analysis. For each of these cases, we can assume there is a distressing daily life problem.

First, there are clients for whom "asking for help" with a particular problem has, in the past, been reinforced by actually being helped with that problem. This history probably involved childhood experiences with parents who were good at providing help when asked; later, similar experiences with doctors, ministers, and friends would also be relevant. In "asking for help," the client acts toward the behavior therapist in a manner that resembles similar past relationships; thus, it is a social interaction and an aspect of the therapist-client relationship. We will term this type of history the *face value history*.

Behavior therapists are not inclined to pay much attention to the client's "asking for help" as a behavior to be analyzed or to the therapist-client relationship as central issues. Thus, the "asking" is probably not considered in terms of its history or as a social interaction or as a behavior that reflects experiences in past relationships. Instead, behavior therapists tend to implicitly assume a face value history and do not see the "asking" as an important aspect of the therapist-client relationship.

In response to the client asking for help, the behavior therapist assesses by requesting information (in-

---

[4]Truth, according to contextual theory as described by Pepper (1957), is based on its usefulness.

cluding data collection and so forth) about what happens during his or her daily life. The behavior therapist then classifies the client's problem (for example, agoraphobia, marital distress, anger problems, depression, lack of assertive skills), and a treatment is selected and applied. In the case of a client with a face value history, the behavior therapist's neglect of analyzing the client's verbal behavior and viewing it in the context of the client-therapist relationship is of little consequence, and a favorable outcome can be expected.

Second, in contrast to the face value history, there are clients whose "asking for help" for one problem has been reinforced in the past by the avoidance of other unrelated, negative situations or is a means to find out what they really feel and want. In this case, the problem presented to the behavior therapist is not the client's most important daily life problem. For example, a client asking for help in saving his or her marriage may actually wish to end the marriage and may not even be able to admit this to himself or herself. Another example is a client who asks for help with agoraphobia but who has learned to accept the phobic responses. Instead, this client is asking for help as a means to stop a spouse from pressuring him or her to go into feared places or to avoid conflict in the relationship. In these cases, the verbal behavior of "asking for help for a particular problem" cannot be taken at face value. These clients do need help—but not for the problem presented. In these cases, the inclination of behavior therapists to avoid viewing the "asking" as a verbal behavior to be analyzed may have deleterious effects. The behavior therapy interventions selected are likely not to be appropriate and improvements will be minimal.

Third, another type of non–face value history could result in the client "asking for help" to obtain the attention and caring of the therapist. Histories leading to this type of asking for help involved parents or other caretakers who gave attention and care only when the client was dysfunctional and requested help. The client continues to approach relationships in this manner, including the client-therapist relationship. These clients are sometimes known as dependent personalities whose daily life problems involve an overreliance on others. The presenting symptoms, such as anxiety or depression, are only indirectly related to their main daily life problem. The within-session behavior of the client is thus an in vivo instance of his or her daily life problems. In this instance, the behavior therapist may inadvertently strengthen the problematic behavior if he or she fails to view the "asking" as a behavior to be analyzed and fails to understand that the client-therapist relationship has properties that evoke the same behavior that occurs in other problematic relationships.

The didactic, programmatic nature of the behavior therapist's interventions are prone to evoke important, unintended effects. For example, clients who need help for depression may also have serious deficits in their ability to form intimate relationships. The intimacy problems may have persisted because these clients avoided such relationships and were deprived of the opportunity to develop better intimate relating behavior. Nonbehavioral therapies emphasizing the therapist-client relationship might provide such an opportunity, but the client might drop out or avoid such treatment for the same reasons that intimate relationships are avoided in daily life. On the other hand, such clients could be attracted to and remain in behavior therapy because its didactic nature and relative lack of focus on the therapist-client relationship does not evoke interpersonal anxiety. In this case, the client may avoid intimacy by being a good client who follows the prescribed steps of treatment. In this way, the behavior therapist inadvertently reinforces the avoidance of intimacy.

B. The Therapeutic Relationship in Behavior Therapy

A functional analysis of behavior therapy underscores the significance of certain aspects of the therapeutic relationship. In particular, the therapeutic relationship is an environment that can evoke clinically relevant behaviors—the client's daily life problems (and improvements) that actually occur during the session in relationship to the therapist (Kohlenberg & Tsai, 1991). The therapist's activities of "doing therapy" can inadvertently strengthen or weaken these problematic behaviors.

Rarely have these aspects of the therapeutic relationship been mentioned by behavior therapists. In standard behavior therapy textbooks, the subject of the therapy relationship is dealt with in a cursory manner, if at all (Nelson & Barlow, 1981; Rimm & Masters, 1977; Wilson & O'Leary, 1980).

Some notable exceptions include Goldfried (1982), Goldfried and Davison (1976) and, more recently, Safran (1990a, 1990b) and Safran and Segal (1990). Safran's and Safran and Segal's views are discussed later in the section on functional analysis of cognitive therapy. Goldfried and Davison pointed out that within-session behavior could be useful in the process of behavior therapy, and Goldfried saw the client-therapist relationship as central to the understanding of resistance during behavior therapy. He viewed resistance as "a mixed blessing in that [it] interfere[s] with the course of therapy but at the same time provide[s] the therapist with a first hand sample of the client's problem" (1982, p. 105). Even though these authors acknowledged the occurrence of client problems during the session and their potential role in treatment, they also saw these problems as playing a relatively minor role in the methods of behavior therapy.

Furthermore, their views seem to have had little impact in the field. For instance, when behavior therapists talk about the therapeutic relationship and recognize its importance, it often has been viewed as (1) ancillary to technique (Rimm & Masters, 1979;Wilson & O'Leary, 1980; Wolpe, 1958), (2) a technique itself to be employed to then introduce and render other more effective, primary techniques (Paul, 1966; Turkat & Brantley, 1981), or (3) something that enhances the therapist's technical influence over the client (DeVoge & Beck, 1978; Rimm & Masters, 1979; Wilson & Evans, 1977; Wilson & O'Leary, 1980).

Even when behavior therapists do identify relationship variables, they generally do not direct attention (as suggested by a functional analysis) to the clinically relevant behaviors occurring during the session (for example, the client experiencing daily life problems such as fear of intimacy with the therapist). Even though the stated purpose of a study by DeRubeis and Feely (1990) was to explore the relationship between the outcome of cognitive therapy and in-session relationship behaviors, the study did not involve observation or measurement of clinically relevant behavior.

This difference in focus is also illustrated in Sweet's (1984) review of therapeutic relationship issues attended to by behavior therapists that include such factors as the impact of the relationship, therapist time, and social reinforcement. None of the reviewed studies mentioned the importance of the client's presenting problem behaviors that occur during the session, even when such problems attracted the attention of the therapist. For example, Sweet described a case in which a client was frightened of making progress in treatment that was manifested, in part, by her negative reactions to the therapist's praise. The therapist used flooding to "overcome this impasse." In citing this case as an example of overcoming a technical difficulty, "fear of success," in doing the therapy, Sweet overlooked the potential importance of the "fear of success" in the therapeutic relationship as an occurrence of a problem that had a significant impact in other areas of this client's life. Furthermore, no consideration was given to the potential benefits that "overcoming a technical difficulty" may have had for the client in her daily life.

Taking the meaning of a client's behavior (such as their asking for help) at face value is known as a formal or structural approach. Taking meaning to be variable and dependent on its context, for example, history and the current therapeutic relationship, is known as a functional approach.

The functional approach can be illustrated by this story about the friendly challenge to behaviorism by Alfred North Whitehead. While dining with Skinner in 1934, Whitehead said to him, "Let me see you account for my behavior as I sit here saying, 'no black scorpion is falling on this table.'" The very next morning, Skinner started writing *Verbal Behavior* (1957), a behavioral account of language. In the epilogue of this book, which took 23 years to complete, Skinner used functional analysis to account for Whitehead's statement. One conclusion was that the meaning of Whitehead's "black scorpion" was behaviorism. Variable and symbolic meanings of what the client says are part of the functional analytic approach to therapy (Glenn, 1983; Hamilton, 1988; Hayes, 1987; Kohlenberg & Tsai, 1991).

A premise of this chapter is that behavior therapists are inclined toward formal analysis and thus depreciate the importance of (1) reinforcement history and variable meanings of their clients' behavior (including verbal behavior), (2) client behavior during the session as being instances of their problem (for example, clinically relevant behavior), and (3) within-session contingencies that affect the strength of clinically relevant behavior. An important issue concerns the history that has led behavior therapists to eschew functional analysis, to adapt formal analysis, and to disregard the three factors just listed.

IV. Historical Factors

Lack of emphasis by behavior therapists on the therapeutic relationship as an environment in which important client problems are evoked and modified stands in stark contrast to other approaches in which the analysis of the client-therapist interaction constitutes the essence of the therapeutic process (Brenner, 1978; Strupp, 1968, 1989; Sullivan, 1953; Wolberg, 1977; Wolman, 1967) and to findings that suggest that the qualities of the interaction are related to outcome (Howard & Orlinsky, 1972; Orlinsky & Howard, 1978). Acceptance of client verbal behavior at face value is also a characteristic of behavior therapy[5] and can be contrasted with other approaches that emphasize variable meanings and symbolism (for example, Frank, 1972; Freud, 1965; Russell, 1987).

To understand the current behavior therapy positions on functional analysis, the therapy relationship, and client verbal behavior, we will examine the historical contexts of the animal model and empiricism from which the positions emerged.

A. The Animal Model

The earliest behavioral forays into the territory of psychotherapy were based on attempts to apply respondent and operant conditioning principles developed in the animal laboratory to human behavior.

In the first of these studies, a well-known respondent conditioning experiment, Watson and Rayner

(1920) conditioned a child, "little Albert," to respond emotionally to what previously had been a neutral stimulus. Watson did not mention the therapeutic (experimental) relationship, nor was the verbal behavior of Albert analyzed (he didn't have much). The focus, however, was entirely on within-session behavior (Albert's emotional reaction in vivo) and on within-session agents of change (the metal bar was paired with other stimuli in vivo). Although not labeled as such, Watson was very aware of the experimenter-client relationship—that is, Albert's reactions to him. This corresponds to the animal experiments in which in-session behavior was also (exclusively) observed and altered. Jones (1924) later employed countercondi-tioning principles to eliminate a fear of rabbits in a boy—research that was both interesting scientifically and valuable in human terms. Again, the relationship was not discussed, but within-session, clinically relevant behavior and the impact of the therapist's actions on such behavior were the focus. A functional analysis was not required or mentioned in these instances because it was too obvious—the entire focus was on in-session therapist (experimenter) and client behavior and their interaction.

A study conducted by Fuller in 1940 is commonly cited as the first systematic application of operant principles. Fuller shaped arm movements using a sugar-milk solution in a "vegetative idiot" (Krasner, 1982; Lutzker & Martin, 1981). Then, in the 1960s there was a virtual explosion of research examining behavior change techniques based on operant principles (for example, Ayllon & Azrin, 1965; O'Leary & Becker, 1967; Wolf, Risley, & Mees, 1964). As in the case of early classical conditioning applications, the focus was on in-session occurrences of the client's problems and how the therapist's contingent treatment produced behavior change in the session. The critical role of the therapist-client interaction in directly evoking and shaping clinically relevant behavior was so obvious that it was not mentioned or formally discussed.

As long as the clinical populations included residents of hospitals, students in classrooms, and young or severely disturbed children, it was not necessary to do a functional analysis of the therapeutic relationship since it was implied by the necessity of focusing on clinically relevant behavior.

---

[5]Although metaphor and language distortion are recognized and used heuristically in cognitive therapy (for example, Guidano & Liotti, 1983), an analysis of meaning is not intrinsic to the approach.

Confusion concerning reinforcement in treating outpatient adults was another factor that inhibited the use of functional analysis in modern behavior therapy. When laboratory reinforcement procedures in animal studies were extended to human adults, they produced incongruous treatments—giving tokens for smiling and giving fines for crying in a depressed client (Reisinger, 1972) or giving tokens to a multiple personality client for maintaining one personality (Kohlenberg, 1973).

The purpose of the laboratory experiments that were emulated by clinicians was to study the parameters of reinforcement. This was useful to the experimenter but was not meant to benefit the participant or to obtain generalization for his or her daily life. The kind of reinforcement used in experiments is referred to as *arbitrary reinforcement*; this can be contrasted with natural reinforcement, which tends to occur in daily life. Skinner (1982) and Ferster (1967, 1972b) discussed the problems that occur using arbitrary reinforcers; for example, clients can perceive such reinforcers to be coercive, and power struggles can ensue. Clients who are arbitrarily reinforced may also regard the therapist as insincere. This problem was alluded to by Wachtel (1977), who observed that behavior therapists were overly exuberant in their use of praise, which "cheapened" the interaction. Since the arbitrary reinforcement problem in adult therapy has just begun to be addressed (Kohlenberg & Tsai, 1987, 1991), behavior therapists avoided functional analysis and its emphasis on reinforcement.

The early work did not highlight functional analysis of the client-therapist interaction. On the other hand, the implications of a functional analysis were incorporated in the model it provided for a behavior therapy. That is, it was assumed that the client's problem occurred within the context of the therapeutic session and was directly changed by contingencies therein. This model, and the apparent absence of functional analysis, had significant repercussions when behavior therapy was applied to outpatient adults.

B. Empiricism

A characteristic of the application of operant principles to clinical populations was the emphasis on empiricism and on experimentation. As a result, behavioral approaches to therapy have accumulated the most impressive track record of any psychotherapy modality for rigorous, controlled outcome research (Kazdin & Wilson, 1978). While this research emphasis has allowed precise documentation of the effects of behavioral techniques, it also has had a down side.

Some of the central problems resulting from the emphasis on experimentation are these. First, emphasis on research has led the clinical researcher to examine issues that were relatively easy to specify, measure, and manipulate. When complex issues such as emotion and meaning in life were examined, it was done in a manner so simplistic as to contribute very little useful information to the practicing clinician. For example, Ramsey (1974) attempted to develop a procedure for a client to help him have more positive feelings. The procedure consisted of relaxation, thinking pleasant thoughts, and then activating a vibrating apparatus. The point was that when the vibrating stimulus (the controlled response) was present, so was "happiness."

The research approach has also resulted in a tendency to focus on modification of isolated behaviors that are not essential parts of clinical disorders (Jacobson, 1987). For example, in a case of intense interpersonal anxiety, "hand clenching" would become the target behavior (Kim, 1979), or in the case of a hospitalized psychotic woman, "towel hoarding" was the target behavior (Ayllon, 1963). Use of such target behaviors surely helped the experimenter/therapist demonstrate efficacy of behavioral principles, and they also had some use clinically. However, many clinicians might regard the behavior therapy exemplified in these kinds of studies as trivial.

It is of interest to note that Skinner (1953) viewed experimentation as only one source of material relevant to a functional analysis; he also mentioned casual observations, controlled field observations, and clinical observations. Examples of alternative approaches to functional analysis are the present chapter, Ferster's functional analysis of depression (1973), and most of Skinner's publications, including his functional analysis of language, *Verbal Behavior* (1957). In this tradition, Willard Day (1969) has elaborated on the compatibility of phenomenology and functional analysis (also see Leigland, 1992). Dougher (1989) applied Day's approach and concluded that it offered promise as an empirical epistemology for the analysis of verbal behavior in therapeutic contexts.

In any event, the behavior therapist's historical emphasis on experimentation and the focus on the exact specification of the dependent and independent variables naturally led to a deemphasis of the therapy relationship. The therapist was portrayed as someone who delivered specific techniques to the client and then documented the effect on the dependent measure. Hersen (1970) noted that those behavior therapists who have had training in traditional psychotherapy generally retain an interest in relationship issues, while those who have had only behavioral training do not. Furthermore, he noted that a great deal more may have occurred in the therapy relationship than was reported in the research literature. It seems clear that the experimental approach to therapy heightened the discriminability of the specified techniques employed, yet it obscured what might be important about the therapy relationship.

V. The Adult Outpatient Within-Session Behavior Conundrum

The historical antecedents of functional behavior therapy resulted in the behavior therapist using formal analysis (for example, the application of well-specified treatments for specific problems). An analysis of verbal behavior or attention to the therapeutic relationship was not part of the process. The within-session observation of the problem behavior and the within-session application of the treatments to change that behavior, however, were integral parts of the process. For this reason, it was superfluous to discuss the client-therapist relationship as an environment that evokes daily life problems. These behavior therapy methods, however, were not well suited for outpatient adults because their problematic behavior presumably did not occur in the session. This was a conundrum for behavior therapists, and they tried to solve it by devising the following types of treatments.

A. Psychotherapy by Reciprocal Inhibition

Wolpe (1958) arranged conditions in the session that were thought to evoke the client's problems. He treated imagined stimuli as though they were equivalent to daily life stimuli. In this tradition, other behavior therapy methods, such as covert reinforcement (Cautela, 1970), relied on imagery to bring the client's problems into the session. Based on principles arrived at in the animal laboratory, Wolpe (1958, 1981) concluded that the active ingredient in psychotherapy was counterconditioning. He strongly advocated the position that counterconditioning can be implemented best by applying specific techniques within the context of therapy (for example, systematic desensitization) and that what was important in effecting change was the specific technique implemented. Consistent with the historical precedents, the process of imagination or how instructions were able to bring about imagination were not analyzed. In addition to the deliberate techniques used, Wolpe noted that emotional responses were also induced in many patients by the interpersonal aspects of therapy itself. These responses, however, constituted data to be used in creating a more sensitive and accurate anxiety hierarchy.

When techniques such as systematic desensitization were first researched, some claimed that the therapeutic relationship was of secondary or of no importance (Lang, 1969; Wolpe, 1958). Foa and Steketee (1987) stated that "it is likely that the more powerful the therapeutic procedure employed, the less pronounced will be the effect of the therapist" (p. 109).

B. Social Skills Training

In social skills training, the client's problems and improvements are brought into the session by role playing, acting, and rehearsal. Such training rarely involves direct observation of symptoms or the conditions that bring them about, and therefore it is difficult to describe the specific components of the target behavior (Ciminero, Calhoun, & Adams, 1977; Conger & Conger, 1982). This approach epitomizes the formal analysts' assumption that behavior has meaning independent of context. That is, behavior acquired via coaching, modeling, role playing, and behavioral rehearsal during the session is functionally different from the behavior that is supposed to occur in daily life even though it might look the same. Ignoring the functional aspects of the behavior is like ignoring the difference between rote learning a sentence in French and learning the same sounds with an understanding of their meaning. The sentences may sound exactly the same to a listener, but they are functionally very different. An allusion to this problem can be found in a review of the literature on social skills training generalization by Scott, Himadi, and Keane (1983). They concluded that the lack of demonstrable generalization is responsible for the limited acceptability of social skills training as a viable treatment. From a functional viewpoint, lack of functional similarity between training and natural environments that typifies social skills training provides no guarantee that trained behavior will transfer. Explanations are needed to account for those instances in which it does.

C. Cognitive Therapy

By proposing that faulty cognition was the cause of the client's problem, therapy could then be directed at the dysfunctional cognition. Cognitive therapy is discussed more completely in the next section.

VI. A Functional Analysis of Cognitive Therapy

The central theme of cognitive therapy is that cognition causes subsequent behavior and that treatment involves changing dysfunctional cognition. We will examine the cognitive therapist's view on the nature of the cognition-behavior relationship, the clinical phenomena that support this view, and some of the theoretical and clinical problems that have emerged. We will then show how an improved version of cognitive therapy results from a consideration of the contingencies that cause dysfunctional cognition and that cause the relationship between cognition and subsequent behavior.

Considerable diversity exists in the underlying theory and practice of cognitive therapy and the manner in which the thought-behavior relationship is defined. For example, Albert Ellis (1962, 1970), a pioneer in cognitive therapy, introduced the idea that a client's

thoughts and feelings could be analyzed using an *ABC* model, in which *A* represents external environmental events, *B* represents cognition, and *C* is the resulting action or emotion (see Figure 1.1[a]). For Ellis, clinical treatment involved explaining the *ABC* paradigm to clients and then helping them to change *B* so that it was no longer dysfunctional.

There are problems with this *ABC* paradigm, and, accordingly, it has been revised (Beck, Rush, Shaw, & Emery, 1979; Guidano & Liotti, 1983; Hollon & Kriss, 1984; Turk & Salovey, 1985). A functional analysis, however, suggests that the revised cognitive therapy formulation has lost some of the clinically useful features of the *ABC* formulation and has not adequately addressed the problems.

A. Problems with Cognitive Therapy and the *ABC* Paradigm

First, the *ABC* paradigm excludes alternative ways in which cognition and behavior could be related. For example, Russell and Brandsma (1974) suggested that client problems could start out fitting the $A \rightarrow B \rightarrow C$ paradigm. Then, after numerous repetitions of the *ABC* sequence during the client's life, classical conditioning would obviate the occurrence of *B*. In other words, *A* becomes a second-order conditioned stimulus that directly elicits *C*. Another possibility suggested by Klein (1974) is that the depressed patient's

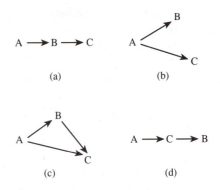

Figure 1.1 Paradigms showing relationships between *A* (antecedent event), *B* (belief or thinking), and *C* (consequent behavior or feeling): (a) thinking influences behavior, (b) thinking has no influence on behavior, (c) thinking partially influences behavior, and (d) behavior influences thinking.

negative self-concept, helplessness, and self-blame are best viewed as an effect rather than a cause of the condition. In other words, the client first feels depressed and then has negative cognitions.

Client statements also indicate alternative paradigms. Comments such as "I intellectually accept that I do not need to be loved by everyone but I still feel devastated when I'm rejected" suggest the presence of a *B* that is inconsistent with the *C*. On the other hand, some clients claim that they experience no *B* that precedes their problematic *C*, thus indicating that *B* either doesn't exist or is unconscious.

Second, the *ABC* paradigm can lead to some questionable clinical procedures. For example, if the cognitive therapist truly believes the *ABC* hypothesis, the client's rejection of it is challenged by directly questioning the client's logic or sincerity or by proposing that there are additional, unconscious cognitions to be discovered. Challenges can also be indirect, such as giving additional homework or assumption-testing assignments. Such nonacceptance of alternative paradigms is found in the cognitive therapy of Beck (1976), even though he rejects the theory implied by the *ABC* model. For example, Beck suggested that clients who say that they intellectually "know" they are not worthless but who do not accept this on an emotional level need more cognitive therapy because the dysfunctional feelings can only occur when they do not "truly believe" the rational thought (Beck et al., 1979, p. 302). The need for more flexible models is demonstrated by the tendency for cognitive therapists (as well as other types) to persist in their approach even though the client is not progressing (Kendall, Kipnis, & Otto-Salaj, 1992). Given the complexity of human behavior, the exclusion of coexistent, noncognitive mediated explanations as demanded by the *ABC* model seems unreasonable.

Furthermore, a client's objecting to cognitive interventions could be desirable behavior. If such a client were seeking help with becoming more assertive or more confident with opinions, then objecting to the therapist's *ABC* theory would be an improvement occurring in vivo within the context of the therapy relationship. Ideally, this within-session improvement should be reinforced by the therapist's acceptance and not punished by the challenges.

Third, evidence used to support the notion that dysfunctional feelings and actions are caused by deviant, irrational, or pathological *B*s is problematic. One type of supportive evidence compares the thoughts and attributions of clients to "normal" subjects (for a review of the issues, see Beidel & Turner, 1986). Not surprisingly, clients tend to have more dysfunctional thoughts than do normals. Such research is problematic because it only demonstrates that people with clinical problems also have irrational thoughts, and it does not demonstrate that the thoughts actually cause the problem feelings. It is possible that dysfunctional feelings cause the cognitions or that both the cognitions and the feelings (actions) are caused by some third variable. Some data even indicate that depressed persons may assess reality more accurately than normals (Krantz, 1985). A recent review of the experimental literature on the relation between internal states and actions also supports the notion that *B* (the internal state) and *C* (the action) are sometimes not congruent (Quattrone, 1985).

Fourth, in terms of the theory-practice connection, it is unclear how the cognitive hypothesis is related to many of the specific treatment procedures. Why and how, for example, does logical argument or evidence change a cognitive structure? How does cognitive theory support Beck's advocacy of a Socratic approach in which clients must discover for themselves their underlying assumptions? How is it relevant to Ellis's direct instruction to clients to adapt new beliefs? What are the theoretical principles involved in accounting for cognitive change as a result of clients' performing experiments in their daily lives to check out hypotheses? How does the client's talk about cognitions and their relation to symptoms (metacognition) help to change structures? How is it possible to have cognitive therapies that are not metacognitive (Hollon & Kriss, 1984)? How does "new interpersonal experience" in the therapeutic interaction (Safran, 1990a, p. 111) produce new behavior in the client in daily life?

That cognitive therapy is often effective is not an issue. What is problematic is the adequacy of the theory to account for treatment outcomes. As expressed by Silverman, Silverman, and Eardley (1984, p. 1112), the clinical effects that occur as a result of cognitive therapy are "awaiting for a convincing rationale."

B. Revised Formulation of Cognitive Therapy

As a step toward improving the *ABC* model, cognitive therapists have turned to basic cognitive theory and have revised or more precisely specified what is meant by *B* (cognition) and how it is related to clinical problems. For example, Hollon and Kriss (1984) delineated the different uses of the term *cognition* and distinguished between cognitive products and cognitive structures (and associated cognitive processes). Cognitive products are directly accessible, conscious, private behaviors, such as thoughts, self-statements, and automatic thoughts. Cognitive structures—for instance, "schemas"—are the underlying organizational entities that play an active role in processing information. Structures, however, operate at an unconscious level since their content cannot be known directly and must be inferred from the products.

As pointed out by Hollon and Kriss, this distinction is similar to the difference between the linguist's surface and deep structures. Surface structures refer to what is said (overt verbalizations) or thought (covert self-statements), whereas deep structures refer to what is meant. From the Hollon and Kriss perspective, the causal factor is the cognitive structure, whereas the thinking or the cognitive products (irrational thoughts, self-statements, automatic thoughts) constitute "signs or hints of the nature of one's knowledge structures" (1984, p. 39).

Therefore, Hollon and Kriss suggest that any clinical interventions that change cognitive products are merely symptomatic treatments. In a similar vein, Safran, Vallis, Segal, and Shaw (1986) warned that changing products have limited clinical effects, and efforts should be directed to "core" processes. Correspondingly, Beck (1984) warned that relapse can be expected unless underlying cognitive structures are changed, and he states that the notion that cognitive phenomena cause depression is "far-fetched." Presumably, the "cognitive phenomena" whose causality Beck rejected are cognitive products, whereas core structures or schema are still viewed as causal.

Although in the theoretical realm the causality of cognitive products has been replaced by structures, a corresponding shift has not occurred in the trenches where cognitive therapy is actually practiced. The same cognitive therapists who reject the causative role of cognitive products are the ones who provide treatment manuals and clinical examples that focus on changing cognitive products. For example, Beck, Emery, and Greenberg (1986) stated that the therapist "must be able to communicate clearly that anxiety is maintained by mistaken or dysfunctional appraisal of a situation" and "gives this explanation . . . in the first session and reiterates it throughout therapy" (p. 168). Guidano and Liotti (1983) stated that the first important step in therapy occurs "when patients understand that their suffering is mediated by their own opinions" (p. 138).

If clinical practice followed the shift in cognitive theory, the obvious focus would be on changing the "underlying" structures. From a functional analytic view, the theory-practice schism in cognitive therapy makes sense. Since the only contact the therapist has with the client is with his or her behavior, and since cognitive products are defined in terms of behavior, the clinical intervention can be specified as a behavior change process. Cognitive structures, however, are defined as nonbehavioral entities that cannot be directly contacted by the therapist. Since clinical interventions are always limited to the behavioral realm—the client's thinking, feeling, talking, theorizing, free-associating, and the like—it is impossible to devise treatments that focus on structures that do not involve these client behaviors. Thus, it is difficult to come up with interventions aimed at structures that are different from those aimed at products.

For example, Beck et al. (1979) stated that "the cognitive and behavioral interventions [used] to modify thoughts . . . are the same as those . . . used to change hidden assumptions" (p. 252). The only procedures that differentiate the clinical treatment of products from structures is that the latter must first be inferred (for example, the client must abstract or deduce the existence of the structure). Once identified, however, the same therapeutic methods used to change products are applied. Directed by theory to change a nonbehavioral entity (the underlying structure) while restricted to working with the behavior (products) of the client, the practicing cognitive therapist is in an untenable position. These theoretically posited difficulties in changing schemas and the tenuous link between theory and how change occurs have been termed a dilemma by Hollon and Kriss (1984, pp. 46–48). Although they and other cognitive psychologists, including Guidano and Liotti (1983), are trying to find ways out of this dilemma, the jury is out as to whether satisfactory resolutions have or can be developed. It is not surprising, therefore, that the actual nuts-and-bolts practice of therapy seems, of necessity, to focus on products.

C. A Functional Analytic Revision

As an alternative, a functional analysis leads to a formulation of the thought-behavior relationship that retains the clinical usefulness but avoids the problems of the original *ABC* hypothesis. Within this framework, cognitions can play a major, minor, or no role in the client's problems. Correspondingly, cognitive therapy methods will be of varying effectiveness with different clients depending on the role that cognition has in the clinical problem.

As detailed in the following discussion, the functional analytic conception of cognition is based on an analysis of the client's verbal behavior involving "tacts" (that is, descriptions) and "mands," (that is, demands or requests) and the distinction between contingency-shaped behavior and rule-governed behavior. Of particular importance to this analysis are tacting-to-self and manding-to-self behaviors.

1. CONTINGENCY-SHAPED BEHAVIOR

Contingency-shaped behaviors are those behaviors that have been directly strengthened by reinforcement. Many behaviors, however, have not been directly reinforced and instead are more a function of the prior stimulus. For example, instructions are a prior stimulus that can evoke complex behaviors that have never before been directly reinforced. Similarly, an instructor demonstrating what to do can evoke behavior not previously reinforced. In these cases, the contingencies have shaped the more global behavior (for example, imitating the instructor or following instructions) but have not yet had a chance to exert much influence on the specific behavior being imitated or the instructed behavior. Thus, all behavior is ultimately contingency-shaped.

As pointed out earlier, even if a conscious experience of pleasure often accompanies contingencies involving positive reinforcement, it is not a necessary part of the shaping and strengthening process and should not be confused with it. Within the functional analytic view, almost all of our behavior (talking, walking, running, and so forth) is there ultimately because of the strengthening effects of reinforcement, and these behaviors were strengthened mostly without our awareness of the process. Conscious experiences (to be discussed later) do play an important albeit different role from that of behavior that is directly shaped by contingencies. However, the fact that conscious experience is more directly felt than the unconscious effects of reinforcement can easily lead to the latter's being overlooked.

To illustrate the application of these concepts, consider the following interaction between Harriet, a client, and the first author, her therapist.

Harriet was asked to change her regular appointment time from 5:00 P.M. Mondays to 3:00 P.M. Tuesdays. Although she consented, Harriet revealed several weeks later that the change had caused a great deal of hardship. To accommodate the change, she had to rearrange her work and school schedules, and her presenting problems of anxiety and depression were exacerbated. When asked why she did not refuse the request or explain how the change would be difficult, Harriet gave the following interpretation. She said that she acquiesced because of what she was thinking at that time: "My willingness to give in to you shows how much I care about you, and besides, I do not want you to get angry at me. I can't stand to have people I care about get angry at me."

Several interpretations of Harriet's behavior can be given in terms of reinforcement history, and we will describe these throughout this section. For now, let us consider the possibility that her acquiescence was purely contingency-shaped and was not influenced by her preceding thoughts, even though she felt it was. From this standpoint, her acquiescence would have been shaped directly by childhood experiences such as being punished in various ways for making her wishes known (for example, anger or refusal to accommodate her desires) combined with the reinforcement of acquiescence. The result was that certain responses (for example, acquiescence) are stronger than others (for example, assertiveness), and it is quite possible for Harriet to be unaware or unconscious of the causes of her behavior. In terms of the *ABC* paradigm, contingency-shaped behavior would correspond to $A \rightarrow C$. The fact that other people would respond differently to the same A reflects the difference in their past experiences when in A situations.

2. TACTS AND MANDS: TWO TYPES OF VERBAL BEHAVIOR

The contingency-shaped explanation, however, does not account for B, the thinking that Harriet described. Our analysis of Harriet's thinking focuses on the concepts of tacts and mands and is based on Skinner's *Verbal Behavior* (1957) in which he accounted for the full range of verbal behavior (including thinking, science, believing, and writing) in terms of reinforcement history. Contrary to popular opinion, Skinner's approach to verbal behavior is alive and well. Chomsky's (1959) widely accepted critique mistakenly confused Skinner's functional approach with the formal analysis that was used by non-Skinnerian behaviorists (MacCorquodale, 1970; Zuriff, 1985).

Tacts include labeling and describing events and objects. Examples of tacts are "That is water," "I screamed at him," and "I can't stand this."

Mands, on the other hand, include commands, threats, and requests. The defining characteristic of a mand is that it is strengthened by a very narrow range of contingencies. For example, the mand "I would like some water" will be strengthened only if it results in the listener providing water or some other thirst quencher.

Tacts and mands are learned in the same way that any other behaviors are learned. Thus, when and how we tact or mand varies from person to person depending on our particular experiences. As an example of how tacting is acquired, consider a child who learns to say "truck" when one goes by because that is how the parent described it. The child is reinforced directly (for example, "that's right, that's a truck") and indirectly as "truck" enters into other contexts (for example, the child says, "I want a truck"). In the same way that an individual learns to describe inanimate objects or such past events as "it rained last Tuesday," he or she also learns to describe others' and his or her own present behavior and past experiences. A man who approaches the dentist's chair and says "This is going to hurt and I am afraid" is probably tacting (1) past experiences of being hurt by dentists, (2) his feelings of fear, and (3) a prediction of how he is going to react when in the chair.

Up to this point, the tacting and manding we have discussed have been said out loud to another person. Of course, tacting and manding also occur when the only person hearing the description or demand is the speaker. From our standpoint, tacting and manding to oneself silently is functionally the same as tacting and manding out loud when no other person is present. These two cases differ mainly in the intensity of the response. Tacting and manding to oneself, in fact, constitute our definition of thinking.

We will now address why thinking (and the similar tacting and manding out loud without a listening audience) occurs. We have explained why a person would tact and mand when others can hear, as in "This is terrible," "I'm anxious," "Be patient," "Keep your mouth shut," "Get out of bed," and "Do it now." It is less clear why these would be thought or said aloud when no one is around.

We are particularly interested in tacting-to-self and manding-to-self because they often encompass what is meant by B in cognitive therapy. For example, the words *must* and *should* are viewed as a cause of neurosis by rational-emotive behavior therapists, and their clinical interventions are aimed at eliminating such words from their client's thinking (Ellis, 1970). Typically, the words *must* and *should* are also found in manding-to-self statements such as "I must never make mistakes" and "I should be happy." Similarly, the thought "I am unlovable," a tact made to oneself, would be viewed by cognitive therapists as an irrational thought or dysfunctional hypothesis that causes client problems. Therefore, a behavioral explanation of why tacting-to-self and manding-to-self occur and how they affect client problems is important in our account of cognition and cognitive therapy.

Generalized tacts and mands that have no influence on subsequent behavior. We believe that the *ABC* model encompasses several types of B–C relationships. The first case we will consider is an absence of relationship between *B* and *C*, which occurs when tacting-to-self or manding-to-self is simply due to stimulus generalization and not because of its effects on subsequent behavior. Thus, we are so used to tacting or manding to others that some persistence would be expected when we are alone (for example, a child saying "truck" out loud even when a parent is not around). Generalization from public reactions to the private realm is particularly expected to occur if its public form is strong. For example, the considerable strength of manding-to-others is illustrated by its frequent generalization to inanimate objects, such as shouting "Start!" to a stalled car or screaming warnings of a blitz to a football team on television. Obviously, these tacts and mands have no effects on the objects.

Let us return to the case of Harriet and describe how she could have thoughts (a behavior) that appear to be linked causally to a subsequent behavior when in reality they are not linked. In this illustration, we posit that her thinking is tacting-to-self due to generalization and her acquiescing has been purely contingency-shaped. For Harriet to tact-to-self due to generalization, she would have had a history in which she learned to describe her own behavior and experiences to others, such as telling her mother, "When I said no, daddy got angry" (a tact). Then, because of stimulus generalization, she tacts recent experiences even when others are not around. As her father's reactions were directly shaping her acquiescence behavior pattern and evoking associated feelings, she also described to herself the contingencies (for example, "Daddy just pushed me away when I asked him for attention") and her own operant and respondent behaviors ("I ran to my room and started to cry"). Thus, at the same time that the acquiescence and lack of assertiveness were being shaped she also described to herself the events as they were unfolding—the thinking and acquiescing were independent of each other. Now, in similar situations Harriet will engage in both behaviors; that is, she will think and acquiesce. In terms of the *ABC* paradigm, these actions are represented by Figure 1.1(b). It just so happens that the *B* precedes the *C* in time, but *B* has no effect on *C*.

The combination of the two separate behaviors, contingency-shaped acquiescence and generaliza-tion-induced tacting-to-self or manding-to-self, offers an account of how a person can have thoughts (thinking behavior) and behavior (a subsequent behavior) that are not causally linked although they may appear to be. If this set of circumstances actually occurs for some clients, it would be a mistake to take their thoughts as causal, to fit them into an *ABC* paradigm, and (compounding the error) to ignore the role that contingencies played in forming the behavior.

Generalized tacts and mands that influence subsequent behavior.   Up to this point, we have looked at thinking as behavior that does not enter into the causal chain of events leading to *C*. Now we will examine circumstances in which tacting-to-self and manding-to-self can have considerable effect on subsequent behavior. Before we do so, however, it is important to clarify a semantic problem concerning the word *cause*. Cognitive psychologists and radical behaviorists mean different things when they refer to cause. To the cognitive psychologist, the effect of a person's thoughts on behavior represents a type of causal relationship—whether it be partial, contributory, or otherwise. The term *cause* simply means that thoughts are considered to bring about a change in behavior. As pointed out earlier, the radical behaviorist uses the term *cause* to refer to contingencies. The same effects that are called *causal* by cognitivists—that is, the effects of thoughts on the behavior that follows—are seen to exist but are described differently by radical behaviorists.

Tacting and manding-to-self can increase a person's effectiveness at the task at hand. Such a case is illustrated in Skinner's (1957, p. 444) observations of a little girl who talked out loud to herself while practicing the piano—"That's in the key of G." Such a tact-to-self could have helped to reduce errors in the way that the same statement made by her teacher would have. Similarly, the mands that she made to herself—"No, wait," "Just a minute," and "Is that right?"—may have helped to strengthen the subsequent behaviors of stopping and listening. Originally, the child said these mands due to generalization from hearing these statements and perhaps saying these statements to others. Eventually, with enough experience, the contingencies of improved piano-playing (that is, the useful purpose) will influence whether or not the child continues to make and follow these mands to herself (whether out loud or in thought).

The case in which tacting-to-self and manding-to-self do lead to useful strengthening of subsequent behavior will now be applied to Harriet's case. Suppose Harriet had learned to describe certain requests made by others (no matter how innocuous) as a test of her love for them. She could have learned this as a child from a narcissistic mother who often needed affirmations of love and who would ask questions with a hidden agenda. For example, when her mother asked, "Did you like the pie I made for you?" she really meant, "Do you love me and appreciate what I do? If you do not, I will get depressed and withdraw."

Since a child would have difficulty in discriminating a "real" question from a test one, Harriet might have experienced unpredictable punishment and reward. Furthermore, suppose that she discussed this problem with friends and became aware of the conditions that differentiated an ordinary question from a "test" question. Thereafter, when confronted with a question, Harriet would privately review (tact) the conditions to decide (discriminate) whether or not it was a test. Then, to herself, she might say, "This is a test of love. If I act in a way that is rejecting, she will get angry; if I go along with the program, she will be happy." In terms of the *ABC* paradigm, this is represented by Figure 1.1(a).

Of course, this description of Harriet's thinking corresponds more closely to the cognitive therapy paradigm in which *B* is a cognitive product, such as conscious experiences of thoughts or self-statements. Such a model assumes that there is little or no independently shaped or conditioned *C*.

Our position, however, is that even though Harriet's behavior was influenced by her thinking and thus corresponds to the $A \rightarrow B \rightarrow C$ paradigm, she would, in time, experience the success or failure of her decision process. Then her acquiescence would be influenced more by the unconscious effects of the contingencies and less by the conscious decision process. This process, in which contingency-shaped behaviors and tacting-to-self and manding-to-self start out as independent but then come to interact with one

another, represents another possible arrangement of the thought-behavior relationship. Thus, in time, a reaction that is first brought about by tacting-to-self or manding-to-self would become contingency-shaped.

A slightly different interpretation of Harriet's thinking is to view *C* as contingency-shaped and, in addition, to posit a *B* that also strengthens *C*. In other words, Harriet could have had the unconscious effects of reinforcement that made her acquiescence more likely, and at the same time, engaged in a conscious tacting-to-herself that would strengthen her acquiescing. In this case, the *C* would be stronger than the *C* that is just contingency-shaped or one that was only evoked by *B*. This paradigm is represented by Figure 1.1(c).

The formulations of thought-behavior relations discussed so far do not exhaust all possibilities. It is possible to have the case represented by Figure 1.1(d), in which emotional reactions and behavior are directly evoked, and then in James-Lange fashion, clients figure out what they must have been thinking. It is also possible for the occurrence of an independent *B* to have an effect on subsequent behavior because of a consistency effect, which occurs in people who have learned that "one should practice what one preaches" or "not say one thing and do another." In the case of consistency, thoughts influence subsequent behavior because these individuals have been reinforced for doing what they said they would do and punished when their actions were not consistent with their verbal behavior.

It is also important to mention some of the special problems engendered by the fact that *B*s cannot be observed directly and must either be inferred or based on self-descriptions. Thus, it is possible that a self-description of a *B*, like the one given by Harriet, may be a fabrication or one that is required by social convention. Even when the client is giving his or her best description of *B*, such introspection can be unreliable and subject to many current influences.

Although a complete account of thought-behavior relationships would include these as well as other paradigms and influencing factors, the major theoretical implications of a functional analysis of cognitive therapy are conveyed by the paradigms we have delineated.

3. RULE-GOVERNED BEHAVIOR

The literature on rules and rule-governed behavior (Skinner, 1966; Zettle & Hayes, 1982) is relevant to the functional analytic concept of the thought-behavior relationship.

When a tact or mand specifies a contingency and the behavior required, it is referred to as a rule. The example of Harriet's tacting-to-self is an instance of a rule because it specifies the required behavior (acquiescence) and the contingency (avoid trouble). A parent's statement, "You must do your homework or you can't go out to play," is a mand that is a rule because it specifies a behavior (doing homework) and a contingency (playing). Thus, laws, logical principles, instruction manuals, injunctions, maxims, and threats are tacts and mands that are also rules. The behavior that occurs as a result of the rule being issued is referred to as rule-governed behavior.

As discussed for tacts and mands, rules are extracted from our own or others' direct experience of the contingencies of reinforcement or from the study of systems that arrange them. The development of rule-extracting and rule-governed behavior becomes a large part of a person's behavior because it helps to shorten the tedious process of shaping. The tacting-to-self that Harriet developed is an example.

The distinction between rule-governed and contingency-shaped behavior is used by Skinner (1974) in his reconceptualization of many common polarizations, including: deliberation versus impulse, contrived versus natural, intellect versus emotion, logic versus intuition, conscious versus unconscious, surface versus depth, and truth versus belief. Skinner's distinction between rule-governed behavior and contingency-shaped behavior bears a striking resemblance to cognitive therapy's distinction between cognitive products and structures.

4. COGNITIVE STRUCTURES AND CONTINGENCY-SHAPED BEHAVIOR

As pointed out previously, some forms of cognitive therapy underscore the importance of changing structures (as opposed to products) yet lack theoretically based means for doing so. Since behavior analysis is primarily a theory of behavior change, it would be useful to translate "cognitive structure" into behavioral terms to devise methods of change.

In addition to the polarizations referred to in the previous section, the characteristics of contingency-shaped behavior and cognitive structures are similar in other ways. First, the effects of reinforcement occur at an unconscious level and structures are also unconscious. Second, the effects of reinforcement are functionally defined (that is, behaviors different in appearance can achieve the same effect), which is consistent with the deep meaning attributed to cognitive structures. Third, reinforced behavior is changed through experience with contingencies and not through "talking about the contingencies," which corresponds to the nonessential presence of metacognition in changing cognitive structures.

Thus, if the core structures referred to by cognitive therapists are contingency-shaped behaviors, then more attention should be paid to contingencies when attempting to change core structures. Paying attention to contingencies is exactly what Jacobson (1989) did when he described how he used the therapist-client relationship to change a client's core belief about her "badness." According to Jacobson, the core structure was changed by the client's taking "the risk of being known intimately" to him, and the client's risk "paid off" in his continued acceptance and positive regard.

Safran and colleagues (Safran, 1990a, 1990b; Safran, McMain, Crocker, & Murray, 1990; Safran & Segal, 1990) offer a significant modification of cognitive therapy that gives a central role to the therapist-client interaction in the change process. They suggest that within-session instances of the client's problems offer an opportunity to change cognitive structures. However, Safran views the therapeutic interaction primarily as providing an opportunity to modify interpersonal schemas and not behavior. Consequently, the therapist's reactions are seen in their role as reinforcing the client's mental models but not their behavior. Consistent with its history, the focus on within-session behavior was not derived from the practice or theory of cognitive therapy. Instead, Safran drew on a nonbehavioral perspective, interpersonal theory, which has psychodynamic historical roots (Sullivan, 1953), as the source for the focus on the therapeutic interaction. The net result is an integration of the two approaches, and no specific cognitive or behavioral rationale for the interpersonal focus is given.

A conceptual difference between contingency-shaped behavior and cognitive structures is that the former is a behavioral entity and the latter is a nonbehavioral entity. Viewing structures as nonbehavioral entities has the unfortunate effect of distracting attention from external variables and behavioral processes. Coyne and Gotlib (1983), for example, conclude that cognitive models of depression fail to account for external factors. Similarly, cognitive therapists often do not acknowledge that contingencies (an external variable) are an inherent part of their procedures. The effect of a therapist's reaction can have a significant impact on what a client says or does. Regardless of theoretical orientation, it is reasonable to assume that reinforcement is a factor to be considered at least some of the time. Yet cognitive therapists in their theoretical analyses seem to have a phobia concerning the term *reinforcement*. Neither Hollon and Kriss (1984) nor Safran and Segal (1990) made even a passing reference to it. Similarly, in the foregoing case described by Jacobson (1989), the operations of reinforcement were described but the term *reinforcement* was not used. Even Wessells (1982), in an elegant defense of cognitive psychology, lamented that cognitivists, unfortunately, have neglected the role of contingencies in explaining behavior.

5. CLINICAL IMPLICATIONS

Although a functional analysis is consistent with the cognitive therapy position that thinking can precede actions, we regard the thought-behavior relationship always as a behavior-behavior relationship. When thoughts are considered as behavior, the therapist is led to consider the various origins of the thinking behaviors involved and the arbitrary nature of their connection to other behavior as well as to pay attention to the ongoing contingencies of reinforcement in their development and modification.

A focus on thinking in the here and now. The client's thinking will be most subject to change if it occurs close in time and place to relevant contingencies and stimulus control. Thus, whenever possible, we recommend focusing on thinking, believing, and other relevant behaviors that occur during the session. Opportunities to directly shape more adaptive *B*s frequently occur as the client's dysfunctional thinking is brought into the client-therapist relationship. For example, if we assume that Harriet's problem is of the $A \rightarrow B \rightarrow C$ variety, then her acquiescing occurs because she thought it showed how much she cares and because she thought doing otherwise would have evoked the therapist's anger. These are examples of *B*s occurring within the context of the relationship. Harriet's thinking could have been challenged and reinterpreted on the spot, and a new behavior could have been encouraged.

With the notable exception of Safran and colleagues (Safran, 1990a, 1990b; Safran et al., 1990; Safran & Segal, 1990), cognitive therapists usually focus on behavior occurring elsewhere, thereby avoiding or preventing therapeutic opportunities provided by the therapist-client interaction. For example, in a discussion of "technical problems" in doing cognitive therapy for depression, Beck et al. (1979) raised the problem of a client who says, "You are more interested in doing research than in helping me." First, Beck wisely pointed out that even if nothing is said, a client who is in a clinical research project may be secretly harboring such thoughts. However, the reason such thoughts occur, according to Beck, is that depressed clients may be distorting what the therapist does. He then suggested that the therapist inquire if any such notions are present and put these worries to rest. According to Beck, if possible, the therapist should avoid such problems in the first place by anticipating their occurrence and giving complete explanations to the client.

Our functional analysis of that situation would be somewhat different. A depressed client who feels unimportant to the therapist highlights the fact that the therapy situation could be evoking the same problem that the client experiences with others (for example, not acting important and not asking for what she wants). This would not be viewed as a technical problem to be disposed of but as a situation that provides an important therapeutic opportunity. Also, it would not be assumed that the client is distorting, just that the therapist and the client are contacting different aspects of the situation. It is even possible that the research is more important to the therapist than the client is, and in that sense, the client would not be "distorting." The notion that the client might be secretly harboring such ideas rather than telling the therapist suggests the clinical problem of the client not being direct, open, or assertive during the session.

Although Beck's theory may, in general, lead the cognitive therapist to overlook situations of interest according to functional analysis, he recognized that certain therapist-client interactions can provide therapeutic opportunity. For example, in discussing ways to strengthen collaboration, he pointed out that a client may react to a homework assignment as a test of self-worth and that the therapist should use this as an opportunity to correct faulty cognitions. Beck, however, gave no special significance to the fact that the therapeutic work focused on behavior as it is occurring. Instead, he viewed it as having the same effects as dealing with a cognition that occurs elsewhere. Jacobson (1989), on the other hand, discussed the importance of focusing on behavior during the session when doing Beck's cognitive therapy. Furthermore, he suggested that this factor be incorporated in the conceptual underpinnings of cognitive therapy for depression.

Take into account the varying role that thoughts can play.   In addition to viewing thoughts as behavior, it is possible to have Bs that may or may not play a role in the client's problem. Recalling our previous discussion, we examined three possibilities: thoughts influence subsequent behavior, thoughts do not influence subsequent behavior, and thoughts contribute to the strength of a contingency-shaped subsequent behavior. In other words, the degree of control exerted by thinking over clinical symptoms is on a continuum. At one end is the pure $A \rightarrow B \rightarrow C$ type, where the preceding B is a behavior that corresponds to a cognitive product and has an influence on the client's problem. Treatment for this type is aimed at changing Bs, and the cognitive therapy techniques are appropriate.

At the other end of the continuum is the $A \rightarrow C$ type, in which the symptom has been shaped purely by contingencies. In this case, treatment is aimed at directly changing the Cs—the focus would be on exposing the client to positive reinforcement in the

therapy session and in the natural environment that would shape and sustain new Cs. The interpretations given to clients also would correspond to $A \rightarrow C$ (Kohlenberg & Tsai, 1991).

Offer relevant explanations of client problems.   Our analysis also has implications for explanations offered to clients about their problems. Although it is possible for a client with an $A \rightarrow C$ problem to improve when given an $A \rightarrow B \rightarrow C$ interpretation, less favorable outcomes are also possible. This is especially true for clients who grew up in dysfunctional families where they were abused, neglected, negated, or otherwise punished for expressing their feelings. Children who are repeatedly told, either directly or indirectly, that "there's no reason for you to feel or think that way" mistrust their feelings and are unsure of who they are. Suggesting to such clients that their beliefs are dysfunctional or irrational can replay the contingencies associated with the invalidation and alienation they experienced while growing up. $A \rightarrow C$ clients who are treated as though their problem were $A \rightarrow B \rightarrow C$ may drop out of treatment if they feel invalidated.

Use direct cognitive manipulation with caution.   Although difficulties may arise when treating an $A \rightarrow C$ problem as if it were an $A \rightarrow B \rightarrow C$ problem, direct cognitive manipulations can sometimes benefit clients even if their problems are mainly $A \rightarrow C$ types. We define direct cognitive manipulation as therapist behaviors that involve appeals to reason, logical arguments, or telling the client that a particular belief does not match the therapist's observations. Thus, direct cognitive manipulation is primarily rule-giving.

When clients respond to rules by changing their Bs, these changes are rule-governed behavior. This process can benefit the client for several reasons. First, beliefs contribute, at least to some degree, to many client problems even if the primary factor is the result of contingencies. This paradigm is illustrated by Figure 1.1(c). Cognitive therapy methods aimed at directly changing B would be helpful, particularly if the client was also exposed to contingencies for improved behavior. Second, cognitive techniques for $A \rightarrow C$ problems also may benefit clients who are linear and logical thinkers and who already interpret their problem according to the *ABC* hypothesis (even though their problem is $A \rightarrow C$). The benefit occurs because these individuals have learned to be consistent. That is, they grew up in environments where "practicing what you preach" was highly valued and "saying one thing and doing another" was not. Inclination exists for this type of client to act in accordance with instructed "beliefs." The strength of such inclinations, however, is generally weak and is dependent on how much emphasis was placed on consistency in the client's subculture. Third, direct cognitive manipulation can help with $A \rightarrow C$ problems through engendering covert contingencies and rules. For example, an unintended effect of rationally convincing clients to hold a certain belief is that it involves a therapist demand or description implying that if the clients behave as told they will get better (a rule). If the clients do behave differently, and this new way of behaving is naturally reinforced, the clients improve. For example, Beck et al. (1979) encouraged clients to act against their assumptions because it is "the most powerful way to change it" (p. 264). Although Beck preferred to view this intervention as changing a cognition (an assumption), it can also be seen as the therapist issuing a rule and the client following a rule that results in exposing the client's behavior to contingencies that directly strengthen the improved behavior. This emphasis on building in new behavior is consistent with a functional analysis.

When the client changes to please the therapist, however, it can be countertherapeutic. The danger is that improvements will not be maintained by the natural reinforcers in the client's daily life and the gains made in therapy will be lost when therapy ends. Since direct cognitive manipulations involve instructions on how to think or behave and make explicit demands for improvements, it is difficult to avoid pleasing the therapist. A notable exception is the use in Beck et al. (1979) of the Socratic method and "hypothesis testing," which we view as ingenious ways of reducing motivation to please the therapist and of bringing clients into contact with natural reinforcers.

Although appeals to reason are consistent with a functional analytic approach, when such interventions are not successful, they are treated differently from what a therapist would do within a cognitive frame-

work (for example, raise additional arguments as to why the client's thoughts are incorrect). From a functional analytic perspective, getting Harriet, for example, to change her belief by rationally convincing her that "she *can* stand anger" is not guaranteed to have a favorable result. No guarantee exists because it is unclear what behavior has been changed due to the convincing other than her saying, "OK, I believe I can stand it."

When a client changes a belief statement because of a therapist's logical arguments, the meaning of the statement changes. Before the therapeutic intervention, the belief statement had the property of being a description of past experiences or an indication of the likelihood of certain actions. After the client's belief is changed due to the therapist's logical arguments, it is no longer derived from experience but is instead a response made to please the therapist or to conform to the rules of logic. It is therefore not surprising that many clients who have been "convinced" to change their beliefs subsequently do not change their behavior in the problem situation. Such "failures" are usually accompanied by explanations such as, "I believe it intellectually, but I do not accept it on an emotional level." From a functional analytic standpoint, this inconsistency is not perplexing since there is no reason to expect anything else. Strategies to deal with such inconsistencies would be to accept them and to identify variables that account for behaviors, such as espousing belief *X* and acting consistent with belief *Y*, trying to be consistent in espousing and acting, or trying to please the therapist by being rational.

VII. New Directions

Although there have been several functional analyses of outpatient treatment of adults (Ferster, 1972a, 1972b; Glenn, 1983; Greenspoon & Brownstein, 1967; Hamilton, 1988; Skinner, 1953), they were primarily intended to offer behavioral descriptions of the process and did not add to technique. Recent extensions of this work, Hayes's (Hayes, 1987; Hayes & Melancon, 1989) acceptance and commitment therapy (ACT) and Kohlenberg and Tsai's (1991) functional analytic psychotherapy (FAP), have produced new approaches to treatment that expand the goals and populations encompassed by behavior therapy.

ACT gives clients a counterintuitive method of experiencing and accepting troublesome thoughts, feelings, memories, bodily states, and behavioral predispositions without necessarily having to change them, escape from them, do what they say, or avoid them. Although acceptance has long been a component in nonbehavioral approaches, with some important exceptions (Jacobson, 1992; Linehan, 1993), it has largely been neglected in behavior therapy. ACT encourages clients to feel and emotionally respond. ACT is based on recent laboratory findings on stimulus equivalence, a uniquely human phenomenon that accounts for the symbolic nature of verbal stimuli and the role verbal stimuli play in generalization (Devany, Hayes, & Nelson, 1986; Hayes, 1991; Hayes, Brownstein, Devany, Kohlenberg, & Shelby, 1987; Hayes, Kohlenberg, & Hayes, 1991; Kohlenberg, Hayes, & Hayes, 1991; Wulfert & Hayes, 1988).

FAP is informed by the literature and laboratory findings of radical behaviorism and by Kohlenberg and Tsai's (1991) observations of clients who changed dramatically when involved in intense client-therapist relationships. FAP relies on an involved, emotional, nonmanipulative, client-therapist relationship as the vehicle of change. A therapy environment is constructed in which the client's daily life problems can occur in the session and be changed by the naturally reinforcing reactions of the therapist. Consistent with functional analysis, there is an emphasis on affective response and on natural rather than arbitrary reinforcement. The emotional responses of the client indicates that he or she is in touch with clinically relevant behavior, and the emotional responses of the therapist are potentially similar to those in the community and can thus facilitate natural reinforcement during the session.

ACT is intended for "therapy-wise" clients who have not improved with previous treatment. FAP is aimed at problems that are not usually dealt with by behavior therapists. For example, Kohlenberg and Tsai (1991) illustrate behavioral approaches to diffuse and pervasive interpersonal problems as well as to problems of the self, such as multiple personality disorder, narcissistic personality disorder, borderline personality disorder, and the experience of an unstable and insecure self as described by object relations therapists (Cashdan, 1988).

Stanley Greben (1981), a psychodynamic therapist, described the "heat" in the therapeutic relationship that he held responsible for exceptional improvements in clients. Many behavior therapists have had memorable clients with whom they had especially intense relationships who also improved in ways beyond the goals of treatment. Although behavior therapists would not refer to it as "heat," something important transpired in the client-therapist relationships in those cases. A reintroduction of functional analysis into behavior therapy offers promise in understanding the therapeutic interaction and, perhaps, of bringing the "heat" into the behavioral realm.

References

AYLLON, T. (1963). Intensive treatment of psychotic behavior by stimulus satiation and food reinforcement. *Behaviour Research and Therapy, 1,* 53–62.

AYLLON, T., & Azrin, N. H. (1965). The measurement and reinforcement of behavior of psychotics. *Journal of the Experimental Analysis of Behavior, 8,* 357–387.

BECK, A. T. (1976). *Cognitive therapy and the emotional disorders.* New York: International Universities Press.

BECK, A. T. (1984). Cognition and therapy. *Archives of General Psychiatry, 41,* 1112–1114.

BECK, A. T., Emery, G., & Greenberg, R. L. (1986). *Anxiety disorders and phobias: A cognitive perspective.* New York: Basic Books.

BECK, A. T., Rush, A., Shaw, B., & Emery, G. (1979). *Cognitive therapy of depression.* New York: Guilford Press.

BEIDEL, B., & Turner, S. (1986). A critique of the theoretical bases of cognitive behavioral theories and therapy. *Clinical Psychology Review, 6,* 177–197.

BRANCH, M. N. (1987). Behavior analysis: A conceptual and empirical base for behavior therapy. *The Behavior Therapist, 4,* 79–84.

BRENNER, C. (1978). Working alliance, therapeutic alliance, and transference. *Journal of the American Psychoanalytic Association, 27,* 137–157.

CASHDAN, S. (1988). *Object relations therapy.* New York: Norton.

CATANIA, A. C. (1991). The gifts of culture and eloquence: An open letter to Michael J. Mahoney in reply to his article "Scientific psychology and radical behaviorism." *The Behavior Analyst, 14,* 61–72.

CAUTELA, J. R. (1970). Covert reinforcement. *Behavior Therapy, 1,* 33–50.

CHOMSKY, N. (1959). Review of Skinner's *Verbal behavior. Language, 35,* 26–58.

CIMINERO, A. R., Calhoun, S. K., & Adams, H. E. (1977). *Handbook of behavioral assessment.* New York: Wiley.

CONGER, J. C., & Conger, A. J. (1982). Components of heterosocial competence. In J. P. Curran & P. M. Monti (Eds.), *Social skills training* (pp. 313–347). New York: Guilford Press.

COYNE, J. C., & Gotlib, I. H. (1983) The role of cognition in depression: A critical appraisal. *Psychological Bulletin, 94,* 472–505.

DAY, W. (1969). Radical behaviorism in reconciliation with phenomenology. *Journal of the Experimental Analysis of Behavior, 12,* 315–328.

DERUBEIS, R., & Feely, M. (1990). Determinants of change in cognitive therapy for depression. *Cognitive Therapy and Research, 14,* 469–482.

DEVANY, J. M., Hayes, S. C., & Nelson, R. O. (1986). Equivalence class formation in language-able and language-disabled children. *Journal of the Experimental Analysis of Behavior, 46,* 243–257.

DEVOGE, J. T., & Beck, S. (1978). The therapist-client relationship in behavior therapy. In M. Hersen, R. M. Eisler, & P. M. Miller (Eds.), *Progress in behavior modification: Volume 6* (pp. 204–248). New York: Academic Press.

DOUGHER, M. J. (1989). A functional analysis of a behavior analyst's functional analysis. *The Analysis of Verbal Behavior, 7,* 19–23.

ELLIS, A. (1962). *Reason and emotion in psychotherapy.* New York: Lyle Stuart.

ELLIS, A. (1970). *The essence of rational emotive therapy: A comprehensive approach to treatment.* New York: Institute for Rational Living.

FERSTER, C. B. (1967). Arbitrary and natural reinforcement. *The Psychological Record, 22,* 1–16.

FERSTER, C. B. (1972a). An experimental analysis of clinical phenomena. *The Psychological Record, 22,* 1–16.

FERSTER, C. B. (1972b). Psychotherapy from the standpoint of a behaviorist. In J. D. Keehn (Ed.), *Psychopathology in animals: Research and clinical implications* (pp. 279–304). New York: Academic Press.

FERSTER, C. B. (1973). A functional analysis of depression. *American Psychologist, 28,* 857–870.

FOA, E. B., & Steketee, G. (1987). Behavioral treatment of phobics and obsessive-compulsives. In N. S. Jacobson (Ed.), *Psychotherapists in clinical practice: Cognitive and behavioral perspectives* (pp. 78–120). New York: Guilford Press.

FRANK, J. D. (1972). *Persuasion and healing.* Baltimore, MD: Johns Hopkins University Press.

FREUD, S. (1965). *The interpretation of dreams.* New York: Avon Books. (First German edition, 1900)

GLENN, S. (1983). Maladaptive functional relations in client verbal behavior. *The Behavior Analyst, 6,* 47–56.

GOLDFRIED, M. R. (1982). Resistance and clinical behavior therapy. In P. L. Wachtel (Ed.), *Resistance: Psychodynamic and behavioral approaches* (pp. 95–113). New York: Plenum.

GOLDFRIED, M. R., & Davison, G. C. (1976). *Clinical behavior therapy.* New York: Holt, Rinehart & Winston.

GREBEN, S. E. (1981). The essence of psychotherapy. *British Journal of Psychiatry, 138,* 449–455.

GREENSPOON, J., & Brownstein, A. J. (1967). Psychotherapy from the standpoint of a behaviorist. *The Psychological Record, 17,* 401–416.

GUIDANO, V. F., & Liotti, G. (1983). *Cognitive processes and emotional disorders.* New York: Guilford Press.

HAMILTON, S. A. (1988). Behavioral formulations of verbal behavior in therapy. *Clinical Psychology Review, 8,* 181–193.

HAYES, S. C. (1987). A contextual approach to therapeutic change. In N. S. Jacobson (Ed.), *Psychotherapists in clinical practice: Cognitive and behavioral perspectives* (pp. 327–387). New York: Guilford Press.

HAYES, S. C. (1991). A relational control theory of stimulus equivalence. In L. J. Hayes & P. N. Chase (Eds.), *Dialogues on verbal behavior* (pp. 19–40). Reno, NV: Context Press.

HAYES, S. C., & Brownstein, A. J. (1986). Mentalism, behavior-behavior relations, and a behavior analytic view of the purpose of science. *The Behavior Analyst, 9,* 175–190.

HAYES, S. C., Brownstein, A. J., Devany, J. M., Kohlenberg, B. S., & Shelby, J. (1987). Stimulus equivalence and the symbolic control of behavior. *Mexican Journal of Behavior Analysis, 13,* 361–374.

HAYES, S. C., Hayes, L. J., & Reese, S. W. (1988). Finding the philosophical core: A revue of Stephen C. Pepper's *World hypotheses. Journal of the Experimental Analysis of Behavior, 8,* 357–387.

HAYES, S. C., Kohlenberg, B. K., & Hayes, L. J. (1991). Transfer of consequential functions through simple and conditional equivalence classes. *Journal of the Experimental Analysis of Behavior, 56,* 119–139.

HAYES, S. C., & Melancon, S. M. (1989). Comprehensive distancing, paradox, and the treatment of emotional avoidance. In M. Ascher (Ed.), *Paradoxical procedures in psychotherapy* (pp. 184–218). New York: Guilford Press.

HAYNES, S. N., & O'Brien, W. H. (1990). Functional analysis in behavior therapy. *Clinical Psychology Review, 10,* 649–668.

HERSEN, M. (1970). The complementary use of behavior therapy and psychotherapy: Some comments. *The Psychological Record, 20,* 395–402.

HOLLON, S. D., & Kriss, M. R. (1984). Cognitive factors in clinical research and practice. *Clinical Psychology Review, 4,* 35–76.

HOWARD, K. I., & Orlinsky, D. I. (1972). Psychotherapeutic processes. *Annual Review of Psychology, 23,* 615–668.

JACOBSON, N. S. (1987). Cognitive and behavior therapists in clinical practice: An introduction. In N. Jacobson (Ed.), *Psychotherapists in clinical practice: Cognitive and behavioral perspectives* (pp. 1–9). New York: Guilford Press.

JACOBSON, N. S. (1989). The therapist-client relationship in cognitive behavior therapy: Implications for treating depression. *Journal of Cognitive Psychotherapy, 3,* 85–96.

JACOBSON, N. S. (1992). Behavioral couple therapy: A new beginning. *Behavior Therapy, 23,* 493–506.

JONES, M. C. (1924). The elimination of children's fears. *Journal of Experimental Psychology, 1,* 383–390.

KAZDIN, A. E., & Wilson, G. T. (1978). *Evaluation of behavior therapy: Issues, evidence, and research strategies.* Cambridge, MA: Ballinger.

KENDALL, P. C., Kipnis, D., & Otto-Salaj, L. (1992). When clients do not progress: Influences on and explanations for lack of progress. *Cognitive Therapy and Research, 16,* 269–281.

KIM, N. S. (1979). Multidimensional-behavioral treatment of interpersonal anxiety. *The Behavior Therapist, 2,* 33–35.

KLEIN, D. F. (1974). Endogenomorphic depression. *Archives of General Psychiatry, 31,* 447–454.

KOHLENBERG, B. S., Hayes, S. C., & Hayes, L. J. (1991). The transfer of contextual control over equivalence classes through equivalence classes: A possible model of social stereotyping. *Journal of the Experimental Analysis of Behavior, 56,* 505–525.

KOHLENBERG, R. J. (1973). Operant control of multiple personality. *Behavior Therapy, 4,* 137–140.

KOHLENBERG, R. J., & Tsai, M. (1987). Functional analytic psychotherapy. In N. Jacobson (Ed.), *Psychotherapists in clinical practice: Cognitive and behavioral perspectives* (pp. 388–443). New York: Guilford Press.

KOHLENBERG, R. J., & Tsai, M. (1991). *Functional analytic psychotherapy: Creating intense and curative therapeutic relationships.* New York: Plenum.

KRANTZ, S. E. (1985). When depressive cognitions reflect negative realities. *Cognitive Therapy and Research, 9*(6), 595–610.

KRASNER, L. (1982). Behavior therapy: On roots, contexts, and growth. In G. T. Wilson & C. M. Franks (Eds.), *Contemporary behavior therapy* (pp. 11–62). New York: Guilford Press.

LANG, P. J. (1969). Desensitization and the laboratory study of human fear. In C. M. Franks (Ed.), *Behavior therapy: Appraisal and status* (pp. 160–191). New York: McGraw-Hill.

LEIGLAND, S. (Ed.). (1992). *Radical behaviorism: Willard Day on psychology and philosophy.* Reno, NV: Context Press.

LINEHAN, M. M. (1993). *Cognitive behavioral treatment of borderline personality disorder: The dialectics of effective treatment.* New York: Guilford Press.

LUTZKER, J., & Martin, G. (1981). *Behavior change.* Pacific Grove, CA: Brooks/Cole.

MacCORQUODALE, K. (1970). On Chomsky's review of Skinner's *Verbal behavior. Journal of the Experimental Analysis of Behavior, 13.*

MORRIS, E. K. (1990). What Mahoney "knows." *American Psychologist, 45,* 1178–1179.

NELSON, R. O., & Barlow, D. H. (1981). Behavioral assessment: Basic strategies and initial procedures. In D. Barlow (Ed.), *Behavioral assessment of adult disorders* (pp. 13–44). New York: Guilford Press.

O'LEARY, K. D., & Becker, W. C. (1967). Behavior modification of an adjustment class: A token reinforcement program. *Exceptional Children, 33,* 637–642.

ORLINSKY, D., & Howard, K. (1978). Relation of process and outcome in psychotherapy. In S. Garfield & A. Bergin (Eds.), *Handbook of psychotherapy and behavior change: An empirical analysis* (2nd ed., pp. 283–329). New York: Wiley.

PAUL, G. (1966). *Insight versus desensitization: An experiment in anxiety reduction.* Stanford: Stanford University Press.

PEPPER, S. C. (1957). *World hypotheses.* Berkeley: University of California Press.

QUATTRONE, G. A. (1985). On the congruity between internal states and action. *Psychological Bulletin, 98,* 3–30.

RAMSEY, R. W. (1974). Emotional training: An extension of desensitization. *Behavioral Engineering, 2,* 24–27.

REISINGER, J. J. (1972). The treatment of anxiety-depression via positive reinforcement and response cost. *Journal of Applied Behavior Analysis, 5,* 125–130.

RIMM, D. C., & Masters, J. C. (1979). *Behavior therapy: Techniques and empirical findings* (2nd ed.). San Francisco: Academic Press.

RUSSELL, P. L., & Brandsma, J. M. (1974). A theoretical and empirical integration of the rational emotive and classical conditioning theories. *Journal of Consulting and Clinical Psychology, 42*(3), 389–397.

RUSSELL, R. L. (Ed.). (1987). *Language and psychotherapy.* New York: Plenum.

SAFRAN, J. D. (1990a). Towards a refinement of cognitive therapy in light of interpersonal theory: I. Theory. *Clinical Psychology Review, 10,* 87–105.

SAFRAN, J. D. (1990b). Towards a refinement of cognitive therapy in light of interpersonal theory: II. Practice. *Clinical Psychology Review, 10,* 107–121.

SAFRAN, J. D., McMain, S., Crocker, P., & Murray, P. (1990). Therapeutic alliance rupture as a therapy event for empirical investigation. *Psychotherapy: Theory, Research and Practice, 27,* 154–165.

SAFRAN, J. D., & Segal, Z. V. (1990). *Interpersonal process in cognitive therapy.* New York: Basic Books.

SAFRAN, J. D., Vallis, T. M., Segal, Z. V., & Shaw, B. F. (1986). Assessment of core cognitive processes in cognitive therapy. *Cognitive Therapy and Research, 10*(5), 509–526.

SCOTT, R., Himadi, W., & Keane, T. (1983). Generalization of social skills. In M. Hersen, R. Eisler, & P. Miller (Eds.), *Progress in behavior modification: Volume 15* (pp. 114–172). New York: Academic Press.

SILVERMAN, J., Silverman, J. D., & Eardley, D. (1984). In reply. *Archives of General Psychiatry, 41,* 1112.

SKINNER, B. F. (1953). *Science and human behavior.* New York: Macmillan.

SKINNER, B. F. (1957). *Verbal behavior.* New York: Appleton-Century-Crofts.

SKINNER, B. F. (1966). An operant analysis of problem solving. In B. Kleinmuntz (Ed.), *Problem-solving: Research, method, and theory* (pp. 225–257). New York: Wiley.

SKINNER, B. F. (1969). *Contingencies of reinforcement.* New York: Appleton-Century-Crofts.

SKINNER, B. F. (1974). *About behaviorism.* New York: Knopf.

SKINNER, B. F. (1982). Contrived reinforcement. *The Behavior Analyst, 5,* 3–8.

STRUPP, H. (1968). Psychoanalytic therapy of the individual. In J. Marmor (Ed.), *Modern psychoanalysis: New directions and perspectives* (pp. 293–342). New York: Basic Books.

STRUPP, H. (1989). Psychotherapy: Can the practitioner learn from the researcher? *American Psychologist, 44,* 712–724.

SULLIVAN, H. S. (1953). *The interpersonal theory of psychiatry.* New York: Norton.

SWEET, A. A. (1984). The therapeutic relationship in behavior therapy. *Clinical Psychology Review, 4,* 253–272.

TURK, D., & Salovey, P. (1985). Cognitive structures, processes and cognitive behavior modification. *Cognitive Therapy and Research, 9,* 1–17.

TURKAT, I. D., & Brantley, P. J. (1981). On the therapeutic relationship in behavior therapy. *The Behavior Therapist, 4,* 16–17.

WACHTEL, P. L. (1977). *Psychoanalysis and behavior therapy: Toward an integration.* New York: Basic Books.

WATSON, J. B., & Rayner, M. (1920). Conditioned emotional reactions. *Journal of Experimental Psychology, 3,* 1–14.

WESSELLS, M. G. (1982). A critique on Skinner's views of the obstructive character of cognitive theories. *Behaviorism, 10,* 65–84.

WILSON, G. T., & O'Leary, K. D. (1980). *Principles of behavior therapy.* New Jersey: Prentice-Hall.

WILSON, T. G., & Evans, I. M. (1977). The therapist-client relationship in behavior therapy. In A. Gurman & A. Razin (Eds.), *Effective psychotherapy: A handbook of research* (pp. 544–565). New York: Pergamon Press.

WOLBERG, L. (1977). *The technique of psychotherapy.* San Francisco: Grune & Stratton.

WOLF, M. M., Risley, T., & Mees, H. L. (1964). Application of operant conditioning procedures to the behavior problems of an autistic child. *Behaviour Research and Therapy, 1,* 305–312.

WOLMAN, B. (1967). *Psychoanalytic techniques.* New York: Basic Books.

WOLPE, J. (1958). *Psychotherapy by reciprocal inhibition.* Stanford: Stanford University Press.

WOLPE, J. (1981). Behavior therapy versus psychoanalysis: Therapeutic and social implications. *American Psychologist, 36,* 159–164.

WULFERT, E., & Hayes, S. C. (1988). The transfer of conditional sequencing through conditional equivalence classes. *Journal of the Experimental Analysis of Behavior, 50,* 125–144.

ZETTLE, R. D., & Hayes, S. C. (1982). Rule governed behavior: A potential theoretical framework for cognitive-behavioral therapy. In P. C. Kendall (Ed.), *Advances in cognitive behavioral research and therapy* (Vol. 1, pp. 73–118). New York: Academic Press.

ZURIFF, G. (1985). *Behaviorism: A conceptual reconstruction.* New York: Columbia University Press.

CHAPTER 2

Psychosocial Interventions for Adolescent Depression: Issues, Evidence, and Future Directions

Harry M. Hoberman
Gregory N. Clarke
Stephen M. Saunders

I. Introduction
II. Adolescent Psychotherapy Research
III. The Nature of Depressive Disorders among Adolescents
   A. Definition
   B. Phenomenology of Adolescent Depression
   C. Epidemiology of Adolescent Depression
   D. Associated Clinical Characteristics of Depressive Episodes during Adolescence
     1. Comorbidity
     2. Psychosocial Impairment
     3. Residual Functioning
     4. Recurrence and Follow-Up
   E. Psychosocial Correlates and Antecedents of Adolescent Depression
   F. Developmental Factors in Increased Risk for Depressive Episodes during Adolescence
   G. Mental Health Services Utilization among Depressed Youth
IV. Etiological Theories and Models of Psychosocial Treatment of Depressive Episodes
V. Efficacy of Psychotherapy of Depressive Episodes among Adults
VI. Theories and Issues in the Psychosocial Treatment of Depressed Adolescents
   A. Etiological and Maintenance Factors in Adolescent Depression: Common Targets in the Treatment of Depressed Adolescents
   B. Models of Treatment of Depressive Disorders in Adolescents
     1. Cognitive Behavioral Models
     2. An Integrative Cognitive Behavioral Intervention: The Adolescent Coping With Depression Course
     3. Interpersonal Psychotherapy
     4. Psychodynamic Therapy
     5. Family Therapy
VII. Treatment Outcome Research for Depressive Disorders among Adolescents
   A. Pharmacological Treatment of Adolescent Depression
   B. Psychotherapy Case Studies
   C. Uncontrolled Psychotherapy Studies
   D. Controlled Psychotherapy Outcome Studies
   E. Comparative Psychotherapy Outcome Studies
VIII. Psychosocial Treatments of Suicidal Adolescents
IX. Prevention of Adolescent Depression
X. Common Tactics and Developmental Considerations in Psychosocial Treatments for Depressed Adolescents
XI. Critique and Future Direction of Psychosocial Treatments for Adolescent Depression
XII. Conclusion
References

I. Introduction

Progress in understanding the psychological treatment of adolescents with psychiatric disorders is in its nascent period. While preliminary data have accumulated that outline certain parameters and themes of effective psychotherapy with youth, much work remains to be done to identify specific interventions for particular psychiatric disorders. After years of relative neglect and disavowal, adolescent depression has emerged as a psychiatric condition of considerable scientific interest. A veritable explosion of basic research investigations of the depressive disorders among youth has occurred over the past ten years. Important information regarding the epidemiology, clinical characteristics, and outcome of depressive episodes during adolescence is increasingly available. It has become apparent that depression during adolescence should be viewed as a central public health issue.

Despite the improved understanding regarding the nature of depressive disorders, however, the literature on psychosocial treatments of these disorders has received surprisingly little attention until quite recently. Both the theories of the etiology of adolescent depression and the theories of appropriate interventions remain quite limited. Moreover, they are primarily downward extensions of models developed for adult depression and typically lack a developmental perspective. Actual studies of psychotherapies of depressed youth are very much in a preliminary phase. However, the limited results of existing studies are suggestive of certain critical ingredients involved in effective interventions for adolescents who are depressed. In contrast, more extensive clinical and research efforts have been directed at evaluating pharmacological interventions for depressive disorders in youth. Unfortunately, the available results of such somatotherapies indicate that a variety of active medications are relatively ineffective in treating depressed adolescents; this increases the importance of identifying one or more psychosocial interventions that can be successful in ameliorating adolescent depression.

The writing of this article by the first author was supported by a research grant R01MH47786 from the National Institute of Mental Health.

The purpose of this chapter is to provide a framework for understanding the current theoretical and empirical bases for psychosocial treatments for depressive disorders during adolescence. To this end, two important domains are initially reviewed. First, the empirical literature concerning psychotherapy with adolescents is examined to provide a context for discussing both available theories and investigations of the specific interventions for depressed youth. Second, the relevant clinical characteristics of depressions in adolescents are reviewed to allow for an adequate understanding of the relevant treatment concerns among such youth. Following this, descriptions are provided for the major etiological and psychotherapeutic models of depression in adults and adolescents. In particular, the most well-developed intervention for depressed adolescents, the Adolescent Coping With Depression Course, is described in detail as an examplar of potential interventions for this population. Next, the available outcome data on the effectiveness of specific intervention strategies for adolescent depression are then reviewed. Treatments for suicidal adolescents and for the prevention of depressive disorders among youth are also considered. Finally, remaining issues of treatment theory and practice are noted to provide the basis for future directions in research.

II. Adolescent Psychotherapy Research

A large body of research exists on psychotherapy with adults, and its efficacy has been repeatedly demonstrated (for example, Smith, Glass, & Miller, 1980). In contrast, relatively little systematic research exists regarding the effectiveness of psychotherapy for adolescents with psychiatric disorders. Early reviews of child psychotherapy literature (for example, Levitt, 1957, 1963, 1971) suggested that such interventions had little impact on youth with psychiatric problems. Subsequent reviews have generally argued that it was too early to conclude anything definitive about general efficacy but that the available evidence demonstrating effectiveness was positive. For example, Tramontana (1980) reviewed studies of psychotherapy with adolescents published between 1967 and 1977. He judged that only five of the available experimental studies of therapy outcome were "exemplary" in methodology. Fortunately, all five indicated significantly better outcome for the adolescents who received therapy.

More recent reviews of the literature are even more reassuring. Casey and Berman (1985) examined 75 outcome studies that compared a therapy condition with either a control or different treatment condition. The subjects in these studies were children ages 3 through 15. This meta-analysis concluded that therapy with children was equivalent in effectiveness to therapy with adults. The authors also concluded, however, that methodological weaknesses, such as vague diagnostic categorizations and lack of treatment specificity ("particularly for nonbehavioral therapies" [p. 397]), were quite common.

Likewise, Weisz, Weiss, Alicke, and Klotz (1987) conducted a meta-analysis of the existing controlled outcome studies with youths ages 4 to 18. Only about 30% of the studies in their analysis were also included in the analysis by Casey and Berman (1985). Weisz et al. (1987) also found that psychotherapy with youth appears similar in effectiveness to that with adult populations. They determined that the effect size (ES) for treatment (versus a control condition) was statistically significant, with an average ES of 0.79. In particular, their analysis suggested that behavioral techniques were more effective than nonbehavioral ones, but this may have been because nonbehavioral interventions were more poorly specified (compare with Casey & Berman, 1985). Effect sizes were not significantly different for studies that focused on overcontrolled versus undercontrolled behaviors. Of the 108 therapy outcome studies reviewed, however, only 61 involved adolescents (ages 13 to 18), and these yielded a mean treatment ES of 0.58. This was significantly smaller than the mean ES of 0.92 in comparisons involving children (ages 4 to 12). Thus, psychotherapy with adolescents appeared less effective compared to such therapy with younger children.

In a meta-analysis of 20 studies of family therapies, Hazelrigg, Cooper, and Borduin (1987) also found that such therapies were generally effective, with mean ESs of between 0.45 and 0.50.

Although Weisz et al. (1987) concluded that their results were encouraging regarding the effectiveness

of psychotherapy with youth, they noted that "the number of available outcome studies is still much too modest to permit definitive analysis" (p. 548). Furthermore, the relevance of existing psychotherapy research to actual clinical practice has been called into question by a number of writers. Kazdin, Bass, Ayers, and Rodgers (1990) evaluated 223 studies that were deemed adequate for inclusion in their review. However, over 75% of the available studies involved cases solicited by the researchers, only 36% investigated individual treatment—forms of behavior modification were the treatment modality in almost half the studies (with cognitive behavioral therapies accounting for an additional 22%)—and less than 1% of the studies involved psychodynamic therapy. Barrnett, Docherty, and Frommelt (1991) reported a review of nonbehavioral child and adolescent psychotherapy but concluded that little could be determined from the available data. Similar conclusions were offered by Shirk and Russell (1992) regarding such therapies; however, they noted that the available studies did not allow ruling out the effectiveness of nonbehavioral interventions.

Furthermore, Kazdin et al. (1990) noted that the relationship between the process and outcome of therapy was investigated in less than 3% of the studies and that most of the available studies were marked by the inclusion of subjects with mild symptomatology, small sample sizes, and a lack of specification of treatment strategies. Similarly, most of the studies in the Weisz et al. (1987) review involved a relatively homogeneous sample of youth (with respect to the targeted problem) who were recruited to the study; in contrast, most clinical work is done with a fairly heterogeneous population of youth who are symptomatic enough to have been referred for treatment. Barrnett et al. (1991) also noted a high number of methodological errors in available studies of nonbehavioral psychotherapy; among other issues, they noted that only 23% focused on adolescents of age 13 or more and that the vast majority of such interventions were of less than six months duration. As Barrnett et al. argued, many questions regarding adolescent psychotherapy remain "largely *untested* according to contemporary methodological standards" (p. 11).

The most common psychosocial interventions practiced in the community involve a traditional form of individual psychotherapy, predominantly psychodynamic in nature (Kovacs & Paulauskas, 1986; Tuma & Sobotka, 1993), quite different from the types of psychotherapeutic modalities most commonly evaluated in treatment outcome studies. As Kazdin et al. (1990) argued, "many of the techniques frequently used in clinical work (for example, psychodynamically oriented therapy, family therapy, play therapy) suffer from empirical neglect" (p. 738). They pointed out that 89% of child psychiatrists and 50% of child psychologists rate psychodynamic therapy as useful most or all of the time, and they noted data indicating that most mental health professionals are quite convinced of the superior efficacy of individual psychotherapy. Yet these modalities of psychotherapy are significantly underrepresented in available studies of treatments for youth with mental health problems (for example, Shirk & Russell, 1992). Further, as Kazdin et al. (1990) showed, the mean numbers of sessions for practicing child psychiatrists and child psychologists were 35 and 21, respectively, whereas most research studies utilized much briefer interventions.

Compounding the controversy of the mismatch of research and actual clinical practice, Weisz and Weiss (1989) examined the effectiveness of therapy as actually practiced in nine public outpatient clinics in the community. They found that youth who completed a course of such "representative" therapy did not significantly differ from those who dropped out of treatment with respect to a variety of outcome measures. In short, it appeared as if treatment as typically practiced in the community was not especially effective. In a more recent review of a number of clinic-based studies, Weisz, Weiss, and Donenberg (1992) concluded that studies of clinic-referred children treated by practicing clinicians in clinic settings have not shown statistically significant effects of psychotherapy. As they state:

> Currently, we lack convincing evidence that the large positive effects of psychotherapy demonstrated in controlled psychotherapy research . . . are being replicated in the clinic and community settings where most real-life interventions actually occur. (p. 1584)

Weisz and Weiss theorized that subjects in clinical research studies may actually fare better than patients in the community because of the presumed greater reliance on more structured and controlled interven-

tion practices as well as the possibility of less disturbed adolescents being represented in research studies. Clearly, while the empirical evidence indicates that psychotherapy with adolescents appears to be better than no treatment, it must be concluded that extant research tells us little about the effectiveness of adolescent psychotherapy as it is actually practiced.

As Barrnett et al. (1991) concluded at the end of their recent review of child psychotherapy research:

> At this juncture, there is a critical need in the area of child psychotherapy for the development of well-delineated, measurable, and differentiated models of treatment that will lend themselves to basic and comparative study. . . .
>
> Child psychotherapy research is a ripe area for investigation, and the methodology of adult psychotherapy research can be readily applied. Any such study will represent a major contribution. (pp. 11–12)

Perhaps it is not surprising, given early pessimistic conclusions about the efficacy of psychosocial interventions with adolescents, that relatively little knowledge exists about how this population fares in psychotherapy in general and about the relative efficacy of particular interventions. While a generic and limited sense of the efficacy of research-based interventions now exists, it is significant that little knowledge is available about the treatment of adolescents with specific disorders (for example, depression) and about the aspects of therapeutic encounter (for example, process variables) that are associated with successful and unsuccessful treatment experiences. If effect sizes for specific research interventions are substantially smaller for adolescents (who generally receive similar types of treatment packages as children), as Weisz et al. demonstrated, then such process variables would be especially important to investigate.

III. The Nature of Depressive Disorders among Adolescents

A. Definition

According to the DSM-III-R (APA, 1987), two types of depressive disorders are defined. Major depressive disorder (MDD) is defined as relatively pronounced change in a youth's overall functioning characterized by a constellation of symptoms. Dysphoric mood (either sadness or irritability) or anhedonia (loss of interest or enjoyment in most activities) must be present along with at least four other symptoms: sleep disturbances, appetite disturbances, fatigue, psychomotor agitation or retardation, concentration difficulties and impairment in decision making, feelings of worthlessness or guilt, or suicidal ideation or behavior. Thus, a minimum of five symptoms must be present for nearly every day for a minimum of two weeks.

Dysthymic disorder (DD) is conceptualized as a more chronic depressive disorder, defined by less intense symptoms. The mood disturbance, which can be persistent or phasic in nature, is defined by sad or irritable mood, most of the day, for most of a one-year period. During this year, periods of up to two months can occur where the dysphoric mood dissipates. In addition, at least two of the following other symptoms must also be present over the one-year period of the mood disturbance: sleep disturbances, appetite disturbances, fatigue, concentration difficulties and impairment in decision making, low self-esteem, or hopelessness. Thus, MDD and DD differ from one another primarily in the length and topography of the mood disturbance and in the types of accompanying cognitive symptoms (for example, MDD: worthlessness or guilt, suicidal ideation versus DD: hopelessness, low self-esteem). Double depression (Keller & Shapiro, 1982) refers to a condition where an individual meets diagnostic criteria for both a present episode of DD and MDD, where a chronic depressive disorder overlaps in time with a more pronounced deterioration in mood and functioning; the DD can either precede or follow the occurrence of the episode of MDD.

B. Phenomenology of Adolescent Depression

Until recently, what we knew about the clinical picture or phenomenology of adolescent depressive disorders had to be extrapolated from studies of adults. This problem has been rectified by recent studies. Ryan and colleagues (1987) assessed the frequency and severity of the various symptoms associated with depression in a clinical sample of adolescents using the Schedule for Affective Disorders and Schizophrenia for School-Aged Children, Present Episodes (K-SADS-P) (Chambers et al., 1985). Of the 92 adolescents (average age 14.7) who met criteria for a diagnosis of major depressive disorder, 88% were found to have moderately or severely depressed mood. The other most frequently reported symptoms, rated as at least mild for over half the sample, were: mood reactivity, decreased concentration, and anhedonia (each 87%); anger or irritability (83%); fatigue (82%); negative self-image (75%); insomnia and social withdrawal (each 73%); psychomotor retardation (71%); hopelessness or helplessness (68%); somatic complaints (66%); psychomotor agitation and suicidal ideation (each 61%); guilt (53%); and anorexia (52%). Fully 34% of the depressed adolescents had made a suicide attempt during their present episode of MDD. It is noteworthy that only 47% exhibited the physical appearance of even mild depression, which may help account for the frequent finding that adolescent depression is largely unrecognized and vastly undertreated. In another study, Kutcher, Marton, and Korenblum (1989) found that among depressed adolescents classic vegetative symptoms were less prevalent than negative cognitions.

No detailed study of the clinical picture of DD in adolescents has yet been published. However, Ryan et al. (1987) described features of patients who had been ill for at least two years—a group with either chronic MDD or overlapping MDD and DD. These more chronic patients were characterized by greater severity of depressed mood, psychomotor agitation, and irritability or anger. In addition, they manifested more severe suicidal ideation, greater seriousness and lethality of suicide attempts, and a greater number of suicide attempts.

Changes in the phenomenology of depression across the life span have also been examined. Carlson and Kashani (1988) used data from three studies to compare the frequency of depressive symptoms among patients diagnosed as having a major depressive disorder in preschool youth (Kashani & Carlson, 1987), prepubertal and adolescent youth (Ryan et al., 1987), and adults (Baker et al., 1971). Results suggested that adolescents are more likely than younger children, but less likely than adults, to exhibit the following symptoms: anhedonia, hopelessness, psychomotor retardation, fatigue, and anorexia. Adolescents are more likely than adults, but less likely than younger children, to exhibit depressed appearance, negative self-image, somatic complaints, and hallucinations. Among the three groups, adolescents were the least likely to exhibit diurnal variations in mood and psychomotor agitation but were the most likely to have made a suicide attempt.

C. Epidemiology of Adolescent Depression

Prevalence estimates for adolescent depression in the community have been generated by numerous studies, many of which are reviewed by Fleming and Offord (1990). Deykin, Levy, and Wells (1987) noted a prevalence of 7% MDD in a group of adolescents 16 to 19 years old. Kashani and colleagues (1987) interviewed a sample of 150 adolescents (ages 14 to 16) living in the community, and they found that 8% of their sample (2.7% males, 13.3% females) met criteria for a depressive disorder (4.7% MDD, 3.3% DD). In the Ontario Child Health Study (OCHS), Fleming, Offord, and Boyle (1989) found that the prevalence rate of major depression was 7.2% for females and 2.5% for males between the ages of 12 and 16. A community sample of high school students identified lifetime prevalence rates of 4% for MDD and of 4.9% for DD (Whitaker et al., 1990).

Most recently, a large epidemiological investigation of rates of depressive disorders was conducted by Lewinsohn, Hops, Roberts, Seeley, and Andrews (1993). Two panels of youth (panel 1 = 1710, panel 2 =1508) were assessed via the K-SADS. The point prevalence of MDD was 2.6% and 3.1% and for DD was 0.5 and 0.13 for panels 1 and 2 respectively. MDD had the highest lifetime prevalence (18.5% and 24.0%) of any psychiatric disorder in the samples, while the comparable figures for DD were (3.2% and 3.0%). First incidence rates of depressive disorders were 5.72% for MDD and 0.07% for DD.

Clinically, youth with depressive disorders constitute a significant proportion of those referred for treatment. Carlson and Cantwell (1980) reported that 23% of juvenile outpatients had a depressive disorder. Kolvin et al. (1991) found that 25% of referrals to a university-based child psychiatric clinic had MDD. In the U.S., at least 18% of children and adolescents admitted to psychiatric settings and nonfederal hospi-

tals had an initial diagnosis of an affective disorder (Silver, 1988).

Research has shown that adolescence appears to be a period of dramatically increased risk for the onset of episodes of depression, particularly for females. Several studies indicated that a progressive increase in rates of depression has occurred, with earlier age of onsets of episodes, in successive birth cohorts of adults (Klerman et al., 1985) and youth (Ryan et al., 1992). Typical age of onset for DD is between 6 and 13, while that for MDD is later; younger age of onset for DD predicts a more protracted episode (Kovacs, Feinberg, Crouse-Novak, Paulauskas, & Finkelstein, 1984a). In a community sample (Lewinsohn, Hops, et al., 1993), the ages of onset for MDD were 13.9 and 14.2 years for female and male subjects, while those for DD were 10.9 and 11.3 years. In a clinical sample, available evidence indicates that MDD is a disorder of relatively long duration, with the mean episode length of between seven and nine months; similarly, the average length of DD appears to be over 3.5 years (Kovacs, 1989). In contrast, in a community sample (Keller et al., 1988), the median duration of MDD for all cases was 16 weeks, while that for youth with a history of a psychiatric condition was 25 weeks, and that for youth with a concurrent nonaffective disorder was 32 weeks. However, the median duration of DD was 240 weeks. In another community sample (Lewinsohn et al., 1993), the mean duration of MDD was 24 weeks and for DD was 134 weeks; females were characterized by significantly longer episodes of DD but not MDD. However, most cases of MDD and DD are characterized by a high rate of eventual recovery, including those in community (Keller et al., 1988) and clinical (Kovacs et al., 1984a) samples.

D. Associated Clinical Characteristics of Depressive Episodes during Adolescence

As with adult populations (for example, Maser & Cloninger, 1990), there is increasing evidence that adolescent depression is a serious problem, often of long duration, that is typically comorbid with other psychiatric disorders and psychosocial problems. Moreover, depressive disorders during adolescence are associated with profound and long-lasting psychosocial impairment that exacerbates the present difficulties and elevates the risk of future depression episodes and other problems.

1. COMORBIDITY

There is a plethora of research indicating that when depressive disorders occur they are often comorbid with a variety of other psychiatric disorders, including the following conditions: anxiety disorders (for example, Kashani et al., 1987; Kovacs, Gatsonis, Paulauskas, & Richards, 1989), conduct disorders (for example, Kovacs, Paulauskas, Gatsonis, & Richards, 1988; Puig-Antich, 1982; Withers & Kaplan, 1987), learning disorders (for example, Weinberg, Rutman, Sullivan, Pencik, & Dietz, 1973), substance abuse disorders (for example, Friedman et al., 1982; Kashani et al., 1985), and personality disorders (for example, Friedman, Corn, Aronoff, Hurt, & Clarkin, 1984). Indeed, comorbid psychiatric disorders in youths with obsessive disorders appear to be the rule rather than the exception.

In their clinical sample, Ryan et al. (1987) found mild to severe conduct problems in 25% of the adolescents in their study. These researchers also reported fairly high levels of other comorbid symptoms and disorders. Moderate to severe separation anxiety disorder was found in 37% of the adolescent subjects, and there were high rates of phobia (27%), overanxious disorder (20%), and obsessive-compulsive disorder (11%). They likewise found that 22% of the depressed adolescents had used drugs during the depressive episode, and 16% reported drinking alcohol in a problematic manner. In a different sample of psychiatric inpatients, Friedman et al. (1984) reported that two-thirds of patients with MDD also met criteria for borderline personality disorder.

The rate of double depression among these adolescents was 58%. Similarly, Lewinsohn, Rohde, Seeley, and Hops (1991) examined the comorbidity of major depression and dysthymia among adolescents in the community. They reported that "the degree of current comorbidity was approximately twenty times greater than expected by chance; lifetime comorbidity was over three times greater than expected by chance" (p. 208). They also found that for adolescents who had double depression, 91% had developed the dysthymia prior to the major depres-

sion. Similar results were reported by Keller and colleagues (1988).

In this same community sample of adolescents, Rohde, Lewinsohn, and Seeley (1991) examined the comorbidity in adolescents with depressive disorders. Of the 50 adolescents who were determined to have a lifetime history of depressive disorder, 42% met criteria for another psychiatric disorder. The most common comorbid disorders were the anxiety disorders (18%), substance use disorder (14%), and the disruptive behavior disorders (8%). For those adolescents with a current episode of either MDD or DD, 66% had a history of another psychiatric disorder (Rohde, Lewinsohn, & Seeley, 1994). In the community sample studied by Kashani et al. (1987), all of the teenagers who met criteria for a diagnosis of a depressive disorder also met criteria for additional psychiatric diagnoses. Keller et al. (1988) found that 53% of youth with MDD had a history of at least one other psychiatric disorder, with the MDD secondary in every case. It should be reiterated that this last study also found that concurrent comorbidity of depressive and nonaffective disorders carried increased risk of chronicity of the depressive episode.

2. PSYCHOSOCIAL IMPAIRMENT

Puig-Antich and colleagues (1985a) contrasted impairment in the psychosocial functioning of prepubertal children who carried a diagnosis of major depression relative to two psychiatric and one normal control group. They found evidence of profound disturbances in psychosocial relationships for the three psychiatric groups, and this impairment was generally worse in children experiencing a major depressive disorder. The parent-child relationships of depressed youth were characterized by poor communication, absence of warmth, high levels of irritability, hostility, and tension. The psychiatric subjects in the study were also found to have profoundly impaired sibling and peer relationships. More recently, Puig-Antich et al. (1993) found that 90% of referred adolescents with MDD had scores greater than two standard deviations (SD) above the mean of normal controls in the following domains: mother-child relations, father-child relations, spousal relations, sibling relations, peer relations, and school performance. In addition, those depressed adolescents with difficulties in parent-child relations were more likely than those without such problems to also have difficulties with peer relations and school performance.

Kovacs and Goldston (1991) reviewed several studies that indicate that depressed youth are less socially adept, less liked, more peer-rejected, and more isolated. They also concluded that the depressed youths' nonverbal intelligence was adversely affected by episodes of depression.

3. RESIDUAL FUNCTIONING

Moreover, Puig-Antich and colleagues (1985b) examined the psychosocial functioning of a group of prepubertal children who had recovered from an episode of major depression. The results of this study indicated that recovery from the depressive disorder did not automatically entail improvement in psychosocial functioning. They found that severity of psychosocial functioning deficits prior to treatment and during the depressive episode was predictive of level of impairment—even if improved—after treatment. The pattern of improvement suggested that school functioning improved fairly quickly, peer relationships improved incompletely, parent-child relationships improved only partially, and sibling relationships continued to be disturbed. Similarly, Fleming et al. (1989) found that 67% of depressed adolescents in their community sample were having significant problems getting along with others. In contrast to the study by Puig-Antich et al. (1985b), Kovacs and Goldston (1991) found that longitudinal studies of youth with a history of depressive disorders indicated enduring effects on school performance, particularly for those youth with longer lasting episodes. Rohde, Lewinsohn, and Seeley (1994) demonstrated that if formerly depressed adolescents are followed longitudinally, they continue to manifest residual differences in a variety of psychiatric and psychosocial domains even after controlling for current depression level. Unlike former adult depressives, they noted that the picture of a formerly depressed adolescent is "one of an individual who exhibits most of the characteristics of depressed individuals, albeit to a reduced extent" (p. 36). Similarly, Nolen-Hoeksema, Girgus, and Seligman (1992)

found that periods of elevated rates of depressive symptomatology can lead to development of a greater and more persistent pessimistic explanatory style.

4. RECURRENCE AND FOLLOW-UP

Research indicates that formerly depressed adolescents are at elevated risk for additional depressive episodes as well as other psychosocial difficulties. Kovacs et al. (1984b) reported that 70% of adolescents originally meeting criteria for either MDD or DD developed a new episode of MDD during a five-year follow-up. In addition, this longitudinal study also showed that individuals with either MDD or DD exhibited an elevated risk for developing new episodes of anxiety disorders, conduct disorders, and mania (that is, converting to bipolar disorders). In a study of depressed child psychiatric inpatients, Asarnow et al. (1988) reported rehospitalization rates of 35% and 45%, respectively, in the first and second years after initial discharge. They also reported that 15% of the depressed children were placed out of their homes within the first year of discharge, indicating substantial family problems. Kandel and Davies (1986) noted a strong connection between depressive symptoms during childhood and those occurring during adulthood. In addition, they noted a variety of "high risk" negative psychosocial outcomes for persons depressed as adolescents, including higher rates of marital and employment problems, accidents, and psychiatric conditions. Harrington, Fudge, Rutter, Pickles, and Hill (1990) reported that the children who had been seen for a "depressive syndrome" during childhood were at significantly higher risk for developing a depressive disorder in adulthood but were not at increased risk for other nondepressive disorders. Harrington and colleagues (1991) found that depressed children with comorbid conduct problems had significantly poorer short-term outcomes (in terms of degree of recovery and degree of handicap at the time of discharge from treatment) and exhibited a significantly higher rate of adult antisocial behavior or a diagnosis of antisocial personality disorder than depressed children who did not have comorbid conduct problems. In brief, juvenile depressive disorders are highly recurrent disorders, both during adolescence and early adulthood, and they are associated with increased risk of the onset of additional psychiatric disorders.

E. Psychosocial Correlates and Antecedents of Adolescent Depression

Allgood-Merten, Lewinsohn, and Hops (1990), in a one-month prospective study of 664 adolescents, found that earlier depressive symptoms, negative body image, lower self-esteem, and recent life events were most strongly predictive of adolescents who reported more depressive symptoms at a second assessment. Utilizing path analysis for an urban sample of 9th and 11th graders, Kandel, Raveis, and Davies (1991) showed that poor interpersonal interactions with parents, absence of peer interactions, and life events were associated with depression; in particular, use of illicit drugs manifested a strong relationship to depression in girls. In a more sophisticated study, Lewinsohn, Roberts, et al. (1993) reported on the results of a prospective study of the development of episodes of depression over a one-year period. They found that many psychosocial variables were correlated with a current diagnosis of depression, especially past and present episodes of psychopathology, including internalizing psychiatric symptoms, suicidal behavior, and past substance use disorders. Beyond such episodes, four psychosocial variables made unique contributions to the variance in current depressive disorders: social support from friends, coping skills, emotional reliance on others, and physical symptoms. Prospectively, five variables predicted future episodes of depression: past suicide attempt, past depressive disorders, low energy level, comorbid internalizing disorders, and physical symptoms. Further, evidence indicated that stressful life events and daily hassles were elevated before, during, and after depressive episodes, suggesting that current, former, and future depressed adolescents live in chronically more stressful environments. Despite elevated rates of current and future depressive disorders among females, the variance accounted for by gender was not significant when differences in psychiatric and psychosocial functioning were taken into account.

Correlational data indicate that depressed youth exhibit negative views of themselves, the world, and the future (Kazdin, French, Unis, Esveldt-Dawson, & Sherick, 1983). Results of investigations of the role of attributions in the development of depression in youth have been mixed (Hammen, Adrian, & Hiroto, 1988; McCauley, Mitchell, Burke, & Moss, 1988; Nolen-Hoeksema, Girgus, & Seligman, 1986). Most recently, reporting on the results of a longitudinal study, Nolen-Hoeksema et al. (1992) showed that in older children a pessimistic explanatory style predicted higher levels of depressive symptoms both six months and five years later. Furthermore, they found that the strength of this association increased with the age of the youth; with increased age, explanatory style and negative life events showed an increased relationship to depression.

Burbach and Borduin (1986) reviewed the available research regarding parent-child relations and depression during childhood. They noted that research consistently demonstrates the existence of maladaptive relationships between parents and their depressed children. Among the characteristics identified were emotional detachment, hostility, punitiveness, cruelty, and physical or sexual abuse. Thus, while studies cited earlier suggest that depressive episodes complicate parent-child relations (for example, Puig-Antich et al., 1985a), considerable evidence exists to suggest that family dysfunction may also be a critical precursor of adolescent depression.

F. Developmental Factors in Increased Risk for Depressive Episodes during Adolescence

Given the sharp increase in rates of depressive episodes among adolescents, especially females, it is useful to briefly consider developmental changes that might underlie or at least potentiate the heightened risk for such episodes. Descriptions of the variety of changes are provided by Steinberg (1989) and Petersen and Hamburg (1986).

Obviously, physical changes entailed in pubertal maturation have an impact on an individual's self-concept, with the need to accommodate to a rapidly changing body and body image. In addition, the increased social comparison among adolescents and their peers and changed interactions between adolescents and their parents and other adults constitute indirect effects of pubertal change. In addition, asynchrony of pubertal development relative to same and other gender peers can be pronounced, and there is evidence indicating that early maturing girls manifest increased risk for a variety of psychosocial problems (for example, Blyth, Simmons, & Zakin, 1985; Magnusson, Stattin, & Allen, 1986). Regarding emotional development, affective experience intensifies during this stage, and adolescents struggle to appreciate the complexity of such experiences. In their attempts to integrate complex emotions, adolescents often vacillate between affective poles (Harter, 1992).

Self-concept during early-middle adolescence tends to be rooted in social approval and disapproval (Harter, 1992) and, like affects, the valence of self-conceptions appear "split" between positive and negative as youths attempt to integrate situation-specific and, sometimes, contradictory abstractions of behaviors. Overall, relationships tend to be in a state of flux. Early adolescence is a time of at least temporarily increased conflict and distance between adolescents and their parents, particularly at the peak of pubertal maturation (Hill, Holmbeck, Marlow, Green, & Lynch, 1985; Steinberg, 1993). While considered normal, this change in the potential valence and closeness of these relationships might nonetheless constitute a loss of social support. Superimposed on already dysfunctional parent-child relations, the further deterioration of such relations during adolescence, at least in certain cases, may exacerbate the risk of depressive reactions. Another social change in early adolescence typically involves changing schools, moving from a more personal elementary school setting to the less personal, more complicated environment of a junior high school. In addition, early and middle adolescence are typically times when social pressure, applied both by peers and through perceived cultural values, increases; relatedly, the cognitive development of adolescents is such that they are especially oriented to concerns of social convention and thus particularly susceptible to real and perceived negative reactions from peers. Evidence indicates that the degree and concurrence of changes can have a strong impact on adolescents. Simmons, Burgeson, Carlton-Ford, and Blyth (1987) found that youth who experienced cumulative change with regard to pubertal maturation, changing schools, and initiating dating evinced greater difficulties in self-esteem than peers who experienced these changes in a more sequential fashion.

In addition, a variety of cognitive changes follow pubertal maturation, and these changes may create increased vulnerability to depression. Leahy (1988) has noted several such aspects of cognitive development, including the increased capacity for self-reflections that establishes the cognitive basis for self-observation and self-criticism; the increased capacity for appreciating disparity between real and ideal self-images; and the increased differentiation of self-image and the greater internalization of standards and norms. Similarly, Elkind (1978) has pointed to two psychological phenomena as especially characteristic of younger adolescents. The first, the imaginary audience, refers to adolescents generalizing their own heightened self-consciousness to others and feeling unrealistically under social observation. The second, the personal fable, in its negative form refers to a sense that the adolescent is relatively unique in his or her degree of distress and apparent dysfunction, and consequently, others are not able to appreciate these unique experiences. Thus, during adolescence, a heightened potential for self-consciousness, stringent self-evaluation, self-criticism, and self-devaluation may in some cases contribute to increased demoralization and thus to depressive episodes.

G. Mental Health Services Utilization among Depressed Youth

Research is consistent in demonstrating that, in general, most emotionally disturbed adolescents do not receive appropriate professional assistance (Dubow, Lovko, & Kausch, 1990; Hodgson, Feldman, Corber, & Quinn 1986; Keller, Lavori, Beardslee, Wunder, & Ryan, 1991; Offer, Howard, Schonert, & Ostrov, 1991; Seiffge-Krenke, 1989; Whitaker et al., 1990). Hodgson and colleagues (1986) found that only 26.3% of adolescents who reported emotional problems had sought professional help. Whitaker and colleagues (1990) estimated that about 35% of the emotionally disturbed youth in their study had made a mental health visit for the problem, and Offord et al. (1987) estimated the rate for their subjects to be only about 13%. Such findings focus attention on the help-seeking behavior of adolescents experiencing emotional problems.

Kellam, Branch, Brown, and Russell (1981) found that the likelihood of accepting help was unrelated to the level of experienced distress but was related to the characteristics of the person offering help. Dubow et al. (1990) reported that adolescents were more likely to seek help from informal (for example, family and friends) than formal (for example, mental health professional) sources because they were generally unaware of formal helping resources, they felt the problem could be handled without such help, they felt that no one could help, they were concerned about privacy, and they felt the problem was too personal to discuss (see also Balassone, Bell, & Peterfreund, 1991; Marks, Malizio, Hoch, Brody, & Fisher, 1983; Riggs & Cheng, 1988). Other studies have found that the best predictor of help-seeking was emotional distress (Balassone et al., 1991; Riggs & Cheng, 1988).

It has been estimated that up to 80% of depressed youth do not receive treatment (Keller et al., 1991; Rohde, Lewinsohn, & Seeley, 1991). Only 18% of a community sample of depressed youth received treatment during their episode of depression (Keller et al., 1988). Stiffman, Earls, Robins, and Jung (1988) reported that less than half of the adolescents with diagnosable depression and only one-third with suicide ideation had sought or received help. Comparing community samples of adolescents and adults, Lewinsohn and colleagues (Lewinsohn et al., 1991; Rohde et al., 1991) reported that only 24% of the adolescents with a depressive disorder had received treatment for the depression in comparison to a rate of 45% among the adult depressives. There was a trend for adolescents with MDD to be less likely to receive treatment than depressed adolescents who had either pure or comorbid DD. These results were reversed in the adult sample: the purely dysthymic group was the least likely to obtain treatment. They concluded that "it seems as if seeking treatment for depression is driven by chronicity in adolescents and by severity in adults" (Rohde et al., p. 211). Rohde et al. (1991) reported that depressed adolescents with a comorbid psychiatric diagnosis were the most likely to have received treatment (45%), followed by adolescents who only had a nondepressive diagnosis (30%). Adolescents diagnosed with depression only were the least likely to receive treatment (24%). Thus, "the result suggests

that the presence of the other disorders substantially augmented the likelihood that a depressed adolescent received treatment" (p. 221). This result was not found with the adult sample, suggesting that adults may be more ready to accept, expect, and act on the symptoms of a depressive episode in themselves or others.

In summary, there appear to be several factors contributing to low mental health care seeking or utilization among depressed adolescents. Evidence suggests that both nondepression- and depression-specific factors play a role. Youth report that their own attitudes towards the help source are an important barrier (for example, Balassone et al., 1991). Further, aspects of depressive episodes in particular may also act as a barrier to treatment. Regarding the latter, the nature of depressive symptoms is such that deficits in motivation (anhedonia), psychomotor retardation, hopelessness, and fatigue all may compromise an individual's ability to seek help. This may be particularly true for adolescent depressives. Further, no information is currently available that clarifies whether depressed adolescents themselves recognize that they are experiencing a clinical condition that might require and respond to intervention.

Moreover, it appears that significant differences characterize the psychosocial characteristics of depressed adolescents who seek help from those who do not. As Lewinsohn, Clarke, and Rohde (1994) note, adolescents who sought treatment reported higher levels of major stressful events, heightened self-consciousness, less social confidence and less perceived social support from their friends, and more conflict with their parents. They suggested that the psychosocial circumstances of a depressed adolescent may be an important determinant in the help-seeking process.

Finally, it must be noted that of those relatively few depressed youth who do, in fact, make contact with the mental health system, many are not helped. In her longitudinal sample, Kovacs et al. (1984b) found that 14% of the depressed youth had received assessment contacts only, while 63% received treatment—primarily "conventional psychosocial care"—at some point during their episode. No difference in rate of recovery was found for DD regardless of receiving treatment or not. Surprisingly, for MDD, untreated cases went into remission several months prior to treated cases, suggesting that conventional care was not effective. Alternatively, relatively more intractable cases may be most likely to enter treatment, while youth predisposed to spontaneous remission may be most likely to refrain from or delay seeking mental health care.

IV. Etiological Theories and Models of Psychosocial Treatment of Depressive Episodes

Certainly there are a number of separate, well-defined cognitive and behavioral theories of depression onset in adults. Historically, the central theoretical construct of behavior therapy (BT) theories of depression (for example, Lewinsohn, Youngren, & Grosscup, 1979) has been that relatively low rates of positive experiences, especially those contingent on an individual's behavior (for example, mastery, positive social interactions), constitute the critical factor for the occurrence of a depressive episode. According to this theory, mood disorders like depression are the result of an imbalance of affective experiences, with negative ones exceeding positive ones. Behavioral theories of depression place considerable weight, etiologically speaking, on an increase in competence-enhancing and pleasurable activities, particularly where there are specific performance and skill deficits. Hence, a significant aspect of all behavioral treatment programs for depression involves the systematic remediation of the performance and skill deficits presented by depressed patients. Behavioral treatment approaches thus focus on teaching depressed patients skills they can use to change detrimental patterns of interaction with their environment as well as the skills needed to maintain these changes after termination of therapy. Among the variety of skills a therapist might employ in the treatment of depression are self-change skills, contingency management skills, social skills such as assertiveness and communication skills, relaxation and stress-management skills, and the identification of and increases in rewarding activities. Training typically involves didactic elements, modeling and coaching by the therapist, role playing and rehearsal by the patient, and practice or the application of skills, particu-

larly in everyday life. In brief, the goal of behavior therapy is to teach the depressed person skills to change the quality of their interaction with the environment.

Several other theories implicate particular types of cognitions and cognitive processing relative to an individual's behavior in the development of depression. Thus, writers have argued that the beliefs individuals hold and the manners in which they process information play the significant role in determining negative affective states and related psychiatric disorders. The reformulated learned helplessness theory (RLHT) (Abramson, Seligman, & Teasdale, 1978) argues that depressogenic attributional style involves internal, stable, and global attributions for failure and external, unstable, and situational attributions for success.

Beck and a variety of colleagues (for example, Beck, 1967; Beck, Rush, Shaw, & Emery, 1979) have described an evolving theory of depression centered around a so-called negative cognitive triad, consisting of negative views of self, the environment, and the future. Maladaptive (that is, negative) personal attitudes, assumptions, or beliefs (schemata) develop early in life from experiences. Particularly in stressful circumstances, repetitious and negative automatic thoughts, cognitive distortions, and errors in logical reasoning lead to the facilitation of interpretation of information so that it is consistent with the negative schemata. The occurrence of predominantly negative thoughts and the selective processing of negatively valenced information lead to depressive episodes. Cognitive therapy (CT) aims to reduce depression by altering depressed individuals' beliefs and information-processing strategies, in part, by teaching them to think about and act on their own belief systems (Hollon & Garber, 1989). In particular, depressed patients are taught to do the following:

- Monitor and examine the relationship between their thoughts, feelings, and behavior
- Identify and challenge their negative thoughts with behavioral evidence
- Substitute more realistic cognitions

A model of depression in adults based on self-control deficits, primarily in the areas of self-monitoring, self-evaluation, and self-reinforcement, and its related treatment, self-control therapy (SCT), was offered by Rehm (1977). Treatment consists of training patients to pay less attention to negative events and greater attention to positive events, to moderate standards for self-evaluation and make more accurate attributions, and to be more appropriate in their self-reinforcement.

While each of these theories and therapies for depression is often viewed as separate and distinct, it is clear that they overlap to a considerable degree. Addressing this, an integrative model of the etiology and maintenance of depression has been proposed by Lewinsohn, Hoberman, Teri, and Hautzinger (1985). Echoing earlier work by Akiskal and McKinney (1975), depression is viewed as an end product of a number of potential risk factors acting transactionally to transform the affects, actions, and cognitions of individuals encountering differing levels of adversity. The integrative model of depression is multifactorial; that is, increased dysphoria or depression is presumed to be the result of multiple etiological elements acting either alone or in combination, including negative cognitions, stressful events, predisposing vulnerabilities or risk factors (for example, being female or having a previous history of depression), and immunities to depression (for example, high self-esteem, coping skills, high frequency of pleasant events and activities). Individuals who become depressed are viewed as experiencing state-dependent and state-maintaining moods, behaviors, and thoughts. A similar biobehavioral model of depression has been proposed by Whybrow, Akiskal, and McKinney (1984), including the identification of a variety of predisposing and precipitating characteristics that lead to depressive episodes through a final common biological pathway. Given the multiple number of influences in the development of depressions, these integrative models suggest that a variety of interventions will be efficacious in ameliorating depressive episodes because they can have an impact on one or many of the variables involved in the onset and maintenance of such episodes and that there are many paths likely to reverse the momentum of depressive experiences.

V. Efficacy of Psychotherapy of Depressive Episodes among Adults

Numerous reviews have appeared in the literature concerning psychosocial treatments for unipolar depression, particularly those of a behavioral or cognitive behavioral nature (for example, Beckham, 1990; Hoberman, 1990; McLean & Carr, 1989; Robinson, Berman, & Neimeyer, 1990). A number of psychotherapeutic programs consisting of theory-driven strategies and tactics have been evaluated for their efficacy in treating depressive episodes, including: cognitive therapy (Beck, 1967; Beck, Rush, Shaw, & Emery, 1979); social skills training (Becker, Heimberg, & Bellack, 1987); self-control therapy (Fuchs & Rehm, 1977); interpersonal psychotherapy (Klerman, Weissman, Rounsaville, & Chevron, 1984); decreasing unpleasant events and increasing pleasant events (Lewinsohn, Sullivan, & Grosscup, 1980); the coping with depression course (Lewinsohn, Antonuccio, Steinmetz, & Teri, 1984); and social interaction therapy (McLean, 1981). As the various reviews make clear, considerable evidence demonstrates that each of these intervention packages is effective at ameliorating depression. Further, while no one particular short-term psychodynamic treatment of depression has emerged as the treatment of choice, such interventions have been evaluated in six comparative treatment outcome studies (Beckham, 1990).

Overall, the empirical data indicate that there is little or no differential effectiveness for any of the aforementioned interventions, particularly when investigator allegiance to specific theoretical models was controlled. No particular psychosocial intervention appears to possess greater efficacy than any other, despite substantial differences in their etiological explanations for the onset of depressive episodes. In part, this speaks to the necessity and value of integrative models of depression. Similarly, evidence is generally inconclusive as to whether combinations of interventions (for example, cognitive and behavioral) are more effective than either by itself, although Robinson et al. (1990) found that combined cognitive behavioral interventions produced more improvement than simple reliance on behavioral methods. Results of the NIMH Collaborative Study of the Treatment of Depression (Elkin et al., 1989) demonstrated that for the majority of depressed adults there is no superiority of medication over psychosocial treatments (cognitive or interpersonal therapy). Similar results were reported in a meta-analysis of psychotherapy and pharmacotherapy

(Steinbrueck, Maxwell, & Howard, 1983); in fact, findings indicated that the effect sizes were nearly twice as high for psychosocial relative to drug interventions. Robinson et al.'s (1990) results revealed that neither the duration of treatment nor the total number of sessions was related to outcome; a tendency was noted for individual therapy to produce better results than group therapy for adults. In another meta-analysis of psychotherapy for depression, Nietzel, Russell, Hemmings, and Gretter (1987) showed that individual therapy was associated with greater clinical improvement than group interventions.

Overall, the results of their comparisons of different treatments led Robinson et al. (1990) to conclude that for treated adult depressives "the magnitude of improvement over the course of therapy appeared impressive" (p. 40). However, they noted that it remains unclear which aspects of the psychotherapeutic process were central to producing symptomatic and other improvement. McLean and Carr (1989), echoing Frank (1973) and Zeiss, Lewinsohn, and Munoz (1979), argue that nonspecific effects account for 50% to 70% of treatment outcome results, based largely on the findings that active therapies are only modestly superior to well-designed attention control conditions. In addition, it is clear that many of these psychotherapy programs, while based on different etiological models, rely on a very similar set of treatment strategies and tactics. Not surprisingly, few mode-specific effects (for example, cognitive change subsequent to cognitive versus interpersonal therapy) have been identified in treatments of adult depressives (for example, Beckham, 1990). This lack of specificity and the failure to find differential effectiveness argue for the necessity and value of integrative models of the etiology and treatment of depressive disorders.

VI. Theories and Issues in the Psychosocial Treatment of Depressed Adolescents

Particularly in the last five years, descriptions of a variety of models for the psychosocial treatment of adolescent depression have appeared in the literature. Almost exclusively, writers have increasingly suggested that psychotherapeutic practices developed and evaluated for adult depressives could be productively applied to adolescents with depressive disorders. Each of these models of psychosocial intervention is based on a particular model of the critical elements of the presumed etiology of depression and, consequently, each typically identifies specific phenomena and strategies for the successful amelioration of depressive episodes. Earlier reviews of the application of these theories to depression in youth include those of Clarizio (1985).

A. Etiological and Maintenance Factors in Adolescent Depression: Common Targets in the Treatment of Depressed Adolescents

It is interesting that, to date, no truly unique theories of depressive disorders among adolescents have been developed within the cognitive behavioral tradition. Rather, each particular theory has been extended downward from parallel adult models with little variation, developmental or otherwise, in its proposed model of how adolescents become and remain depressed. In fact, most of the current models of treatment for depression in adolescence eschew detailed discussions of etiology. While a well-conceived model of the etiology of adolescent depression has yet to be fully described, it seems clear from the literature briefly reviewed earlier that an integrative model of depressive onset seems especially appropriate for adolescents. In particular, an etiological model of depressive episodes in adolescence must necessarily be even more transactional than that for adult depressions, given the multiple developmental transformations within which psychopathological experiences in adolescence occur. In particular, life change is elevated, especially among early adolescents. Additionally, self-consciousness and self-evaluation also increase during the teenage years. Thus, many of the factors implicated by the original integrative model of depression are likely to be more potent as risk factors for adolescent depression. Further, it is also clear from the literature on the characteristics of depressive episodes during adolescence that, as with adults, there are many psychosocial concomitants and consequences of the disorder (for example, Lewinsohn et al., 1993).

Consequently, the accumulated available evidence about the antecedent and other characteristics of MDD and DD in adolescents directly suggest that a multiple of domains might be especially appropriate targets of interventions:

- Depression-evoking events or triggers, including acute life events, chronic stressors, and daily hassles or unpleasant events
- Inappropriate or inadequate coping mechanisms
- Acute drops or chronically impoverished self-esteem
- Heightened self-consciousness or self-criticism
- Identity issues, including identity diffusion or fore-closure, or a negative identity
- Social skills and perceived social competence
- Physical well-being
- Family problems, including parental psychopathology, marital discord, and maladaptive family interaction patterns

At the same time, several points need to be kept in mind. Although symptom reduction or relief is a primary goal of interventions (Rutter, 1983) in the treatment of all psychiatric disorders, Kazdin (1990) has pointed out that the overlap between symptom reduction and prosocial functioning may be modest. Consequently, in the treatment of depressive episodes, both the goals of relieving distress and of improved psychosocial functioning must be considered and targeted by interventions, particularly if impaired psychosocial functioning heightens the risk for future depressive episodes. By addressing both these domains, change of both statistical and clinical significance is more likely to be achieved.

B. Models of Treatment of Depressive Disorders in Adolescents

Currently, almost all models of treatment for adolescent depression are downward extensions of treatment programs developed for adult depressives. Most recently, Holmes and Wagner (1992) have provided a succinct review of a number of potential psychotherapy programs for depressed adolescents with brief examples of the application and empirical evidence for a variety of interventions. For the purposes of this review, the current cognitive behavioral models are discussed first and in greater detail, in part, because such models have received greater attention in the

literature. In particular, one such model, the adolescent coping with depression course, is described as an exemplar of such an intervention. Several other models of treatment are also described to provide a basis for comparison of similarities and differences among the models.

1. Cognitive Behavioral Models

The degree of overlap among the so-called cognitive and behavioral perspectives on depression becomes especially striking when the strategies and tactics of these various models of treating adolescent depression are examined; most such treatment descriptions are clearly cognitive behavioral therapy (CBT) in nature. Application of behavioral interventions for childhood depression was first described by Petti (1983, 1985). While not articulating a particular behavioral model for the occurrence of depressive episodes in youth, Petti reviewed a variety of behavioral interventions applied to children with other psychiatric conditions and suggested their application to depressed children. Fine et al. (1989) described the characteristics of a short-term group therapy with depressed adolescent outpatients. The group therapy was a manual-based social skills intervention encompassing seven skill areas, including:

1. Recognizing feelings in oneself and others;
2. Assertiveness;
3. Conversational skills;
4. Giving and receiving positive feedback;
5. Giving and receiving negative feedback;
6. Social problem solving;
7. Negotiation to resolve social conflicts.

For each group, skill areas would be introduced, examples from group members solicited, and role playing was videotaped. Group leaders were expected to act as role models and written, home practice exercises would be utilized.

To date, no particular model of psychotherapy has been developed for depression in either adults or children based upon the RLHT. In contrast, several writers have attempted to apply the writings of Beck and cognitive therapy to depressed adolescents. Emery, Bedrosian, and Garber (1983) were among the first to describe specific techniques of CT with depressed youth. Among the behavioral techniques they suggested as treatment tactics were self-monitoring of mood, ongoing activities, pleasant events and mastery experiences, activity scheduling, and contingent positive reinforcement both for purposes of mood alteration and to increase engagement in therapy-prescribed behavior, scheduling pleasant activities, and grade task assignments. Regarding efforts to promote cognitive change, Emery et al. recommended the use of self-, parent-, and therapist-monitoring of youths' thoughts in general and in specific situations as a means of assessment. Change tactics include the use of coping self-statements, attribution retraining procedures, and interpersonal cognitive problem solving. Perhaps most central are attempts to assist depressed youths to examine the validity of their own beliefs by (1) looking at the evidence for a thought, (2) exploring alternative explanations, and (3) examining the consequences of the original and alternative thoughts. Emery et al. suggest that adolescents may learn the most by challenging inaccurate, maladaptive beliefs by "hypothesis testing" via obtaining concrete evidence from their own actions.

More recently, Wilkes and Rush (1988) suggested methods for adapting cognitive behavioral therapy for depressed adolescents. They noted that adolescents may experience difficulty with a traditional application of cognitive changes developed for adults. As a result of limitations in cognitive development, youth may have difficulty understanding the notion of logical errors in thinking and consequential thinking, and they thereby recommended that therapists simply assist the teenager to consider alternative ways of perceiving events. Wilkes and Rush describe a number of other modifications of cognitive therapy approaches, including: to have youth draw out a continuum of best to worst situations to combat exaggerated thinking; to behaviorally operationalize the meaning of their negative or maladaptive constructs (for example, what does it mean to be "a loser") to identify the pros and cons of particular actions; and to work with both parents and adolescents around the cognitive error of "mind reading" to clarify hidden expectations and beliefs.

Self-control therapy was modified for youth by Stark, Reynolds, and Kaslow (1987) and aims to teach

depressed youth to be more accurate and adaptive in their self-control strategies. Stark and colleagues (Stark, Best, & Sellstrom, 1989; Stark, Rouse, & Livingston, 1991) describe a variety of techniques to be employed in treating depressed youth. Within the area of affective education, several games were designed as a medium for teaching children about their emotions. They note that depressed youth typically need to be taught what to self-monitor, not how to self-monitor. Role playing is encouraged as an active method of involving and creating new experiences for the depressed youth. Specific instruments are utilized to identify personal standards and to examine the relative stringency with which these are applied to the self. Regarding cognitive restructuring, Stark et al. recommended that depressed children be taught to be "thought detectives" in identifying and evaluating potentially maladaptive thoughts.

Winnett, Bornstein, Cogswell, and Paris (1987) described a "levels of treatment" approach for the application of CBT for depressed youth. Level I focuses on behavioral interventions, with the emphasis on increasing positive behaviors and activities in the youth, especially social interaction, and selective inattention to negative, nonreinforcing behavior. In level II, the youth's lack of motivation or perceived ability is targeted, with various tactics to facilitate the depressed adolescent's reattribution of successful experiences. Social skills training and problem solving, especially in social situations, comprise the interventions in level III. Finally, self-control skills are applied in level IV, with emphasis on self-monitoring and self-rewards.

An integration of cognitive and behavioral therapy has been offered by Trautman and Rotheram-Borus (1988). Among the tactics of their program for depressed youth, they include: developing a list of problems and strengths; emphasizing identification of types and intensity of feelings; utilizing a thought-action worksheet that facilitates identifying problems, automatic feelings, and thoughts; setting goals for a positive outcome for the situation with accompanying alternative behaviors; and making coping self-statements to combat negative self-attributions. Several characteristics suggested by these writers are relatively unique and intriguing. First, they emphasize the importance of a therapist aiming to increase "idealistically" positive thoughts, feelings, and actions even though initially unrealistic; that is, adolescents are encouraged to attempt to act "as if" their lives were happier. In addition, they encourage the therapist to model what they are trying to change in the child or family by self-disclosure of positive events, personal solutions identified to daily problems, and verbalizing their own coping self-instructional talk.

2. AN INTEGRATIVE COGNITIVE BEHAVIORAL INTERVENTION: THE ADOLESCENT COPING WITH DEPRESSION COURSE

Currently, the most developed intervention for treating adolescents experiencing depressive episodes is the Adolescent Coping With Depression course (CWDA) (Clarke, Lewinsohn, & Hops, 1990), modeled after the adult Coping With Depression course (Lewinsohn, Antonuccio, Steinmetz, & Teri, 1984). The most recent version of the CWDA course (Clarke et al., 1990) consists of 16 two-hour sessions, typically conducted over an eight-week period. The course is conducted like a class or workshop, providing training in skills such as relaxation, increasing pleasant events, controlling negative thoughts, interpersonal problem solving, and increasing social skills. Each adolescent is provided with a participant workbook that is closely integrated with the group activities. An associated workbook for adolescents provides participants with short explanations of key concepts, quizzes on the knowledge presented in each session, structured in-session exercises, and forms for homework assignments.

Theoretical background.   The theoretical orientation of the CWDA group treatment is best represented by the multifactorial model of depression proposed by Lewinsohn et al. (1985). Development of the CWDA course was guided by the hypothesis that teaching individuals new coping mechanisms and strategies provides them with the ability to counteract the putative causal elements of their depressive episode. For example, at least some of these adolescents are presumed to be depressed (at least in part) because they are predisposed to experiencing depressogenic negative/irrational cognitions (Beck et al., 1979). The CWDA course trains adolescents in cognitive-restruc-

turing skills to permit them to reduce these negative cognitions and thereby overcome their depression. This same rationale holds true for the other skill areas covered in the course, which are described in the next section.

CWDA skill training domains.   The first CWDA session reviews the group rules or guidelines and the rationale of the treatment. The social learning view of depression is also presented in which depression is described as a result of difficulty dealing with significant life stresses. The CWDA course is described as focusing on new skills that will help adolescents gain control over their mood and better deal with the stressors that contributed to their depression; these specific skills are described in the following discussion. Although these techniques are presented in the specific sessions indicated, the homework for these skills is spread over many other sessions, with homework for skills presented early in the course repeated in later sessions.

Relaxation training, presented in sessions 3 and 8, teaches adolescents to alternately tense and then relax major muscle groups throughout the body until fully relaxed. The rationale for including this skill is the social anxiety reported by many depressed adolescents in peer/family/school situations, which may contribute to the poor social relations often associated with depression. Teaching depressed adolescents to relax in typically stressful situations enables them to improve their social relationships and to more effectively employ the social skills taught elsewhere in the course.

Pleasant activity training (sessions 2, 4, and 5) is based on the behavioral theory of depression (Lewinsohn, Biglan, & Zeiss, 1976), in which relatively low rates of response-contingent positive reinforcement (for example, positive social interactions, pleasant activities and events, and so forth) are thought to contribute to depression. Depressed adolescents are taught both to increase the quantity and quality of their positive activities and to decrease their level of negative or punishing activities. These sessions begin by teaching adolescents to identify personally relevant pleasant activities, using the pleasant events schedule (PES) (MacPhillamy & Lewinsohn, 1982). The PES consists of 320 potentially pleasant activities (for example, "Taking a walk," "Reading a book"); adolescents rate how often they did each activity over the past 30 days and how much they enjoyed the activity (or would have enjoyed it had they done it). The PES provides each adolescent with an individualized list of potential target pleasant activities for change. Adolescents then track and monitor specific behaviors targeted for change, establishing a baseline over a week period. With assistance from the therapist, adolescents set realistic goals for increasing pleasant activities and sign a contract to make changes in their behavior (complete with self-rewards).

Cognitive therapy sessions 5 through 10 incorporate elements of interventions developed by Beck et al. (1979) and Ellis and Harper (1961) for identifying and challenging negative and irrational thoughts, which are hypothesized to both cause and maintain depression. However, in the CWDA course these techniques have been greatly simplified for use with adolescents, using cartoon strips with popular characters (for example, Garfield) to introduce adolescents to the basic concepts of cognitive therapy. Through progressively more advanced exercises, adolescents apply cognitive techniques to their own personal thoughts. The group assists the therapist to identify and challenge irrational thoughts and to help adolescents generate their own counterarguments to irrational or excessively negative beliefs.

The social skills training (sessions 1–3, 5, and 8) focuses on conversation techniques, planning more social activities, and strategies for making more friends. These techniques appear to be more relevant for younger adolescents; older teens are more likely to know how to act in social situations, although they may fail to use this knowledge consistently. Social skills are spread throughout the course to better integrate them with the other techniques and target skills. This is especially true of the pleasant activities section, since so many of the relevant activities are social in nature.

Sessions 9 through 14 incorporate basic communication, negotiation, and conflict resolution skills. These skills are included in the CWDA course because conflict often escalates as teenagers progressively assert their independence from their parents, which, in turn, may contribute to the adolescent's

depression. The specific negotiation and communication techniques were modified from materials developed by Robin and colleagues (Robin, 1979; Robin, Kent, O'Leary, Foster, & Prinz, 1977), and emphasize teaching problem-solving and communication skills with the assumption that negative communication habits interfere with effective problem solving (Alexander, Barton, Schiavo, & Parsons, 1976). The training uses a four-step model of problem solving:

1. Define the problem concisely and without accusations.
2. Brainstorm alternative solutions.
3. Decide on a mutually satisfactory solution by projecting positive and negative consequences, assigning solutions positive or negative ratings, adopting one or more solutions rated positively by everyone.
4. Specify the details for implementing the agreement.

The final two sessions (15 and 16) focus on problem-solving techniques in anticipating future problems and associated group-generated solutions. Adolescents also develop a life plan and personal goals and create a plan for the prevention of relapse should depressive symptoms recur in the future. Adolescents identify skill areas that were personally most effective for overcoming depressed mood, and they include workbook references to these skills in their relapse prevention plan.

A complementary but separate group for the parents of the depressed teenagers has been developed (Lewinsohn, Rohde, Hops, & Clarke, 1991). The parents' group consists of eight two-hour sessions meeting once per week on one of the same nights as the adolescents' group (adolescent and parent groups typically have separate leaders). The parent group was developed to provide parents with an overview of the skills and techniques taught in the adolescent group sessions to promote parental acceptance and reinforcement of the expected positive changes in their teenagers. The parent group also provides parents with training in the same communication, negotiating, and problem-solving techniques taught to their teenagers. Combined parent and adolescent sessions, in which families use their problem solving without resorting to arguments or fights, are sometimes held.

3. INTERPERSONAL PSYCHOTHERAPY

Emphasizing the interpersonal context of current relationships, interpersonal psychotherapy (IPT) was also developed as a treatment for depressed adults (Klerman et al., 1984). In treating depressive symptoms, IPT targets several of four problem areas associated with the onset of depression: grief, interpersonal role disputes, role transitions, and interpersonal deficits. Therapy focuses on current rather than past interpersonal relationships and is administered in an individual rather than a group format. A modification of IPT for adolescents (IPT-A) is described by Moreau, Mufson, Weissman, and Klerman (1991). IPT-A is a time-limited intervention in which weekly therapy sessions are interspersed with telephone contacts between therapist and patient. In addition to the four problem areas considered in treating depression in adults, a fifth area relating to single-parent families can also be a focus of intervention. While treatment primarily focuses on the adolescent, parents play an integral role in the initial phase during which the therapist discusses with them the adolescent's symptoms and need for treatment. Parents may also be seen during the course of therapy regarding changes needed at home and at school. As with IPT, therapy sessions concentrate on interpersonal relationships, but social circumstances particularly salient in adolescence are addressed in more detail, including parent-adolescent conflicts (particularly regarding authority and autonomy), peer pressures (for example, pressure to engage in drug use), and hetero- and homosocial relationships. The development of a treatment manual and associated materials is currently in process, but a number of case vignettes for interventions in each of the five problem areas are presented by Moreau et al. (1991).

4. PSYCHODYNAMIC THERAPY

Numerous writers have argued for the value of psychodynamic psychotherapeutic approaches for the treatment of depression in adults (for example, Rosenberg, 1985; Strupp, Sandell, Waterhouse, et al., 1982). In the adolescent psychotherapy literature, psychodynamic interventions have generally found empirical support (for example, Casey & Berman, 1985; Shirk & Russell, 1992). As Marans (1989) has noted, the field of dynamic child psychotherapy research is growing, with an interest in questions of both outcome and process. Several writers have described psychodynamic approaches to the treatment of depressive disorders in adolescence, including Toolan (1978), Bemporad (1982, 1988), and Rossman (1982).

More than many writers, Bemporad has attempted to incorporate a developmental perspective in his conceptualization of adolescent depression. He notes that the youth's egocentrism, relative dependence upon the environment, and increased intensity of affective experiences all result in increased risk for depressive episodes. In a recent article, Bemporad (1988) conceptualized depression as a reaction to the deprivation of anything that is important to the maintenance of the depression-prone individual's self-esteem or self-worth (for example, failure on an exam, personal rejection). Due to a lack of internal psychological resources, depression-prone individuals rely excessively on external support and help to deal with stressful life events. External support is inherently less dependable than internal resources and leaves the youth more vulnerable to blows to his or her sense of self-worth. Bemporad distinguishes two types of depressive experiences in adolescence. The first, the anaclitic type, refers to adolescents who have failed to adequately emancipate themselves from their familial role and have difficulty with age-appropriate dependence and independence. The second, the introjective type, is defined more by internalized unrealistic demands and expectations, where an adolescent becomes depressed under the belief that he or she will lose the love or support of others unless the adolescent complies with perceived directives.

Psychodynamic treatment is generally individual and long term, with an early emphasis on development of a working therapeutic alliance largely through the creation of a supportive and nonjudgmental "holding environment" by the therapist. Sessions typically occur twice a week to enhance the therapist-patient relationship and to maintain the momentum of treatment. An exploration of the patient's developmental history is an important component of treatment. In their study of psychoanalytic therapy with children, Heinicke and Ramsey-Klee (1986) identified four domains of improvements, including effective adaptation and adequate self-esteem, capacity for relationships, frustration tolerance and the ability to work, and flexible adaptation. As in psychoanalytic therapy with adults, treatment tactics emphasize a focus on the interactions between youth and therapist, especially the interpretation of transference (the degree to which previous intrapsychic conflicts are re-experienced in relation to the therapist).

Bemporad (1982, 1988) has suggested important themes that might be appropriate targets of intervention in psychodynamic treatment of depressed adolescents. An excellent description of the psychodynamics of working with depressed, acting-out adolescents is provided by Rossman (1982). He speaks to the importance of a number of factors involved in engaging the adolescent in the therapy process, including clarifying distrust of the therapist and therapy, identifying realistic benefits of treatment, providing acceptance and reassurance of the adolescent's maladaptive behavior, exploring and interpreting the functional meaning of maladaptive behavior, promoting identification with the therapist as a person who is flexible and able to tolerate mistakes, and establishing an authoritative stance regarding the need for adolescent autonomy and their subsequent responsibility to make their own choices.

5. Family Therapy

It is noteworthy that no particular model of family treatments for depression in adolescents has been developed outside of the application of family conflict-resolution techniques in the CWDA course with joint parent-adolescent sessions. However, this is not primarily a family-oriented therapy.

VII. Treatment Outcome Research for Depressive Disorders among Adolescents

A. Pharmacologic Treatment of Adolescent Depression

Although a recent meta-analysis of antidepressant outcome under "blinder" conditions indicated that patient ratings revealed no advantage for medications beyond the placebo effect (Greenberg, Bornstein, Greenberg, & Fisher, 1992), the effectiveness of psychopharmacologic treatment of depression in adults

has generally been demonstrated (for example, Elkin et al., 1989; Morris & Beck, 1974) and certainly been widely accepted. In contrast, efficacy of pharmacologic treatment of adolescent depression has not yet been established, despite a number of investigations of the possible effectiveness of a variety of medications. While somewhat limited in number, controlled studies currently available have not yet demonstrated either a plasma level/response relationship or the superiority of tricyclic antidepressants (TCAs) or other antidepressants over placebo conditions.

Several double-blind, placebo-controlled investigations have failed to demonstrate the utility of antidepressant medications with depressed youth. For example, Puig-Antich and colleagues (1987) examined the clinical efficacy of imipramine (IMI) in a sample of 38 depressed prepubertal children, and they found that the placebo was more effective than the drug treatment condition. Kramer and Feiguine (1981), examining amitriptyline, reported no difference in effectiveness between the drug and placebo conditions. Simeon, Dinicola, Phil, Ferguson, and Copping (1990) examined the effectiveness of fluoxetine in the double-blind treatment of 40 depressed adolescents between the ages of 13 and 18 and found that placebo and fluoxetine were equally effective. Geller, Graham, Marsteller, and Bryant (1990) looked at the effectiveness of nortriptyline (NTP) in 52 depressed youth ages 12 to 17. Seventeen participants responded to placebo washout; of the 31 participants who completed the study, only one showed a clinical response to NTP, and the study was therefore discontinued early. Initial reports of relatively large scale, in-progress studies by Ryan and Perel (1989) and Koplewicz, Klass, and Klein (1990) have yielded similar reports (compared with Jensen, Ryan, & Prien, 1992).

In his review of the methodological quality of this literature, Conners (1992) concluded that response to TCAs ranged from less than 10% up to 60%, while the range of placebo response has been between 20% and 68%. However, he noted that most of the available studies of the effectiveness of pharmacotherapy for depressed youth are limited by "fundamental" methodological problems such as small sample size, unreliability of measurement instruments, and failure to examine subtypes of adolescent depression. Nonetheless, it is also possible that the psychobiology of adolescence itself may interfere with the efficacy of medications proven useful with adult depressives. However, despite the fact that "to date, no study has shown that any antidepressant is unequivocally superior to placebo" (Elliott, 1992, p. 7), "clinicians have come to use antidepressants to treat adolescent depression on such a wide scale that it has become essentially a standard of practice in many locales" (Popper, 1992, p. 1). Further problems exist with the use of pharmacological agents, including the potential of annoying side effects of TCAs, which interfere with medication compliance, as well as more serious consequences of both TCAs (for example, cardiac toxicity, reduced thresholds for seizures) and monoamine oxidase inhibitors (MAOIs) (for example, hypertensive episodes). In addition, both TCAs and MAOIs may cause hypomanic reactions in susceptible individuals (for example, Harrington, 1992). Given both lack of demonstrated efficacy of pharmacotherapy and the potential negative consequences, pharmacological interventions seem problematic choices in treating depressive episodes in adolescents. In any case, the relative inefficacy of medications clearly points to the importance of developing and studying psychosocial interventions for depressive episodes among youth.

B. Psychotherapy Case Studies

Available descriptions and results of psychotherapy studies of depressed youth are reported in Table 2.1. Several case studies primarily involving multimodal and behavioral treatments have been published. Petti, Bornstein, Delamater, and Conners (1980) reported on the use of affective education, academic tutoring, improving peer interactions, supportive family therapy, social skills training, and antidepressant medication in the inpatient treatment of a 10 1/2-year-old girl. The patient, who also received year-long outpatient treatment as well, reportedly recovered from her depression. Frame, Matson, Sonis, Fialkov, and Kazdin (1982) reported on the behavioral treatment of a 10-year-old boy. Verbal and nonverbal social behavior was treated via instructions, modeling, role playing, and feedback. These authors concluded that the treatment was effective in reducing the fre-

quency of problem behaviors in all the targeted areas both at posttreatment and at follow-up. More recently, Asarnow and Carlson (1988) reported on the five-year outcome for a depressed 10-year-old patient treated with a combination of cognitive behavioral treatment and pharmacotherapy. Treatment was conducted initially during an inpatient hospitalization, with imipramine beginning in the third week after admission and CBT initiated a week later. CBT consisted of self-monitoring of mood, thought, and activities; activity scheduling; cognitive restructuring; and problem solving. Medication was terminated at the end of hospitalization. Outpatient therapy (presumably CBT but not specified) was continued biweekly, and supportive family counseling was conducted weekly during outpatient treatment. Over five years later, the patient was described as never having experienced a recurrence of depression or a bipolar conversion. Finally, Stark and Brookman (1992) describe a combined family-school intervention for a depressed 11-year-old girl. Treatment included both didactic and directive components that were designed to reduce family chaos through the establishment of family routines; to strengthen the family dyad; to reduce mother-daughter enmeshment and engage the stepfather in the patient's life; and to establish a line of communication between school and home through meetings and consultations between the therapist and teachers.

C. Uncontrolled Psychotherapy Studies

In an uncontrolled pilot study of 38 hospitalized adolescents 13 to 17 years old, Robbins, Alessi, and Colfer (1989) examined the efficacy of an intensive, multimodal intervention program that included psychodynamically and IPT-oriented individual therapy sessions three times weekly, group therapy sessions twice weekly, family therapy sessions weekly, and a cognitive behaviorally oriented inpatient ward therapeutic milieu. After six weeks of psychotherapy and milieu intervention without pharmacological intervention, 18 (47%) patients exhibited a positive response. The remaining psychotherapy-nonresponsive patients were entered into a subsequent trial of antidepressant medication with continued psychotherapy, with a 92% positive response rate. It was noted that in a number of cases comorbid psychiatric symptoms,

Table 2.1 Description of published literature on psychosocial treatment of depressed adolescents

Study Citation	Definition of and Means of Assessing Depression[a]	Exclusion Criteria	Participants	Characteristics of Study and Interventions[b]	Posttreatment Outcome	Follow-Up Outcome
Frame et al. (1982)	S met DSM-III criteria for MDD via DI (psychiatric interview, BID) and PR (CDI, CBCL).	NA	$N = 1$, male, age = 10, IQ = 79	S was inpatient at intensive care psychiatric unit, referred for treatment for suicidal ideation and gestures and violent behavior. Four target behaviors selected for modification via 20 sessions of 20-minute individual behavior-therapy skills training; that is, instructions, modeling, role playing, and feedback. No mention of manual or adherence measures.	Each of the four target behaviors was reduced in frequency by the end of therapy (no statistical analyses conducted).	At 12-week follow-up, treatment gains were maintained.
Stark and Brookman (1992)	S identified by school counselor; scores on CDI of 39 and 46 on two consecutive admissions. K-SADS-P with youth and mother.	NA	$N = 1$, age = 11	S identified by school counselor as potentially depressed because of academic difficulties, alienation from peers, and negative attitudes. Family-school interventions: (1) reduce family chaos through the establishment of routine; (2) strengthen the parent dyad; (3) reduce mother-daughter enmeshment and increase involvement with stepfather; (4) establish line of communication between school and family.	No data reported. Anecdotal information suggested that improvement occurred for each of the targeted areas.	

Table 2.1   (continued)

Study Citation	Definition of and Means of Assessing Depression[a]	Exclusion Criteria	Participants	Characteristics of Study and Interventions[b]	Posttreatment Outcome	Follow-Up Outcome
Asarnow and Carlson (1988)	S hospitalized on psychiatric ward and assessed via K-SADS.	NA	Age = 10	Transferred from a pediatric ward for refusal to eat and weight loss; also reported auditory hallucinations. Initial four weeks of milieu treatment failed to produce improvement; cognitive-behavioral psychotherapy initiated and continued for ten weeks of inpatient treatment and for three months of outpatient treatment. Imipramine initiated in week 7 of hospitalization and continued for seven weeks; discontinued at discharge.	At discharge scores on DSRS and CDRS were below clinical cutoffs.	S reevaluated at age 16, 5.5 years after hospitalization; initial episode ended just prior to termination of outpatient psychotherapy. During follow-up, no further depressive episodes or anxiety symptoms; some intermittent nonaggressive conduct problems.
Robbins et al. (1989)	Ss selected via DSM-III criteria as per SADS.	Medical illness; pscho- tropic medica- tion.	N = 38, mean age = 15.6, range 13–17	Ss hospitalized on adoles- cent psychiatric unit. All adolescents received intensive psychosocial treatment alone for six weeks of a psychodynamic- interpersonal nature (three times weekly), group therapy (twice per week), family therapy (once per week), and a cognitive behavioral milieu. At six weeks, if nonresponse to psychosocial treatment, a trial of TCA was added.	18/38 (47%) responded to psychosocial treatment alone; 12 of 15 nonresponders to psychosocial treatment given trials of TCA; of 12 who completed trial, 11 (92%) had positive response.	NA

Table 2.1   (continued)

Study Citation	Definition of and Means of Assessing Depression[a]	Exclusion Criteria	Participants	Characteristics of Study and Interventions[b]	Posttreatment Outcome	Follow-Up Outcome
Butler et al. (1980)	Ss selected via SR (scores on Depression Battery, a composite of measures of self-esteem, depressive symptoms, cognitive distortions, and locus of control) and identified by teacher, via research interview, as exhibiting depressive problems.	Ss described by teacher as "well-adjusted socially and academically" (despite battery score).	$N = 56$ (35 male), grades 5–6	Ss recruited from school; assigned to four cells: attention-placebo; no-treatment control; role playing (RP); cognitive restructuring (CR). The active treatments and the placebo condition consisted of 10 one-hour sessions, delivered in group format. RP was designed to: "sensitize" child to thoughts and feelings; enhance social skills; teach problem-solving skill. CR was designed to teach listening skills and how to recognize and change negative thoughts. No mention of manual or adherence measures.	Active treatment Ss showed significantly greater improvement on depression symptoms and locus of control measures.	NA
Reynolds and Coats (1986)	Ss selected via SR (BDI and RADS) and DI (BID).	Not currently in treatment or taking medication for emotional disorder.	$N = 30$ (11 male), grades 9–12, average age = 15.6 years	Ss recruited from school; randomly assigned to: wait-list control; CBT; relaxation training (RT). Active conditions consisted of 10 50-minute sessions, delivered in group format. CBT emphasized self-control skills, especially monitoring, evaluation, and reinforcement. RT via progressive muscle relaxation. No mention of manual or adherence measures.	Treated Ss groups improved significantly more on SR and DI measures of depression; no difference between CBT and relaxation training.	Treatment gains maintained at five-week follow-up.

Table 2.1 (continued)

Study Citation	Definition of and Means of Assessing Depression[a]	Exclusion Criteria	Participants	Characteristics of Study and Interventions[b]	Posttreatment Outcome	Follow-Up Outcome
Stark et al. (1987)	Ss selected via SR (CDI score); other depression severity measures: DI (CDRS-R), SR (CDS), and PR (CBCL).	One S excluded after CDRS "revealed additional serious nondepressive pathology."	$N = 28$ (16 male), average age $= 134$ months	Ss recruited from school; randomly assigned to: wait-list control; self-control (SC); behavioral problem-solving therapy (BPS). Active conditions consisted of 12 45–50-minute sessions, delivered in group format. SC focused on cognitive and behavioral skills training, especially self-monitoring, self-evaluating, and self-rewarding. BPS also involved self-monitoring but emphasized social skills via group problem solving. Interventions were manualized and adherence was monitored.	Both SC and BPS groups improved significantly on DI and SR measures; no difference between active treatment conditions.	At eight-week follow-up, improvements by SC and BPS groups on DI and SR measures were maintained; PR indicated additional gains for BPS group.
Kahn et al. (1990)	Ss selected via DI (BID) and SR (CDI & RADS); outcome assessed using these measures and PR (CDI and RADS).	Not currently in treatment or taking medication for depression.	$N = 68$ (33 male), grades 6–9	Ss recruited from school; randomly assigned to: wait-list control; CBT; relaxation training (RT); self-modeling (SM). CBT and RT consisted of 12 50-minute sessions, delivered in group format. SM was administered individually in 10–12-minute sessions, CBT utilized CWD, modified for younger adolescents. RT via progressive muscle relaxation. SM Ss observed themselves on videotape exhibiting nondepressive behaviors. All interventions were manualized; no mention of adherence measurement.	Treated Ss groups improved significantly more on SR and DI measures; no difference between active treatment conditions.	One-month follow-up indicated maintenance of treatment gains.

Table 2.1 (continued)

Study Citation	Definition of and Means of Assessing Depression[a]	Exclusion Criteria	Participants	Characteristics of Study and Interventions[b]	Posttreatment Outcome	Follow-Up Outcome
Liddle and Spence (1990)	Ss selected via SR (CDI) and DI (CDRS-R).	Intellectually handicapped children.				
Lewinsohn et al. (1990)	Ss selected met criteria for DSM-III MDD or RDC minor or intermittent depressive disorder determined via DI (K-SADS); other measures of depression symptoms: SR (BDI, CES-D) and PR (CBCL).	Other major psychiatric illness (e.g., bipolar, drug use, or conduct disorder); history of schizophrenia; MDD psychotic subtype; organic brain syndrome or mental retardation; need for immediate treatment or hospitalization or actively suicidal.	N = 59 (23 male), age = 14–18 (average ≈ 16)	Ss recruited from school; randomly assigned to: wait-list control; coping with depression (CWD)–adolescent only; CWD–adolescent and parent. CWD conditions were 14 two-hour sessions, group format. CWD is a CBT-based psychoeducational treatment that includes training in relaxation, controlling thoughts, social skills, and conflict resolution. Interventions were manualized and adherence was measured.	Both CWD groups improved significantly on measures of depression; no difference between CWD conditions.	Treatment gains maintained at two-year follow-up.

Table 2.1 (continued)

Study Citation	Definition of and Means of Assessing Depression[a]	Exclusion Criteria	Participants	Characteristics of Study and Interventions[b]	Posttreatment Outcome	Follow-Up Outcome
Fine et al. (1991)	Ss selected met criteria for DSM-III-R MDD or dysthymic disorder, determined via consensus between interviewer and chief child psychiatrist. Depression severity also rated via DI (K-SADS) and SR (CDI).	Younger than 13 or older than 17; evidence of neurologic damage; borderline intellectual functioning or lower.	N = 66 (11 male), age = 13–17 (average = 15.1)	Ss referred to outpatient psychiatry, recruited nonrandomly to either therapeutic support (TS) or social skills (SS) group. Each ran for 10 weeks. TS group primary aim was to improve self-concept via sharing of concerns, discussion, and mutual support. SS group primary aim was to enhance social skills including feelings recognition, conversation skill, and conflict resolution. No treatment manual or adherence measures, although SS group followed a manual that delineated social skills to be learned.	Both groups improved significantly on DI and SR measures of depression; TS group demonstrated significantly more improvement than SS group.	At nine-month follow-up, treatment gains were sustained; no detectable difference between TS and SS, indicating that SS group had "caught up."

[a]The method used to determine whether Ss were depressed was also used to evaluate the effectiveness of the treatment. DI = Diagnostic interview; SR = Self-report instrument; PR = Parent-report instrument.

[b]The following characteristics were assessed: how participants were recruited; whether randomly assigned to treatment; group versus individual treatment; length of treatments; whether the treatment was manualized; a brief description of the interventions; whether adherence to treatment (integrity) was monitored or measured.

Note: CDI = Children's Depression Inventory (both parent- and self-report versions); BID = Bellevue Index of Depression; CBCL = Achenbach Child Behavior Checklist; BDI = Beck Depression Inventory; RADS = Reynolds Adolescent Depression Scale; CES-D = Center for Epidemiological Studies–Depression Scale; K-SADS = Children's Schedule for Affective Disorders and Schizophrenia; CDRS-R = Children's Depression Rating Scale–Revised; SADS = Schedule for Affective Disorders and Schizophrenia; DSRS = Depression of Self-Rating Scale.

including depressive ones, persisted but became more amenable to psychosocial intervention. The multicomponent intervention makes it difficult to attribute the results to any specific component. Nevertheless, this study may be representative of what is actually done in many inpatient settings.

Employing an early version of the CWDA course, 21 adolescents were treated in an uncontrolled pilot study (Clarke, 1985). Fourteen (66%) of the 21 adolescents met RDC/K-SADS criteria (Orvaschel & Puig-Antich, 1986) for either MDD or intermittent depression at intake. From intake to posttreatment, the mean BDI score of those clinically depressed adolescents following treatment dropped significantly, from 15 to 4.

A feasibility study of cognitive therapy for depressed adolescents is currently being conducted at four sites in the United States and Canada by Wilkes and colleagues (Wilkes & Belsher, 1992). Up to 12 sessions of treatment are provided, using different types of therapist background (for example, M.D., Ph.D., and M.S.W.). Intervention is not manual-directed; while the principles of cognitive therapy (for example, Beck et al., 1979) direct the content and flow of sessions, psychotherapy is provided in a flexible, client-centered manner. The relative inclusion of the family of the adolescent in treatment is also handled in a flexible manner, with no family involvement in most cases. To date, 21 participants with MDD have been enrolled in the study: 50% with double depression and 33% with other psychiatric disorders. Thirteen participants have finished treatment, while three have dropped out. Nineteen percent of the improved adolescents negotiated to leave treatment prior to the 12th session. Most of the clinical improvement occurred within the first six sessions of intervention, and comorbidity did not have an impact on the length of treatment.

Similarly, Mufson, Moreau, Weissman, and Klerman (1992) reported on the results of two feasibility studies of IPT with depressed adolescents. Initially, five youths were treated according to the principles of IPT; the length of treatment varied from 12 to 28 weeks. More recently, 14 clinically depressed adolescents received IPT. For those who remained in treatment (two participants were early terminators), the mean number of sessions was ten. For the majority of depressed adolescents (7/12) the primary interpersonal issue targeted in treatment was the area of role disputes. By the end of treatment, scores on the Beck Depression Inventory (BDI) (Beck, Ward, Mendelson, Mock, & Erbaugh, 1961) declined an average of 17 points; scores on a measure of social adjustment also declined but the change was not clinically significant.

D. Controlled Psychotherapy Outcome Studies

In the last decade, several investigators have begun examining psychological treatments (primarily cognitive behavioral interventions) for depressed adolescents in a randomized controlled design. Relatively few studies have been completed, but several are in progress. Only three published studies have addressed the treatment of adolescent depression in randomized controlled trials with a no-treatment control condition.

In a randomized outcome trial (Lewinsohn, Clarke, Hops, & Andrews, 1990), 59 adolescents meeting DSM-III criteria for unipolar affective disorder were randomly assigned to one of three conditions: (a) a cognitive behavioral, psychoeducational group for adolescents ($n = 21$); (b) an identical group for adolescents, but with their parents enrolled in a separate parent group ($n = 19$); and (c) a wait-list condition ($n = 19$). Overall, multivariate analyses demonstrated significant pre- to posttreatment change on all dependent variables, which was accounted for by the two active treatment conditions. However, contrary to expectations, there was no significant advantage for the condition with parental involvement. At the end of treatment, 52% of the adolescent-parent group and 57% of the adolescent-only group met criteria for depression, compared to 95% of the waiting list control group. Similarly, BDI scores dropped from the moderate range to the none-mild range for both active treatments, while they remained in the moderate range for the control group. Lewinsohn, Clarke, Hops, and Andrews (1990) found that treated adolescents exhibited declining rates of depressive disorders over the two-year postintervention follow-up period, with the percentage of such disorders decreasing from 54% to 15%. Again, trends indicated that youth who participated in the combined adolescent and parent intervention exhibited a greater degree of recovery. Concerning predictors of positive clinical outcome, Clarke et al. (1992) found that initially lower levels of depression and anxiety, greater enjoyment and frequency of pleasant activities, and more rational thinking were associated with overcoming a depressive episode by the end of active treatment. Better outcome, as defined by residual BDI scores, was also found to be associated with a greater number of past psychiatric diagnoses, parent involvement in treatment, and younger age at first depressive episode.

Lewinsohn, Clarke, Hops, and Rohde are currently replicating the findings of these first two studies in a five-year investigation of the psychosocial treatment of adolescent depression. Over 150 adolescents meeting DSM-III-R criteria for MDD or DD have been randomly assigned to one of the three treatment conditions described above, with 24-month follow-up interviews still in progress. Preliminary findings appear to replicate the results of the previous two findings, including the unexpected outcome that parental participation was not associated with significantly better outcome.

In a different study, Liddle and Spence (1990) randomly assigned 31 children to one of three groups: social competence training (which addressed overt social skills, cognitive restructuring, and interpersonal problem-solving skills), attention placebo control (a program to teach drama), and no-treatment control. Depression status was defined by scores on both the Children's Depression Inventory (CDI) (Kovacs, 1980/1981) and the Children's Depression Rating Scale (CDRS) (Poznanski, 1984). Active interventions consisted of eight weekly one-hour group sessions conducted by the same school psychologist. Results indicated that youth in all three conditions improved over the two-month period; thus, no differential intervention effect was noted. However, neither self- nor teacher-rated social competence exhibited changes as a function of active interventions.

Stark, Rouse, and Livingston (1991) reported on an unpublished study in which 24 children were randomly assigned to a cognitive behavioral treatment or to traditional counseling conditions. Children met in groups of four with pairs of therapists; intervention consisted of 24 to 26 sessions conducted over a three-month period. Initially, groups met twice per week for

eight weeks and once a week thereafter. Monthly family sessions were also held. The cognitive behavioral treatment consisted of training in self-control skills, social skills, and cognitive restructuring. Parents were taught to encourage their child to use new skills and to increase their engagement in more pleasant family events. While no specific data are reported, the findings described indicate that both treatment conditions resulted in significantly fewer depressive symptoms at posttreatment and fewer depressive cognitions. These gains were maintained at a seven-month follow-up. Results were generally better for the cognitive behavioral treatment at posttreatment.

E. Comparative Psychotherapy Outcome Studies

Butler, Miezitis, Friedman, and Cole (1980) assigned 56 late elementary school-aged children who were determined to be depressed based upon elevated scores on the Children's Depression Inventory (CDI) (Kovacs, 1980/1981) to one of four conditions: (a) role play, which focused on problems relevant to the depressed children and served as a medium for social problem solving; (b) cognitive restructuring, which emphasized the identification of negative automatic thoughts and the relationship between such thoughts and negative feelings; (c) attention-placebo, which emphasized a cooperative group problem-solving approach relying on shared research and information; and (d) classroom control. Fourteen children were assigned to each of the four conditions and met with a graduate student leader for one hour each week for a ten-week period. The best results were obtained in the role-play intervention, which demonstrated the greatest improvement in depression severity and self-esteem. One of the cognitive restructuring groups showed significant improvement, while the other did not. Although some children in the control condition did exhibit improvement in depression level, this finding was probably accounted for by their additional participation in concurrent self-esteem improvement sessions with a resource teacher.

Reynolds and Coats (1986) identified depressed adolescents on the basis of elevated scores on two schoolwide administrations of the Beck Depression Inventory (Beck et al., 1961), the Reynolds Adolescent Depression Scale (RADS) (Reynolds, 1986), and a single administration of the Bellevue Index of Depression (BID) (Petti, 1978). The 30 persons culled from this case-finding process were randomly assigned to one of three conditions: (a) a cognitive behavioral group, largely based on self-control therapy; (b) a relaxation therapy group; and (c) a wait-list control. The active treatments were highly structured and were administered in ten 50-minute sessions conducted over a five-week period; one therapist administered all the treatment conditions. Participants attended an average of eight sessions and completed approximately 67% of homework assignments. Retained participants in both active treatments showed substantial and equal improvement, which was maintained at a five-week follow-up. Subjects in the wait-list control group exhibited little improvement at any of the assessments, suggesting that spontaneous recovery is uncommon among untreated adolescent depressives.

Stark, Reynolds, and Kaslow (1987) compared the relative efficacy of a self-control therapy intervention (SCT), a behavioral problem-solving (BPS) intervention, and a waiting list control condition for 29 youth (ages 9 to 13) with depressive symptoms. Treatment was provided in a school setting, and subjects were randomly assigned to treatment conditions. Therapy conditions met 12 times for 45 to 50 minutes over a five-week period. The BPS condition targeted improved social behavior via education, self-monitoring, and group problem solving. In addition to emphasizing principles and practices of self-control therapy, the SCT condition also included attention to increasing adaptive attributions. Youth who participated in either active treatment reported significant improvements in depressive and anxiety symptomatology posttreatment and at an eight-week follow-up. Those who received SCT exhibited continued improvement during follow-up as well as improvement in self-concept. It is noteworthy that mothers of the participants in each condition did not report significant improvements in depressive symptomatology.

Kahn, Kehle, Jenson, and Clark (1990) examined the effectiveness of three active interventions and a wait-list control in the treatment of depressive symptomatology in middle school adolescents aged 10 to 14 years old. Potential participants were identified

using a two-stage, school-based screening procedure similar to that employed by Reynolds and Coats (1986). Two initial screening administrations utilizing the CDI and the Reynolds Adolescent Depression Scale (RADS) (Reynolds, 1986) identified an initial pool of individuals who were then interviewed with the Bellevue Inventory for Depression (Petti, 1978). The 68 identified participants were randomly assigned to one of four conditions: (a) a progressive muscle relaxation group therapy; (b) a cognitive behavioral group therapy, modeled after the Adolescent Coping With Depression course (CWD-A) (Clarke, Lewinsohn, & Hops, 1990); (c) a self-modeling intervention (Prince & Dowrick, 1984) in which participants watched videotaped samples of their own behavior selectively edited to show only desired, nondepressive behaviors; and (d) a wait-list control condition. The active treatment conditions resulted in significantly more improvement in both depressive symptoms and self-concept. While not significantly different from the other active interventions, participants in the cognitive behavioral group exhibited greater positive effects across all outcome measures. Intervention gains were maintained at one-month posttreatment follow-up, although more self-modeling participants regressed into the dysfunctional range. The majority of members of the relaxation and cognitive behavioral groups reported that intervention was at least somewhat helpful and somewhat enjoyable.

Fine, Forth, Gilbert, and Haley (1991) compared two short-term group treatments for adolescents meeting diagnostic criteria for MDD or DD. Sixty-six teenagers aged 13 to 17 were assigned to either a social skills group (SSG) or a therapeutic support group (TSG). The SSG targeted enhancing social skills such as communication, assertiveness, and giving and receiving feedback. The TSG was conceived of as a more unstructured therapeutic discussion group, an attempt to create an atmosphere where adolescents could experience and express personal and interpersonal concerns in a secure setting. The therapist's role shifted from leader to facilitator of discussion over time. At the conclusion of the 12-week treatment, adolescents in the TSG evinced greater improvements in the rate of depressive disorders and symptoms and a multidimensional measure of self-image than those in the SSG. However, the two groups were comparable at nine months posttreatment, indicating that the SSG participants caught up with the TSG participants during the follow-up period.

Brent, Kolko, Boylan, Holder, Feinberg-Steinberg, and Birmaher (1992) are currently conducting a comparative outcome study of depressed or suicidal adolescents randomly assigned to one of three treatment conditions: CBT derived from Beck et al. (1979); systemic-behavioral family therapy, which involves engagement of the family and training in communication and problem-solving skills; and a nondirective treatment based on client-centered counseling, which was designed to provide a limited but supportive intervention. Initial data demonstrated that each of the three conditions achieved relatively positive outcome over 12 to 16 sessions over a 12-week period (Brent et al., 1992).

VIII. Psychosocial Treatments of Suicidal Adolescents

It is well known that there is a substantial association between depression and suicidal behavior (for example, Andrews & Lewinsohn, 1992; Crumley, 1979). In part, this association is artifactual because suicidal ideation and behavior are one of the eight potentially defining symptoms of MDD according to DSM-III-R. Nonetheless, suicidal ideation and behavior are often characteristic of depressed adolescents, and it may be worthwhile to review treatment interventions that have been specifically developed to address suicidal behavior in adolescents.

An early but seminal article on the active treatment of depressed and suicidal individuals was authored by Kiev (1975). His crisis intervention therapy (CIT) was an integrative model of intervention combining supportive psychotherapy, chemotherapy, and life strategy skills. Kiev emphasized the critical importance of a warm, understanding, and reality-oriented patient-therapist relationship. He also argued that:

> personality changes do not come about in the therapy session but in real life situations, particularly when patients are able to experiment with new ways of being and behaving . . . treatment moves most rapidly when pa-

tients can focus on concrete problems . . . [which] offer the greatest opportunity for trying new ways of dealing with others, which can in turn lead to new attitudes and greater opportunities for self-realization. (p. 347)

A group counseling program for suicidal adolescents was described by Ross and Motto (1984). Labeled a "peer befriender group," the intervention had five goals:

1. To provide a supplemental support network for the members
2. To help the participants learn strategies and skills for dealing with stress
3. To improve self-esteem
4. To learn supportive or "befriending" techniques
5. To develop effective means of handling distress as alternatives to suicidal behavior

Originally, the group was conceived of as an adjunct to psychotherapy, but for many members it served as the primary psychosocial intervention. While the group leaders provided ongoing support for group members, the extreme neediness of the participants spurred identification of volunteer befrienders or "therapeutic friends" for the group members to create expanded social resources. The counseling emphasis of the program included a number of components. First, the importance of acknowledgment and acceptance of feelings was stressed. Second, it was emphasized that when participants felt threatened or overwhelmed by negative feelings, they could identify individuals who cared about them (for example, group leaders or members or befrienders) and seek assistance. That is, members were encouraged to realize that if caring others were given an opportunity to express that caring, the participant could be helped. Finally, group members were directly encouraged to take constructive action to initiate learning new coping behaviors. Seventeen participants began the group; however, three dropped out within the first two meetings leaving 14 adolescents who completed the group. Although originally planned as a time-limited intervention of 12 weeks, the duration of the group was extended at the request of its members. Thirty-five sessions were held over a 40-week period. The average number of adolescents who attended each group was 6, and the mean number of sessions attended was 13. The authors postulated that the critical factors in the group process were understanding and involvement of the leaders and subsequent facilitation of open communication within the group. In particular, issues around dysfunctional family functioning, peer relationships, and dealing with painful affects were common and central issues for most of the participants. Telephone follow-up indicated no further suicidal behavior, although two members experienced brief psychiatric hospitalizations.

A model of a cognitive behavioral treatment of an adolescent who had attempted suicide was presented by Overholser and Spirito (1990). An acute stage of treatment involved assessment of suicidal ideation and ongoing risk factors for further suicidal behavior. During the following convalescent phase, cognitive therapy for depressive cognitive distortions was conducted. Reattribution training was utilized to promote more realistic expectations, and reasons for living were reinforced. Thought stopping was used to reduce negative ruminations over perceived failures, and assertiveness training and role playing ways of dealing with anger were also utilized. During the recovery phase, problem-solving skills to help in developing active coping strategies were promoted. In addition, the development of adequate social support was addressed, as were relapse prevention tactics.

Another promising treatment intervention for suicidal behavior is a social problem-solving therapy developed by Lerner and Clum (1990). The treatment is based on the assumption that the key deficit of suicidal individuals is poor interpersonal problem-solving ability in the face of high stress. Eighteen participants, ages 18 to 24, were assigned to either problem-solving therapy or supportive therapy. Both treatments consisted of ten sessions conducted over a five- to seven-week period. Individuals in problem-solving therapy showed greater improvement in regard to depression and problem-solving self-efficacy than those in supportive therapy. Improvements in problem-solving ability and in suicidal ideation were greater for the problem-solving condition, but the differences were not statistically significant. Further research is needed to determine whether comparable findings can be obtained with younger adolescents.

A pilot study of cognitive behavioral family therapy for suicidal adolescents and children has been reported by Sanchez-Lacay, Trautman, and Lewin (1991). The treatment is based on the model described by Trautman and Rotheram-Borus (1988) that incorporates elements of cognitive therapy, social problem solving, and family communication skills training designed to reduce conflict. All pertinent family members are asked to take part in treatment, although typically this has involved the mother-daughter dyad. Sanchez-Lacay et al. (1991) randomly assigned female adolescent suicide attempters to either cognitive behavioral family therapy or to an "unstructured family treatment," which focused discussion on a particular family theme or interaction. Parents and adolescents in both conditions reported decreased levels of symptomatology at posttreatment and at a five-week follow-up assessment with both. Generally, participants reported satisfaction with both treatment conditions, although parents indicated a preference for the more structured intervention.

Working from the premise that a primary dysfunction of parasuicidal individuals is inadequate affective regulation, Linehan (1987) has developed a sophisticated biosocial model of the functional deficits that characterize those who attempt suicide. Theorizing that an initial affective vulnerability interacts with a social-developmental environment that invalidates individual affective experiences, she has developed a type of cognitive behavioral treatment termed dialectical behavior therapy (DBT). DBT includes both individual and group treatment. While the group treatment primarily addresses skills enhancement, treatment targets in individual therapy follow a hierarchical plan: (1) suicidal behaviors; (2) behaviors interfering with the conduct of therapy; (3) avoidance and escape behaviors interfering with a reasonable quality of life; (4) behavioral skill acquisition; and (5) idiographic issues. The central behavioral skills addressed in both individual and group treatment include emotional regulation, interpersonal effectiveness, distress tolerance, and self-management. Regarding suicidal behavior, DBT is designed to validate negative affect, to teach more adaptive means of coping with problematic situations, and to use contingency strategies to highlight the relative outcomes of suicidal and nonsuicidal behavior. In a recent outcome study with adult parasuicidal borderline patients, Linehan, Armstrong, Suarez, Allmon, and Heard (1991) compared a sample randomized to DBT or to "treatment as usual" in the community. Patients who received DBT had fewer and less medically severe incidences of parasuicide, were more likely to remain in treatment, and had fewer inpatient psychiatric days.

IX. Prevention of Adolescent Depression

In contrast to the promising advances in the treatment of adolescent depression, there have been few systematic efforts either to develop or evaluate programs directed at the prevention of depression in youth. This is particularly disappointing because of the significance of adolescent depression as a public health problem and because effective preventive interventions might be well suited to reducing first and repeated depressive episodes, especially in high-risk populations.

The only randomized, controlled prevention study conducted to date is that conducted by Clarke and colleagues (1994). These researchers are currently completing a school-based prevention program to evaluate the possibility of reducing the incidence of unipolar affective disorders and depressive symptomatology in high school adolescents who were identified as being at an increased risk of future depression because of elevated but subdiagnostic levels of depressive symptomatology (Weissman, Myers, Thompson, & Belanger, 1986). Roberts (1987) and Dorenwhend, Shrout, Egri, and Mendelsohn (1980) have defined this state of subdiagnostic depressive symptomatology as "demoralization."

In this investigation, demoralized adolescents were identified by a two-stage screening procedure. A self-report screening instrument, the Center for Epidemiological Studies–Depression Scale (CES-D) (Radloff, 1977), was administered in all 9th grade health classes. This was followed by a confirmatory structured diagnostic interview with adolescents exhibiting elevated scores on the screen. Adolescents who were determined to meet diagnostic criteria for current DSM-III-R MDD or DD were diverted to a nonexperimental CWDA treatment group. The remaining 148 subdiagnostic, demoralized adolescents were randomly assigned either to a 15-session, after-school, cognitive-restructuring preventive intervention (Clarke & Lewinsohn, 1991) or to a "usual care" control condition. While the demoralized group was diagnostically heterogeneous and included some youth with anxiety or conduct disorders, the vast majority (> 85%) had only subdiagnostic depressive symptoms with no current DSM-III-R disorder. All participants are being followed at six and 12 months postintervention to evaluate the impact of the secondary preventive intervention on affective symptomatology and the development of episodes of depression, appropriate treatment-seeking, suicide attempts, school attendance, and other individual and community indices of health and prosocial behaviors. Currently, six-month follow-up results are quite positive: the Life Table results shown in Figure 2.1 indicate significantly fewer cases of either MDD or DD in the experimental group over the six-month follow-up period.

Only two other groups have conducted outcome trials of the prevention of adolescent depression. Klein, Greist, Bass, and Lohr (1987) developed a school-based "wellness" prevention intervention that was tested in a midwestern high school. The program emphasized aerobic exercise and made use of an interactive computer program to provide information about depression and other health problems (for example, venereal disease, drug use/abuse). The aerobic exercise program included before and after school jogging, indoor roller-skating, and soccer. Other group activities offered as part of the program included classroom demonstrations, canoeing, and nature trips. Near the end of the school year, 89% of the students had heard of the program and 34% had participated in at least one aspect of the program. Participation was greater for females and for the younger students. Although the program attracted some of the more depressed adolescents, no evidence exists that indicates participation in the program reduced depression as measured with the depression cluster of the Symptom Checklist-90-Revised (Derogatis, Lipman, & Covi, 1973).

At another site, Beardslee and colleagues have conducted initial safety and feasibility studies of an

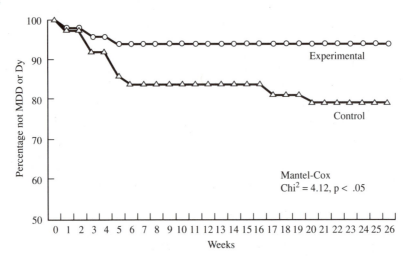

Figure 2.1   Six-month Life Table results for prevention of major depression or dysthymia in demoralized adolescents

intervention designed to prevent depression in the offspring of depressed parents (Beardslee et al., 1993). They have just begun a five-year randomized outcome trial based on the cognitive-restructuring therapy approach (Beck et al., 1979).

X. Common Tactics and Developmental Considerations in Psychosocial Treatments for Depressed Adolescents

A number of principles have emerged concerning psychosocial treatment for depressed adults (for example, McLean & Hakstian, 1979; Zeiss et al., 1979). There is a general consensus that psychotherapy should:

• Possess a well-developed rationale
• Be structured with a goal attainment focus
• Provide training and encourage independent use of life skills that patients can apply in their daily life
• Encourage the patient's attributions that improvement is a function of the patient's efforts

Given the existing literature on adolescent depression, these same principles would seem equally applicable.

In addition, commonalities in recommended modifications of psychosocial treatments for depressed adolescents are found among a number of writers of various theoretical persuasions (Emery et al., 1983;

Hoberman & Peterson, 1990; Leahy, 1988; Rossman, 1982; Trautman & Rotheram-Borus, 1988; Wilkes & Rush, 1988). Preeminent among these considerations is the increased emphasis placed on developing the therapeutic alliance by actively cultivating rapport with the adolescents, particularly by attending to the depressed adolescent's affect and concerns. Maintaining an empathic stance, the therapist attempts to cultivate a collaborative relationship by developing an explicit contract regarding the adolescent's concerns and needs. Two studies of especially effective therapists with youth (Kolvin et al., 1981; Ricks, 1974) have demonstrated the importance of therapist personal characteristics. In the former study, the "supershrink" was an active, responsive therapist who educated the patient and dealt primarily with reality issues; worked to increase the youth's autonomy and frequently utilized outside resources; and included nonpsychological issues within therapy sessions. In the latter study, the best therapeutic outcomes were achieved by extroverted, assertive, and open therapists.

· Given their lack of appreciation of the extent or phenomenology of depression as a disorder, depressed youth may not consider themselves as having a psychiatric condition and may not recognize that they might benefit from intervention. In addition, adolescents typically have misconceptions about the nature and outcome of psychotherapy. They may need to be educated about depression and psychotherapy, including encouraging realistic expectations about the likely benefits of treatment.

There are a number of developmental considerations when conducting psychotherapy with adolescents, and the following tactics and considerations are especially appropriate. Psychotherapy with depressed adolescents should be positive in its orientation with special emphasis on the existing strengths of the adolescent, given the heightened self-consciousness and potential self-criticism that increases during adolescence. Likewise, therapy with adolescents needs to attend to individual or idiosyncratic factors. The nature of the specific interventions should be developmentally informed, with particular consideration of the individual's cognitive development. Given the heterogeneity of adolescent depressions—the diversity of the clinical presentations, the varying developmental level of depressed adolescents, and the potential multiplicity of etiological and maintaining factors involved in depressive episodes—the role of therapeutic decision making is of obvious importance. As Harrington (1992) has written, "Wherever treatment is carried out, it should be tailored to the needs of the individual child, rather than prescribed as a standard "package" . . . [given] the multiple problems of the depressed child" (p. 1292).

Therapists need to be both creative and relatively concrete in their application of intervention methods. Metaphors, storytelling, art, creative writing, role playing, and videotaping can all be useful clinical tactics. Therapists need to be flexible in their treatment plan and able to think strategically to maximize therapeutic outcome. Indeed, evidence from current treatment programs indicates that flexibility in treatment tactics, rather than rigid adherence to therapy manuals, is the norm, not the exception, in effective treatment (for example, Brent et al., 1992; Wilkes & Belsher, 1992). Furthermore, given the range of antecedent conditions to depressive episodes, it is likely that treatment may be most successful if it possesses the potential for broad, multidimensional interventions.

Existing studies also indicate that psychotherapy with adolescents will be most beneficial if it is active, both in terms of the patient-therapist interactions and in the focus on the actual life experiences and responses of the youth (for example, Kolvin et al., 1981; Ricks, 1974). Efforts to minimize silence during sessions to reduce the potential discomfort experienced by the adolescent client is an example of the need for an active therapeutic stance. Early success experiences to reinforce the process or attendance at therapy may also be useful. Generally speaking, the available manuals on psychosocial interventions emphasize behavioral tactics early in treatment to facilitate success or mastery experiences; cognitive tactics are employed later in therapy as distorted thinking and core negative schemas become apparent. In particular, affect identification and affect management seem critical early in treatment to provide depressed adolescents the means of containing the increased distress that can be associated with the tasks of identifying and exploring the content of cognitive distortions.

Adolescent needs for autonomy and control may lead to testing behavior and noncompliance, and therapists must be able to tolerate such behavior and to understand when it might be appropriate to challenge such actions as interfering with the process of therapy. Regarding parameters of psychotherapy, a number of considerations are applicable to adolescents. Therapy sessions might be briefer and faster paced. More frequent sessions at the beginning of treatment (for example, twice per week) may be especially valuable in containing or reducing symptomatic distress and generating a sense of hope regarding improvement. Further, shorter, simpler, and more concrete homework assignments are probably preferable to maximize compliance. In cases where the adolescent does not complete homework, it may be useful to complete the assignment in the session. In addition, several writers emphasize the use of phone contact with depressed adolescents between sessions, especially with those who are characterized by suicidal ideation (Linehan, 1987; Mufson et al., 1992). For those depressed youth who are experiencing premorbid academic problems or depression-augmented or -induced academic difficulties, regular contacts with school personnel may be helpful in providing the school with education about the nature and consequences of depressive disorders, and in creating the opportunity to work collaboratively with school personnel on cognitive processing problems (for example, attention, comprehension, decision making) and the promotion of academic achievement.

Finally, work with depressed adolescents should attempt to include family members in both the assessment and treatment process. At a minimum, family members benefit from an education as to the true phenomenology of depressions as well as their severity, chronicity, and broad psychosocial impairment. With the support of informed family members, it is likely that a variety of interventions can be useful in improving the context for recovery from depression and perhaps in restructuring maladaptive family interactions that contributed to both the development and maintenance of depressive episodes. To these ends, family homework might be especially useful.

XI. Critique and Future Direction of Psychosocial Treatments for Adolescent Depression

Undoubtedly, substantial progress has been made in the development of treatment models for depressive episodes in adolescence. A small but convergent empirical base currently exists for a variety of psychosocial treatments of adolescent depression. However, this base possesses a number of methodological limitations.

Overall, it would appear that many of the conditions of the empirical literature on psychosocial treatments of adolescent depression depart greatly from those of actual clinical practice and thus raise concerns about external validity (for example, Kazdin, Siegel, & Bass, 1990). To begin with, it is not clear that most of the participants treated in these studies were truly experiencing depressive episodes. In the typical treatment study, participants were solicited from school populations and were identified as depressed by self-report questionnaires. In contrast, therapy clients tend to be self-, parent-, or school-referred (that is, to seek help of their own accord, albeit infrequently). Furthermore, at least three of the available outcome studies focused on school-age children, with only two studies including substantial numbers of adolescents. Exclusion criteria for studies were such that, for the most part, only adolescents with pure MDD or DD were included. Yet, such adolescents are quite atypical depressives; the majority of adolescents with depressive episodes have comorbid psychiatric conditions, including both internalizing disorders (for example, overanxious disorder) and externalizing disorders (for example, conduct disorder, substance abuse). Given the degree to which comorbidity is associated both with the recognition that there is a problem and, ultimately, with the treatment outcome, available studies likely share little in common with community-based processes and outcomes of interventions for depressed youth. Thus, it is doubtful that existing results possess true clinical significance.

Available controlled treatment outcome studies have employed group interventions. This appears to be more a matter of experimental convenience than either empirical or theoretical substance. In a meta-analysis of nine studies that contrasted group and individual treatment for adults, adolescents, and children, Tillitski (1990) found a trend for group treatments to be more effective with adolescents than with children. However, in their considerably more comprehensive meta-analysis, Weisz et al. (1987) found larger effect sizes for individual versus group treatment. Further, both the Weisz et al. and Kazdin et al. studies, which examined both research and clinical practice, respectively, reported that adolescents are more difficult to treat. This suggests that individual approaches might provide additional benefits for depressed adolescents. Further, the broad consensus on the importance of the therapeutic relationship as a necessary condition of change may best be maximized in individual treatment. As Kazdin, Siegel, and Bass (1990) point out, only 37% of psychologists or psychiatrists believe that group interventions are effective; while this belief may be erroneous, the data indicate that clinical practice in the community is characterized by a pronounced preference for individual therapy. Finally, on a practical note, Fine et al. (1991) noted unexpected difficulties in recruiting depressed adolescents to participate in group interventions for depression. The reliance on group interventions clearly limits the ecological validity of available studies.

Likewise, the fact that most participants in published studies were recruited and identified as having a problem by the researchers significantly limits generalizability. Community-based studies indicate that psychiatrically disturbed youth—especially ones suffering from depression—are very poor help-seekers; that is, they have difficulty recognizing problems, believing formal help sources are useful, and using those resources. Clearly, more research investigating the help-seeking behavior of depressed youth needs to be conducted. Similarly, prevention programs directed at enhancing help-seeking willingness and ability of depressed adolescents would be useful (for example, extensions of the Depression Awareness, Recognition, and Treatment (DART) program (Garfinkel, Jensen, & Hoberman, 1988).

Other limitations of the available treatment outcome studies exist. First, no study of psychosocial interventions for adolescent depression has examined potential mechanisms of change. Second, most have not examined individual predictors of clinical outcome. Finally, follow-up assessments for controlled studies of the treatment of depressed adolescents generally range from one to nine months; only the study by Clarke, Lewinsohn, Hops, and Andrews (1991) has reported two-year follow-up data. Lewinsohn, Clarke, and Rohde (1994) noted that approximately 23% of the adolescents treated with the CWDA course relapse and experience additional depressive episodes. Given the consistent body of data indicating that adult and, even more so, juvenile depressives are at great risk of relapse or recurrence of depressive episodes, longer follow-up periods are clearly essential to determine whether psychosocial interventions have long-term prophylactic effects.

A number of suggestions for future research regarding the psychosocial treatment of adolescent depression can be offered. Many of these issues are ones commonly noted by recent reviews of the child psychotherapy literature, including those by Kazdin (1990; Kazdin, Bass, et al., 1990), Kendall and Morris (1991), and Mash (1990). To begin with, greater precision and specificity of measurements are needed. Regarding assessment, attempts should be made to identify a core set of diagnostic, psychosocial, and biological variables that should be included across studies by investigators of different theoretical allegiance. Moreover, such assessments must necessarily involve multiple informants to adequately capture the contextual or situational specificity of both dysfunction and improvement. Further, measurement needs to be conducted both at the *impact* level (for example, traditional outcome measures such as symptom severity or school performance) and at the *specifying* level (Kendall & Morris, 1991), the latter to indicate the specific affect-behavior-cognitions relationships that may have changed as a result of the intervention. Impact level assessments must indicate the degree to which interventions have achieved clinical as well as statistical significance.

In addition, future studies need to be more ecologically valid. They therefore should not exclude depressed adolescents with comorbid psychiatric diagnoses since they are by far the norm. Thus, existing studies with extensive exclusionary criteria may lack clinical significance, which raises questions about the generalizability of their results. Consequently, in future research the extent and degree of comorbidity should be identified and quantified and examined as a covariate of process and outcome. Similarly, parental psychiatric disorder, family adversity, and family conflict should also be carefully evaluated and studied in relation to the therapeutic process. In a related manner, broader domains of psychosocial problems (for example, school problems, maladaptive sexual behavior) should also be assessed given their association with depression. These issues have particular implications for managed care, which may adopt given research protocols based upon the *apparent* effectiveness of existing outcome results without an appreciation for the lack of ecological validity.

Given the apparent similarity of the actual strategies and tactics employed in existing psychotherapy studies for adolescent depression, it would make sense to examine an expanded range of interventions, especially psychodynamic and family therapies, within the framework of randomly assigned, controlled studies. Although a recent meta-analysis of brief psychodynamic psychotherapy indicated that such interventions were as or more effective compared to other types of psychosocial interventions (Crits-Christoph, 1992), to date no psychotherapy outcome studies have been conducted utilizing a psychodynamic-based intervention to treat depressive disorders among adolescents. Given the recurrent nature of adolescent depression, it is possible that psychodynamic interventions might offer prophylactic potential, both in their emphasis on the interpersonal relationships and in their emphasis on broader individual change. Similarly, with evidence for both parental and family interaction dysfunction, systematic family interventions might also offer the potential for contextual change which, in turn, can lower the risk for future depressive and other disorders and dysfunction.

In addition, while there are both overlaps and differences in MDD and DD, the development of disorder-specific interventions might be of great interest. With DD characterized by, at least, greater chronicity, modifications of process or technical factors may be called for, and these issues deserve investigation. For example, McCullough (1984) has suggested that an interpersonal focus may be of particular importance in treating adult patients with DD; in addition, emphasis is placed on dysthymic individuals to accept responsibility for their depression and by implication control over their moods, and to develop strategies to achieve and maintain control over their moods.

Major questions remain concerning the critical ingredients involved in positive outcome for depressed adolescents. In their comprehensive review of the empirical literature, Lambert, Shapiro, and Bergin (1986) found that only 15% of the variance in clinical outcome can be attributed to specific technical factors; up to 45% of the variance can be attributed to nonspecific factors in an intervention. Applicability of this finding for treatment of adult depressives is echoed by McLean and Carr (1991). Certainly, CBT interventions emphasize the role of learning specific skills, especially by in vivo practice. Yet one has to question the degree and robustness of learning new skills after only one or at best a few sessions devoted to learning a particular skill. Further, the Lewinsohn et al. (1990) study indicated that the rate of homework completion by depressed adolescents was under 50%, further questioning the practice and true acquisition of new skills. Such data highlight both the theoretical and empirical salience of nonspecific factors (for example, the therapeutic alliance) to clinical outcome and call attention to the need to better understand the nature of such factors.

Beyond an exploration of the importance of nonspecific factors, studies need to devote attention to understanding the mechanisms of clinical change in depressed adolescents. Multiple assessments of both process and putative etiological factors need to be made at several points during the treatment process to assess both the levels of impact and specification. To date, this has only been accomplished in a few studies. Further, in adults, there appears to be a lack of specificity of treatment effects related to different interventions (Rude & Rehm, 1991); this also appears to be the case for treatments of adolescent depression, although definitive comparisons have yet to be made. Clarification of the mechanism of change has important implications as to whether psychotherapy for depressed adolescents operates via a model of compensation (for example, by addressing patient deficits) or of capitalization (for example, by addressing patients' preexisting competencies). An alternative approach to better understanding critical ingredients in the treatment process would be to undertake dismantling studies and to compare the effects of presumably critical intervention components to one another. Finally, another avenue to a broader understanding of the treatment process would be to examine the sequencing of psychotherapeutic tactics with depressed adolescents.

Another important area for further investigation concerns combinations of different intervention modalities and tactics. While comparisons among alternative psychosocial and pharmacological interventions offer the potential for understanding both similarities and differences in the outcome and mediating processes of recovery from depressive disorders, studies of combinations of treatment are also needed. Less illuminating from an empirical perspective, combinations of treatment modalities and tactics may have much to offer the clinician. A high research priority, for instance, is the examination of combinations of family and individual adolescent therapy. In the Lewinsohn et al. study of the CWDA course, the group of depressed adolescents with a parallel parent group, a relatively weak family intervention, tended to do better than the other active treatment. That result suggests that stronger, more active family interventions could improve the outcome of depressed adolescents. Likewise, given that common clinical practice in the community is to treat depressed adolescents with a combination of psychotherapy and pharmacotherapy, it is important to provide an empirical perspective for this strategy.

A related issue involves the lack of empirical guidelines concerning the selection and implementation of the variety of clinical strategies available to the clinician and the evaluation of how effective specific interventions are with particular types of patients (Beckham, 1990). Further studies are needed of those variables that predict positive and negative outcome in treatment trials. Beyond these group predictors, there is an increasing need to understand the role of individual differences in the process and outcome of psychotherapy, particularly treatment-specific strengths and deficiencies of both patients and therapists (Beckham, 1990). For example, since antidepressants do not appear to be efficacious in group trials, it makes sense to study the individualized response of those adolescents who do and do not respond to medication. While gender differences in etiologic-related variables appear to be more quantitative than qualitative in nature, it would be useful to determine whether treatment tactics might be modified to enhance their differential effectiveness with female and male patients. Beckham (1990) reviewed several studies of patient difficulty and suggested that treatment-specific deficiencies may characterize certain patients and moderate treatment outcome. Since 35% to 65% of adult and adolescent depressives do not respond to a particular intervention, nonresponders to specific treatment interventions should be carefully evaluated to gain an understanding of factors in treatment failure. More broadly, future investigations should attempt to analyze patterns of response among treatment study participants, both in outcome and in the process of treatment. Clinically speaking, all of these issues suggest the potential significance of clinical decision making in tailoring interventions to the specific needs of particular depressed individuals and of the value of evaluating the actual process of treatment planning, implementation, and modification.

Perhaps most important, the time has come to attempt to identify critical components of different modes of psychotherapy and to integrate them into a more coherent and integrated whole. Such multidimensional interventions take the best of different theoretical orientations, regarding both etiology and treatment tactics, and apply them to the particular needs of the patient. Hoberman and Peterson (1990) have discussed the value of integrating psychodynamic and cognitive behavioral tactics in the treatment of childhood psychiatric disorders in general. Hoberman (1993) has described multidimensional developmental psychotherapy (MDP), a developmentally informed psychotherapy for adolescents that describes the value and means of integrating multiple psychotherapeutic approaches. Similar attempts to describe the mutual benefits of integrating more theoretically disparate elements into a more comprehensive treatment program have also been provided by Linehan (1987), Safran and Segal (1990), and Westen (1991).

To date, however, no such interventions have been systematically studied with depressed adolescents. Again, the ecological validity and utility of such approaches and research might be great, given that many clinicians described themselves as eclectic—that is, ascribing to a combination of theoretical and strategic orientations. The potential for integrating research findings on both the etiology and treatment of adolescent depression as well as developmental considerations deserves fuller exploration. For example, one possible explanation of the efficacy of fairly nonintensive group treatments is that they address the interaction between etiological and developmental issues. Many depressed adolescents do not know that they are depressed and are unaware that treatments are available; that is, they simply don't recognize that this distress is not normal and is not necessary. Likewise, depression-related psychosocial impairment—that is, increased conflict or withdrawal and isolation—may be particularly depressogenic or depression-maintaining for adolescents. Group psychoeducational treatments address all of these issues, some explicitly (for example, psychosocial deficits) and some implicitly (for example, social isolation and lack of a sense of belonging). Integrative models can explicitly combine specific and nonspecific curative factors.

The consistent positive outcomes of a variety of relatively short-term group interventions in treating adolescent depressive episodes are somewhat paradoxical. The phenomenological and natural history literature on adolescent depression characterizes these episodes as relatively severe, of long duration, and recurrent. As the study by Kovacs et al. (1984b) indicated, most young depressives, despite psychosocial treatment in the community, continued to demonstrate these clinical characteristics and, worse yet, were at elevated risk for a variety of additional psychiatric conditions. Yet in every study to date, a majority of depressed adolescents provided with group psychosocial treatment recovered with brief interventions. Similarly, depressed adolescent participants in medication trials have consistently demonstrated high placebo response rates despite the lack of an active intervention. These findings appear paradoxical and remain central issues for future studies to clarify.

In the area of outcome, several issues remain to be clarified. Obviously, more long-term follow-up studies need to be conducted to better understand the eventual outcome of depressed adolescents receiving different treatments and of the variety of subsequent events that influence later adolescent psychiatric symptomatology and psychosocial functioning. The evidence that IPT in adults with recurrent depression lowers the chance of additional depressive episodes (Frank, 1991), particularly to the degree that intervention focuses on interpersonal issues (Frank, Kupfer, Wagner, McEachran, & Cornes, 1991), suggests the value of exploring its prophylactic effects with adolescents treated with a variety of primary interventions.

Finally, two additional concerns regarding interventions with depressed adolescents bear consideration. Both concern the dynamic nature of the juvenile population and the health care system that serves most of them. First, researchers must bear in mind the nature of the demographic composition of American youth. Presently, nonwhite persons constitute 21% of the total U.S. population; by the year 2020, this percentage will enlarge to 40%, with increasing numbers of African Americans, Hispanics, Asian Americans, and Native Americans. Minority populations are disproportionately young, meaning they contain increasing percentages of adolescents. As Hoberman (1992) points out in his recent review, minority adolescents are more likely than white adolescents to live in conditions of poverty, disrupted family life, and single-parent homes; they also exhibit high rates of high school drop-out and unemployment. Each of these factors is associated with higher rates of psychiatric disorders, including depression. In short, while no definitive data currently exist as to the association of ethnic minority status and elevated rates of psychiatric disorder, it is likely that an increasing number of adolescents with depressive disorders will be youth of color. This points to the urgent need to extend treatment outcome studies to include significant portions of minority youth and to examine potential ethnicity-related differences in the process and outcome of psychosocial treatments for youth of color. At this point in time, there is no database to direct modifications of existing interventions to enhance their cultural appropriateness.

Second, a variety of issues currently characterizes the funding and accessibility of health and mental health services in general, and the particular issues that adolescents face in seeking and obtaining necessary services (for example, Hoberman, 1992). Such issues are especially significant given the evidence that most depressed adolescents are not identified or provided with treatment. School-based health clinics or school-adjacent comprehensive community service centers may offer the best means of providing mental health services to adolescents in general and to depressed or suicidal adolescents in particular (Office of Technology Assessment, 1991). Users of school-based clinics (Balassone, Bell, & Peterfreund, 1991) are more likely to be knowledgeable of where to seek mental health services; further, several studies have indicated that depressed or suicidal youth are actually more willing or interested in seeking intervention from school-based clinics than are their nondepressed peers (Hawkins, Spigner, & Murphy, 1990; Riggs & Cheng, 1988). Similarly, given the elevated rates of conduct disorder and delinquency associated with depressed youth, improved mental health assessment and clinical services in the juvenile justice system would also be an appropriate means of serving samples of youth with depressive disorders.

XII. Conclusion

As Cantwell (1992) recently stated: "Probably no area related to childhood depression needs more investigation than that of treatment" (p. 291). There can be no question that he is correct. Fortunately, basic foundations have been laid for the process of conceptualizing and implementing elements of psychosocial interventions for depressive episodes in adolescence. With increasing recognition of the current and future implications of high rates of severely impairing adolescent depression, delineating the important elements of the process and outcome of psychosocial therapies for this condition must be a critical clinical research priority.

References

ABRAMSON, L. Y., Seligman, M. E. P., & Teasdale, J. D. (1978). Learned helplessness in humans: Critique and reformulation. *Journal of Abnormal Psychology, 87,* 49–74.

AKISKAL, H. S., & McKinney, W. T. (1975). Overview of recent research in depression: Integration of ten conceptual models into a comprehensive clinical frame. *Archives of General Psychiatry, 32,* 285–305.

ALEXANDER, J. F., Barton, C., Schiavo, R. S., & Parsons, B. V. (1976). Systems-behavioral intervention with families of delinquents: Therapist characteristics, family behavior, and outcome. *Journal of Consulting and Clinical Psychology, 44,* 656–664.

ALLGOOD-MERTEN, B., Lewinsohn, P. M., & Hops, H. (1990). Sex differences and adolescent depression. *Journal of Abnormal Psychology, 99,* 55–63.

AMERICAN Psychiatric Association. (1987). *Diagnostic and statistical manual of mental disorders (3rd ed., rev.).* Washington, DC: Author.

ANDREWS, J. A., & Lewinsohn, P. M. (1992). Suicidal attempts among older adolescents: Prevalence and co-occurrence with psychiatric disorders. *Journal of the American Academy of Child and Adolescent Psychiatry, 31,* 655–662.

ASARNOW, J. R., & Carlson, G. A. (1988). Childhood depression: Five-year outcome following combined cognitive-behavior therapy and pharmacotherapy. *American Journal of Psychotherapy, 42,* 456–464.

ASARNOW, J. R., Goldstein, M. J., Carlson, G. A., Perdue, S., Bates, S., & Keller, J. (1988). Childhood-onset depressive disorders: A follow-up study of rates of re-hospitalization and out-of-home placement among child psychiatric inpatients. *Journal of Affective Disorders, 15,* 245–253.

BAKER, M., Dorzob, J., Winokur, G., et al. (1971). Depressive disease: Classification and clinical characteristics. *Comprehensive Psychiatry, 12,* 354–365.

BALASSONE, M. L., Bell, M., & Peterfreund, N. (1991). A comparison of users and nonusers of a school-based health and mental health clinic. *Journal of Adolescent Health Care, 12,* 240–246, 450–458.

BARRNETT, R. J., Docherty, J. P., & Frommelt, G. M. (1991). A review of child psychotherapy research since 1963. *Journal of the American Academy of Child and Adolescent Psychiatry, 30*(1), 1–14.

BEARDSLEE, W. R., Hoke, L., Wheelock, I., Rothberg, P. C., van de Velde, P., & Swatling, S. (1992). Preventative intervention for families with parental affective disorders: Initial findings. *American Journal of Psychiatry, 149,* 1335–1340.

BEARDSLEE, W. R., Salt, P., Porterfield, K., Rothberg, P. C., van de Velde, P., Swatling, S., Hoke, L., Moilanen, D. L., & Wheelock, I. (1993). Comparison of preventative interventions for families with parental affective disorder. *Journal of the American Academy of Child and Adolescent Psychiatry, 32,* 254–263.

BECK, A. (1967). *Depression: Clinical, experimental, and theoretical aspects.* New York: Harper & Row.

BECK, A. T., Rush, A. J., Shaw, B. F., & Emery, G. (1979). *Cognitive therapy of depression.* New York: Guilford Press.

BECK, A. T., Ward, C. H., Mendelson, M., Mock, J. E., & Erbaugh, J. K. (1961). An inventory for measuring depression. *Archives of General Psychiatry, 4,* 561–571.

BECKER, R. E., Heimberg, R. G., & Bellack, A. S. (1987). *Social skills training treatment for depression.* New York: Pergamon.

BECKHAM, E. E. (1990). Psychotherapy of depression research at a crossroads: Directions for the 1990s. *Clinical Psychology Review, 10,* 207–228.

BEMPORAD, J. (1978). Psychodynamics of depression and suicide in children and adolescents. In S. Arieti & J. Bemporad (Eds.), *Severe and mild depression: The psychotherapeutic approach* (pp. 185–207). New York: Basic Books.

BEMPORAD, J. (1982). Management of childhood depression: Developmental considerations. *Psychosomatics, 23,* 272–279.

BEMPORAD, J. R. (1988). Psychodynamic treatment of depressed adolescents. *Journal of Clinical Psychiatry, 49* (Suppl.), 26–31.

BLYTH, D., Simmons, R., & Zakin, D. (1985). Satisfaction with body image for early adolescent females: The impact of pubertal timing within different school environments. *Journal of Youth and Adolescence, 14,* 227–236.

BRENT, D., Kolko, D., Boylan, M., Holder, D., Feinberg-Steinberg, T., & Birmaher, B. (1992). *Cognitive therapy in depressed suicidal adolescents*. Paper presented at the annual meeting of the American Academy of Child and Adolescent Psychiatry, Washington, DC.

BURBACH, D. J., & Borduin, C. M. (1986). Parent-child relations and the etiology of depression: A review of methods and findings. *Clinical Psychology Review, 6*, 133–153.

BUTLER, L., Miezitis, S., Friedman, R., & Cole, E. (1980). The effect of two school-based intervention programs on depressive symptoms in preadolescents. *American Educational Research Journal, 17*, 111–119.

CANTWELL, D. P. (1992). Directions for future research. In M. Lewis & D. P. Cantwell (Eds.), *Child and adolescent psychiatric clinics of North America: Mood disorders* (pp. 285–292). Philadelphia: Saunders.

CARLSON, G. A., & Cantwell, D. P. (1980). Unmasking depression in children and adolescents. *American Journal of Psychiatry, 137*, 445–449.

CARLSON, G. A., & Kashani, J. H. (1988). Phenomenology of major depression from childhood through adulthood: Analysis of three studies. *American Journal of Psychiatry, 145*, 1222–1225.

CASEY, R. J., & Berman, J. S. (1985). The outcome of psychotherapy with children. *Psychological Bulletin, 98*, 388–400.

CHAMBERS, W., Puig-Antich, J., Hirsch, M., Paez, P., Ambrosini, P., Tabrizi, M., & Davies, M. (1985). The assessment of affective disorders in children and adolescents by semistructured interview. *Archives of General Psychiatry, 42*, 696–702.

CLARIZIO, H. F. (1985). Cognitive-behavioral treatment of childhood depression. *Psychology in the Schools, 22*, 308–322.

CLARKE, G. N. (1985). *A psychoeducational approach to the treatment of depressed adolescents*. Unpublished dissertation, University of Oregon, Eugene, OR.

CLARKE, G. N., Hawkins, W., Murphy, M., & Sheeber, L. (1993). School-based prevention of depressive symptomatology in adolescents: Findings from two studies. *Journal of Adolescent Research, 8*, 183–204.

CLARKE, G. N., Hawkins, W., Murphy, M., Sheeber, L. B., Lewinsohn, P. M., & Seeley, J. R. (1994). Targeted prevention of unipolar depressive disorder in an at-risk sample of high school adolescents: A randomized trial of a group cognitive intervention. *Journal of the American Academy of Child and Adolescent Psychiatry*.

CLARKE, G. N., Hops, H., Lewinsohn, P. M., Andrews, J., Seeley, J. R., & Williams, J. (1992). Cognitive-behavioral group treatment of adolescent depression: Prediction of outcome. *Behavior Therapy, 23*, 341–354.

CLARKE, G. N., & Lewinsohn, P. M. (1991). *The coping with stress course: A group, psycho-educational cognitive-restructuring intervention for the secondary prevention of adolescent affective disorders*. Unpublished therapy manual, Oregon Health Sciences University.

CLARKE, G. N., Lewinsohn, P. M., & Hops, H. (1990). *Instructor's manual for the adolescent coping with depression course*. Eugene, OR: Castalia Press.

CLARKE, G. N., Lewinsohn, P., Hops, H., & Andrews, J. (1991). *Two-year treatment outcome follow-up of depressed adolescents*. Paper presented at the annual meeting of the Association for the Advancement of Behavior Therapy, New York, NY.

CONNERS, C. K. (1992). Methodology of antidepressant drug trials for treating depression in adolescents. *Journal of Child and Adolescent Pharmacology, 2*, 11–22.

CRITS-CHRISTOPH, P. (1992). The efficacy of brief dynamic psychotherapy: A meta-analysis. *American Journal of Psychiatry, 149*, 151–158.

CRUMLEY, F. E. (1979). Adolescent suicide attempts. *Journal of the American Medical Association, 241*, 2404–2407.

DEROGATIS, L., Lipman, R., & Covi, L. (1973). SCL-90: An outpatient psychiatric scale: Preliminary report. *Psychopharmacology Bulletin, 9*, 13.

DEYKIN, E. Y., Levy, J. C., & Wells, V. (1987). Adolescent depression, alcohol and drug abuse. *American Journal of Public Health, 77*, 178–182.

DORENWHEND, B. P., Shrout, P. E., Egri, G., & Mendelsohn, F. S. (1980). Nonspecific psychological distress and other dimensions of psychopathology. *Archives of General Psychology, 37*, 1229–1236.

DUBOW, E. F., Lovko, K. R., & Kausch, D. F. (1990). Demographic differences in adolescents' health concerns and perceptions of helping agents. *Journal of Clinical Child Psychology, 19*(1), 44–54.

ELKIN, I., Shea, M. T., Watkins, J. T., Imber, S. D., Sotsky, S. M., Collins, J. F., Glass, D. R., Pilkonis, P. A., Leber, W. R., Docherty, J. P., Fiester, S. J., & Parloff, M. B. (1989). National Institute of Mental Health treatment of depression collaborative research program. *Archives of General Psychiatry, 46*, 971–982.

ELKIND, D. (1978). Understanding the young adolescent. *Adolescence, 13*, 127–134.

ELLIOTT, G. R. (1992). Dilemmas for clinicians and researchers using anti-depressants to treat adolescents with depression. *Journal of Child and Adolescent Pharmacology, 2*, 7–9.

ELLIS, A., & Harper, R. A. (1961). *A guide to rational living*. Hollywood, CA: Wilshire Books.

EMERY, G., Bedrosian, R., & Garber, J. (Ed.). (1983). Cognitive therapy with depressed children and adolescents. In D. P. Cantwell & G. A. Carlson (Eds.), *Affective disorders in childhood and adolescence—An update* (pp. 445–471). New York: Spectrum.

FINE, S., Forth, A., Gilbert, M., & Haley, G. (1991). Group therapy for adolescent depressive disorder: A comparison of social skills and therapeutic support. *Journal of the American Academy of Child and Adolescent Psychiatry, 30*(1), 79–85.

FINE, S., Gilbert, M., Schmidt, L., Haley, G., Maxwell, A., & Forth, A. (1989). Short-term group therapy with depressed adolescent outpatients. *Canadian Journal of Psychiatry, 34*, 97–102.

FLEMING, J., & Offord, D. (1990). Epidemiology of childhood depressive disorders: A critical review. *Journal of the American Academy of Child and Adolescent Psychiatry, 29*, 571–580.

FLEMING, J., Offord, D., & Boyle, M. (1989). Prevalence of childhood and adolescent depression in the community: Ontario child health study. *British Journal of Psychiatry, 155*, 647–654.

FRAME, C., Matson, J. L., Sonis, W. A., Fialkov, M. J., & Kazdin, A. E. (1982). Behavioral treatment of depression in a prepubertal child. *Journal of Behavior Therapy and Experimental Psychiatry, 13*(3), 239–243.

FRANK, E. (1991). Interpersonal psychotherapy as a maintenance treatment for patients with recurrent depression. *Psychotherapy, 28*, 259–266.

FRANK, E., Kupfer, D. J., Wagner, E. F., McEachran, A. B., & Cornes, C. (1991). Efficacy of interpersonal psychotherapy as a maintenance treatment of recurrent depression: Contributing factors. *Archives of General Psychiatry, 48*, 1053–1059.

FRANK, J. D. (1973). *Persuasion and healing*. Baltimore, MD: Johns Hopkins University Press.

FRIEDMAN, R. C., Clarkin, J. F., Corn, R., Aronoff, M. S., Hurt, S. W., & Murphy, M. C. (1983). DSM-III and affective pathology in hospitalized adolescents. *Journal of Nervous and Mental Disorders, 170*, 511–521.

FRIEDMAN, R. C., Corn, R., Aronoff, M. S., Hurt, S. W., & Clarkin, J. F. (1984). The seriously suicidal adolescent: Affective and character pathology. In H. S. Sudak, A. Ford, & N. B. Rushforth (Eds.), *Suicide in the young* (pp. 209–226). Boston: John Wright.

FUCHS, C., & Rehm, L. (1977). A self-control behavior therapy program for depression. *Journal of Clinical and Consulting Psychology, 48*, 206–215.

GARFINKEL, B. D., Jensen, J. B., & Hoberman, H. M. (1988). *Depression: Awareness, recognition, and treatment in children and adolescents*. Unpublished manuscript, University of Minnesota.

GELLER, B., Graham, D. L., Marsteller, F. A., & Bryant, M. (1990). Double-blind placebo-controlled study of nortriptyline in depressed adolescents using a "fixed plasma level" design. *Psychopharmacology Bulletin, 26*, 85–90.

GREENBERG, R. P., Bornstein, R. F., Greenberg, M. D., & Fisher, S. (1992). A meta-analysis of antidepressant outcome under "blinder" conditions. *Journal of Consulting and Clinical Psychology, 60*(5), 664–669.

HARRINGTON, R. (1992). Annotation: The natural history and treatment of child and adolescent affective disorders. *Journal of Child Psychology & Psychiatry, 33*(8), 1287–1302.

HARRINGTON, R., Fudge, H., Rutter, M., Pickles, A., & Hill, J. (1990). Adult outcomes of childhood and adolescent depression: I. Psychiatric status. *Archives of General Psychiatry, 47*, 465–473.

HARRINGTON, R., Fudge, H., Rutter, M., Pickles, A., & Hill, J. (1991). Adult outcomes of childhood and adolescent depression: II. Risk for antisocial disorders. *Journal of the American Academy of Child and Adolescent Psychiatry, 30*, 434–439.

HARTER, S. (1992). Intrapersonal development. In *NIMH Conference on Developmental Approaches to the Assessment of Psychopathology*, Rockville, MD.

HAWKINS, W. E., Spigner, C., & Murphy, M. (1990). Perceived use of health education services in a school-based clinic. *Perceptual and Motor Skills, 70*, 1075–1078.

HAZELRIGG, M. D., Cooper, H. M., & Borduin, C. M. (1987). Evaluation of the effectiveness of family therapies: An integrative review and analysis. *Psychological Bulletin, 101*, 428–443.

HEINICKE, C. M., & Ramsey-Klee, D. M. (1986). Outcome of child psychotherapy as a function of frequency of session. *Journal of the American Academy of Child Psychiatry, 25*, 247–253.

HILL, J., Holmbeck, G., Marlow, L., Green, T., & Lynch, M. (1985). Menarcheal status and parent-child relations in families of seventh-grade girls. *Journal of Youth and Adolescence, 14*, 301–316.

HOBERMAN, H. M. (1990). Behavioral treatments for unipolar depression. In B. Wolman & G. Stricker (Eds.), *Affective disorders facts, theories, and treatment methods*. New York: Wiley.

HOBERMAN, H. M. (1992). Ethnic minority status and adolescent mental health services utilization. *Journal of Mental Health Administration, 19*, 246–267.

HOBERMAN, H. M. (1993). *Multidimensional developmental psychotherapy for dysthymic disorder*. Unpublished manuscript, University of Minnesota Medical School.

HOBERMAN, H. M., & Peterson, C. B. (1990). Multidimensional psychotherapy for children and adolescents. In B. D. Garfinkel, G. A. Carlson, & E. B. Weller (Eds.), *Psychiatric disorders in children and adolescents* (pp. 503–536). Philadelphia: Saunders.

HODGSON, C., Feldman, W., Corber, S., & Quinn, A. (1986). Adolescent health needs II: Utilization of health care by adolescents. *Adolescence, 21*, 383–390.

HOLLON, S. D., & Garber, J. (1989). Cognitive therapy. In L. Y. Abramson (Ed.), *Social cognition and clinical psychology: A synthesis* (pp. 204–253). New York: Guilford Press.

HOLMES, W. E., & Wagner, K. D. (1992). Psychotherapy treatments for depression in children and adolescents. *Journal of Psychotherapy Practice and Research, 1*, 313–323.

JENSEN, P. S., Ryan, N. D., & Prien, R. (1992). Psychopharmacology of child and adolescent major depression: Present status and future directions. *Journal of Child and Adolescent Psychopharmacology, 2*, 31–45.

KAHN, J. S., Kehle, T. J., Jenson, W. R., & Clark, E. (1990). Comparison of cognitive-behavioral, relaxation, and self-modeling interventions for depression among middle-school students. *School Psychology Review, 19*, 196–211.

KANDEL, D., & Davies, M. (1986). Adult sequelae of adolescent depressive symptoms. *Archives of General Psychiatry, 43*, 255–262.

KANDEL, D., Raveis, V., & Davies, M. (1991). Suicidal ideation in adolescence: Depression, substance use, and other risk factors. *Journal of Youth and Adolescence, 20*(2), 289–309.

KASHANI, J., & Carlson, G. (1987). Seriously depressed preschoolers. *American Journal of Psychiatry, 144*, 348–350.

KASHANI, J. H., Carlson, G. A., Beck, N. C., Hoeper, E. W., Corcoran, C. M., McAllister, J. A., Fallahi, C., Rosenberg, T. K., & Reid, J. C. (1987). Depression, depressive symptoms, and depressed mood among a community sample of adolescents. *American Journal of Psychiatry, 144*, 931–934.

KASHANI, J. H., Keller, M. B., Solomon, N., Reid, J. C., & Mazzola, D. (1985). Double depression in adolescent substance abusers. *Journal of Affective Disorders, 8*, 153–157.

KAZDIN, A. E. (1990). Psychotherapy for children and adolescents. *Annual Review of Psychology, 41*, 21–54.

KAZDIN, A. E., Bass, D., Ayers, W. A., & Rodgers, A. (1990). Empirical and clinical focus of child and adolescent psychotherapy research. *Journal of Consulting and Clinical Psychology, 58*(6), 729–740.

KAZDIN, A. E., French, N. H., Unis, A. S., Esveldt-Dawson, K., & Sherick, R. B. (1983). Hopelessness, depression and suicidal intent among psychiatrically disturbed inpatient children. *Journal of Consulting and Clinical Psychology, 51*, 504–510.

KAZDIN, A. E., Siegel, T. C., & Bass, D. (1990). Drawing on clinical practice to inform research on child and adolescent psychotherapy: Survey of practitioners. *Professional Psychology: Research and Practice, 20*(3), 189–198.

KELLAM, S. G., Branch, J. D., Brown, C. H., & Russell, G. (1981). Why teenagers come for treatment. *Journal of the American Academy of Child Psychiatry, 20*, 477–495.

KELLER, M. B., Beardslee, W., Lavori, P. W., Wunder, J., Drs, D. L., & Samuelson, H. (1988). Course of major depression in non-referred adolescents: A retrospective study. *Journal of Affective Disorders, 15*, 235–243.

KELLER, M. B., Lavori, P. W., Beardslee, W. R., Wunder, J., & Ryan, N. (1991). Depression in children and adolescents: New data on "undertreatment" and a literature review on the efficacy of available treatments. *Journal of Affective Disorders, 21*, 163–171.

KELLER, M. B., & Shapiro, R. W. (1982). "Double depression": Superimposition of acute depressive episodes on chronic depressive disorders. *American Journal of Psychiatry, 139*, 438–442.

KENDALL, P. C., & Morris, R. J. (1991). Child therapy: Issues and recommendations. *Journal of Consulting and Clinical Psychology, 59*(6), 777–784.

KIEV, A. (1975). Psychotherapeutic strategies in the management of depressed and suicidal patients. *American Journal of Psychotherapy, 29*, 345–354.

KLEIN, M. H., Greist, L. H., Bass, S. M., & Lohr, M. (1987). Autonomy and self-control: Key concepts for the prevention of depression in adolescents. In R. F. Muñoz (Ed.), *Depression prevention: Research directions* (pp. 103–124). Washington, DC: Hemisphere.

KLERMAN, G. L., Lavori, P. W., Rice, J., Reich, T., Endicott, J., Andreasen, N. C., Keller, M. B., & Hirschfield, R. M. A. (1985). Birth-cohort trends in rates of major depressive disorder among relatives of patients with affective disorder. *Archives of General Psychiatry, 42*, 689–693.

KLERMAN, G., Weissman, M., Rounsaville, B., & Chevron, E. (1984). *Interpersonal psychotherapy of depression.* New York: Wiley.

KOLVIN, I., Barrett, M., Bhate, S., Berney, T., Famuyiwa, O., Fundudis, T., & Tyrer, S. (1991). The Newcastle child depression project: Diagnosis and classification of depression. *British Journal of Psychiatry, 159* (Suppl. 11), 9–21.

KOLVIN, I., Garside, R. E., Nicol, A., et al. (1981). *Help starts here: The maladjusted child in the ordinary school.* London: Tavistock.

KOPLEWICZ, H., Klass, E., & Klein, R. (1990). *Preliminary data of a study of the efficacy of amitriptyline in the treatment of adolescents with major depressive disorder.* Paper presented at the 30th annual meeting of the NIMH New Clinical Drug Evaluation Unit, Key Biscayne, FL.

KOVACS, M. (1980/1981). Rating scales to assess depression in school-aged children. *Acta Paedopsychiatrica, 46*, 305–315.

KOVACS, M. (1989). Affective disorders in children and adolescents. *American Psychologist, 44*, 209–215.

KOVACS, M., Feinberg, T., Crouse-Novak, M., Paulauskas, S., & Finkelstein, R. (1984a). Depressive disorders in childhood: I. A longitudinal prospective study of characteristics and recovery. *Archives of General Psychiatry, 41*, 643–649.

KOVACS, M., Feinberg, T. L., Crouse-Novak, M., Paulauskas, S. L., Pollock, M., & Finkelstein, R. (1984b). Depressive disorders in childhood: II. A longitudinal study of the risk for a subsequent major depression. *Archives of General Psychiatry, 41*, 643–649.

KOVACS, M., Gatsonis, C., Paulauskas, S. L., & Richards, C. (1989). Depressive disorders in childhood: III. A longitudinal study of comorbidity with and risk for anxiety disorders. *Archives of General Psychiatry, 46*, 776–782.

KOVACS, M., & Goldston, D. (1991). Cognitive and social cognitive development of depressed children and adolescents. *Journal of the American Academy of Child and Adolescent Psychiatry, 30*, 388–392.

KOVACS, M., & Paulauskas, S. (1986). The traditional psychotherapies in child psychotherapy. In H. C. Quay & J. S. Werry (Eds.), *Psychopathological disorders of childhood* (pp. 496–522). New York: Wiley.

KOVACS, M., Paulauskas, S., Gatsonis, C., & Richards, C. (1988). Depressive disorders in childhood: III. A longitudinal study of comorbidity with and risk for conduct disorders. *Journal of Affective Disorders, 15*, 205–217.

KRAMER, A. D., & Feiguine, R. J. (1981). Clinical effects of amitriptyline in adolescent depression: A pilot study. *Journal of the American Academy of Child and Adolescent Psychiatry, 20*, 636–644.

KUTCHER, S. P., Marton, P., & Korenblum, M. (1989). Relationship between psychiatric illness and conduct disorder in adolescents. *Canadian Journal of Psychiatry, 34*, 526–529.

LAMBERT, M. J., Shapiro, D. A., & Bergin, A. E. (1986). The effectiveness of psychotherapy. In S. L. Garfield & A. E. Bergin (Eds.), *Handbook of psychotherapy and behavior change* (pp. 157–216). New York: Wiley.

LEAHY, R. L. (1988). Cognitive therapy of childhood depression: Developmental considerations. In S. R. Shirk (Ed.), *Cognitive development and child psychotherapy* (pp. 187–204). New York: Plenum.

LERNER, M. S., & Clum, G. A. (1990). Treatment of suicide ideators: A problem-solving approach. *Behavior Therapy, 21*, 403–411.

LEVITT, E. E. (1957). The results of psychotherapy with children: An evaluation. *Journal of Consulting Psychology, 21*, 186–189.

LEVITT, E. E. (1963). Psychotherapy with children: A further evaluation. *Behavior Therapy and Research, 60*, 326–329.

LEVITT, E. E. (Ed.). (1971). *Research on psychotherapy with children.* New York: Wiley.

LEWINSOHN, P. M., Antonuccio, D. O., Steinmetz, J. L., & Teri, L. (1984). *The coping with depression course: A psychoeducational intervention for unipolar depression.* Eugene, OR: Castalia Press.

LEWINSOHN, P. M., Biglan, A., & Zeiss, T. (1976). Behavior treatment of depression. In P. O. Davidson (Ed.), *The behavioral management of anxiety, depression, and pain* (pp. 91–146). New York: Brunner/Mazel.

LEWINSOHN, P. M., Clarke, G. N., Hops, H., & Andrews, J. (1990). Cognitive-behavioral treatment for depressed adolescents. *Behavior Therapy, 21*, 385–401.

LEWINSOHN, P. M., Clarke, G. N., & Rohde, P. (1994). Psychological approaches with adolescents. In W. M. Reynolds & H. F. Johnston (Eds.), *Handbook of depression in children and adolescents.* New York: Plenum.

LEWINSOHN, P. M., Hoberman, H. M., Teri, L., & Hautzinger, M. (1985). An integrative theory of unipolar depression. In S. Reiss & R. R. Bootzin (Eds.), *Theoretical issues in behavioral therapy* (pp. 313–359). New York: Academic Press.

LEWINSOHN, P. M., Hops, H., Roberts, R. E., Seeley, J. R., & Andrews, J. (1993). Adolescent psychopathology: I. Prevalence and incidence of depression and other DSM-III-R disorders in high school students. *Journal of Abnormal Psychology, 102*, 133–144.

LEWINSOHN, P. M., Roberts, R. E., Seeley, J. R., Rohde, P., Gotlib, I. H., & Hops, H. (1993) Adolescent depression: II. Psychosocial risk factors. *Journal of Abnormal Psychology, 2*, 302–315.

LEWINSOHN, P. M., Rohde, P., Hops, H., & Clarke, G. N. (1991). *Instructor's manual for course for parents of adolescents enrolled in the adolescent coping with depression course.* Eugene, OR: Castalia Press.

LEWINSOHN, P. M., Rohde, P., Seeley, J. R., & Hops, H. (1991). Cormorbidity of unipolar depression: I. Major depression with dysthymia. *Journal of Abnormal Psychology, 100*, 205–213.

LEWINSOHN, P. M., Sullivan, J. M., & Grosscup, S. J. (1980). Changing reinforcing events: An approach to the treatment of depression. *Psychotherapy: Theory, Research, and Practice, 17*, 322–334.

LIDDLE, B., & Spence, S. H. (1990). Cognitive-behavior therapy with depressed primary school children: A cautionary note. *Behavioral Psychotherapy, 18*, 85–102.

LINEHAN, M. M. (1987). Dialectical behavior therapy: A cognitive behavioral approach to parasuicide. *Journal of Personality Disorders, 1*, 328–333.

LINEHAN, M. M., Armstrong, H. E., Suarez, A., Allmon, D., & Heard, H. L. (1991). Cognitive-behavioral treatment of chronically parasuicidal borderline patients. *Archives of General Psychiatry, 48*, 1060–1064.

MacPHILLAMY, D. J., & Lewinsohn, P. M. (1982). The pleasant events schedule: Studies on reliability, validity, and scale intercorrelation. *Journal of Consulting and Clinical Psychology, 50*, 363–380.

MAGNUSSON, D., Stattin, H., & Allen, V. (1986). Differential maturation among girls and its relation to social adjustment in a longitudinal perspective. In P. Baltes, D. Featherman, & R. Lerner (Eds.), *Life span development and behavior.* Hillsdale, NJ: Erlbaum.

MARANS, S. (1989). Psychoanalytic psychotherapy with children: Current research trends and challenges. *Journal of the American Academy of Child Psychiatry, 28*, 669–674.

MARKS, A., Malizio, J., Hoch, J., Brody, R., & Fisher, M. (1983). Assessment of health needs and willingness to utilize health care resources of adolescents in a suburban population. *Journal of Pediatrics, 102*, 456–460.

MASER, J. D., & Cloninger, C. R. (Ed.). (1990). *Comorbidity in anxiety and mood disorders.* Washington, DC: American Psychiatric Press.

MASH, E. J. (1990). Treatment of child and family disturbance: A behavioral-systems perspective. In E. J. Mash

& R. A. Barkley (Eds.), *Treatment of childhood disorders* (pp. 3–36). New York: Guilford Press.

McCAULEY, E., Mitchell, J., Burke, P., & Moss, S. (1988). Cognitive attributes of depression in children and adolescents. *Journal of Clinical and Consulting Psychology, 56*, 903–908.

McCULLOUGH, J. P. (1984). Cognitive-behavioral analysis system of psychotherapy: An interactional treatment approach for dysthymic disorder. *Psychiatry, 47*, 234–250.

McLEAN, P. D. (1981). Matching treatment to patient characteristics in an outpatient setting. In L. P. Rehm (Ed.), *Behavior therapy for depression: Present status and future directions* (pp. 197–207). New York: Academic Press.

McLEAN, P. D., & Carr, S. (1989). The psychological treatment of unipolar depression: Progress and limitations. *Canadian Journal of Behavioural Science, 21*, 452–469.

McLEAN, P., & Hakstian, R. (1979). Clinical depression: Comparative efficacy of outpatient treatments. *Journal of Clinical and Consulting Psychology, 47*, 818–836.

MOREAU, D., Mufson, L., Weissman, M. M., & Klerman, G. L. (1991). Interpersonal psychotherapy for adolescent depression: Description of modification and preliminary application. *Journal of the American Academy of Child and Adolescent Psychiatry, 30*(4), 642–651.

MORRIS, J. B., & Beck, A. T. (1974). The efficacy of anti-depressant drugs. *Archives of General Psychiatry, 30*, 667–674.

MUFSON, L., Moreau, D., Weissman, M., & Klerman, G. (1992). *Preliminary findings on the use of interpersonal psychotherapy with depressed adolescents.* Paper presented at the annual meeting of the American Academy of Child and Adolescent Psychiatry, Washington, DC.

NIETZEL, M. T., Russell, R. L., Hemmings, K. A., & Gretter, M. L. (1987). Clinical significance of psychotherapy for unipolar depression: A meta-analytic approach to social comparison. *Journal of Consulting and Clinical Psychology, 55*, 156–161.

NOLEN-HOEKSEMA, S., Girgus, J. S., & Seligman, M. E. P. (1986). Learned helplessness in children: A longitudinal study of depression, achievement, and explanatory style. *Journal of Personality and Social Psychology, 51*, 435–442.

NOLEN-HOEKSEMA, S., Girgus, J. S., & Seligman, M. E. P. (1992). Predictors and consequences of childhood depressive symptoms: A 5-year longitudinal study. *Journal of Abnormal Psychology, 101*, 405–422.

OFFER, D., Howard, K. I., Schonert, K. A., & Ostrov, E. (1991). To whom do adolescents turn for help? Differences between disturbed and nondisturbed adolescents. *Journal of the American Academy of Child and Adolescent Psychiatry, 4*, 623–630.

OFFICE of Technology Assessment. (1991). *Adolescent health III: Cross cutting issues under the delivery of health and related services.* Washington, DC: Author.

OFFORD, D. R., Boyle, M. H., Szatmari, P., et al. (1987). Ontario child health study: II. Six-month prevalence of disorder and rates of service utilization. *Archives of General Psychiatry, 44*, 832–836.

ORVASCHEL, H., & Puig-Antich, J. (1986). *Schedule for affective disorder and schizophrenia for school-age children. Epidemiologic version: Kiddie-SADS-E (K-SADS-E) (4th version).* Pittsburgh, PA: Western Psychiatric Institute and Clinic.

OVERHOLSER, J. C., & Spirito, A. (1990). Cognitive-behavioral treatment of suicidal depression. In E. L. Feindler & G. R. Kalfus (Eds.), *Adolescent behavior therapy handbook* (pp. 211–231). New York: Springer.

PETERSEN, A. C., & Hamburg, B. A. (1986). Adolescence: A developmental approach to problems and psychopathology. *Behavior Therapy, 17*, 480–499.

PETTI, T. A. (1978). Depression in hospitalized child psychiatry patients: Approaches to measuring depression. *Journal of the American Academy of Child Psychiatry, 17*, 49–59.

PETTI, T. A. (1983). Imipramine in the treatment of depressed children. In D. P. Cantwell & G. A. Carlson (Eds.), *Affective disorders in childhood and adolescence—An update* (pp. 375–415). New York: Spectrum.

PETTI, T. A. (1985). Active treatment of childhood depression. In J. F. Clarkin & H. I. Glazer (Eds.), *Depression: Behavioral and directive intervention strategies* (pp. 311–343). New York: Garland.

PETTI, T. A., Bornstein, M., Delamater, A., & Conners, C. K. (1980). Evaluation and multimodality treatment of a depressed prepubertal girl. *Journal of the American Academy of Child Psychiatry, 19*, 690–702.

POPPER, C. (1992). Are clinicians ahead of researchers in finding a treatment for adolescent depression? *Journal of Child and Adolescent Psychopharmacology, 2*, 1–3.

PRINCE, D., & Dowrick, P. W. (1984). *Self modeling in the treatment of depression: Implications for video in behavior therapy.* Paper presented at the annual conference of the Association for Advancement of Behavior Therapy, Philadelphia.

PUIG-ANTICH, J. (1982). Major depression and conduct disorder in prepuberty. *Journal of the American Academy of Child Psychiatry, 21*, 118–128.

PUIG-ANTICH, J., Dahl, R., Ryan, N., et al. (1989). Cortisol secretion in prepubertal children with major depressive disorder. *Archives of General Psychiatry, 46*, 801–809.

PUIG-ANTICH, J., Kaufman, J., Ryan, N. D., Williamson, D. E., Dahl, R. E., Lukens, E., Todak, G., Ambrosini, P., Rabinovich, H., & Nelson, B. (1993). The psychosocial functioning and family environment of depressed adolescents. *Journal of the American Academy of Child and Adolescent Psychiatry, 32*, 244–253.

PUIG-ANTICH, J., Lukens, E., Davies, M., Goetz, D., Brennan-Quattrock, J., & Todak, G. (1985a). Psychosocial functioning in prepubertal major depressive disorders: I. Interpersonal relationships during the depressive episode. *Archives of General Psychiatry, 42*, 500–507.

PUIG-ANTICH, J., Lukens, E., Davies, M., Goetz, D., Brennan-Quattrock, J., & Todak, G. (1985b). Psychosocial functioning in prepubertal major depressive disorders: II. Interpersonal relationships after sustained recovery from affective episode. *Archives of General Psychiatry, 42*, 511–517.

PUIG-ANTICH, J., Perel, J. M., Lupatkin, W., Chambers, W. J., Tabrizi, M. A., Ping, J., Goetz, R., Davies, M., & Stiller, R. L. (1987). Imipramine in prepubertal major depressive disorders. *Archives of General Psychiatry, 44*, 81–89.

RADLOFF, L. S. (1977). A CES-D scale: A self-report depression scale for research in the general population. *Applied Psychological Measurement, 1*, 385–401.

REHM, L. P. (1977). A self-control model of depression. *Behavior Therapy, 8*, 787–804.

REYNOLDS, W. M. (1986). *Assessment of depression in adolescents: Manual for the Reynolds adolescent depression scale*. Odessa, FL: Psychological Assessment Resources.

REYNOLDS, W. M., & Coats, K. I. (1986). A comparison of cognitive-behavioral therapy and relaxation training for the treatment of depression in adolescents. *Journal of Consulting and Clinical Psychology, 54*(5), 653–660.

RICKS, D. F. (1974). Supershrink: Methods of a therapist judged successful on the basis of adult outcomes of adolescent patients. In D. F. Ricks, A. Thomas, & M. Roff (Eds.), *Life history research in psychopathology* (pp. 275–297). Minneapolis: University of Minnesota Press.

RIGGS, S., & Cheng, T. (1988). Adolescents' willingness to use a school-based clinic in view of expressed health concerns. *Journal of Adolescent Health Care, 9*, 208–213.

ROBBINS, D., Alessi, N., & Colfer, M. (1989). Treatment of adolescents with major depression: Implications of the DST and the melancholic subtype. *Journal of Affective Disorders, 17*, 99–104.

ROBERTS, R. E. (1987). Epidemiological issues in measuring preventive effects. In R. F. Munoz (Ed.), *Depression prevention: Research directions* (pp. 45–69). New York: Hemisphere.

ROBIN, A. L. (1979). Problem-solving communication training: A behavioral approach to the treatment of parent-adolescent conflict. *American Journal of Family Therapy, 7*, 69–82.

ROBIN, A. L., Kent, R. N., O'Leary, K. D., Foster, S., & Prinz, R. J. (1977). An approach to teaching parents and adolescents problem-solving communication skills: A preliminary report. *Behavior Therapy, 8*, 639–643.

ROBINSON, L. A., Berman, J. S., & Neimeyer, R. A. (1990). Psychotherapy for the treatment of depression: A comprehensive review of controlled outcome research. *Psychological Bulletin, 108*(1), 30–49.

ROHDE, P., Lewinsohn, P. M., & Seeley, J. R. (1991). Cormorbidity of unipolar depression: II. Cormorbidity

with other mental disorders in adolescents and adults. *Journal of Abnormal Psychology, 100*(2), 214–222.

ROHDE, P., Lewinsohn, P. M., & Seeley, J. R. (1994). Are adolescents changed by an episode of depression? *Journal of the American Academy of Child and Adolescent Psychiatry, 33*, 1289–1298.

ROSENBERG, S. E. (1985). Brief dynamic psychotherapy for depression. In E. E. Becham & W. R. Lieber (Eds.), *Handbook of depression: Treatment, assessment, and research* (pp. 100–123). Belmont, CA: Wadsworth.

ROSS, C. P., & Motto, J. A. (1984). Group counseling for suicidal adolescents. In H. S. Sudak, A. B. Ford, & N. B. Rushford (Eds.), *Suicide in the young* (pp. 369–391). Boston: John Wright PSG Inc.

ROSSMAN, P. G. (1982). Psychotherapeutic approaches with depressed, acting-out adolescents: Interpretive tactics and their rationale. In S. C. Feinstein, J. G. Looney, A. Z. Schwartzberg, & A. D. Sorosky (Eds.), *Adolescent psychiatry: Developmental and clinical studies* (pp. 455–468). Chicago: University of Chicago Press.

RUDE, S. S., & Rehm, L. P. (1991). Response to treatments for depression: The role of initial status on targeted cognitive and behavioral skills. *Clinical Psychology Review, 11*, 493–514.

RUTTER, M. (1983). Psychological therapies: Issues and prospects. In S. B. Guze, F. J. Earls, & J. E. Barrett (Eds.), *Childhood psychopathology and development* (pp. 139–164). New York: Raven Press.

RYAN, N. D., & Perel, J. (1989). *A controlled study of amitriptyline versus placebo in adolescent MDD*. Paper presented at 36th annual meeting of the American Academy of Child and Adolescent Psychiatry, New York.

RYAN, N. D., Puig-Antich, J., Ambrosini, P., Rabinovich, H., Robinson, D., Nelson, B., Iyengar, S., & Twomey, J. (1987). The clinical picture of major depression in children and adolescents. *Archives of General Psychiatry, 44*, 854–861.

RYAN, N. D., Williamson, D. E., Iyengar, S., Orvaschel, H., Reich, T., Dahl, R. E., & Puig-Antich, J. (1992). A secular increase in child and adolescent onset affective disorder. *Journal of the American Academy of Child and Adolescent Psychiatry, 31*(4), 600–605.

SAFRAN, J. D., & Segal, Z. V. (1990). *Interpersonal process in cognitive therapy*. New York: Basic Books.

SANCHEZ-LACAY, A., Trautman, P. D., & Lewin, N. (1991). *Expressed emotion and cognitive family therapy of suicide attempters*. Paper presented at the annual meeting of the American Academy of Child and Adolescent Psychiatry, San Francisco, CA.

SEIFFGE-KRENKE, I. (1989). Problem intensity and the disposition of adolescents to take therapeutic advice. In M. Brambrin, F. Losel, & H. Skowronek (Eds.), *Children at risk: Assessment, longitudinal research and intervention* (pp. 457–477). New York: Walter de Gruyter.

SHIRK, S. R., & Russell, R. L. (1992). A reevaluation of estimates of child therapy effectiveness. *Journal of the*

American Academy of Child and Adolescent Psychiatry, 31(4), 703–710.

SILVER, L. (Ed.). (1988). The scope of the problem in children and adolescents. In J. G. Looney (Ed.), *Chronic mental illness in children and adolescents* (pp. 39–51). Washington, DC: American Psychiatric Press.

SIMEON, J., Dinicola, V., Phil, M., Ferguson, H., & Copping, W. (1990). Adolescent depression: A placebo-controlled fluoxetine treatment study and follow-up. *Progress in Neuro-Psychopharmacology and Biological Psychiatry*, 791–795.

SIMMONS, R., Burgeson, R., Carlton-Ford, S., & Blyth, D. (1987). The impact of cumulative change in early adolescence. *Child Development, 58*, 1220–1234.

SMITH, M. L., Glass, G. V., & Miller, T. I. (1980). *Benefits of psychotherapy*. Baltimore, MD: Johns Hopkins University Press.

STARK, K., Best, L., & Sellstrom, E. (1989). A cognitive-behavioral approach to the treatment of childhood depression. In J. N. Hughes & R. J. Hall (Eds.), *Cognitive-behavioral psychology in the schools: A comprehensive handbook* (pp. 389–433). New York: Guilford Press.

STARK, K., & Brookman, C. S. (1992). Childhood depression: Theory and family-school intervention. In M. J. Fine & C. Carlson (Eds.), *The handbook of family-school intervention: A systems perspective* (pp. 247–271). Boston: Allyn & Bacon.

STARK, K. D., Reynolds, W. M., & Kaslow, N. J. (1987). A comparison of the relative efficacy of self-control therapy and a behavioral problem-solving therapy for depression in children. *Journal of Abnormal Child Psychology, 15*(1), 91–113.

STARK, K. D., Rouse, L. W., & Livingston, R. (1991). Treatment of depression during childhood and adolescence: Cognitive-behavioral procedures for the individual and family. In P. C. Kendall (Ed.), *Child and adolescent therapy: Cognitive-behavioral procedures* (pp. 165–206). New York: Guilford Press.

STEINBERG, L. (1989). *Adolescence*. New York: Knopf.

STEINBRUECK, S. M., Maxwell, S. C., & Howard, G. S. (1983). A meta-analysis of psychotherapy and drug therapy in the treatment of unipolar depression with adults. *Journal of Consulting and Clinical Psychology, 51*(6), 856–863.

STIFFMAN, A., Earls, F., Robins, L., & Jung, K. (1988). Problems and help-seeking in high-risk adolescent patients of health clinics. *Journal of Adolescent Health Care, 9*, 305–309.

STRUPP, H. H., Sandell, J. A., Waterhouse, G. J., O'Malley, S. S., & Anderson, J. L. (1982). Psychodynamic therapy: Theory and research. In A. J. Rush (Ed.), *Short-term psychotherapies for depression* (pp. 215–250). New York: Guilford Press.

TILLITSKI, C. J. (1990). A meta-analysis of estimated effect sizes for group versus individual versus control treatments. *International Journal of Group Psychotherapy, 40*(2), 215–224.

TOOLAN, J. (1978). Therapy of depressed and suicidal children. *American Journal of Psychotherapy, 32*, 243–251.

TRAMONTANA, M. (1980). Critical review of research on psychotherapy outcome with adolescents: 1967–1977. *Psychological Bulletin, 88*, 429–450.

TRAUTMAN, P., & Rotheram-Borus, M. (1988). Cognitive-behavioral therapy with children and adolescents. In A. Frances & R. Hales (Eds.), *Annual review of psychiatry, 7* (pp. 584–607). Washington, DC: American Psychiatric Press.

TUMA, J. M., & Sobotka, K. R. (1993). Traditional therapies with children. In T. Ollendick & M. Hersen (Eds.), *Handbook of child psychopathology* (pp. 391–426). New York: Plenum.

WEINBERG, W. A., Rutman, J., Sullivan, L., Pencik, E. C., & Dietz, S. G. (1973). Depression in children referred to an education diagnostic center. *Journal of Pediatrics, 83*, 1065–1072.

WEISSMAN, M. W., Myers, J. K., Thompson, W. C., & Belanger, A. (1986). Depressive symptoms as a risk factor for major depression. In L. Erlenmeyer-Kimling & N. E. Miller (Eds.), *Life-span research on the prediction of psychopathology* (pp. 251–260). Hillsdale, NJ: Erlbaum.

WEISZ, J., Weiss, B., & Donenberg, G. (1992). The lab versus the clinic: Effects of child and adolescent psychotherapy. *American Psychologist, 47*(12), 1578–1585.

WEISZ, J. R., & Weiss, B. (1989). Assessing the effects of clinic-based psychotherapy with children and adolescents. *Journal of Consulting and Clinical Psychology, 57*(6), 741–746.

WEISZ, J. R., Weiss, B., Alicke, M. D., & Klotz, M. L. (1987). Effectiveness of psychotherapy with children and adolescents: A meta-analysis for clinicians. *Journal of Consulting and Clinical Psychology, 55*, 542–549.

WESTEN, D. (1991). Cognitive-behavioral interventions in the psychoanalytic psychotherapy of borderline personality disorders. *Clinical Psychology Review, 11*, 211–230.

WHITAKER, A., Johnson, J., Shaffer, D., Rappoport, J., Kalikow, K., Walsh, B., Davies, M., Braiman, S., & Dolinsky, A. (1990). Uncommon troubles in young people: Prevalence estimates of selected psychiatric disorders in a nonreferred adolescent population. *Archives of General Psychiatry, 47*, 487–496.

WHYBROW, P. C., Akiskal, H. S., & McKinney, W. T. (Eds.). (1984). *Mood disorders: Toward a new psychobiology*. New York: Plenum.

WILKES, T., & Belsher, G. (1992). *Adapting cognitive therapy for depressed adolescents*. Paper presented at the annual meeting of the American Academy of Child and Adolescent Psychiatry, Washington, DC.

WILKES, T. C. R., & Rush, J. A. (1988). Adaptations of cognitive therapy for depressed adolescents. *Journal of the American Academy of Child and Adolescent Psychiatry, 27*, 381–386.

WINNETT, R. L., Bornstein, P. H., Cogswell, K. A., & Paris, A. E. (1987). Cognitive-behavioral therapy for childhood depression: A levels-of-treatment approach. *Journal of Child and Adolescent Psychotherapy, 4,* 283–286.

WITHERS, L. D., & Kaplan, D. W. (1987). Adolescents who attempt suicide: A retrospective clinical chart review of hospitalized patients. *Professional Psychology: Research and Practice, 18,* 341–393.

ZEISS, A., Lewinsohn, P., & Munoz, R. (1979). Nonspecific improvement effects in depression using interpersonal skills training, pleasant activity schedules, or cognitive training. *Journal of Clinical and Consulting Psychology, 47,* 427–439.

CHAPTER 3

Social Phobia: Diagnostic Issues and Review of Cognitive Behavioral Treatment Strategies

Harlan R. Juster
Richard G. Heimberg
Craig S. Holt

I. Introduction
II. Diagnostic Issues
    A. Diagnostic Criteria for Social Phobia
    B. Empirical Support for Subtypes of Social Phobia
    C. Generalized Social Phobia and Avoidant
       Personality Disorder
    D. Situationist Perspective
    E. DSM-IV
III. Treatment Review
    A. Social Skills Training
    B. Exposure
    C. Cognitive Interventions
IV. Conclusions and Recommendations
    References

I. Introduction

Anxiety experienced in social interaction or in anticipation of public performance is common. The vast majority of people describe themselves as either currently shy or as having once been shy (Zimbardo, 1977; Zimbardo, Pilkonis, & Norwood, 1975). Virtually everyone reading this chapter has experienced physiological symptoms of anxiety, self-doubt, or concern with being evaluated in connection with an important presentation. While these examples may be representative of commonly experienced social anxiety, they may also be symptoms of social phobia, an anxiety disorder marked by fear (and sometimes avoidance) of situations in which the phobic individual might act in embarrassing ways while in the presence of others. Because nonclinical levels of social anxiety are so common, however, the impact of the social phobic's anxiety experience is often minimized by others. In our experience at the Center for Stress and Anxiety Disorders, social phobic clients have been routinely told by friends and family that they are just shy and not to worry, or in the case of public speaking, that everyone gets anxious in those types of situations. While social and evaluative anxiety may be common, the social phobic individual's experience of anxiety is more severe and personally distressing. It remains unclear whether social phobics experience higher levels of anxiety (quantitative difference) or are hypersensitive to normal levels of anxiety (qualitative difference) or whether both conditions may exist in different individuals. Regardless, the result is often a cyclical pattern of anxiety, avoidance, marked distress, and impaired functioning.

While Schneier, Spitzer, Gibbon, Fyer, and Liebowitz (1991) have cited references to social phobia in the literature as early as 1903 (Janet, 1903), it is generally accepted that Marks and Gelder (1966) first

described social phobia as a disorder distinct from others. However, social phobia received scant attention in the research literature before it was included in the third edition of the *Diagnostic and Statistical Manual of Mental Disorders* (DSM-III) (American Psychiatric Association, 1980). Since the late 1970s, interest in developing effective treatments for social phobia has increased.

The purpose of this chapter is to review the research on the behavioral and cognitive behavioral treatment of social phobia. We will update previous reviews (for example, Heimberg, 1989; Heimberg & Barlow, 1991), paying particular attention to the theoretical, applied, and research issues important to our understanding of social phobia and our approaches to its treatment. In the first section, a range of diagnostic issues will be briefly considered. While these may not bear directly on treatment outcome, it is important for the reader to be aware of these issues and how they may shape the samples from which our research is derived. Past and current conceptualizations of social phobia and considerations for future changes in the diagnostic criteria will be discussed. The review of treatment studies follows and is divided into three main sections, addressing studies of social skills training, exposure-based methods, and cognitive interventions including integrated cognitive behavioral treatments. The inclusion of a specific study in a particular section is somewhat arbitrary, since multiple treatments are often incorporated into a single study and others have an empirical base too limited for separate consideration. Finally, conclusions are presented with suggestions for future research.

II. Diagnostic Issues

The diagnosis of social phobia has undergone considerable change and refinement since its introduction in DSM-III. Changes in the diagnostic criteria in DSM-III-R (American Psychiatric Association, 1987) reflect greater understanding of the diversity of situations that may elicit anxiety among social phobic clients and increasing acknowledgment that social phobic clients may be more impaired than was originally believed. The hierarchical relationship of social

Preparation of this chapter was facilitated by Grant R01MH4419 from the National Institute of Mental Health to Richard G. Heimberg.

Correspondence concerning this article should be addressed to Richard G. Heimberg, Center for Stress and Anxiety Disorders, University at Albany, State University of New York, Pine West Plaza, Building 4, Washington Avenue Extension, Albany, New York, 12205.

phobia and avoidant personality disorder has also evolved, although it is less clear that this is consistent with empirical findings. These changes, and the efforts in progress for DSM-IV, will be discussed briefly to provide a conceptual framework from which to better understand social phobia, its treatment, and the differences in participant sampling procedures among studies included in this treatment review.

A. Diagnostic Criteria for Social Phobia

The essential feature of social phobia in DSM-III was "a persistent, irrational fear of, and compelling desire to avoid, a situation in which the individual is exposed to possible scrutiny by others and fears that he or she may act in a way that will be humiliating or embarrassing" (American Psychiatric Association, 1980, p. 228). It was further noted that social phobics usually feared only one of several possible circumscribed situations, such as public speaking, writing in the presence of others, or eating in public. Despite the criterion of significant distress noted in DSM-III, social phobia, in this circumscribed form, was rarely viewed as incapacitating. However, several studies have since reported that clients meeting DSM-III criteria for social phobia experience significant degrees of functional impairment, typically in more than a single domain. For example, Turner, Beidel, Dancu, and Keys (1986) demonstrated that social phobics meeting DSM-III criteria report fear in multiple situations. Impairment due to the effects of social phobia may limit educational attainment, career advancement, and social functioning (Amies, Gelder, & Shaw, 1983; Liebowitz, Gorman, Fyer, & Klein, 1985; Turner et al., 1986). DSM-III social phobia may be frequently associated with alcohol abuse (Amies et al., 1983), tranquilizer abuse (Sanderson, DiNardo, Rapee, & Barlow, 1990), dysthymia (Sanderson et al., 1990), depression (Heimberg et al., 1989), and suicide attempts (Amies et al., 1983; Schneier, Johnson, Hornig, Liebowitz, & Weissman, 1992).

DSM-III criteria for social phobia described clients who feared specific situations involving performing a task in the presence of others. The diagnosis of avoidant personality disorder (APD) was to be considered for the client who feared multiple social situations. While the essential feature of the diagnosis of social phobia remained substantively unchanged in DSM-III-R, changes in other diagnostic criteria were implemented in recognition that social phobics' fears may occur in a wider array of social situations than was previously considered and that impairment caused by the disorder may be extensive. A *generalized subtype* was added if the person reported fear in most social situations, although no operational definition of the number of situations that must be feared to meet the criteria of "most" social situations was provided. Social phobics not meeting criteria for the generalized subtype were grouped together by exclusion with no implication that they necessarily represent a homogeneous subtype group. We now turn our attention to the empirical studies of subtyping. However, the reader should also bear in mind that changes in the diagnostic criteria for social phobia also brought it into direct competition with APD. Changes in the diagnostic criteria for APD, the exclusionary rules, and overlap between APD and social phobia will be discussed in a later section.

B. Empirical Support for Subtypes of Social Phobia

Several studies support the differentiation of social phobia into subtypes, which may have implications for treatment (extensively reviewed by Heimberg et al., 1993). Heimberg, Hope, Dodge, and Becker (1990) compared generalized social phobics (GSPs) with social phobics fearing only public speaking situations. Compared to public speaking phobics, GSPs were younger at the time of presentation, less educated, and less likely to be employed. GSPs reported greater fear of the phobic situation and more avoidance, general anxiety, and depression than public speaking phobics and were rated by observers as more anxious and exhibiting poorer performance during an individualized behavior test. Despite the greater impairment of GSPs, public speaking phobics exhibited greater cardiac reactivity during the behavior test. Levin et al. (1993) reported a similar study comparing generalized and circumscribed social phobics and normal controls, essentially replicating the results of Heimberg, Hope, et al. (1990) but using a standardized situation (public speaking task) for the behavior test.

Although these results support subtyping at the diagnostic extremes of severity and impairment, little information is provided about the potentially large number of social phobics who do not meet criteria for the generalized subtype but who appear to fear more than circumscribed, performance-based situations. In a report to the subworkgroup on social phobia for DSM-IV, Heimberg and Holt (1989) suggested the addition of a third classification (labeled "nongeneralized") to describe the subgroup of social phobics who may or may not have circumscribed fears but experience significant social interactional anxiety in one or more domains while coping without significant anxiety in at least one other major class of these situations, thus not appearing to meet the criterion of fear in most social situations. An example is the individual who experiences much anxiety in heterosocial situations while functioning virtually anxiety-free while interacting with same-sex friends or while at work. Thus, this system categorizes social phobics into one of three groups—circumscribed, nongeneralized, or generalized.

There is some evidence in support of the distinction between generalized and nongeneralized subtypes. Herbert, Hope, and Bellack (1992) found that GSPs had more comorbid Axis I and Axis II diagnoses and were rated as more impaired by structured interviewers than nongeneralized social phobics. They also displayed poorer social skills and reported higher levels of anxiety during a behavior test. Holt, Heimberg, and Hope (1992) similarly compared generalized and nongeneralized social phobics. GSPs were more impaired, fearful, and avoidant than nongeneralized social phobics when assessed by an independent rater and on self-report measures of social anxiety and depression.

Heimberg, Mueller, Holt, Hope, and Liebowitz (1992) compared responses of social phobics on two instruments designed to measure different social concerns hypothesized to be differentially endorsed by generalized and nongeneralized social phobics. The Social Interaction Anxiety Scale (SIAS) (Mattick & Clarke, 1989) was constructed to assess reactions to a variety of social interaction situations while the Social Phobia Scale (SPS) (Mattick & Clarke, 1989) was specifically designed to assess social phobics' reac-

tions to being observed. As predicted, generalized social phobia was associated with more extreme scores on the SIAS than nongeneralized social phobia, while the two groups did not differ on the SPS. Finally, Bruch and Heimberg (1992) reported that GSPs, compared with nongeneralized social phobics, were more likely to describe their mothers as shy or social phobic and their families as more overprotective and less likely to engage in social activities with other families.

Evidence has been presented that differentiates generalized from circumscribed social phobics or nongeneralized social phobics using demographic, socio-familial, and other clinically relevant measures of social anxiety and general psychopathology. No data are currently available examining the differentiation of nongeneralized and circumscribed social phobics.

Since the evidence suggests that social phobics of different subtypes are unlike each other in clinically significant ways, it might be expected that they would respond differently to treatment. For example, it may be that GSPs with their greater severity, broader range of feared situations, and fewer available coping resources, may be more difficult to treat than circumscribed social phobics or require interventions capable of targeting the wider spectrum of feared situations while addressing ancillary problems like general anxiety and depression. However, controlled outcome research examining differential response to treatment by subtypes is virtually nonexistent. One study currently in progress will examine differential response of social phobic subtypes to cognitive behavioral group therapy and pharmacotherapy with the monoamine oxidase inhibitor phenelzine, but data on subtype response are not yet available (Heimberg & Liebowitz, 1992). Some nonexperimental studies address the question of subtype and outcome. Heimberg (1986) used regression analysis and found subtype (generalized versus public speaking phobic) to account for the largest proportion of variance in outcome using preliminary data from the treatment trial by Heimberg, Dodge, Hope, Kennedy, Zollo, and Becker (1990). However, in a subsequent analysis with a larger sample, Holt, Heimberg, and Hope (1990) found that once initial severity was controlled, subtype no longer predicted treatment outcome, suggesting that subtype exists along a continuum of severity.

There are some data, reviewed by Schneier, Levin, and Liebowitz (1990) and Levin, Schneier, and Liebowitz (1989), on the response of social phobics to pharmacological treatment. The data on differential response to treatment by subtype are, again, scanty, but some investigators have hypothesized differential response to treatment with beta-blockers versus monoamine oxidase inhibitors (MAOIs). Liebowitz et al. (1985) suggested that circumscribed social phobics are similar to normal participants with performance anxiety and might show a similar positive response to treatment with beta-blockers. They also noted that GSPs share the symptom of rejection sensitivity with atypical depressives, a group known to be responsive to the MAOI phenelzine (Liebowitz, Quitkin, et al., 1988; Liebowitz et al., 1984) and suggested that GSPs might be preferentially responsive to phenelzine. Liebowitz, Gorman, and colleagues (1988) and Liebowitz, Schneier, and colleagues (1992) tested these hypotheses and found that after eight weeks of treatment GSPs treated with phenelzine were more likely to be classified as improved than GSPs treated with the beta-blocker atenolol or a placebo. After 16 weeks of treatment, phenelzine was still more effective among GSPs than the beta-blocker, but this difference was no longer statistically significant. A scarcity of circumscribed participants precluded analysis of treatment effectiveness within this subtype group.

C. Generalized Social Phobia and Avoidant Personality Disorder

Further complicating the diagnostic picture of social phobia are changes in criteria for APD and in the hierarchical exclusionary rules for social phobia and APD from DSM-III to DSM-III-R. In DSM-III, APD was characterized by rejection sensitivity, unwillingness to enter relationships without guarantees of acceptance, social withdrawal, and low self-esteem. A diagnosis of social phobia was indicative of more circumscribed fears, while a diagnosis of APD meant greater fear and avoidance of social interaction and greater impairment than was expected with social phobics. Although empirical justification was lacking, a diagnosis of APD precluded a diagnosis of social phobia. This diagnostic strategy appeared to have validity in describing the extremes of social anxiety, although it did so by crossing the boundary between Axis I (clinical syndromes) and Axis II (personality disorders).

In DSM-III-R, the diagnostic criteria for APD were changed, and the exclusionary rules were dropped. APD was defined as "a pervasive pattern of social discomfort, fear of negative evaluation, and timidity . . . present in a variety of contexts" (American Psychiatric Association, 1987, p. 352). Four of seven diagnostic criteria must be met to receive a diagnosis of APD compared to five of five criteria in DSM-III. At the same time that APD criteria were modified, the generalized subtype was added to the diagnosis of social phobia, and the exclusionary rules between the two diagnoses were abandoned. APD and generalized social phobia could now be comorbid diagnoses with a high likelihood of redundancy and ambiguity.

This ambiguity is clearly apparent when examining the criteria for APD. Three of the criteria appear to conceptually overlap almost completely with the diagnostic criteria for (generalized) social phobia, including avoiding interpersonal contact, reticence in social situations, and fears that anxiety symptoms will be visible to others. Three other criteria that appear to overlap with social phobia include being easily hurt by criticism, having no close friends (or just one), and the need for certainty of being liked to become socially involved. The only criterion conceptually different from the criteria for social phobia involves the exaggeration of potential difficulties in activities beyond an individual's usual routine.

Four studies have addressed the degree of overlap and distinctiveness of APD and GSP (Herbert et al., 1992; Holt, Heimberg, & Hope, 1992; Schneier et al., 1991; Turner, Beidel, & Townsley, 1992). Schneier et al. (1991) reported that 89% of their sample of GSPs were also diagnosed with APD, while just 21% of the circumscribed social phobics met criteria for APD. While this suggests an almost one-to-one correspondence between GSP and APD, other studies report percentages of overlap that are more moderate. Herbert et al. (1992) found 61% of their GSPs to meet criteria for APD, while for the Holt, Heimberg, and Hope (1992) study this figure was 50%. Turner et al.

(1992) reported the lowest percentage of overlap in the four studies with just 25% of their GSP sample meeting criteria for APD. Heimberg, Holt, Schneier, Spitzer, and Liebowitz (in press) suggest that variations in percentages may be due to differences in sampling procedures, subtype definition, diagnostic instruments, or methods. Despite these differences in apparent percentage of overlap between GSP and APD, all authors reached essentially a similar conclusion that GSP and GSP with comorbid APD (GSP-APD) denote similar pathology, with the combination representing the most severe manifestation of this disorder (Widiger, 1992).

Conceptual similarities between the criteria for GSP and APD, noted earlier, further suggest that GSP and APD may not be distinct diagnostic entities. However, there is some evidence reported by Holt, Heimberg, and Hope (1992) that indicates that real differences may exist. Holt, Heimberg, and Hope (1992) compared nongeneralized social phobics, GSPs, and GSP-APD participants on the frequency with which they met the seven APD criteria. Three of the criteria failed to differentiate between the groups, including being easily hurt by criticism, having no close friends (or just one), and reticence in social situations. GSP-APD participants met two criteria significantly more than either of the other groups, including unwillingness to get involved unless certain of being liked and exaggerating potential difficulties in situations outside the individual's routine. GSP-APD participants were more likely to avoid interpersonal contact than the GSPs and were more likely to fear the visibility of their anxiety symptoms than the nongeneralized social phobics. These differences alone do not suggest a qualitative distinction between the two disorders. Further examination of the frequency with which APD and non-APD participants met criteria, however, found that on three of the four items where significant differences occurred, no participants (or in one case, just one participant) met criteria in the two non-APD groups combined, suggesting that these criteria may have special significance to APD. These items included an unwillingness to get involved unless certain of being liked, avoidance of activities involving significant interpersonal contact, and exaggerating potential difficulties of doing some-

thing ordinary but outside the usual routine. On the fourth item, fears that anxiety symptoms will be observed, one nongeneralized social phobic, four GSPs, and eight GSP-APDs met this criterion. GSPs may be more realistic than GSP-APD participants in their understanding that social reassurances are rarely given and in their willingness, therefore, to proceed without such reassurances. They may also be more willing to attempt to enter social situations despite their anxiety and to attempt novel activities.

The implications of these findings are complex and beyond the scope of the present discussion. Briefly, in his commentary on three of the studies, Widiger (1992) emphasizes the similarities over the differences between GSP and GSP-APD participants. The relationship between GSP and APD is viewed as a "boundary condition" between anxiety disorders and personality disorders, one which Widiger reconciles by noting that "anxiety and personality are not mutually exclusive categories, and the need to differentiate them is to some extent a procrustean artifact of the DSM-III-R categorical nosology" (p. 342). Widiger makes two proposals. First, the GSP-APD comorbid diagnosis could be classified as both an Axis I and Axis II disorder to indicate that this may not be a clinically useful distinction in this case. A second more drastic approach consistent with a quantitative view, classification as either an anxiety disorder or a personality disorder, could be deemphasized altogether with the focus shifted toward better precision in describing the degree of social avoidance. In either case, Widiger (1992) suggests that epidemiologic research with more representative samples could shed light on the currently ambiguous relationship between GSP and APD, either by identifying clear distinctions not yet found between them or by lending further support to current findings.

D. Situationist Perspective

A relatively new approach to the study of social phobia examines the type and range of situations social phobics fear and the relationship between fears in various situations. Using items of the Liebowitz Social Anxiety Scale (LSAS) (Liebowitz, 1987), Holt, Heimberg, Hope, and Liebowitz (1992) rationally derived four situational domains (that is, groups of functionally similar situations). These domains were formal speaking/interaction, informal speaking/interaction, observation by others, and assertion. The formal speaking/interaction domain consisted of items concerned with public speaking and performing in front of a group. The informal speaking/interaction domain was composed of items involving social interaction at parties and other situations when other persons are not well known. The assertive interaction domain contains items that focus on the expression of disagreement, conflict, resisting requests, and talking to people in authority. The observation by others domain involves working, writing, eating, and drinking in the presence of others. Holt, Heimberg, Hope, and Liebowitz (1992) examined the frequency with which social phobics report significant levels of anxiety in each domain and the co-occurrence of anxiety across the four domains.

The most commonly endorsed situational domain was formal speaking/interaction, with 70.3% of the participants reporting moderate or greater anxiety in all or all but one of the situations (termed *anxiety-positive*) in that domain. Using the same criteria, 46.2% of the sample were anxiety-positive for the informal speaking/interaction domain, 30.8% for the assertive interaction domain, and 22.0% for the observation by others domain. When participants were anxiety-positive in more than a single domain, formal speaking/interaction was usually one of them (94.3%).

The conditional probability of being anxiety-positive in a second domain given the knowledge that a participant is anxiety-positive in a particular domain was also examined. When a participant was anxiety-positive for the formal speaking/interaction domain, the conditional probability that he or she was anxiety-positive in any of the other domains was not significantly different from the base rate for that domain. No additional knowledge was gained by knowing that a participant feared formal public speaking situations. In contrast, if a participant was anxiety-positive for any one of the other three domains, the probability of him or her being anxiety-positive in the formal speaking/ interaction domain was at least 85% (compared with the base rate of 70.3%). The remaining probabilities did not result in significant increases over base rate probabilities, suggesting that these domains are relatively independent of one another.

One problem in this study, addressed by Holt, Heimberg, Hope, and Liebowitz (1993), was that domains were derived rationally with no statistical corroboration of the categories. Holt and colleagues performed a cluster analysis on the LSAS items used in the previous study. Three clusters of items were identified. The center of attention cluster contained items related to public speaking and being observed by others. The social interaction cluster contained items related to party situations and interacting with unfamiliar others. The assertion cluster contained items related to interpersonal conflict and displeasure. These statistically derived clusters were essentially similar to three of the four domains described earlier.

This early work examining social phobia from a situational perspective provides information about the ubiquity of public speaking fears, co-occurrence of fears, and the degree of similarity between different situations that may be reported as phobic stimuli. Replication and extension of this effort seems warranted as it might provide important information regarding subtype boundaries formerly unavailable.

E. DSM-IV

The DSM-IV subworkgroup for social phobia considered two options for delineating subtypes. The first considered expanding the number of subtypes of social phobia to three, depending on pervasiveness of the disorder and the types of situations feared (Task Force on DSM-IV, 1991). Similar in concept to the proposal by Heimberg and Holt (1989), situations feared by social phobic clients are characterized as primarily involving social interaction or performing in front of others. A *performance subtype* is assigned to individuals who fear public performance of activities that can be engaged in comfortably if performed alone and is most similar to the original DSM-III conception of social phobia. A *limited-interactional subtype* would be assigned if the phobic stimulus is restricted to one or two socially interactive situations. The *generalized subtype* continues to be defined by the phrase "most social situations." There remains a lack of clarity regarding the number of situations required to meet this criterion, and there are insufficient data differentiating limited interactional and performance subtypes (Heimberg et al., 1993). Thus, DSM-IV retains essentially the same subtyping scheme from DSM-III-R, noting that social phobics not meeting the generalized subtype represent a heterogeneous group.

III. Treatment Review

We now turn to an examination of treatments of social phobia. Consistent with previous reviews (for example, Heimberg, 1989), the remainder of this chapter will focus on studies of treatment of clearly identifiable social phobic individuals as defined in DSM-III or DSM-III-R or of individuals who would have met these criteria had they been applied. Three major treatment categories are reviewed including social skills training, exposure-based methods, and cognitive interventions. As noted earlier, placement of studies in a particular section may be arbitrary either because multiple treatments are compared or because a particular treatment may have a limited empirical base yet be considered important enough to warrant consideration in this review.

A. Social Skills Training

Initial treatment efforts with social phobia presumed that clients' anxiety was related to deficient social skills at both verbal (for example, appropriate speech content) and nonverbal (for example, maintaining acceptable levels of eye contact and appropriate body posture) levels. Social skills training (SST) interventions were presumed to enhance proficiency in these behavioral skills, thereby alleviating the cause of the anxiety. Social skills training includes components of modeling, role playing, feedback, social reinforcement, and homework assignments (Taylor & Arnow, 1988). To date, eight studies of SST as a treatment for social phobia have been conducted.

Marzillier, Lambert, and Kellet (1976) compared SST with systematic desensitization (SD) in the treatment of twenty psychiatric outpatients and one inpatient who received a diagnosis of personality disorder or neurosis. Since this study predated the inclusion of social phobia in the DSM, no official diagnosis of social phobia could have been assigned. However, the inclusion criteria were a primary complaint of interpersonal or social difficulties, complaints of anxiety in a wide range of social situations, and deficits in social skills, suggesting that these individuals could have met current criteria for social phobia, generalized subtype (and possibly APD as well).

Participants randomly assigned to either SD or SST were individually treated for 15 weekly, 45-minute sessions and compared with participants randomly assigned to a wait-list control group. Pretreatment, posttreatment, and six-month follow-up assessments were conducted. While participants from both treatment groups improved on most measures from pretreatment to posttreatment, these within-group changes were not generally reflected in significant improvement over the wait-list control group. However, participants in the SST group did increase their range of social activities, while participants in both treatment groups increased their range of social contacts significantly more than did subjects in the wait-list group. No differences were found between the two treatment groups, suggesting little advantage for one treatment over the other. While a six-month follow-up assessment was planned, numerous drop-outs in the SD group precluded any comparison of treatments at this assessment point. The SST group maintained their increased range of social activities, although no additional gains were made during the follow-up period.

The authors concluded that SST had some beneficial effect on limited aspects of the social lives of these dysfunctional individuals, including increased social activities and social contacts. However, treatment did not result in improved social skills or reduced anxiety and had little effect on numerous other measures of clinical improvement. It is also unclear to what extent these limited changes were due to the specific treatment provided or to other nonspecific factors. These results underscore the importance of including appropriate control conditions in the design of a treatment outcome study. Wait-list participants showed improvements on several measures similar to those demonstrated by SST and SD participants. The decision of Marzillier et al. (1976) to include an untreated group greatly clarified the meaning of changes in the other conditions but did not reflect well on either SST or SD.

Trower, Yardley, Bryant, and Shaw (1978) also examined the comparative efficacy of SST and SD in the treatment of subgroups of socially anxious individuals. Two subgroups of individuals were defined by clinical judgment. The first consisted of individuals with demonstrable deficits in social skills. The second consisted of persons who possessed adequate social skills but, because of excessive levels of anxiety, were unable to apply those skills appropriately. These individuals experienced excessive anxiety in and a tendency to avoid situations in which they might be evaluated, such as meals, meetings, interviews, making complaints, and being watched while doing something. The latter group appears to match current definitions of a more circumscribed social phobia. It has been argued elsewhere that the skills deficit group might be better described by a diagnosis of APD according to criteria in DSM-III (Heimberg, 1989). By later standards (DSM-III-R), it is possible that comorbid diagnoses of social phobia and APD could be applied to this subgroup. Nevertheless, it was hypothesized that SD, with its emphasis on maintaining a low arousal state while imagining feared situations, would reduce fear for the anxious subgroup, allowing available skills to be more adequately applied. SST was expected to provide the necessary training for those whose primary problem was deficient social skills.

Participants in each group were randomly assigned to either SST or SD and received ten individual sessions of their assigned treatment. The skill deficit and anxious subgroups evidenced significant pretreatment-to-posttreatment reductions in phobic severity, social inadequacy, and general anxiety, regardless of treatment received. Skill deficit participants receiving SST, compared with those receiving SD, experienced less difficulty in social situations and a greater frequency of social activities, lending some support to a treatment-matching hypothesis. No such interaction occurred for the anxious subgroup, who appeared to benefit equally from either treatment. Gains were maintained at six-month follow-up.

Shaw (1979) utilized the data for the anxious subgroup treated by Trower et al. (1978) and treated an additional ten phobic individuals with imaginal flooding. Similar reductions in phobic severity, social inadequacy, and general anxiety occurred in all three groups with gains maintained at six-month follow-up assessment. Combining the results of these two studies, phobic participants benefited equally when treated with SST, SD, or flooding. Skill deficit participants treated with SST evidenced some advantage in social functioning not evident in participants treated with SD; however, no differences were found on clinical measures of phobic severity, depression, and general anxiety. Since the results of the various treatments tested in these two studies were so similar, and so few differential effects were found, the lack of a credible control group is problematic. Given the results of Marzillier et al. (1976), in which within-group changes were not reflected in differences between a control group and treatment groups, the lack of a wait-list control makes the results of Trower et al. (1978) and Shaw (1979) inconclusive.

Stravynski, Marks, and Yule (1982) compared SST alone with SST plus cognitive modification administered in individual and group sessions in the treatment of 22 social phobic individuals diagnosed by DSM-III criteria. Prior to treatment onset, no changes occurred during a control waiting period in which participants were repeatedly assessed. Treatment consisted of twelve 1.5-hour weekly individual or group sessions. Participants in both conditions improved significantly, reporting increases in social interaction, reduced levels of depression, and reduced irrational beliefs regarding social situations. Results for the group and individually administered treatment were very similar, although it was noted that this assignment was not made randomly. At six-month follow-up, improvement was maintained in both conditions with no apparent benefit from the addition of cognitive modification procedures. The lack of enhancement of SST by the cognitive intervention may be attributed to procedural factors in the latter treatment. These will be discussed in a later section.

In a similarly designed study, Falloon, Lloyd, and Harpin (1981) treated 16 individuals meeting DSM-III criteria for social phobia with either SST plus propranolol, a beta-blocker, or SST plus placebo in a double-blind trial. Treatments began after a four-week waiting period, which served as a within-subjects control for the treatments to follow. Two problem situations for each participant were targeted for treatment with SST, each being the focus of one-half the treatment. SST began with a six-hour marathon session in which individual participants met with one other participant and a nonprofessional "therapist" to practice the skills required for the targeted situations. For the next two weeks, the participant and the therapist practiced these skills in the natural environment. This procedure was repeated for another two-week treatment period addressing the second targeted situation.

Assessments prior to and following the pretreatment waiting period (control condition) indicated no changes on self-report measures. Pretreatment-to-posttreatment analyses revealed reductions in social anxiety and difficulty with reported problems and increases in positive self-image. While therapists and other participants observed significant reductions in anxiety during the six-hour session, no equivalent change occurred in real-life rehearsal. Gains were maintained in the 81% of participants who responded to the follow-up six months later. Drug therapy did not enhance the effects of SST at either posttest or follow-up.

Öst, Jerremalm, and Johansson (1981) attempted to match treatment to specific subtypes of individual phobic response patterns, although their methods were quite different from those utilized by Trower et al. (1978). By examining cardiac response and overt behavioral signs of anxiety during a role-played social interaction, the authors classified 32 social phobic individuals as either "behavioral reactors" or "physiological reactors." Behavioral reactors exhibited a relatively larger number of overt signs of anxiety during a conversation with a confederate. Physiological reactors showed relatively larger differences between resting heart rate and mean heart rate during the conversation. Half of the participants in each group were treated with a behaviorally focused method (SST), while the other half received a physiologically focused method (applied relaxation, AR). AR combines progressive, cue-controlled, and differential relaxation procedures. Participants learn these techniques and apply them in role-play situations in the last several sessions of treatment. The authors hypothesized that individuals treated with the method matching their particular response pattern would achieve better results than the group treated with the mismatched method.

Behavioral reactors receiving SST exhibited significantly greater improvements than behavioral reactors receiving AR on several self-report measures. Specifically, SST-treated behavioral reactors reported less social fear, less difficulty in and avoidance of previously troublesome social situations, and reduced subjective anxiety during the behavioral test. They also reported increased social activities and social contacts. Physiological reactors receiving AR participated in more social activities, made more social contacts, and evidenced fewer observed signs of anxiety during the behavioral test than SST-treated physiological reactors. This study provides some support for the treatment-matching hypothesis; however, the findings are mixed. Behavioral reactors appeared to respond in keeping with the hypothesis, but only on self-report measures. Physiological reactors showed change supporting the treatment-matching hypothesis on two self-report measures and on one behavioral measure. Most analyses resulted in no differences between the groups. It should be noted that individuals were excluded if they were high or low in both the behavioral and physiological domains, thus limiting generalizability of the findings to the specific subgroups studied. As in previous studies, there was no control condition to test for changes in responses due to time, repeated testing, or other nonspecific factors.

Mersch, Emmelkamp, Bögels, and van der Sleen (1989) used a similar strategy to extend the results of Öst et al. (1981) to behavioral reactors and cognitive reactors. Behavioral reactors were identified using the procedures of the previous study. Cognitive reactors, first studied by Jerremalm, Johansson, and Öst (1986) in a study to be reviewed later, scored lower on a measure of rational thinking. Individuals scoring high or low in both domains were excluded. Using a group therapy format, social skills training was provided to half the behavioral reactors and to half the cognitive reactors while rational-emotive therapy (RET) (Ellis, 1962) was provided to the remaining participants in both groups. All four treatment groups showed pretreatment to posttreatment reductions in social anxiety. Behavioral and cognitive reactors receiving SST, for example, reported more positive self-statements and were rated as being less anxious and more skillful on a behavior test from pretreatment to posttreatment assessment. Behavioral and cognitive reactors receiving RET rated themselves as more skillful and less anxious from pretreatment to posttreatment and from posttreatment to six-week follow-up. There were virtually no significant differences between behavioral and cognitive reactors treated either with SST or RET. In one of the rare long-term follow-up assessments of the treatment of social phobia, within-group gains were maintained 14 months later, but there was no difference in outcome as a result of treatment condition or subject-by-treatment matching (Mersch, Emmelkamp, & Lips, 1991).

Wlazlo, Schroeder-Hartwig, Hand, Kaiser, and Münchau (1990) compared a semi-structured, individually tailored SST program with individual exposure (IE) and group exposure (GE). A total of 78 participants, judged to have either a primary social skills deficit or a primary social phobia, similar to the subgrouping procedure of Trower et al. (1978), were randomly assigned to groups of six to eight in one of the three conditions. Both groups of participants receiving SST evidenced reduced social anxiety, avoidance, and interference of symptoms with daily life activities as well as reductions in global symptoms of depression and obsessional rumination. These benefits were not significantly different from gains made in either of the exposure conditions. Follow-up assessment was conducted at a mean of 2.5 years (range = 1.5–5.5 years) after treatment. Primary phobic individuals receiving GE evidenced less fear of social contacts and a greater ability to refuse unreasonable requests than the social skills deficit group receiving GE. Individuals with social skills deficits receiving SST were more depressed at follow-up assessment. While SST appeared to produce significant benefit, it was not superior to exposure on any measure. In addition, direct exposure was "strongly emphasized in all treatment rationales" (p. 190) as part of the homework component. Individuals were encouraged to self-expose, although degree of compliance with this procedure was not reported. Unfortunately, several measures were not administered to treatment groups at all assessment points, thereby preventing possible between-group comparisons. The self-report nature of all measures and the lack of a credible comparison group further reduces confidence in these findings.

Summary.   Social skills training methods have produced mixed results as treatments for social phobia. In a well-controlled study, SST produced changes similar to SD, and both treatments produced no better outcome than a wait-list control group after 15 weeks of treatment (Marzillier et al., 1976). Only mild benefits were found for increases in social activities and social contacts. In contrast, the results of several other studies suggest that SST resulted in significant improvements in various aspects of social phobia, such as reductions in reported anxiety and depression and less difficulty in social situations (Falloon et al., 1981; Stravynski et al., 1982; Trower et al., 1978). However, it must be noted that these studies lacked the control conditions and distinctiveness of treatment (Wlazlo et al., 1990) that would allow for "strong inference" (Platt, 1964), diminishing confidence in these results. Attempts to match SST and other treatments to specific subgroups of social phobic subjects have produced few strong results, possibly due to the lack of adequate methods of subtyping. The utility of SST as a treatment for social phobia remains unproven at best. A need for controlled outcome studies using credible comparison groups still exists.

In concluding this section, we wish to note that the term *social skills deficit* is often used incorrectly in the social phobia literature. There has been little demonstration that social phobics are, in fact, lacking in social skills (that is, lacking in capacity to execute a behavior), while there are ample data to show that some social phobics show performance deficits (that is, for whatever reasons, including but not limited to social skills deficits, they may not execute a behavior or execute it well). In our clinic, most social phobic persons are found to possess adequate social skills but are inhibited when it comes to applying their skills in social situations. When asked to perform social interaction or public performance as part of a behavior test or exposure exercise during treatment, they are typically capable of such behavior. This also appears to apply to their behavior outside the treatment setting as self-report and behavioral diaries indicate adequate performance is the norm (although avoidance behavior and disruption of performance by anxiety is common). Self-report is usually marked by negative bias regarding the individual's own social skills in both socially anxious persons (Clark & Arkowitz, 1975; Curran, Wallander, & Fischetti, 1980) and social phobics (Rapee & Lim, 1992).

B. Exposure

Confronting a feared stimulus has been the basis of phobia treatment since behavior therapy came to prominence in the 1950s (Barlow, 1988). While exposure continues to be a critical component of social phobia treatment packages, Butler (1985) outlined the difficulties inherent in devising exposure tasks for social phobia not typically encountered when exposure is applied to other types of phobias. First, problems arise in attempting to specify graduated and repeatable tasks, allowing social phobics to practice in incrementally more difficult situations. This is especially true in naturally occurring social situations that do not lend themselves well to imposed control. Actual social situations are also difficult to prolong so that individuals will experience decreasing anxiety or habituation that would naturally occur over time. Many social phobics continue to enter feared situations despite high levels of anxiety, a situation not common in other types of phobias. Despite their self-initiated exposure, anxiety often persists, leading Butler (1985) to conclude that social phobics may fail to become psychologically engaged in exposure treatment. Butler (1985) described individuals who report becoming disengaged from external cues while in feared situations. Others report pretending to be somewhere else or, as in the case of one individual in our lab, pretending to be someone else. In our experience, depersonalization or dissociation is commonly reported by social phobic persons. It is sometimes perceived as a "barrier" between the social phobic and others, or as a feeling that others are at a distance despite being in close proximity. Butler calls these examples of "internal avoidance," which is hypothesized to allow individuals to enter feared situations when they must (for example, an important family event) but may also limit effectiveness of exposure should these symptoms (avoidance strategies) occur during treatment. The final concern noted by Butler (1985) lies in the reported content of social phobics' thoughts, which appear to reflect overconcern with evaluation by others and a negative bias. The significance of such thoughts will be discussed in the introduction to the next section.

Butler (1985) offers suggestions for each of the concerns noted here. To manipulate the physical qualities of the exposure situation (for example, length, content), exposures are best planned within the laboratory or group treatment setting. In this controlled environment, role players can be active or passive and can alter their behavior to gradually increase difficulty level. Length of exposure can be predetermined or adjusted "on the fly" to maximize gains. An example of the latter situation might be when an exposure is extended to provide additional time to allow habituation to occur. To counter the effects of internal avoidance, Butler (1985) suggests including directives for social phobics to practice certain social skills (for example, making eye contact, initiating conversation), to be an active participant (for example, ask questions) in situations in which reticence might make the situation more difficult, and to provoke anxiety symptoms (for example, wearing a sweater when concerned about perspiring), especially during a period of improvement. While these suggestions make intuitive sense, the effectiveness of such methods in improving exposure treatments, especially reducing internal avoidance, is unknown. The degree to which these recommendations are followed in the eight studies reviewed in this section is also unknown.

Biran, Augusto, and Wilson (1981) used a multiple-baseline design to compare in vivo exposure with combined RET and cognitive restructuring (CR) for three females with fears of writing in public. All three appear to have met DSM-III criteria for social phobia, and two of the participants may have met criteria for the DSM-III-R generalized subtype, although the focus of the treatment was restricted to individuals' writing fears. Five sessions of CR were followed by five sessions of exposure for two participants, while the third participant received exposure only. Participants evidenced no change in the number of tasks completed on a behavior test during baseline assessment or following CR. They attained maximal levels of approach after exposure was implemented and maintained these changes through the nine-month follow-up. While increase in approach behavior was highly correlated with exposure, change in subjective fear was much less predictable. Patterns of change in fear differed across participants, with one showing reductions during baseline assessment, the second showing reductions following CR, and the third showing no change until the one-month follow-up. All three participants evidenced increases in fear by the nine-month follow-up. While avoidance was low at that time, fear had returned to pretreatment levels. While exposure appeared to outperform CR, procedures varied from more sophisticated administrations of this treatment. The problems associated with the administration of CR in this study will be discussed in a later section.

Alstrom, Nordlund, Persson, Harding, and Ljungqvist (1984) randomly assigned 42 social phobic individuals to therapist-directed prolonged exposure (EXP), dynamically oriented supportive therapy (ST), or relaxation therapy. Participants also received basal therapy as a component of their treatment, and a fourth group received basal therapy alone. Basal therapy consisted of unspecified anxiolytic medication and encouragement to practice self-exposure but with no actual directed exposure. Participants in the EXP condition were treated with prolonged exposure to moderately difficult but common situations, conducted with the direct aid of a therapist. Participants were instructed to remain in feared situations until anxiety decreased. Situation difficulty was gradually increased, and therapist assistance gradually removed. Exposure in imagination supplemented this procedure for some participants.

Reductions in anticipatory anxiety and in anxiety in difficult situations were most evident for the participants in the EXP condition at the conclusion of treatment. EXP participants avoided less when faced with difficult situations and showed greater improvement on a global rating scale of disturbance than did participants treated with relaxation therapy and basal therapy alone. At nine-month follow-up assessment, most differences between EXP, relaxation therapy, and supportive therapy were no longer evident. However, EXP participants did maintain their advantage over participants receiving basal therapy alone at follow-up for situational and anticipatory anxiety.

Several problems in the design and report of this study make reliance on these findings difficult. For example, persons selected for participation were de-

scribed as unsuitable for insight-oriented psychotherapy. Suitability was reported to be associated with better prognosis, and the authors attempted to create a more homogeneous sample with regard to treatment outcome potential. It is unclear how much of an impact this exclusion had on outcome, since no analysis was conducted nor description provided of individuals in this group. Other difficulties summarized by Heimberg (1989) include gender, demographic, and pretreatment impairment differences across groups, unsystematic administration of treatments within and across groups (imaginal flooding in the exposure condition and medication across conditions), and the inclusion of self-exposure instructions in basal therapy.

Butler, Cullington, Munby, Amies, and Gelder (1984) randomly assigned 45 persons who met DSM-III criteria for social phobia to exposure (EXP), exposure plus anxiety management (EX/AM), or a wait-list control group. Participants met individually with either a clinical psychologist or a social worker for seven weekly one-hour sessions, and booster sessions were provided two weeks and six weeks after treatment concluded. In the EXP condition, participants were encouraged to engage in approximately one hour of exposure each day, focusing on graded tasks that were clearly defined and repeatable and that had previously resulted in anxiety or avoidance. Citing the concerns regarding internal avoidance noted earlier, Butler et al. (1984) hypothesized that the addition of anxiety management techniques might enhance the effects of exposure by reducing psychological disengagement. Anxiety management training consisted of relaxation, distraction, and rational self-talk and was employed to counter the effects of internal avoidance by focusing on the covert aspects of social phobia. To equalize the amount of exposure and therapist attention that each individual received, a filler treatment (associative therapy) was provided as part of the EXP condition. Associative therapy occupied the same amount of time as anxiety management training and included discussion about exposure.

Participants in both exposure conditions evidenced pretreatment-to-posttreatment reductions in phobic severity, difficulty encountered in phobic situations, anxiety experienced during a behavior test, general anxiety, and depression. Except for difficulty encountered in phobic situations, within-group changes in EXP and EX/AM groups were supported by significantly greater improvement in the two treatment groups when compared with the wait-list group. At six-month follow-up, EX/AM was more effective than EXP in reducing phobic severity, fear of negative evaluation, social avoidance, general anxiety, and depression. Forty percent of those receiving EXP requested additional treatment in the following 12 months, while no participant in the combined treatment requested additional intervention. It is unclear whether or not exposure would have fared better under different conditions. Following the initial meeting, the remaining six treatment sessions lasted just one hour each, equally divided between exposure discussion and either anxiety management or associative therapy. EXP consisted primarily of encouragement to confront feared situations outside the treatment setting with some practice asking questions and initiating conversation. This may be less effective than administering exposure in a group setting where practice with several individuals is possible. Exposure in vivo with therapist guidance may be a more effective and credible treatment than exposure encouragement. In fact, credibility ratings for the EXP condition were significantly lower than for the combined group by the fourth week of treatment, although the extent to which this was in response to the filler treatment cannot be determined.

Emmelkamp, Mersch, Vissia, and van der Helm (1985) compared exposure with RET and self-instructional training (SIT) in the treatment of 34 social phobic persons meeting DSM-III criteria. Participants were randomly assigned to one of the three treatment conditions. Treatments were conducted in groups of four to seven participants with each session 2.5 hours in length. The rationale provided to participants in the exposure condition involved the role of avoidance in maintaining the phobia and "the need for continuous exposure in social situations until anxiety dissipated" (p. 366). Exposure consisted of role-played exercises within the group (for example, public speaking) and in vivo exposure (for example, asking questions in shops, speaking to strangers). Cognitive treatments will be described in a later section.

Exposure resulted in reductions in social anxiety and general psychopathology at posttreatment assess-

ment and additional improvement on those measures at one-month follow-up. At posttreatment assessment, exposure participants evidenced significantly more reduction in heart rate before and after a behavior test than participants treated with either cognitive treatment. No other between groups differences favored the exposure treatment at posttest or follow-up. Participants in the cognitive treatment conditions reported fewer irrational beliefs than exposure participants.

Noting the problems with the exposure trial of the Butler et al. (1984) study outlined earlier, Mattick and Peters (1988) compared therapist-assisted guided exposure with and without cognitive restructuring. Direct therapist guidance was hypothesized to provide additional support to individuals entering feared situations and to be more credible to individuals. Therapists accompanied groups to locations where they could engage their feared situation (for example, eating or drinking at a cafe). Difficulty level was gradually increased while direct assistance was gradually withdrawn. The therapist remained available, providing feedback and support, despite providing less direct aid. No filler treatment was used as in the Butler et al. (1984) design, equalizing total active treatment received.

The sample, consisting of 51 participants, was described as having one or more primarily circumscribed fears. It is likely that a substantial proportion of this sample would have met criteria for DSM-III-R generalized subtype since, in a later study, 67% of a similarly selected sample did so (Mattick, Peters, & Clarke, 1989). Treatment was administered in groups of four to seven persons, for six weeks, two hours each week. Both treatments yielded significant reductions in avoidance behavior, phobic severity, and depression from pretreatment to posttreatment assessment. Additional gains were noted from posttreatment to three-month follow-up assessment. While both treatments were effective, the combined treatment was superior to the exposure alone condition, especially on percentage of tasks completed during a behavioral test, phobic avoidance, and composite measures of improvement and end-state functioning.

Mattick et al. (1989) compared exposure, cognitive restructuring, and exposure plus cognitive restructuring to a wait-list control group in an attempt to disentangle the effects found in the previous study.

Forty-three social phobic subjects participated, with approximately two-thirds of the sample meeting criteria for the generalized subtype and the remainder having more circumscribed fears. All three treatments produced improvement at posttreatment assessment when compared with the wait-list condition on percentage of tasks completed during a behavior test and self-report of phobia severity and avoidance. At posttreatment assessment, exposure alone and the combined treatment were more effective than cognitive restructuring alone in increasing the number of tasks completed on a behavior test. At follow-up assessment, subjects in the cognitive restructuring condition and the combined treatment continued to improve, while subjects in the exposure condition deteriorated slightly. Overall, combined treatment subjects completed a higher percentage of behavioral tasks than did subjects in the exposure and cognitive restructuring treatments. There were few significant differences between treatments on self-report measures. While exposure appears to have been somewhat less effective than cognitive restructuring or combined cognitive restructuring plus exposure, the mechanism that led to these findings is unclear. It is possible that the availability of cognitive coping skills allowed an individual to decrease avoidance (increase exposure) of phobic situations after the end of formal treatment.

As reported earlier, Wlazlo et al. (1990) compared social skills training with individual- and group-administered exposure in the treatment of subjects classified as having primary social skills deficits or primary social phobia. All treatments produced significant within-group changes on most measures. Phobic subjects receiving group exposure reported less fear of social contact and greater ability to refuse requests than did subjects with social skills deficits treated with group exposure at a mean follow-up period of 2.5 years. Problems with this study, noted in a previous section, reduce our ability to determine the relative benefits of these treatments.

Summary.   Individual- and group-administered exposure are effective treatments for social phobia. Significant reductions in phobic severity, avoidance, and anticipatory and situational anxiety are common immediately following the conclusion of exposure treatment. However, exposure alone may not produce desired long-term maintenance of gains as evidenced by deterioration at follow-up in three of the studies reviewed (Alstrom et al., 1984; Butler et al., 1984; Mattick et al., 1989). Significant proportions of participants sought additional treatment in an exposure alone condition (Butler et al., 1984), and exposure combined with cognitive restructuring produced more favorable long-term results (Mattick & Peters, 1988; Mattick et al., 1989).

C. Cognitive Interventions

Butler (1985) hypothesized that fear of negative evaluation is especially important in the treatment of social phobia, and there is some research to support this claim. Mattick and Peters (1988) and Mattick et al. (1989) used a composite measure of improvement and end-state functioning, which consisted of a combination of avoidance and severity ratings and percentage of tasks completed on a behavior test as the criterion in a regression analysis to examine possible mediators of long-term improvement. Predictors included pretreatment to posttreatment change in fear of negative evaluation, irrational beliefs, and locus of control. In both studies, change in fear of negative evaluation was most strongly associated with improvement, suggesting that interventions that can effectively alter this fear will more likely result in improvement in the functioning of social phobic individuals. Exposure has not been particularly effective in producing these kinds of changes (Butler et al., 1984; Emmelkamp et al., 1985; Mattick et al., 1989), leading Butler (1985) to conclude that "social phobia might be resistant to treatment . . . which does not include a cognitive element" (p. 655). These results lend support to Butler's (1985) hypothesis regarding the importance of cognitive variables, specifically change in fear of negative evaluation, and their relationship to positive outcome in therapy. In this section, 11 studies will be reviewed in which cognitive behavioral interventions have been studied as singular treatments, as enhancements to other modalities, or as part of integrated treatment strategies.

Kanter and Goldfried (1979) examined a variation of RET in the first test of a cognitive treatment for 68 socially anxious persons who, by description, appear to have met diagnostic criteria for social phobia. In systematic rational restructuring (SRR) (Goldfried, DeCenteceo, & Weinberg, 1974), participants are instructed to utilize imagery of situations from an anxiety hierarchy to identify unrealistic thoughts, overtly challenge these thoughts, and substitute more adaptive ones in their place. Individuals use their experience of anxiety during the imagery process as a cue to begin identifying maladaptive thoughts. SRR was compared with self-control desensitization (SCD) (Goldfried, 1971) in which participants were trained to respond to anxiety experienced during imagery procedures with progressive relaxation. In both treatments, participants gradually progressed up their anxiety hierarchy to more provocative situations. Homework assignments supplemented both treatments. A third treatment condition combined SRR and SCD such that, following imagery-induced anxiety, participants utilized both progressive relaxation and rational restructuring to cope with anxiety. Exposure was held constant across treatment conditions. Participants were treated in groups of eight to ten for seven weekly 1.5-hour sessions. Individuals assigned to a wait-list control condition received pretreatment and posttreatment assessments only, followed by active treatment.

Participants in all three active treatment conditions showed significantly greater improvement than did those in the control group. Participants in the SRR and combined treatment conditions showed significant pretreatment-to-posttreatment improvement on 16 of 19 measures, including reductions in social anxiety, trait anxiety, and irrational beliefs. SCD participants improved on 10 of 19 measures. SRR participants reported lower trait anxiety, fewer irrational beliefs, and lower anxiety during a behavior test than did SCD participants. Combined treatment participants reported less anxiety about the prospect of giving a speech and less anxiety during a behavior test than did SCD participants. The behavior test was not administered at follow-up assessment, limiting results at this assessment point to self-report measures. Within-group changes from pretreatment to nine-week follow-up were evident on all self-report measures for SRR participants. Participants who received SCD or combined treatment improved on 11 of 14 self-report measures. SRR participants, compared with SCD participants, were found to

have significant reductions in trait anxiety, fear of negative evaluation, and irrational beliefs at follow-up.

In a study described earlier, Emmelkamp et al. (1985) compared RET and self-instructional training (SIT) with role-played and in vivo exposure. RET focused on disputing irrational beliefs commonly held by social phobic persons. SIT is a modified version of Meichenbaum's (1985) stress-inoculation training minus relaxation procedures. SIT participants were trained to identify and record negative thoughts and feelings that occurred in social situations. Using imaginal rehearsal, participant and therapist developed and practiced realistic thoughts designed to increase coping with the anticipatory phase of social situations, the situation itself, and the postsituation phase where negative bias regarding performance is common. Neither cognitive treatment included instruction for in vivo exposure. Participants in both cognitive treatments reported pretreatment to posttreatment reductions in social anxiety, general psychopathology, and irrational beliefs. RET participants, compared with SIT participants, reported less social anxiety on one measure at posttest, a difference that was maintained at one-month follow-up. Exposure was superior to both cognitive treatments on the pulse rate measure at posttreatment assessment. At follow-up assessment, RET participants showed additional improvement on social anxiety and irrational beliefs, while SIT participants reported less general psychopathology. RET participants continued to report less social anxiety than SIT participants, and participants in both cognitive treatments reported fewer irrational beliefs than participants in the exposure treatment.

Using a design similar to Öst et al. (1981), Jerremalm et al. (1986) classified 39 social phobic outpatients as physiological reactors or cognitive reactors. Individuals were classified as physiological reactors if relatively large changes in heart rate occurred during a conversation with a confederate. Cognitive reactors were classified, as such, based on a relatively higher frequency of negative thoughts reported during the conversation. As a test of a treatment-matching hypothesis, persons within each classification were randomly assigned to either AR, SIT, or a wait-list condition. Both treatments received high credibility ratings at posttest. Physiological reactors were more improved than wait-list participants on measures of anxiety and heart rate during the behavioral test regardless of treatment condition. Physiological reactors receiving SIT reported more positive thoughts and fewer negative thoughts than the control group. Cognitive reactors receiving either treatment evidenced significant improvement in thought index scores, with SIT resulting in improvement beyond that seen in participants treated with AR. Cognitive reactors treated with SIT improved significantly more than those treated with AR on three of seven self-report measures. Contrary to the hypothesis, no advantage was found for the physiological reactors treated with AR, and on two of the measures SIT was actually a more effective treatment than AR.

The authors advanced several possible explanations for their contrary results. First, classification into cognitive and physiological reactors may not have been successful. The instrument used to classify cognitive reactors, the thought index, was an untested instrument with low test-retest reliability. Reassessment of persons on the wait-list condition after four months found that four persons were reclassified to the other response pattern. It is possible that the physiological classification based on cardiac reactivity may also have been inadequate and that other criteria for classification might improve differentiation. Furthermore, the cognitive treatment may have offered a more robust method of coping to those suffering social fears, regardless of individual response pattern.

Mersch et al. (1989) further tested the treatment-matching hypothesis, comparing RET with SST in the treatment of social phobic individuals classified as cognitive reactors and behavioral reactors. While there were numerous pretreatment-to-posttreatment gains in both treatment conditions, there was virtually no support for the matching of treatment to individual response pattern. This outcome was not different at 14-month follow-up (Mersch et al., 1991).

Integrated cognitive behavioral treatments.   Biran et al. (1981), in a study described earlier, compared exposure and exposure plus combined RET and cognitive restructuring (CR) for the treatment of three social phobics' writing fears. The cognitive component of treatment consisted of an explanation of the rationale underlying cognitive treatment in general,

especially that anxiety results from maladaptive cognitive responses. Participants were trained to identify maladaptive ideas while imagining phobic situations. Through discussion and modeling, a realistic appraisal of the situation was developed, presumably displacing maladaptive thinking and reducing anxiety. As noted earlier, CR appeared to add little to the exposure treatment that resulted in reductions in avoidance. Subjective fears appeared to be unchanged by the active treatment. Stravynski et al. (1982) compared SST alone and in combination with cognitive restructuring in the treatment of DSM-III diagnosed social phobics. Both treatments resulted in reductions in the severity of phobic symptoms, but cognitive restructuring did not enhance the outcome at posttreatment or six-month follow-up.

It has been argued (Heimberg, 1989; Heimberg & Barlow, 1988; Heimberg, Dodge, & Becker, 1987) that the Biran et al. (1981) and Stravynski et al. (1982) studies were methodologically flawed in several ways and that the cognitive restructuring procedures may not have been administered in a maximally effective way. In Stravynski et al. (1982), both treatment groups produced equivalent results; however, there was no comparison group to control for confounding factors (for example, therapist attention) or the fact of being in treatment. In the multiple-baseline design of Biran et al. (1981), change in fear of social situations appeared unrelated to the active treatment. In both studies, questions have been raised about the appropriateness of the participant sample (Heimberg et al., 1987). Stravynski et al. (1982) described their participants as having both social phobia and avoidant personality disorder, in addition to several other functional impairments. These participants are described in ways that suggest a greater degree of impairment than is implied by a diagnosis of social phobia. However, mean scores on self-report measures of social anxiety for Stravynski et al. (1982) and for one of the three participants in Biran et al. (1981) were lower than those reported in other studies of social phobia (Heimberg et al., 1987). In fact, these scores were in the normative range of scores originally reported for these measures (Watson & Friend, 1969).

It has also been suggested that, in both Biran et al. (1981) and Stravynski et al. (1982), cognitive techniques were not administered in a way that would maximize effectiveness of this treatment. Specifically, Heimberg et al. (1987) suggested that cognitive restructuring was administered in isolation from social skills training or exposure, such that each technique remained distinct. Administered in this way, cognitive restructuring techniques are reliant on participants' recall of phobic situations, including their cognition, affect, and behavior in those situations. It is unclear how much of an impact this retrospective technique would have on the accuracy of a participant's report. Instead, Heimberg (1989) called for the integration of cognitive and behavioral techniques. For example, cognitive restructuring could immediately precede and follow exposure simulations, making cognition more readily available for modification. Treatments based on this integration of techniques will be presented later.

Mattick and colleagues examined the relative efficacy of cognitive restructuring, exposure, and combined treatments for social phobia (Mattick & Peters, 1988; Mattick et al., 1989). Cognitive restructuring, as applied in these studies, focused on irrational beliefs regarding social phobics' concerns with others' opinions—that they are being observed and that signs of anxiety were public and could be viewed by others. Thoughts related to these beliefs were identified in the context of past and hypothetical feared situations. The logic and adaptiveness of those thoughts relative to social situations were evaluated. Development of rational and adaptive thoughts was followed by encouragement to actively use these thoughts in feared situations. The results of both studies converge to show that CR was an effective treatment for social phobia and enhanced the effects of exposure. Mattick and Peters (1988) found that CR combined with exposure was more effective than exposure alone in reducing phobic avoidance, increasing the number of tasks completed on a behavior test, and producing positive change on composite indices of improvement and functioning. Mattick et al. (1989) found that CR plus exposure was as effective as exposure alone and more effective than CR alone on behavior test task completion at posttreatment assessment. At follow-up, CR plus exposure was superior to both CR alone and exposure alone, which were equivalent to each other, in effecting the number of behavioral tasks completed.

As noted earlier, Butler et al. (1984) found that a combination of relaxation, distraction, rational self-talk, and exposure was more effective in reducing phobic severity, social avoidance, anxiety, and depression than exposure alone. At 12-month follow-up, no participants in the combined treatment requested additional treatment, while 40% of the exposure alone condition sought additional treatment. While approximately half of the participants reported using one or more of the anxiety management techniques incorporated in the combined treatment strategy prior to treatment, almost 90% of the combined treatment participants reported effective use of these strategies after treatment compared to just 14% of the exposure alone group. The use of rational self-talk appears to have been especially important to the combined treatment participants.

Heimberg, Becker, Goldfinger, and Vermilyea (1985) treated seven social phobic persons in two groups with a combination of imaginal exposure, role-play, cognitive restructuring, and homework assignments. Imaginal exposure was conducted in four of the fourteen 90-minute sessions. These were followed with two sessions (for a total of eight) of combined exposure and cognitive restructuring. Exposure consisted of participants role-playing relevant situations while other group members and therapists played key roles. Cognitive restructuring followed each exposure and focused on identifying thoughts that occurred during the simulation, repeated questioning about the meaning of the thought for that individual (especially long-range consequences), and revealing the faulty logic behind the thought. Personalized homework assignments augmented therapy by having participants engage in exposure and cognitive restructuring in the natural environment.

Significant reductions in social anxiety, general anxiety, and fear of negative evaluation were evident from pretreatment to posttreatment and from pretreatment to six-month follow-up. Attribution of the causes of negative outcomes became less internal and stable, and participants reported taking less responsibility for negative outcomes. Participants reported less anxiety, rated their own behavioral performance as higher in quality, and were rated by observers as exhibiting fewer signs of anxiety during a behavior test from pretreatment to posttreatment. Gains were maintained at six-month follow-up for all but one participant whose anxiety returned to baseline levels.

In our clinic, combined cognitive restructuring and exposure has been integrated into a structured treatment package. The first two sessions of cognitive behavioral group therapy (CBGT) train participants in the basic tenets of cognitive therapy, especially the link between irrational thinking and anxiety. Initial training in cognitive restructuring occurs as individuals learn to identify their own irrational thoughts and to dispute their content. Each of the remaining ten sessions begins with a review of homework assignments followed by two or three restructuring/exposure exercises. Sessions conclude with assignment of homework for each group member. Cognitive restructuring/ exposure exercises constitute the bulk of the CBGT session. For each individual scheduled, a period of cognitive restructuring precedes the role-play of the feared situation. Setup procedures prior to role-play consist of: (a) identification of automatic negative thoughts (ATs) that the participant reports in anticipation of the situation, (b) classification of ATs using a typology of cognitive distortions adapted from Burns (1980) and Persons (1989), (c) disputation of ATs through logical questioning, and (d) development of alternative responses that are more rational and act as cues to participants regarding the disputation process just completed. Following the setup procedures, observable and measurable goals for the exposure are established, usually in the form of number of responses made or number of questions asked during the interaction. Goal setting is an important procedure in the treatment of social phobics who often have vague, unrealistic, and sometimes perfectionistic goals for themselves in social situations. Measurable goals allow for immediate feedback at the conclusion of the exposure, making judgment of success or failure a straightforward process. With practice, focus shifts from the affective experience of the individual in the situation (for example, "I failed because I was anxious") to the tasks required by the situation (for example, "I was able to ask three questions and make three comments").

Exposure situations are based on individualized hierarchies of anxiety-provoking situations and clinical experience with each participant. Exposures last approximately ten minutes, and subjective anxiety ratings are elicited initially and at one-minute intervals. At the same interval, participants are instructed to read their rational responses aloud. Following the exposure, another period of processing is conducted. Participants' goals are reviewed and goal attainment assessed. The occurrence of ATs, expected and unexpected, is reviewed as is the use of rational responses. The covariation of ATs, rational responses, and subjective anxiety ratings is examined. The restructuring/exposure procedure concludes with a summary by the target participant of the main points he or she has learned.

Heimberg, Dodge, et al. (1990) compared CBGT with a placebo therapy group developed to control for therapist attention, treatment credibility, and outcome expectancy. Control group sessions combined educational presentations of material on topics relevant to the problems generally reported by social phobics, including fear of negative evaluation, effective conversation, anticipatory anxiety, physiological factors in anxiety, assertiveness, perfectionism, and need for control. The second half of each group provided time for members to share ideas, insights, and advice with each other in a supportive environment. Heimberg, Dodge, et al. (1990) reported that treatment credibility was virtually equivalent between CBGT and the attention-placebo group when assessed after one or four sessions. Kennedy and Heimberg (1986) reported that the treatment rationales underlying CBGT and the attention-placebo group were regarded similarly to each other and to the rationale for SST in an undergraduate sample.

Forty-nine social phobic persons were randomly assigned to either CBGT or attention-placebo conditions. Four to seven participants met for 12 weekly two-hour sessions conducted by a doctoral-level therapist and an advanced doctoral student, both trained extensively in these procedures. At posttreatment assessment, CBGT participants, as compared to attention-placebo participants, reported less anxiety during an individualized behavior test and were rated as less severely impaired by clinical assessors. At six-month follow-up, CBGT participants maintained their gains and also reported more positive and fewer negative thoughts during the behavior test than did attention-placebo participants. Clinically significant improvement was defined as a 2 point decrease from pretreatment assessment on the assessor's 0 to 8 rating of phobic severity and a score below the clinically significant level (3 or less). Using these criteria, 75% of CBGT participants were improved at posttest, while 40% of attention-placebo participants improved. At six-month follow-up, 81% and 47% of CBGT and placebo participants, respectively, were improved using this index.

While the evidence is strong that these changes are a result of participation in CBGT, the mechanism by which these changes occurred is unknown. Bruch, Heimberg, and Hope (1991) investigated this question, testing Schwartz and Garamoni's (1986, 1989) states of mind (SOM) model with a subset of 30 subjects who participated in the Heimberg, Dodge, et al. (1990) study. Simply stated, the SOM model asserts that varying levels of psychopathology are related to an individual's balance of positive and negative cognitions. The ratio of positive to positive plus negative thoughts (P/P + N) constitutes the SOM ratio. Different states of mind are hypothesized, each characterized by a specific SOM ratio and conceptually linked to varying degrees of psychopathology. SOM ratios of 0.00 to 0.31 (termed negative monologue) and 0.32 to 0.44 (negative dialogue) are presumably linked to severe and moderate psychopathology, respectively. SOM ratios of 0.45 to 0.55 are indicative of a conflicted dialogue and are believed to be associated with milder psychopathology. A shift from a negative monologue or a negative or conflicted dialogue to a positive dialogue (SOM ratio of 0.56 to 0.68) is hypothesized to be a mechanism by which cognitive treatments positively effect change.

Fourteen CBGT participants and 16 attention-placebo participants completed a thought-listing procedure immediately following the behavioral test at pretreatment, posttreatment, and six-month follow-up assessments. The SOM ratio for the entire sample at pretreatment assessment was 0.3, lying just below the boundary between negative dialogue and negative monologue. At posttreatment assessment, participants

in both treatments exhibited similar SOM ratios indicative of conflicted dialogue. At six-month follow-up, however, CBGT participants exhibited a SOM ratio within the theoretical ideal range (0.65) while the ratio for attention-placebo participants returned to pretreatment levels. In a further analysis of the role of state of mind, Bruch, Heimberg, and Hope (1991) examined the association between improvement status and SOM ratio, regardless of treatment condition. Using the same index of improvement as Heimberg, Dodge, et al. (1990), improvers had higher average SOM ratios than nonimprovers at both posttest and follow-up assessment. SOM ratios for improvers were in the theoretical ideal range (positive dialogue) at both posttreatment (0.63) and follow-up (0.67).

Of the 40 participants who completed treatment in the Heimberg, Dodge, et al. (1990) study, 32 were recontacted and 19 agreed to participate in a follow-up evaluation (Heimberg, Salzman, Holt, & Blendell, in press). The range of follow-up was 4.5 to 6.25 years (mean = 5.5 years). Individuals participating in the follow-up differed significantly from those not participating in several ways, indicating that the follow-up sample may have been less impaired than the original sample prior to and following treatment. However, differences were equivalent across CBGT and attention-placebo treatment conditions. CBGT participants, as compared to attention-placebo participants, rated their phobia as less severe and reported less social avoidance. Independent assessors rated CBGT participants' social fear as less severe and their symptoms as interfering less with work, social activities, and family life, compared with attention-placebo participants. Assessors rated CBGT participants as barely symptomatic, while attention-placebo participants maintained a need for continuing treatment. Judges, blind to treatment condition, observed CBGT participants to be significantly less anxious and to exhibit superior performance during a behavior test when compared with attention-placebo participants.

Clearly, these results suggest that an integrated exposure and cognitive restructuring treatment is more effective than a credible attention-placebo in the treatment of social phobia, even five years after treatment. Changes are most evident in self-report and independent ratings of severity of impairment and in judges' ratings of anxiety and performance quality during an individualized behavioral test. While these results must be interpreted in light of the small and somewhat unrepresentative follow-up sample, they provide a cause for optimism about the long-term effectiveness of cognitive behavioral treatments.

While this review does not specifically address pharmacotherapeutic methods in the treatment of social phobia, two studies that compared CBGT with pharmacotherapy methods will be reviewed here. Gelernter et al. (1991) compared CBGT with two pharmacotherapies. Sixty-five participants were randomly assigned to either phenelzine plus exposure instructions, alprazolam (a triazolobenzodiazepine) plus exposure instructions, pill-placebo plus exposure instructions, or CBGT. The four groups differed on only one of several self-report measures. Phenelzine participants reported less trait anxiety at posttest and two-month follow-up than did participants in the other three treatment conditions. Several problems limit conclusions of relative efficacy that can be drawn from this study. First, assessment was limited to self-report questionnaires. No independent assessment was included. While a behavior test was conducted at pretreatment and posttreatment assessment, the only measurement obtained was a frequency checklist of self-statements that occurred during the test. No anxiety ratings or behavioral measures were collected. A second problem concerned CBGT group size and session duration. Ten persons participated in each group, and sessions were just 120 minutes in length. In the current version of the CBGT treatment manual (Heimberg, 1991), the recommended number of persons in each group is six and recommended duration is 2.5 hours. While it is not stated in this report, it is likely that CBGT individuals did not participate in as many cognitive restructuring/exposure exercises as is recommended, possibly reducing the efficacy of this treatment. Third, participants in the other three treatment conditions were instructed to engage in self-exposure activities. These instructions introduced an additional treatment component to the pharmacotherapy treatments, making this more of a comparison between CBGT and pharmacotherapy plus exposure.

Heimberg and Liebowitz (1992) report preliminary results of an ongoing multicenter collaborative study comparing CBGT with phenelzine. Participants were randomly assigned to either CBGT, attention-placebo, phenelzine, or pill-placebo. Following the initial 12 weeks of treatment, attention-placebo and pill-placebo participants were removed from the study and treated or referred for treatment as appropriate. Participants responding to CBGT or phenelzine treatment according to independent assessor ratings are treated for an additional six months in the form of monthly group or medication appointments. In Heimberg and Liebowitz's (1992) preliminary report, CBGT and phenelzine participants were more likely to be classified as positive treatment responders by the independent assessor than participants receiving attention-placebo and pill-placebo but were equivalent to each other. More detailed analysis will be included in future reports.

Summary. Two studies found no enhancement of outcome already produced by social skills training (Stravynski et al., 1982) or exposure (Biran et al., 1981) with the addition of cognitive restructuring procedures. However, the design of these studies has been criticized, and the application of cognitive restructuring procedures may have been less than optimal (Heimberg, 1989). Every other study reviewed showed cognitive restructuring to be an effective treatment for social phobia. A version of RET was more effective than desensitization in reducing self-report of social and general anxiety (Kanter & Goldfried, 1979), and self-instructional training was more robust than hypothesized with subgroups of social phobics regardless of individual response pattern (Jerremalm et al., 1986). The combination of exposure and cognitive restructuring appeared to be a very effective treatment, while exposure without cognitive restructuring failed to produce the same long-term outcome as the combination treatment (Mattick et al., 1989). The effectiveness of combining exposure with cognitive restructuring was further supported by Butler et al. (1984) and extended to group therapy designed specifically for the treatment of social phobia (Heimberg et al., 1985). Refined by Heimberg, Dodge, et al. (1990), cognitive behavioral group therapy was more effective than a credible placebo control and was shown to have long-term benefits (Heimberg, Salzman, Holt, & Blendell, in press).

IV. Conclusions and Recommendations

Social skills training, at first glance, appears to produce significant improvements in social anxiety and other clinically relevant measures of functioning in social phobic clients. Upon closer inspection, however, methodological shortcomings limit the extent to which generalizations regarding the efficacy of this treatment can be made. Only one study included a no-treatment comparison group, and their results suggest only modest improvements in the number of social contacts made by social phobic individuals as a result of social skills training (Marzillier et al., 1976). We have already noted that the term *social skills deficit* may be inappropriately applied to some individuals with this disorder, and this may account for the modest effectiveness of SST. Training designed to teach skills that may already be available is unlikely to be beneficial. Modest benefits could have resulted from the exposure components inherent in social skills training methods such as role playing. Nevertheless, it is clear that social skills training has not been adequately tested as a treatment for social phobia. Replication of previous studies with greater attention to appropriate control conditions is warranted. The use of social skills training as an adjunctive treatment to other therapies has yet to be empirically tested. There may be a subgroup of social phobics, as yet unidentified, that may also have true social skills deficits that might be responsive to social skills training.

In contrast, exposure-based treatments consistently produce significant gains quickly, despite the difficulties of treating social phobics with exposure (Butler, 1985). The most efficacious method of administering exposure is still uncertain, although there is some evidence that group exposure may have more long-term effectiveness than individual exposure (Wlazlo et al., 1990). The relative effectiveness of exposing participants to actual feared situations, role-played situations, or imaginal exposure situations and the role of the therapist during exposure are empirical questions that deserve further attention.

Butler (1985) has hypothesized that treatment for social phobia must address the cognitive component of anxiety to produce sustained gains. Various treatments based on cognitive behavioral principles have been shown to effectively reduce symptoms of social phobia, more so than delayed treatment or anxiety-reduction treatments. Combining exposure and cognitive restructuring into a fully integrated treatment package (Heimberg, 1989) has been especially effective, even beyond gains made by participants in an equally credible educational-support group (Heimberg, Dodge, et al., 1990).

Anxiety-reduction techniques have received less attention in the social phobia treatment literature than might be expected. Systematic desensitization and self-control desensitization served as comparison treatments in tests of other techniques, such as social skills training (Marzillier et al., 1976) and systematic rational restructuring (Kanter & Goldfried, 1979). Interestingly, participants in those studies benefited from these anxiety-reduction techniques as compared to a wait-list condition and on some measures showed improvements equivalent to the competing treatment. Applied relaxation has shown promising results in improving the functioning of social phobics who tend to respond with physiological symptoms in phobic situations (Jerremalm et al., 1986; Öst et al., 1981), although self-instructional training, a cognitive technique, appeared to be more robust regardless of participants' response tendency (Jerremalm et al., 1986). The possible adjunctive role of anxiety-reduction methods is worthy of further study.

Attempts to match specific treatment techniques to specific deficits of social phobic clients has produced few replicated and consistent results. Intuitively, the design of these studies is logical, yet the outcome is sometimes contrary to expectations. One of the problems, noted earlier, may lie within the methods used to classify subgroups. This has been done using either subjective means (for example, Trower et al., 1978) or objective means that sometimes proved unreliable (Jerremalm et al., 1986). It is also possible that attempts to match treatment to subgroup may overemphasize differences among participants that are less critical to treatment outcome than are their similarities. Fear of negative evaluation may be a common underlying theme among social phobics whether they respond to specific phobic situations primarily with physiological symptoms, cognitive symptoms, or with overt signs of anxiety. This may account for the robust findings for cognitive behavioral treatments, regardless of the participants' response tendencies.

References

ALSTROM, J. E., Nordlund, C. L., Persson, G., Harding, M., & Ljungqvist, C. (1984). Effects of four treatment methods on social phobic patients not suitable for insight-oriented psychotherapy. *Acta Psychiatrica Scandinavica, 70,* 97–110.

AMERICAN Psychiatric Association. (1980). *Diagnostic and statistical manual of mental disorders* (3rd ed.). Washington, DC: Author.

AMERICAN Psychiatric Association. (1987). *Diagnostic and statistical manual of mental disorders* (3rd ed., rev.). Washington, DC: Author.

AMIES, P. L., Gelder, M. G., & Shaw, P. M. (1983). Social phobia: A comparative clinical study. *British Journal of Psychiatry, 142,* 174–179.

BARLOW, D. H. (1988). *Anxiety and its disorders.* New York: Guilford Press.

BIRAN, M., Augusto, F., & Wilson, G .T. (1981). In vivo exposure versus cognitive restructuring in the treatment of scriptophobia. *Behaviour Research and Therapy, 19,* 525–532.

BRUCH, M. A., & Heimberg, R. G. (1992). Differences in perceptions of parental and personal characteristics between generalized and nongeneralized social phobics. Manuscript submitted for publication.

BRUCH, M. A., Heimberg, R. G., & Hope, D. A. (1991). States of mind model and cognitive change in treated social phobics. *Cognitive Therapy and Research, 15,* 429–441.

BURNS, D. D. (1980). *Feeling good: The new mood therapy.* New York: Morrow.

BUTLER, G. (1985). Exposure as a treatment for social phobia: Some instructive difficulties. *Behaviour Research and Therapy, 23,* 651–657.

BUTLER, G., Cullington, A., Munby, M., Amies, P., & Gelder, M. (1984). Exposure and anxiety management in the treatment of social phobia. *Journal of Consulting and Clinical Psychology, 52,* 642–650.

CLARK, J. V., & Arkowitz, H. (1975). Social anxiety and self-evaluation of interpersonal performance. *Psychological Reports, 36,* 211–221.

CURRAN, J. P., Wallander, J. L., & Fischetti, M. (1980). The importance of behavioral and cognitive factors in heterosexual-social anxiety. *Journal of Personality, 48,* 285–292.

ELLIS, A. (1962). *Reason and emotion in psychotherapy.* New York: Lyle Stuart.

EMMELKAMP, P. M., Mersch, P. P., Vissia, E., & van der Helm, M. (1985). Social phobia: A comparative evaluation of cognitive and behavioral interventions. *Behaviour Research and Therapy, 23,* 365–369.

FALLOON, I. R. H., Lloyd, G. G., & Harpin, R. E. (1981). The treatment of social phobia: Real-life rehearsal with nonprofessional therapists. *Journal of Nervous and Mental Disease, 169,* 180–184.

GELERNTER, C. S., Uhde, T. W., Cimbolic, P., Arnkoff, D. B., Vittone, B. J., Tancer, M. E., & Bartko, J. J. (1991). Cognitive-behavioral and pharmacological treatments for social phobia: A controlled study. *Archives of General Psychiatry, 48,* 938–945.

GOLDFRIED, M. R. (1971). Systematic desensitization as training in self-control. *Journal of Consulting and Clinical Psychology, 37,* 228–235.

GOLDFRIED, M. R., DeCenteceo, E. T., & Weinberg, L. (1974). Systematic rational restructuring as a self-control technique. *Behavior Therapy, 5,* 247–254.

HEIMBERG, R. G. (1986, June). *Predicting the outcome of cognitive-behavioral treatment of social phobia.* Paper presented at the annual meeting of the Society for Psychotherapy Research, Wellesley, MA.

HEIMBERG, R. G. (1989). Cognitive and behavioral treatments for social phobia: A critical analysis. *Clinical Psychology Review, 9,* 107–128.

HEIMBERG, R. G. (1991). Cognitive-behavioral treatment of social phobia in a group setting: A treatment manual (2nd ed.). Unpublished manuscript.

HEIMBERG, R. G., & Barlow, D. H. (1988). Psychosocial treatments for social phobia. *Psychosomatics, 29,* 27–37.

HEIMBERG, R. G., & Barlow, D. H. (1991). New developments in cognitive-behavioral therapy for social phobia. *Journal of Clinical Psychiatry, 52*(11), 21–30.

HEIMBERG, R. G., Becker, R. E., Goldfinger, K., & Vermilyea, J. A. (1985). Treatment of social phobia by exposure, cognitive restructuring, and homework assignments. *Journal of Nervous and Mental Disease, 173,* 236–245.

HEIMBERG, R. G., Dodge, C. S., & Becker, R. E. (1987). Social phobia. In L. Michelson & M. Ascher (Eds.), *Cognitive behavioral assessment and treatment of anxiety disorders* (pp. 280–309). New York: Plenum.

HEIMBERG, R. G., Dodge, C. S., Hope, D. A., Kennedy, C. R., Zollo, L., & Becker, R. E. (1990). Cognitive-behavioral group treatment of social phobia: Comparison to a credible placebo control. *Cognitive Therapy and Research, 14,* 1–23.

HEIMBERG, R. G., & Holt, C. S. (1989). The issue of subtypes in the diagnosis of social phobia: A report to the social phobia workgroup for DSM-IV. Unpublished manuscript.

HEIMBERG, R. G., Holt, C. S., Schneier, F. R., Spitzer, R. L., & Liebowitz, M. R. (1993). The issue of subtypes in the diagnosis of social phobia. *Journal of Anxiety Disorders, 7,* 249–269.

HEIMBERG, R. G., Hope, D. A., Dodge, C. S., & Becker, R. E. (1990). DSM-III-R subtypes of social phobia: Comparison of generalized social phobics and public speaking phobics. *Journal of Nervous and Mental Disease, 178*, 172–179.

HEIMBERG, R. G., Klosko, J. S., Dodge, C. S., Shadick, R., Becker, R. E., & Barlow, D. H. (1989). Anxiety disorders, depression, and attributional style: A further test of the specificity of depressive attributions. *Cognitive Therapy and Research, 13*, 21–36.

HEIMBERG, R. G., & Liebowitz, M. R. (1992, April). *A multi-center comparison of the efficacy of phenelzine and cognitive-behavioral group treatment for social phobia.* Paper presented at the annual meeting of the Anxiety Disorders Association of America, Houston, TX.

HEIMBERG, R. G., Mueller, G. P., Holt, C. S., Hope, D. A., & Liebowitz, M. R. (1992). Assessment of anxiety in social interaction and being observed by others: The Social Interaction Anxiety Scale and the Social Phobia Scale. *Behavior Therapy, 23*, 53–73.

HEIMBERG, R. G., Salzman, D. G., Holt, C. S., & Blendell, K. A. (in press). Cognitive-behavioral group treatment for social phobia: Effectiveness at five-year follow-up. *Cognitive Therapy and Research.*

HERBERT, J. D., Hope, D. A., & Bellack, A. S. (1992). Validity of the distinction between generalized social phobia and avoidant personality disorder. *Journal of Abnormal Psychology, 101*, 332–339.

HOLT, C. S., Heimberg, R. G., & Hope, D. A. (1990, November). *Success from the outset: Predictors of cognitive-behavioral therapy outcome among social phobics.* Paper presented at the annual meeting of the Association for Advancement of Behavior Therapy, San Francisco, CA.

HOLT, C. S., Heimberg, R. G., & Hope, D. A. (1992). Avoidant personality disorder and the generalized subtype of social phobia. *Journal of Abnormal Psychology, 101*, 318–325.

HOLT, C. S., Heimberg, R. G., Hope, D. A., & Liebowitz, M. R. (1992). Situational domains of social phobia. *Journal of Anxiety Disorders, 6*, 63–77.

HOLT, C. S., Heimberg, R. G., Hope, D. A., & Liebowitz, M. R. (1993). A search for situational features of social phobia: Clustering social situational anxiety. Manuscript in preparation.

JANET, P. (1903). *Les obsessions et la psychasthenie.* Paris: F. Alcan.

JERREMALM, A., Johansson, L., & Öst, L.-G. (1986). Cognitive and physiological reactivity and the effects of different behavioral methods in the treatment of social phobia. *Behaviour Research and Therapy, 24*, 171–180.

KANTER, N. J., & Goldfried, M. R. (1979). Relative effectiveness of rational restructuring and self-control desensitization in the reduction of interpersonal anxiety. *Behavior Therapy, 10*, 472–490.

KENNEDY, C. R., & Heimberg, R. G. (1986, November). *Treatment credibility and client outcome expectancy: An evaluation of five treatment rationales.* Paper presented at the annual meeting of the Association for the Advancement of Behavior Therapy, Chicago, IL.

LEVIN, A. P., Saoud, J. B., Strauman, T., Gorman, J. M., Fyer, A. J., Crawford, R., & Liebowitz, M. R. (1993). Responses of "generalized" and "discrete" social phobics during public speaking. *Journal of Anxiety Disorders, 7*, 207–221.

LEVIN, A. P., Schneier, F. M., & Liebowitz, M. R. (1989). Social phobia: Biology and pharmacology. *Clinical Psychology Review, 9*, 129–140.

LIEBOWITZ, M. R. (1987). Social phobia. *Modern Problems in Pharmacopsychiatry, 22*, 141–173.

LIEBOWITZ, M. R., Gorman, J. M., Fyer, A. J., Campeas, R., Levin, A. P., Sandberg, D., Hollander, E., Papp, L., & Goetz, D. (1988). Pharmacotherapy of social phobia: A placebo controlled comparison of phenelzine and atenolol. *Journal of Clinical Psychiatry, 49*, 252–257.

LIEBOWITZ, M. R., Gorman, J. M., Fyer, A. J., & Klein, D. F. (1985). Social phobia: Review of a neglected anxiety disorder. *Archives of General Psychiatry, 42*, 729–736.

LIEBOWITZ, M. R., Quitkin, F. M., Stewart, J. W., McGrath, P. J., Harrison, W., Markowitz, J. S., Rabkin, J. G., Tricamo, E., Goetz, D. M., & Klein, D. F. (1988). Antidepressant specificity in atypical depression. *Archives of General Psychiatry, 45*, 129–137.

LIEBOWITZ, M. R., Quitkin, F. M., Stewart, J. W., McGrath, P. J., Harrison, W., Rabkin, J., Tricamo, E., Markowitz, J. S., & Klein, D. F. (1984). Phenelzine versus imipramine in atypical depression: A preliminary report. *Archives of General Psychiatry, 41*, 669–677.

LIEBOWITZ, M. R., Schneier, F., Campeas, R., Hollander, E., Hatterer, J., Fyer, A., Gorman, J., Papp, L., Davies, S., Gully, R., & Klein, D. F. (1992). Phenelzine versus atenolol in social phobia: A placebo-controlled comparison. *Archives of General Psychiatry, 49*, 290–300.

MARKS, I. M., & Gelder, M. G. (1966). Different ages of onset in varieties of phobia. *American Journal of Psychiatry, 123*, 218–221.

MARZILLIER, J. S., Lambert, C., & Kellet, J. (1976). A controlled evaluation of systematic desensitization and social skills training for socially inadequate psychiatric patients. *Behaviour Research and Therapy, 14*, 225–238.

MATTICK, R. P., & Clarke, J. C. (1989). Development and validation of measures of social phobia scrutiny fear and social interaction anxiety. Unpublished manuscript.

MATTICK, R. P., & Peters, L. (1988). Treatment of severe social phobia: Effects of guided exposure with and without cognitive restructuring. *Journal of Consulting and Clinical Psychology, 56*, 251–260.

MATTICK, R. P., Peters, L., & Clarke, J. C. (1989). Exposure and cognitive restructuring for social phobia: A controlled study. *Behavior Therapy, 20*, 3–23.

MEICHENBAUM, D. (1985). *Stress inoculation training*. New York: Pergamon Press.

MERSCH, P. P. A., Emmelkamp, P. M. G., Bögels, S. M., & van der Sleen, J. (1989). Social phobia: Individual response patterns and the effects of behavioral and cognitive interventions. *Behaviour Research and Therapy, 27*, 421–434.

MERSCH, P. P. A., Emmelkamp, P. M. G., & Lips, C. (1991). Social phobia: Individual response patterns and the long-term effects of behavioral and cognitive interventions. A follow-up study. *Behaviour Research and Therapy, 29*, 357–362.

ÖST, L.-G., Jerremalm, A., & Johansson, J. (1981). Individual response patterns and the effects of different behavioral methods in the treatment of social phobia. *Behaviour Research and Therapy, 19*, 1–16.

PERSONS, J. B. (1989). *Cognitive therapy in practice: A case formulation approach*. New York: Norton.

PLATT, J. R. (1964). Strong inference. *Science, 146*, 347–353.

RAPEE, R. M., & Lim, L. (1992). Discrepancy between self- and observer ratings of performance in social phobics. *Journal of Abnormal Psychology, 101*, 727–731.

SANDERSON, W. C., DiNardo, P. A., Rapee, R. M., & Barlow, D. H. (1990). Syndrome comorbidity in patients diagnosed with a DSM-III-R anxiety disorder. *Journal of Abnormal Psychology, 99*, 308–312.

SCHNEIER, F. R., Johnson, J., Hornig, C. D., Liebowitz, M. R., & Weissman, M. W. (1992). Social phobia: Comorbidity and morbidity in an epidemiologic sample. *Archives of General Psychiatry, 49*, 282–288.

SCHNEIER, F. R., Levin, A. P., & Liebowitz, M. R. (1990). Pharmacotherapy. In A. S. Bellack & M. Hersen (Eds.), *Handbook of comparative treatments for adult disorders* (pp. 219–239). New York: Wiley.

SCHNEIER, F. R., Spitzer, R. L., Gibbon, M., Fyer, A. J., & Liebowitz, M. R. (1991). The relationship of social phobia subtypes and avoidant personality disorder. *Comprehensive Psychiatry, 32*, 496–502.

SCHWARTZ, R. M., & Garamoni, G. L. (1986). A structural model of positive and negative states of mind: Asymmetry in the internal dialogue. In P. C. Kendall (Ed.), *Advances in cognitive-behavioral research and therapy* (Vol. 5, pp. 1–62). New York: Academic Press.

SCHWARTZ, R. M., & Garamoni, G. L. (1989). Cognitive balance and psychopathology: Evaluation of an information processing model of positive and negative states of mind. *Clinical Psychology Review, 9*, 271–294.

SHAW, P. M. (1979). A comparison of three behaviour therapies in the treatment of social phobia. *British Journal of Psychiatry, 134*, 620–623.

STRAVYNSKI, A., Marks, I., & Yule, W. (1982). Social skills problems in neurotic outpatients: Social skills training with and without cognitive modification. *Archives of General Psychiatry, 39*, 1378–1385.

TASK Force on DSM-IV, American Psychiatric Association. (1991). *DSM–IV options book: Work in progress 9/1/91*. Washington, DC: Author.

TAYLOR, C. B., & Arnow, B. (1988). *The nature and treatment of anxiety disorders*. New York: Macmillan.

TROWER, P., Yardley, K., Bryant, B., & Shaw, P. (1978). The treatment of social failure: A comparison of anxiety-reduction and skills acquisition procedures on two social problems. *Behavior Modification, 2*, 41–60.

TURNER, S. M., Beidel, D. C., Dancu, C. V., & Keys, D. J. (1986). Psychopathology of social phobia and comparison to avoidant personality disorder. *Journal of Abnormal Psychology, 95*, 389–394.

TURNER, S. M., Beidel, D. C., & Townsley, R. M. (1992). Social phobia: A comparison of specific and generalized subtypes and avoidant personality disorder. *Journal of Abnormal Psychology, 101*, 326–331.

WATSON, D., & Friend, R. (1969). Measurement of social-evaluative anxiety. *Journal of Consulting and Clinical Psychology, 33*, 448–457.

WIDIGER, T. A. (1992). Generalized social phobia versus avoidant personality disorder: A commentary on three studies. *Journal of Abnormal Psychology, 101*, 340–343.

WLAZLO, Z., Schroeder-Hartwig, K., Hand, I., Kaiser, G., & Münchau, N. (1990). Exposure in vivo versus social skills training for social phobia: Long-term outcome and differential effects. *Behaviour Research and Therapy, 28*, 181–193.

ZIMBARDO, P. D. (1977). *Shyness: What it is and what to do about it*. New York: Addison-Wesley.

ZIMBARDO, P. D., Pilkonis, P. A., & Norwood, R. M. (1975). The social disease called shyness. *Psychology Today, 8*, 68–72.

CHAPTER 4

Behavioral Treatment of Depression in the Context of Marital Discord

Steven R. H. Beach
Amy E. Brooks
Katherine R. Wright

I. Introduction
II. Depressed Persons and Their Spouses
   A. Magnitude of the Relationship between Marital Discord and Depression
   B. Temporal Patterning of the Relationship between Marital Discord and Depression
   C. Observation of Depressed Persons Interacting with Their Spouses
III. The Marital Discord Model and Basic Points of Intervention
   A. Overview of the Marital Discord Model
IV. Marital Therapy for Depression in the Context of Marital Discord
   A. First Phase of Therapy: Identifying and Eliminating Stressors
     1. Decreasing Stressors
     2. Increasing Cohesion: Caring Gestures
   B. Second Phase of Therapy: Enhancing Communication and Interaction
     1. Communication Training
     2. Problem Solving
     3. Special Problems
   C. Third Phase of Therapy: Enhancing Maintenance
V. Individual Approaches with Maritally Discordant and Depressed Persons
   A. Social Skills Training
   B. Cognitive Therapy
VI. Outcome of Marital Interventions for Depression
   A. Early Investigations of Dyadic Treatment with Heterogeneous Populations
   B. Outcome Work with Depressed Outpatients
     1. O'Leary and Beach (1990)
     2. Jacobson, Dobson, Fruzzetti, Schmaling, and Salusky (1991)
     3. Foley, Rounsaville, Weissman, Sholomaskas, and Chevron (1989)
     4. Summary
   C. Outcome Work with Depressed Inpatients
VII. Can Depression Be Prevented?
VIII. Conclusion
References

I. Introduction

The past decade has seen considerable advance in the treatment of depression. At least two individual behavioral approaches (cognitive therapy and social skills training), at least one nonbehavioral psychotherapeutic approach (interpersonal psychotherapy), as well as a variety of pharmacological approaches have been shown to be effective in the treatment of depression. At the same time, however, data have been accumulating that marital discord is a common and serious complication of depression. When present at the beginning of therapy, discordant family relations often make it more difficult to implement individually based treatments and predict poorer long-term outcomes (Beach & O'Leary, 1992; Swindle, Cronkite, & Moos, 1989). When present at termination, marital discord often maintains residual symptoms and prompts early relapse (Hooley & Teasdale, 1989). In response to the growing evidence that marital discord is a common and consequential complication of depression, the past decade has seen development and preliminary testing of behavioral marital therapy for depression as one possible response to the challenge of depression in the context of marital discord.

How strongly related are marital discord and depression? Is there any reason to believe that marital discord sometimes precipitates, exacerbates, or otherwise influences the level of depression? Is the interrelationship of marital discord and depression due to anything more fundamental than a depression-induced response set on self-report inventories? These are all reasonable questions for responsible clinicians to ask before accepting marital intervention as a potentially useful addition to currently available individual and somatic approaches to the treatment of depression. By reviewing the literature on the magnitude, temporal patterning, and behavioral manifestations of the link between marital discord and depression, we hope to build the case for the importance of being alert to marital processes in many cases

Correspondence and reprint requests should be directed to the first author at Department of Psychology, University of Georgia, Athens, Georgia 30606, telephone number (404) 542-1173. Preparation of this manuscript was made possible by NIMH Grant #41487-05.

of depression. Having laid the foundation for our discussion in this manner, we will present an overview of our marital discord model of depression and then elaborate the therapeutic implications of this model. We will provide sufficient detail of the procedures that anyone already familiar with behavioral marital therapy (BMT) should have little trouble understanding the approach being recommended. For those unfamiliar with basic procedures in BMT, additional references are liberally provided. We also briefly discuss individual approaches and their relevance to the treatment of maritally discordant, depressed persons. In particular, we attempt to highlight circumstances in which an individual approach to the treatment of depression occurring in the context of marital discord might be more advantageous than a couples approach. To move the comparison of approaches to an empirical context, we next review the outcome literature on treatment of depression where marital approaches have been assessed. Finally, we review the available evidence regarding the use of premarital interventions as a means of preventing depression.

In brief, this chapter is meant to provide the empirical foundation for attempting marital therapy with depressed-discordant individuals, to provide detail regarding a specific marital approach to the treatment of depressed-discordant persons and their spouses, and to review the relevant outcome research. As will be clear by the end of the chapter, while research in the area has moved forward rapidly, much remains to be done.

II. Depressed Persons and Their Spouses

A. Magnitude of the Relationship between Marital Discord and Depression

Behavioral theorists have suggested that a central role is played by marriage in the maintenance of depressive symptomatology both recently (Beach, Sandeen, & O'Leary, 1990; Biglan, Lewin, & Hops, 1990) and historically (Lewinsohn & Atwood, 1969; Lewinsohn & Shaffer, 1971). Indeed, considerable empirical evidence exists regarding the strong concurrent relationship between depression and marital satisfaction (see Beach & Nelson, 1990, for a review). Particularly pertinent to the current chapter, Weissman (1987) found a 25-fold increase in the relative risk of major depression for persons in unhappy marriages in her large-scale investigation of the general population. Conversely, in clinical samples, Beach, Jouriles, and O'Leary (1985) report that 50% of couples presenting for marital therapy have at least one spouse who is at least mildly depressed, while Rounsaville, Weissman, Prusoff, and Herceg-Baron (1979) report that about 50% of patients presenting for depression report significant marital disputes. Vaughn and Leff (1976) found that depressives are particularly vulnerable to family tension and to hostile statements made by family members, and Schless, Schwartz, Goetz, and Mendels (1974) demonstrated that this vulnerability to marriage- and family-related stresses persists after depressed patients recover. Accordingly, most therapists working with depressed patients will have occasion to discuss marital problems with them, and most marital therapists will have occasion to work with persons who are mildly to moderately depressed.

B. Temporal Patterning of the Relationship between Marital Discord and Depression

It has been found that negative marital events often precede the onset of depressive symptoms (Paykel, 1979). Paykel and associates (1969) and Paykel and Tanner (1976), for example, used semistructured interviews of hospitalized patients to examine event occurrence and timing. In both cases, marital arguments and other stressors preceded depression, and they were especially prominent during the month preceding depression onset. Using a different methodology, Ilfeld (1976) had community couples make independent judgments of the length of their depression, social stressors, and marital problems. On average, marital distress was of considerably longer duration than the depressive symptomatology. Likewise, using a retrospective interview approach, Brown and Harris (1978) found that lack of a confiding relationship with a boyfriend or spouse was a significant vulnerability factor in the development of depression. Thus, taken together, the data suggest that marital problems are more likely to precede the onset of an episode of depression than vice versa.

There is now also some prospective work examining the impact of marital variables on the development

and remission of depressive symptomatology. Monroe, Bromet, Connell, and Steiner (1986) found that with nonsymptomatic women in nondiscordant marriages, social support within a marriage predicted lower risk for depressive symptoms one year later. More recent longitudinal research (Beach & Nelson, 1990) has also found an effect of marital discord on later depressive symptomatology. It was found that with newly married couples, marital discord at six months predicted higher levels of depressive symptoms at 18 months, even after controlling for initial symptoms and intervening levels of life stress. In addition, the magnitude of the relationship between marital discord and level of depressive symptomatology increased over time. The concurrent correlation between symptoms of depression (Beck Depression Inventory, or BDI) and symptoms of marital discord (Short Marital Adjustment Test, or SMAT) at premarital assessment was −.35; six months after marriage it had increased significantly to −.45; and by an 18-month assessment, the concurrent correlation had increased significantly again to −.56. Thus, the available longitudinal evidence suggests a causal flow from marriage to depression and an increasing interrelationship between marital discord and depression over time (see also Markman, Duncan, Storaasli, & Howes, 1987; Schaefer & Burnett, 1987). Further implicating marriage as an important factor in the maintenance of depressive symptomatology, Rutter and Quinton (1984) report that when women whose marital difficulties precede their depression divorce their husbands their symptomatic outcome is most similar to women in good marriages. That is, terminating a discordant marriage may help terminate an episode of depression for some women.

C. Observation of Depressed Persons Interacting with Their Spouses

The results of a number of self-report studies, many of which we have just reviewed, suggest that the marital relationships of depressed individuals are problematic. One potential difficulty with these data, however, is that they rely on the self-reports of depressed persons. It has been argued that depressed individuals may sometimes demonstrate negatively distorted perceptions of their environments (compare with Beck, Rush, Shaw, & Emery, 1979; Johnson & Magaro, 1987). Further, it is known that negative mood states facilitate the recall of negatively toned information (for example, Bower, 1981; Derry & Kuiper, 1981; Gotlib, 1981, 1983). Accordingly, it is important to corroborate the results of studies relying on self-report with observational studies. Specifically, it is important to establish that depressed persons complaining of marital discord display other characteristics of marital discord as well.

In one of the first observational studies of depressed patients, Hinchliffe, Hooper, and Roberts (1978) examined the behavior of 20 depressives interacting with their spouses and with opposite-sex strangers. Compared to the interactions of nondepressed medical patients, couples with a depressed spouse showed greater conflict and tension. Interestingly, the depressed patients were more verbally productive and more affectively positive with a stranger than with their spouses. In a similar study, Hautzinger, Linden, and Hoffman (1982) assessed the interactions of 26 couples seeking marital therapy, 13 of whom had a depressed spouse. Consistent with Hinchliffe's results, Hautzinger et al. found that communication patterns in couples with a depressed spouse were more disturbed than in couples without a depressed partner. Spouses of depressed partners seldom agreed with their spouse, offered help in an ambivalent manner, and evaluated their depressed partner negatively.

Several other studies have also found the interactions of depressed persons and their spouses to be characterized by hostility. Arkowitz, Holliday, and Hutter (1982) found that following interactions with their wives, husbands of depressed women reported feeling more hostile than did husbands of psychiatric and nonpsychiatric control persons. Comparable findings were reported by Kahn, Coyne, and Margolin (1985), who found that couples with a depressed spouse were sadder and angrier following marital interactions and experienced each other as more negative, hostile, mistrusting, and detached than did nondepressed couples. Kowalik and Gotlib (1987) had depressed and nondepressed psychiatric outpatients and nondepressed nonpsychiatric controls participate in an interactional task with their spouses while simultaneously coding both the intended impact of their own behavior and the perception of their spouses' behavior. These investigators found that the communications of the depressed patients were more intentionally negative and less intentionally positive than were the communications of the nondepressed controls. Ruscher and Gotlib (1988) examined the marital interactions of mildly depressed persons from the community and found that couples in which one partner was depressed emitted a greater proportion of negative verbal and nonverbal behaviors than did nondepressed control couples. Finally, Hooley (1986, 1990; Hooley & Hahlweg, 1986) found that depressed spouses determined to be in high expressed emotion (EE) dyads typically characterized themselves as maritally distressed and demonstrated very striking patterns of verbal and nonverbal escalation of negative behavior. In contrast, depressed spouses determined to be in low EE dyads typically characterized themselves as nondistressed and displayed much less escalation. Taken together, these studies indicate that depressed spouses who report themselves to be in discordant relationships indeed are in such relationships. Further, Hooley's work supports the use of self-report to index the quality of the marital relationship of depressed spouses.

New impetus for the study of interaction in depression was provided by the research team at the Oregon Research Institute when they identified the constellation of behaviors including self-derogation, physical and psychological complaints, and displays of depressed affect as "depressive" (or distressed) behaviors. These researchers hypothesized that depressive behavior might be reinforced through its effects on the behavior of other family members. Three studies, coding depressive behavior in slightly different ways but all staying close to the original definition, have found "depressive" behavior to be elevated among depressed persons but not among their nondepressed partners or in community controls (Biglan et al., 1985; Nelson & Beach, 1990; Schmaling & Jacobson, 1990). The pioneering work by Biglan et al. (1985) found that in the depressed-discordant group, depressive behavior had the effect of suppressing subsequent aggressive spousal responses. However, since there was no discordant, nondepressed comparison group, it was not possible to determine whether the effect was due to depression, marital discord, or their interaction.

A subsequent study by Schmaling and Jacobson (1990) attempted to disentangle the effect of marital discord and depression by comparing nondepressed, nondiscordant; nondepressed, discordant; depressed, nondiscordant; and depressed, discordant couples. Unfortunately they were unable to replicate the basic suppression effect, rendering the issue of the source of the effect moot. However, Schmaling and Jacobson (1990) did find a distinctly different pattern of spousal response to depressive behavior than to aggressive behavior. Specifically, discordant spouses tended to reciprocate aggressive behavior with aggressive responses. Depressive behavior, however, produced no tendency toward increased aggressive behavior on the part of spouses. Accordingly, while failing to replicate the ability of depressive behavior to suppress aggressive responding among discordant couples, Schmaling and Jacobson found depressive behavior and aggressive behavior to be functionally distinct with regard to their effects on subsequent aggressive behavior by the spouse.

Finally, a study by Nelson and Beach (1990) contrasted the interactions of nondepressed, nondiscordant; nondepressed, discordant; and depressed, discordant couples. Again, depressed and aggressive behaviors were found to be functionally distinct with regard to their effects on subsequent spousal aggression. In this case, depressive behavior was found to suppress aggressive responding by the spouse and to do so most strongly in the nondepressed, discordant group. Taken together, the three studies strongly suggest that depressive behavior is functionally distinct from aggressive behavior. In addition, the Schmaling and Jacobson (1990) and Nelson and Beach (1990) studies imply that the effect of depressive behavior on aggressive spousal responding is primarily a function of level of marital discord rather than level of depression. Indeed, Nelson and Beach did not find a significantly stronger suppression effect in the nondepressed, discordant group and found the magnitude of the suppression effect to be correlated with duration of marital discord. For couples who reported long-standing marital discord, the suppression effect was reduced. Thus, Schmaling and Jacobson (1990) may

have failed to find an effect of depressive behavior in reducing subsequent spousal behavior either because their sample was insufficiently maritally discordant (none of the couples was seeking marital therapy) or because those couples who were maritally discordant had been discordant for a long time. Further research is necessary to resolve these issues.

In a follow-up to the Schmaling and Jacobson (1990) study, Schmaling, Whisman, Fruzzetti, and Truax (1991) examined the behavior of 100 couples as they attempted to decide which problem areas to discuss during their upcoming videotaped problem-solving discussion. It was found that both husbands' attempts to involve the interviewer and wives' active summary of proposed topics for discussion predicted the level of the wives' depression. In both cases, more active behavior was associated with less depression in the wife. This result fits well with recent findings by Christian, O'Leary, and Vivian (1991) that depression is associated with self-reported poorer problem-solving skills in both husbands and wives.

Taken together, the data lead to the conclusion that marital problems are robustly related to depression, that marital discord sometimes precipitates or exacerbates level of depression, and that the relationship of marital discord and depression cannot be dismissed as an artifact of depression-induced response bias. The retrospective and cross-sectional research based on self-report data would appear to link marital discord to clinically significant depression, while the longitudinal research to date demonstrates that marital variables can predict future levels of depressive symptomatology. The observational research base is sufficiently strong to provide considerable reassurance that the clinically observed relationship between marital discord and depression is not attributable to depressive distortion. Finally, recent evidence also links the presence of marital discord and perceived criticism by the spouse with relapse following successful somatic treatment for depression (Hooley, Orley, & Teasdale, 1986; Hooley & Teasdale, 1989). Thus, marital discord appears to be a factor in determining the course of depression and one worthy of clinical attention. It appears to be powerful enough to make someone who is already depressed more depressed, and it also seems to be powerful enough to make someone who has recently recovered from a depression more likely to relapse. While additional work is necessary to fully document the influence of marital discord on the course of depression, sufficient evidence is already available to suggest the likely value of attending to and directly addressing marital discord when it co-occurs with depression.

For the maritally discordant, depressed individual, then, it is important to consider the role that may have been played by the marital relationship in the development and maintenance of depression and the potential utility of marital intervention in promoting recovery and maintenance of gains. The marital situation holds, at a minimum, considerable influence over feelings of well-being (Diener, 1984) and often may be playing a central role in the etiology and maintenance of the depressive episode (Beach & Nelson, 1990). The marital discord model of depression is designed to help identify an integrated set of "points of intervention" to guide clinical activity. To the extent that the model achieves this goal, it will help organize clinical activity in a natural and fluid manner, allowing the clinician to tailor interventions to fit the couple while keeping the clinician focused on the mediating goals of therapy—that is, those targets of therapy held to produce positive outcome (Beach & Bauserman, 1990).

III. The Marital Discord Model and Basic Points of Intervention

A model's approach to therapeutic intervention (Beach, Abramson, & Levine, 1981) makes explicit the assumption that basic research findings should guide the development of intervention. Given the evidence that marital discord can exacerbate or maintain clinically significant levels of depression and influence the display of depressive behavior, it follows that a marital discord model of depression should highlight potentially useful avenues for clinical intervention. Toward this end, the marital discord model of depression is designed to highlight an integrated set of points of intervention that can be influenced using techniques from behavioral marital therapy. First, we outline our marital discord model of depression

(Beach, Sandeen, & O'Leary, 1990); then we discuss the specific techniques and patterning of intervention most likely to result in symptomatic improvement among depressed, maritally discordant persons.

A. Overview of the Marital Discord Model

An overview of the basic model can be seen in Figure 4.1. As can be seen, the marital relationship areas highlighted are aspects of support and coping or stress, which most typically are produced in the marital relationship (Beach, Martin, Blum, & Roman, 1993). In particular, the model highlights the support obtainable through couple cohesion, acceptance and encouragement of emotional expression by the spouse, coping assistance provided by the spouse, direct self-esteem support, perception of spousal dependability and enduring commitment to the relationship, and the presence of a confiding and intimate relationship. On the negative stress-enhancing side, the model highlights the marital areas of overt hostility, threats of divorce, severe denigration, severe disruption of marital routines, and other major stressors identified by the couple. Each area represents a relatively distinct facet of marital interaction that has shown some evidence

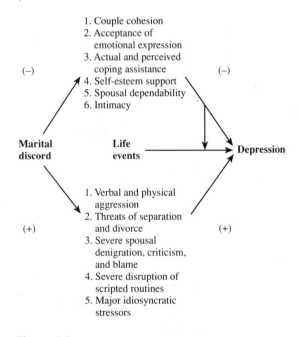

Figure 4.1 The marital discord model of depression

of being related to depressive symptomatology. In each case, the areas highlighted can be a direct focus of attention in marital therapy. Thus, the marital discord model provides a blueprint for marital intervention aimed at relieving depressive symptomatology or maintaining gains.

The marital discord model allows for several ways in which depression and marriage may come to be related over time. One of the ways in which marital discord and depression may come to be related is when marital distress leads directly to the development of a depressive episode. Imagine, for example, a marriage in which neither partner has a history of depression but which becomes discordant and leads to a depressive episode in one of the spouses. This would reflect the direct effect of marital discord on depressive symptomatology highlighted in the marital discord model of depression. Stressful life events may function either as direct or as indirect causes of both marital distress and depression, or they may also function either additively or interactively with marital discord to lead to a depressive episode. For example, job loss might interact with preexisting marital discord to trigger the onset of depressive symptoms in one of the spouses. Finally, the marital discord model allows for depression in one spouse to lead to changes in marital behavior and marital cognition, ultimately leading to marital distress, even in those cases in which the marital relationship may have seemed satisfactory prior to the depressive episode (Barling, MacEwen, & Kelloway, 1991). At a minimum, depression in a person's partner is difficult and draining (Coyne et al., 1987). Furthermore, the marital discord model indicates that a vicious cycle may develop in which marital discord exacerbates or prolongs depressive symptomatology, which in turn exacerbates or prolongs the marital discord (Beach & Fincham, 1994).

It is well known that emotions can prompt attention, influence cognitive capacity, and recruit congruent cognitive material (Bower, 1981, 1991; Clark, Milberg, & Ross, 1983; Forgas, Bower, & Moylan, 1990; Mandler, 1984; Pietromonaco & Rook, 1987). These processes, in turn, can profoundly affect social judgments. Of particular relevance for marital discord and the emergence of depression in the context of marital discord is the likelihood that depressed mood

may facilitate recall of previous anger- or anxiety-provoking situations (compare with Blaney, 1986). Likewise, it seems plausible that depressed spouses will find their attention more readily drawn to small negative behaviors or mannerisms than will nondepressed partners. Depressed spouses also may be particularly likely to recall and react to partner behavior that is nonsupportive or critical of them, further fueling their negative affective response to conflictual marital interactions.

In addition, and perhaps more consequential, it is possible that depressed individuals will be more likely than nondepressed individuals to recruit negatively valenced responsibility attributions for negative partner behavior, inferring negative intent, foresight, and harmful motivation. Indeed, depressed individuals are often characterized as feeling unjustly treated and criticized. Spouses' attributions for marital difficulty correlate with negative marital behavior (Fincham & Bradbury, 1988a) and are strongly related to marital satisfaction (Fincham, Beach, & Nelson, 1987). Further, manipulation of spousal attributions can negatively influence subsequent marital behavior (Fincham & Bradbury, 1988b). Accordingly, the facilitation of this cognitive material in depressed individuals could strongly influence the course of marital satisfaction.

IV. Marital Therapy for Depression in the Context of Marital Discord

Marital therapy for depression is typically time-specified, relatively brief, and focused on changing ongoing problem behavior. As can be seen in Figure 4.2, the therapist using marital therapy for depression applies a series of interventions in three phases. First, the therapist focuses on identifying and rapidly eliminating extreme stressors while reestablishing joint positive activities within the relationship. When successfully implemented, this stage of therapy often produces a substantial elevation in mood for the depressed patient and increased expressions of positive feelings by both spouses. This initial boost in morale and positive feelings allows the couple to confront the second phase of therapy, which involves restructuring the marital relationship.

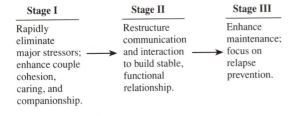

Stage I	Stage II	Stage III
Rapidly eliminate major stressors; enhance couple cohesion, caring, and companionship.	Restructure communication and interaction to build stable, functional relationship.	Enhance maintenance; focus on relapse prevention.

Figure 4.2 The flow of marital therapy for depression

The second phase of therapy is focused on the way spouses communicate, solve problems, and interact on a daily basis. This phase of therapy provides the couple with a more supportive pattern of problem resolution and systematically increases the support value of the relationship in the areas of acceptance of emotional expression, actual and perceived coping assistance, perceived spousal dependability, and couple intimacy. Typically, during this phase of therapy, there will be further decreases in the stress previously associated with coercive patterns of exchange within the dyad. Relationship cohesion and self-esteem support are likely to receive some additional attention during this phase of therapy, but typically will receive less attention than during the first phase of therapy. When successfully implemented, this phase of therapy leaves the couple better integrated and better able to handle difficulties they may encounter in the future.

The third phase of therapy is less directive, prepares the couple for termination, and identifies likely "high-risk" situations that may produce recurrence of symptoms or marital discord. Previously learned successful and appropriate ways to cope with a return of depressive symptoms or marital discord are reviewed. Couples are helped to attribute their gains in therapy to their love and caring for each other as well as to their personal resources.

A. First Phase of Therapy: Identifying and Eliminating Stressors

1. DECREASING STRESSORS

A distressed marital relationship is not only a poor source of marital support but is frequently an active source of stress. Sometimes, before therapy can begin the process of healing the relationship, it is necessary to address the ongoing patterns in the marriage that may be inflicting damage on the depressed as well as the nondepressed spouse. Clearly, it is difficult for old wounds to heal when fresh ones are being inflicted every day. Thus, when we discover salient, ongoing negative behavior, we pinpoint it as a target of immediate change. A number of studies have shown that negative behavior has a stronger association with satisfaction levels than does positive behavior (for example, Broderick & O'Leary, 1986). Thus, a relatively low number of very negative interactions may have the effect of wiping out a greater number of positive interactions. In addition, destructive behavior that is severely distressing in its own right may occur. This is behavior that is so negative in itself as to become a focus of dissatisfaction independent of the issue that elicited it. In particular, we have found that verbal and physical aggression, threats to terminate the relationship, derogating references, high levels of criticism and blame, or behaviors that unilaterally produce severe disruption of marital routine (such as not coming home at night or leaving the house after arguments) can be extremely destructive for both the marriage and the depressed spouse. If allowed to occur, they will completely stop or at least severely impede progress in therapy. We conceptualize these maladaptive behaviors as almost always being methods, albeit coercive methods, of dealing with problems in the relationship (Patterson & Reid, 1970). However, these methods themselves prevent any progress in dealing with the underlying problems. Therefore, we put great emphasis on eliminating these destructive behaviors as early in therapy as possible. When we do so, we emphasize to our clients that this early "suppression" of negative behaviors is not the eventual goal of marital therapy. We assure them that we will deal with problems in therapy but in a much different way, and in a context that allows for positive feelings to coexist with problem discussions. Thus, partners are not asked to "make sacrifices" or "compromises" at this early stage in therapy. They are, however, asked to stop some forms of negative behavior that will prevent them from finding effective ways to deal with problems.

For most moderately discordant couples (Dyadic Adjustment Scale [DAS] scores between 50 and 97), the salient negative behaviors we make the focus of early directives are essentially voluntary and controllable given the context of a program of therapy aimed at resolving grievances in the near future. For some severely discordant couples (DAS scores between 10 and 50), it is our impression that the severely maladaptive behavior patterns that tend to preclude an initial positive focus sometimes may be less voluntary and controllable. For these couples, the therapist's directive to change, even coupled with a strong rationale and reassurance about addressing problems later in the course of therapy, may not be sufficiently potent to produce change. While there is little concrete evidence at present regarding this issue, our clinical impression is that severely discordant couples often show repeated breakthroughs of the high-intensity disruptive interactions described earlier. For these couples, it may be necessary to alter the course of therapy to use structured individual interventions aimed at increasing each spouse's self-control of disruptive behavior before a dyadic focus can prove useful (compare with Jacobson & Margolin, 1979). Alternatively, it may sometimes be possible to effectively address these high-intensity negative interactions by using cognitive marital therapy techniques currently being developed (compare with Baucom & Epstein, 1990; Beach & Bauserman, 1990). A third alternative with these severely discordant couples is suggested by the observation that in some of these cases lifting the depressive episode will occur only if the decision is made to divorce or separate. Thus, it may be appropriate in some cases to focus on individual therapy for the depressed patient and support the process of disengaging from the relationship.

2. INCREASING COHESION: CARING GESTURES

Couples presenting with the joint problems of marital discord and depression appear to be particularly likely to show low levels of couple cohesion (Beach, Nelson, & O'Leary, 1988). These couples tend to be low in the type of shared positive activity expected to have antidepressant properties (Lewinsohn & Arconad, 1981). By addressing cohesion early in therapy, the therapist is attempting to bring about a rapid shift in the amount of positive, enjoyable time spent together by the couple and increase the rate of positive exchange and ongoing displays of affection. The techniques most appropriate for this goal are drawn from the pool of support-understanding strategies currently available to marital therapists (Weiss, 1978). These strategies are particularly useful for the depressed and discordant couple because they are designed to reverse the cycle of coercion and withdrawal exhibited prominently by these couples and to reintroduce fun and mutual involvement.

One of the most valuable techniques in the therapist's armamentarium for enhancing the deteriorated cohesion of the depressed, discordant couple is the prescription of increased caring gestures (Stuart, 1980; Weiss & Birchler, 1978) or "couple pleases" and companionship activities (Jacobson & Margolin, 1979). Caring gestures and "couple pleases" focus on mutual relationship pleasures that the spouses agree on. Caring gestures are any behaviors designed to please the partner and, in so doing, indicate love and caring (for example, kiss of greeting, hold hands). The behaviors to be increased should already be within the response repertoire of the spouses; that is, no new learning should be required in this phase. Also, these are typically rather small actions that could be repeated often. The goal of a caring gestures focus in therapy is to increase the frequency of already learned responses that are readily available but currently underused. Similarly, companionship activities are joint activities that are enjoyable or have been enjoyable for the couple in the past. Companionship activities are typically somewhat larger actions than caring gestures, possibly involving going on a date or talking about each other's day. Once again, however, they should be relatively simple and not require new learning.

Creating a good caring gesture list may take one or more sessions. The exercise of having each spouse generate possible caring items for himself or herself and for the partner is also an excellent introduction to objectification (Weiss, 1978) and rudimentary communication skills. We typically have the couple work together to create one master list of caring items that contains all the items generated by each partner individually as well as by the two of them together. We cut out the center of a normal 8 1/2" x 11" pad of paper and write the items generated on the last page of the pad. The "flaps" of the cut-out pad allow each spouse to monitor his or her own performance of caring items on a daily basis.

It is particularly important that no particular item on the list ever be mandatory. All behaviors are to be exchanged freely and without coercion. This allows more items to be included, with fewer concerns about possible negative reactions. In fact, it can be pointed out that the larger the pool of items the more options each spouse has. Sometimes couples will wonder whether they can add items later. While this type of continuing creative involvement in the assignment should be encouraged, spouses should also be encouraged to bring the new items into the session before actually writing them on the list.

B. Second Phase of Therapy: Enhancing Communication and Interaction

If the first phase of therapy has gone well, the couple will have already shown an enhancement of cohesion and self-esteem support. Simultaneously, stressors associated with spousal denigration, concern over a partner's leaving the relationship, and ongoing disruption of scripted marital behavior will have subsided to a large extent. Although these areas typically continue to require some work, they need less intense, ongoing therapist attention. Thus, the therapist can begin to attend to other relevant relationship areas such as (1) increasing acceptance of emotional expression, (2) increasing the frequency and breadth of intimate exchanges, (3) enhancing perceived and actual coping assistance, (4) enhancing the perception of spousal dependability, (5) continuing to decrease sources of stress within the relationship, and (6) working on special problem areas of the couple. Problems in each of the areas can be glossed over by spouses in the first flush of successful marital change. However, if they are not dealt with during the course of therapy, the marital discord model would predict rapid relapse of marital discord or depressive symptomatology following termination.

1. COMMUNICATION TRAINING

Unfortunately, our clinical experience suggests that encouraging the couple to refocus on more prob-lematic areas of the relationship will commonly result in a temporary increase in felt marital dissatisfaction. Typically, there is a rapid response to the reduction of marital stressors and focus on enhancing marital cohesion and self-esteem support. However, there is a reliable dip in reported satisfaction as the couple begins to focus more on problem areas. We have found it useful to predict this temporary reaction and to interpret it as a normal part of the therapy process. This approach seems to help couples see their fluctuating marital satisfaction in context and prevents catastrophizing.

Nearly all of our depressed, discordant couples receive communication training in one form or another aimed at increasing their ability to accept and listen to their partners. It is common for maritally discordant and depressed spouses to fail to listen to each other in a caring and attentive manner. Nondepressed husbands report that their wives' complaining or whining is aversive and that it has led to avoidance of problem discussion on their part. Depressed wives report that whenever they begin to discuss their feelings they find their husbands "tuning them out." The nondepressed husband also tends to see problem expression and complaining by the depressed wife as a sign of disaffiliation or rejection of the relationship, while she may see this behavior as a means of drawing closer (compare with Guthrie, 1988, cited in Weiss & Heyman, 1990). Thus, misunderstanding and misperception can compound an already poor exchange of information.

Listener skills.   The husbands in our depressed couples have often offered a minimal response or no response to their wives' complaints, as if they believed their lack of response would make the complaining go away. However, such nonresponse has only served to further aggravate their already deteriorated marital situation (Gottman & Krokoff, 1989). On the other hand, depressed wives have often been no better at listening to their husbands than their husbands were at listening to them. Commonly, when a husband would begin to discuss his view of a marital issue, the depressed wife would cut him off or immediately begin to vent emotions in response. This emotional venting serves to powerfully inhibit further discussion on the husband's part, thereby feeding into his pattern of nonresponsiveness and further fueling the vicious cycle of negative exchange and withdrawal. Conversely, in some couples the partner of the depressed person would feel compelled to "cheer up" the depressed individual by giving suggestions about how he or she could feel better and downplaying the seriousness of the complaints voiced (compare with Stephens, Hokanson, & Welker, 1987). Usually, this leads the depressed person to feel misunderstood, angry, and more depressed. Although the fear of the nondepressed spouse is that simply listening to the depressed partner and responding with empathy will increase the depression ("It will only encourage her"), we have found the opposite to be true. When the depressed wife feels that her husband is truly listening to her feelings and problems, she feels more hopeful and feels closer to him (compare with Guthrie, 1988). Accordingly, for both of these patterns, empathic listening training is potentially an effective antidote, one that both spouses need if acceptance of emotional expression is to be available within the context of the dyad. In addition, good listening skills often further increase the level of cohesion in the dyad, allowing for increased self-esteem support, increased perceived availability of spousal support, enhanced couple problem solving, and the development of greater intimacy. Therapists often initiate a number of beneficial processes by increasing empathic listening early in the middle stage of therapy.

It usually makes sense to introduce summarizing skills by first focusing on developing skills at the level of primary empathy (Egan, 1986). This type of summarizing is very content-oriented. Only as this skill is mastered are more inferential, secondary-level empathic statements encouraged. As each spouse begins to practice listening skills, we have found it most effective to focus on one or two relatively salient issues. Typically, this is as much as clients can handle, and focusing on the most salient issues allows clients to perceive more easily that they are changing and making progress.

Feedback.   Giving feedback to a depressed individual must be done with special care. It must be remembered that the depressed person will tend to interpret feedback in a personal and global manner, perhaps concluding: "I can't do anything right; even my therapist says so." The therapist should try to find a positive aspect of the person's performance to comment on along with a negative aspect. The therapist might say something like, "Susan, I like how you kept your voice calm. That was good. But you didn't really summarize my statement. Instead you responded with your own statement. Let's try it again. Keep your nice, calm voice and try to focus on summarizing what I say." Only after the clients have observed the therapist demonstrating the skill and after they have successfully tried it with the therapist role-playing the partner are they encouraged to try it with each other. By starting communication training using the therapist first as a model and then as a surrogate partner, we decrease the likelihood of unsuccessful experiences with the spouse.

Typically, we proceed through an informal hierarchy of problem topics over the course of several sessions, saving more difficult or "hotter" topics for later in therapy when the couple is better equipped to deal with them constructively. If a couple has one or two big issues with which they have struggled unsuccessfully for a long time, we would ask them to "put those issues on the back burner" during the early training phases and use less emotionally charged topics to teach the skills. Since this is difficult for many clients to accept, we have found it helpful to give an actual estimate of a time when the problem issue will be approached.

Speaker skills.   We usually begin by teaching listener skills, despite the fact that spouses are generally equally poor in speaker and listener skills, because we have found that empathic listening is the area that, if changed, has the greatest impact on the depressive cycle. However, it requires almost superhuman powers to maintain empathic listening skills in the face of very poor speaker skills. If the speaker continues to engage in name-calling, derogation, and accusation, and continues to be rambling, vague, and agitated, it is highly unlikely that good listening skills will show maintenance over the long run. Accordingly, guidelines for keeping statements brief and clear are introduced early in communication training.

2. PROBLEM SOLVING

One of the greatest factors influencing the actual coping support forthcoming from the spouse as well as the perceived availability of coping support from the spouse is the extent to which spouses can engage in resolving problems jointly and constructively. Problem-solving training can help to increase the ability of the partners to provide this kind of concrete aid to each other.

It is appropriate to begin problem-solving training when couples have a solid foundation in the speaker and listener skills outlined previously. Because many conflicts are triggered by trivial issues, it is often the process of communication, rather than its content, that leads to the conflict. However, there remain those disagreements that are unsolvable without using the techniques of problem solving. We teach our clients a slightly modified version of the D'Zurilla and Goldfried (1971) model of problem solving. Considerable useful detail on problem solving as a therapeutic modality can also be found in D'Zurilla (1988) and Nezu, Nezu, and Perri (1989). Gains in problem-solving skills may well be central to successful marital therapy for depression since depressed spouses routinely self-report poor problem-solving skills (Christian, O'Leary, & Vivian, 1991).

3. SPECIAL PROBLEMS

Couples present with a variety of concerns in addition to their concerns about their marriage and about the depression being experienced by one or both spouses. Concerns may be raised about long-standing sexual difficulties, such as orgasmic or erectile problems. Concerns may be expressed about previous episodes of extramarital sexual relationships or prior episodes in which one spouse left the home for some period of time. During routine assessment, issues of one or both spouses' use of drugs or alcohol may emerge as salient problem areas. Likewise, it is not uncommon for couples to have questions about how best to handle problems their children are experiencing. In each of these cases, the therapist will need to determine the relative importance of working on one problem as opposed to another. In every case, the therapist will need to realize that not all problems can be worked on at the same time. Therefore, the therapist

and the couple must agree on the order in which problems should be addressed. Most typically, we have found that it is easier to address sexual problems after improvement has occurred both in level of discord and depression. Conversely, when physical abuse is an issue, we have often found it necessary to deal with the abuse at the outset of therapy. Likewise, when alcohol or drugs are being abused, this pattern may need to be among the first issues addressed. Whenever auxiliary issues are to be dealt with in therapy, the therapist must make a clinical decision about the needs of the particular couple and the way in which the auxiliary issues can best be dealt with. It is probably never appropriate simply to assume that these other problems will disappear entirely once the marital problems have been adequately resolved. Rather, it may be necessary to extend the course of therapy to allow a focus on these issues either before or after working on improving the marital relationship in general.

C. Third Phase of Therapy: Enhancing Maintenance

Although maintenance of gains is always a concern for therapists, it is even more of a concern when working with a depressed, discordant population. If it is the case that amelioration of marital stressors and improvement in marital sources of support are important for the prevention of future episodes of depression, then a relapse into marital discord is doubly dangerous. It not only represents a relapse in relationship problems but also poses the threat of a relapse in depression for one or both partners. In addition, it increasingly appears that relapse is relatively common at longer lags posttherapy for discordant couples receiving BMT (Jacobson, Schmaling, & Holtzworth-Munroe, 1987). Thus, for this approach to treatment, the issue of relapse must be considered critical and not yet completely resolved.

We have attempted to address the problem of maintenance of gains after marital therapy of depression with several techniques used during the final phase of therapy. These include fading out the directive role of the therapist, narrowing the scope of therapy to the issues that prove to be most important for the particular couple, and reinforcing problem solving as a skill the couple can use to prevent future difficulties or use to continue making positive changes in their relationship. Additionally, we have included a discussion of "booster sessions." Booster sessions are regularly scheduled sessions that take place several weeks or months after the end of therapy. The underlying assumption behind the inclusion of booster sessions is that the use of skills taught in marital therapy for depression is liable to decrease without explicit efforts at renewal. In addition, couples may be vulnerable to external sources of stress that were not envisioned while therapy was ongoing. Thus, booster sessions allow the therapist to continue working with the couple at a much reduced intensity to further facilitate positive change and prevent relapse (Jacobson, 1989).

Attitudes and expectations regarding the end of therapy also must receive explicit attention, and the therapist must work hard to equip clients with realistic, functional expectations regarding the likely course of their marriage and their moods after the termination of therapy.

As soon as our clients have mastered the rudiments of communication and problem solving, we attempt to sharply curb the extent of the therapist's directiveness. This results in a decrease in the amount of talking done by the therapist in later sessions as compared with earlier ones. In the end state of therapy, the therapist will typically spend most of the therapy hour listening to the clients recount their week, talk to each other (not the therapist) about difficulties or positive experiences they had, and problem solve when necessary. The therapist will guide the interaction by suggesting that the spouses use certain skills or by pinpointing difficulties they are having in communication (for example, "Why don't you try validating Sharon on this, Jack, before you work on problem solving?")

As the therapist is fading out his or her directiveness, the focus of therapy should also be narrowing. Whereas the early and middle phases of therapy presented a variety of techniques to the couple, the final phase should be restricted to practicing those interventions that proved most effective for the particular couple. Again, this narrowing may not be ideal in the eyes of the therapist, who may see that the couple never quite mastered a skill that they could really use. However, the therapist must be realistic about the

capacities of the couple and the length of therapy. It is essential that the therapist help the couple depart therapy with a sense of closure. The final phase of therapy is a time to build on what they have accomplished during the earlier phases, not dwell on what was not accomplished.

For many couples, the best method of addressing new relationship issues or problems as they arise is to use the problem-solving framework they learned in therapy. However, not every couple must use the formal steps of problem solving to benefit from the general problem-solving attitude. Again, during the final phase of therapy we try to reinforce whatever level of problem-solving ability the couple has demonstrated previously. The essential thing for couples to take with them at termination is the realization that there are solutions or partial solutions to problems and that it is worthwhile to try to find them. In addition, therapy should have served to normalize the process of change within the marriage. Asking for wanted changes in a spouse's behavior should have become an accepted part of the relationship by the end of therapy. The major focus of the final stage of therapy can be reinforcing this pattern of raising issues for discussion directly and nonaggressively.

V. Individual Approaches with Maritally Discordant and Depressed Persons

Both social skills training and cognitive therapy for depression have a place in the treatment of persons presenting with marital discord and depression. At a minimum, these individually focused approaches are useful when the nondepressed spouse refuses to participate in therapy or when the depressed patient declines to involve their spouse or when the couple decides to separate or divorce. In addition, our clinical experience suggests that individual therapy is indicated for depressed persons who are acutely suicidal (O'Leary, Sandeen, & Beach, 1987). There is also some basis for suspecting that individual approaches may be the treatment of choice for more severe depression occurring in the context of mild marital discord. We will discuss these issues in more detail as we describe the available outcome work. First, however, we briefly describe each of these widely used behavioral approaches to the treatment of depression.

A. Social Skills Training

This approach to the treatment of depression is conceptually similar to marital therapy for depression in that it is based on the assumption that the social environment is pivotal in the development and maintenance of depression (Becker & Heimberg, 1985). It is proposed that a person having well-developed social skills will show only mild mood disturbance when the interpersonal environment is disrupted, and even this mood disturbance dissipates as the individual takes appropriate corrective action. Conversely, someone with less well-developed social skills might manifest increasingly greater mood disturbance over time because he or she fails to take the appropriate corrective action.

Indeed, depressed persons show a number of deficits in interpersonal behavior that render them more likely to be rejected by others (compare with Coyne, 1976). Accordingly, social skills are likely to be a reasonable target of intervention for many depressed persons. For depression occurring in the context of marital discord, however, we suspect this approach will prove most relevant when marital disruption is already a fait accompli. In these cases, a focus on marital dynamics is likely to be judged fruitless by both patient and clinician. However, exposure to new social situations and support in learning new ways to navigate the changed social environment may seem very appropriate. In addition, social skills training is an approach with documented effectiveness for unipolar depressed women (Bellack, Hersen, & Himmelhoch, 1983; Hersen, Bellack, Himmelhoch, & Thase, 1984).

The clinician attempting to apply social skills training will conduct a thorough assessment of the social environment and the level of interpersonal skill shown by the depressed patient. The specific targets for treatment are typically arranged in a hierarchy based on the patient's report of their subjective difficulty (see Becker, Heimberg, & Bellack, 1987, for more detail). Four types of social skills training procedures are used. First, *direct behavior training* is used to teach basic verbal and nonverbal skills. Second, *practice* is assigned to ensure application of each skill to problem areas. Third, *social perception training* is conducted to increase the salience of important social cues. And fourth, *self-evaluation and self-reinforcement training* is used to change the individual's negative judgments about his or her social performance.

B. Cognitive Therapy

This approach to the treatment of depression is based on the cognitive model of depression, which assumes, in part, that depression occurs when there is vulnerability resulting from depressive schemata and specific stresses, especially stresses that resemble earlier experiences that promoted learning the depressive schemata. There is considerable data supporting the presence of negative statements about the self and cognitive distortions among depressed persons. In addition, cognitive factors appear central in the maintenance of ongoing episodes of depression (Dent & Teasdale, 1988; O'Hara, Rehm, & Campbell, 1982). We suspect that cognitive therapy will be most useful in the treatment of depressed, maritally discordant spouses who believe their depression has caused their marital problems (O'Leary, Risso, & Beach, 1990) and whose marital problems are mild in comparison to their level of self-reported cognitive distortion (Beach & O'Leary, 1992). Reviewed here are two studies that included individual cognitive therapy as a comparison treatment. In both cases, as marital discord lessened, any advantage of marital therapy relative to cognitive therapy lessened as well.

The clinician attempting to apply cognitive therapy for depression will apply a series of therapeutic techniques designed to identify, reality-test, and correct distorted conceptualizations or beliefs. In correcting negative cognitions, the depressed individual learns to overcome obstacles and handle situations previously believed to be overwhelming. Ultimately, the patient is helped to correct the underlying schemata that are presumed to confer the vulnerability to future episodes of depression. More specifically, after carefully assessing symptoms of depression and possible suicidal ideation, the clinician will present the cognitive model of depression and highlight the possibility that much of the patient's current self-criticisms and sense of failure may be signs of depression rather than accurate reflections of ongoing events. Activity scheduling is often used in cognitive therapy and may well involve assignments that overlap in content with those assigned in either marital or social skills training approaches. However, typically the focus of activity scheduling is to increase opportunities for mastery and pleasure and to precipitate opportunities to do cognitive work. After clients have been helped to identify and challenge an array of ongoing dysfunctional cognitions, it is typical for the cognitive therapist to identify a common theme in the dysfunctional cognitions and help the client rethink the underlying propositions. This is presumed to decrease vulnerability to similar dysfunctional cognitions in the future (see Beck, Rush, Shaw, & Emery, 1979, for more detail).

VI. Outcome of Marital Interventions for Depression

Individual approaches to depression are at a fundamental disadvantage in dealing with persons in discordant relationships. Because only one person is attending therapy, it is difficult to change dyadic patterns of interacting. Accordingly, individual work with depressed, discordant couples may be successful in relieving a depressive episode but leave the person in a dysfunctional marital relationship. For most depressed patients, remaining in a destructive marital relationship will prove difficult and lead to elevated levels of divorce (Merikangas, 1984) or create a climate conducive to symptomatic relapse and residual symptomatology (Hooley & Teasdale, 1989). Outcome research examining response to marital intervention for depression suggests that it may be a better alternative for the treatment of co-occurring marital discord and depression in many cases.

A. Early Investigations of Dyadic Treatment with Heterogeneous Populations

Several studies have addressed the issue of spousal involvement in therapy and its potential utility in alleviating depressive symptomatology. For example, McLean, Ogston, and Grauer (1973) demonstrated the superiority of a focused behavioral marital intervention over alternative treatments available in the community (for example, medication, group therapy, individual therapy, and combinations of the former) for a population of apparently discordant, depressed patients. The authors did not use standard measures of marital satisfaction and did not select for maritally discordant couples. However, they reported the presence of marital disputes in all couples. The authors also did not assess depressive symptoms per se. However, they were able to show significant improvement in depressed mood on the Depression Adjective Checklist (Lubin, 1965), improvement on target behaviors, and improvement on positiveness of communication for the group treated with a form of marital therapy. Thus, while diagnostic questions, measurement issues, and the nonstandard nature of the marital intervention limit the interpretability of the study, it still must be viewed as a pioneering study suggesting the potential for marital therapy in the treatment of depression.

Another early controlled study of marital therapy for diagnosed depression was reported by Friedman (1975). While this study is often cited as evidence of the effectiveness of marital therapy for depression, the effects demonstrated were actually quite modest. When analyses using only "completers" of therapy were reported, marital therapy actually looked nonsignificantly worse than placebo–minimal contact on the global rating of therapy outcome. Even when the more favorable analysis—which included drop-outs across all conditions—was reported, marital therapy displayed a rather weak effect on depressive symptoms and on relationship behavior. It is probably only the striking weakness displayed by the antidepressant medication group that allowed the author to say anything positive about marital therapy for depression. It is worth noting, however, that no effort was made in this study to separate maritally discordant from nondiscordant couples. Our expectation is that this should have resulted in the inclusion of a large group of probable nonresponders in the marital therapy condition (compare with Jacobson, Dobson, Fruzzetti, Schmaling, & Salusky, 1991). In addition, the group was very heterogeneous with regard to diagnoses (which were pre–DSM-III diagnoses in any case). The heterogeneity with regard to Axis I and Axis II diagnoses could also increase variability in response to treatment. Thus, while only minimally positive in outcome, the marital therapy study reported by Friedman (1975) was encouraging of further investigation of marital therapy for depression.

Another study that was encouraging of a marital approach to the treatment of psychiatric disorders, including depression, was reported by Hafner, Badenoch, Fisher, and Swift (1983). In this study, patients with a wide variety of psychiatric disorders of a severe and persisting nature were treated with either a marital or an individual approach to therapy. Psychiatric symptoms in general were improved somewhat more by the marital interventions than by the individual approaches. However, it is particularly interesting that individual therapy was found to be associated with improvement in symptomatic status, even while producing an overall increase in marital problems, and increased depression for both partners at a three-month follow-up. Thus, while not a study of a particular diagnostic category, the results once again suggest the promise of a marital approach to the treatment of depression and the likely ineffectiveness of individual approaches in resolving marital disputes.

These early studies, while encouraging, had various limitations that precluded their being taken as a solid foundation for recommending marital therapy for the treatment of depressed, discordant couples. The early studies typically indicated that they had employed one form or another of nonstandard or very loosely specified interventions. Likewise, it was unclear from these studies that individuals meeting current diagnostic criteria for major depressive episode, unipolar type, could benefit from marital approaches.

Building on the foundation of these earlier studies, several outcome studies have examined reasonably well-specified examples of marital therapy for depression and compared their effectiveness to well-specified and widely used individual approaches. Four outcome studies that included specified treatments, random assignment to condition, diagnosis based on structured interview, and assessment of change at posttreatment in level of both marital satisfaction and depression have been reported in the literature. However, one of these studies is better considered pilot work (Beach & O'Leary, 1986) due to its small size and so is not reviewed in detail here.

We will examine the results of each of the other currently available outcome studies in turn.

B. Outcome Work with Depressed Outpatients

1. O'LEARY AND BEACH (1990)

O'Leary and Beach (1990) randomly assigned 36 couples to either individual cognitive therapy (CT), conjoint behavioral marital therapy (BMT), or a 15-week waiting list condition. Both partners had to score in the discordant range of the dyadic adjustment scale as well as present themselves as being discordant. In each couple, the wife met diagnostic criteria for major affective disorder. At both posttherapy and one-year follow-up, CT and BMT were found to be effective in reducing depressive symptomatology. Indeed, at posttherapy 67% of those who received individual cognitive therapy and 83% of those who received marital therapy no longer met the initial symptom level criteria for inclusion in the study (that is, Beck Depression Inventory scores were below 14). There was no significant difference between marital therapy and individual cognitive therapy in terms of effect on depressive symptomatology. However, only BMT was found to be effective in improving the marital relationship. At posttherapy, 25% of persons receiving individual cognitive therapy in contrast to 83% of those receiving behavioral marital therapy had at least 15-point pre-post increases in the marital satisfaction according to the Dyadic Adjustment Scale (Spanier, 1976). The same general pattern of results held at follow-up; that is, both the decreases in depression and the increases in marital satisfaction were maintained for at least one year following treatment.

What can be concluded from this study? If replicated in other labs, the results suggest that individual cognitive therapy (and perhaps other individual behavioral approaches as well) can be a very acceptable intervention for depression occurring in the context of marital discord. Remarkably, this appears to be true even in the face of continuing marital discord. There was no evidence that individual cognitive therapy for depression resulted in increased guilt, shame, or increased depression for study participants. Indeed, cognitive therapy appeared to be quite effective at alleviating these symptoms. However, cognitive therapy was not routinely effective in enhancing marital satisfaction.

At one-year follow-up, the results obtained at posttherapy were maintained, both by the couples who had received marital therapy and by those who had received individual cognitive therapy. There was no significant difference between the two treated groups on level of depression, but there continued to be a significant advantage for the marital therapy condition in level of marital satisfaction. The primary advantage of marital therapy documented in this study is its ability to effectively reduce depressive symptomatology while enhancing marital satisfaction.

Interestingly, subsequent work (O'Leary, Risso, & Beach, 1990) suggests that the unique advantage of marital therapy in producing better outcome on marital measures may be restricted to a subset of the overall population of maritally discordant and depressed— that is, those depressed, discordant couples who reported that their marital problems preceded the onset of their depression. Conversely, depressed, discordant couples who reported that the depressed partner's symptoms preceded the onset of their marital problems responded well to both cognitive therapy and marital therapy, showing improvements both in depressive symptomatology and in marital satisfaction. It appears, then, that persons reporting that their depression preceded their marital discord may respond very well to individual therapy (and also to marital therapy).

2. JACOBSON, DOBSON, FRUZZETTI, SCHMALING, AND SALUSKY (1991)

A recent study conducted by Jacobson and colleagues further suggests that the effects of individual cognitive therapy on depression may be quite robust with regard to the presence of marital discord but also suggest that behavioral marital therapy may have some unique benefits among the maritally discordant-depressed. Jacobson, Dobson, Fruzzetti, Schmaling, and Salusky (1991) randomly assigned 60 married women who had been diagnosed depressed to either individual cognitive therapy, behavioral marital therapy, or a treatment combining BMT and CT. Couples were not selected for the presence of marital discord. Accordingly, it was possible to examine directly the

effect of marital therapy for nondiscordant, depressed couples. Contrary to the authors' predictions, it was found that marital therapy was not helpful for persons who were not maritally discordant. Only persons with at least some significant marital complaints were benefited by marital therapy alone. However, a treatment combining individual cognitive therapy (6 to 12 sessions) with behavioral marital therapy (8 to 14 sessions) was the only condition to produce statistically significant improvement among nondiscordant couples. Accordingly, there may be some merit to including some conjoint sessions focused on the marital relationship even for depressed patients who do not appear maritally discordant.

Replicating O'Leary and Beach (1990), it was found that, within the more discordant half of the sample, BMT was just as effective as CT in reducing depression. Also replicating O'Leary and Beach (1990), it was found that only BMT was successful in enhancing marital satisfaction among discordant, depressed couples. Finally, as in O'Leary and Beach (1990), CT was effective in reducing depressive symptomatology even among the maritally discordant, depressed. However, Jacobson et al. (1991) found no unique advantage of marital therapy over cognitive therapy among the discordant, depressed, with individual cognitive therapy and marital therapy differing nonsignificantly at posttherapy both on measures of depression and on measures of marital discord. No data on long-term follow-up are presented. Thus, the basic analyses suggest that individual cognitive therapy is better than marital therapy for some depressed persons (the nondiscordant, depressed) and as good as marital therapy even for the discordant, depressed.

A major limitation of the Jacobson et al. (1991) study, however, is that there were very few couples in which both members of the dyad met the usual cut-off for marital discord on the Dyadic Adjustment Scale (DAS < 97). In addition, couples were not seeking marital therapy, and so many may not have viewed themselves as having serious marital problems. Although there were too few participants to allow meaningful between-groups comparisons, the authors report some comparisons within and between the small groups of "truly discordant" (both spouses'

DAS < 97) couples. They report that the magnitude of change in marital satisfaction among the "truly discordant" who received marital therapy was greater than that observed in the larger "somewhat distressed" sample. In addition, only BMT showed a significant impact on the marital satisfaction of the truly discordant, while cognitive therapy did not. Also of interest, all the truly discordant persons receiving marital therapy recovered from their depressive episodes, while this was not true of the larger "somewhat distressed" sample, nor was it true of all truly discordant persons receiving individual cognitive therapy. Given this reanalysis, the Jacobson et al. (1991) study again suggests the possibility of unique advantages for marital therapy when administered to a depressed and clearly maritally discordant population.

3. FOLEY, ROUNSAVILLE, WEISSMAN, SHOLOMASKAS, AND CHEVRON (1989)

A third study of direct relevance to marital therapy for co-occurring marital discord and depression has been conducted by Foley, Rounsaville, Weissman, Sholomaskas, and Chevron (1989). In this study, 18 depressed outpatients were randomly assigned to either individual interpersonal psychotherapy (IPT) (Klerman, Weissman, Rounsaville, & Chevron, 1984) or a newly developed couple format version of IPT. Patients appear to have been only slightly more symptomatic than in the O'Leary and Beach (1990) study or the Jacobson et al. (1991) study, but spouses appear to have been considerably more symptomatic, with 78% of spouses having a lifetime history of some form of psychiatric disorder. Unlike the other two studies discussed, patients in this investigation were allowed to be either gender rather than being restricted to wives only. Accordingly, the sample consisted of 5 male and 13 female patients. Individual IPT is designed to handle marital disputes among other interpersonal problems, so the use of a conjoint format represented a minor change only in the format of therapy.

Foley et al. (1989) found that the inclusion of the spouse in cases where there were ongoing marital disputes was well received by patients and, even in their very small sample, resulted in marginally greater improvement in the marital relationship than did the

standard individual format for IPT. Conversely, both formats produced significant and comparable reductions in symptoms of depression. Of interest, given the previous discussion, is the fact that depressed wives had mean Dyadic Adjustment Scale scores of 103 and 90.9 at intake in the individual and conjoint formats, respectively. Given the suggestion of Jacobson et al. (1991) that moderately discordant couples may show a greater advantage in marital therapy than do very mildly discordant couples, it seems possible that the sample may not have been sufficiently discordant to demonstrate the full potential of the conjoint format. Nonetheless, the obtained results suggest that the pattern reported by O'Leary and Beach (1990) and replicated by Jacobson et al. (1991) in his "truly discordant" subsample may be generalizable to other couple formats as well. That is, direct attention to dyadic processes in structured directive couples therapy may enhance marital functioning while providing relief of depressive symptomatology comparable to standard individual treatments. Because follow-up data were not reported, this study also fails to address the relative merits of the two formats in terms of maintenance of gains.

What can be concluded from this study? Again, an individual treatment, in this case interpersonal therapy, appears to be a very robust intervention for depression even in the context of ongoing (mild) marital discord. In addition, however, there is a tantalizing suggestion, based on a small number of participants and marginally significant results, that the conjoint format may offer greater potential for enhancing marital functioning than does the individual format.

4. SUMMARY

Taken together, the studies provide a strong basis for arguing that conjoint format interventions for the maritally discordant and depressed may have some unique benefits with maritally discordant and depressed persons. The apparent consistency in the results, particularly for couples in which both partners are reporting significant levels of marital discord, should excite advocates of marital therapy for depression. Certainly, the results are sufficiently encouraging to support further investigation of the potential effectiveness of marital therapy for depression. At present, the advantage of using marital interventions for depression rather than individual interventions appears to lie primarily in the fact that marital intervention for depression may be more efficient in persons with co-occurring marital discord and depression. For the truly discordant, marital therapy may resolve both marital discord and depression simultaneously.

C. Outcome Work with Depressed Inpatients

As the outcome literature reviewed suggests, behavioral marital therapy for depression is a promising intervention modality for outpatients presenting both depression and concurrent marital discord. However, there is evidence, albeit indirect evidence, that use of conjoint formats for depressed inpatients may be problematic. Two studies have investigated spousal involvement in the treatment of depressed inpatients. In the first, Waring (1988) reported that 27 female inpatients diagnosed with major affective disorder (DSM-III criteria) were randomly assigned to either a conjoint approach labeled "cognitive self-disclosure" or to a control condition involving supportive psychotherapy. In both conditions, the depressed person was given an antidepressant medication in addition to therapy. Waring (1988) reports both a high drop-out rate in the conjoint condition and nonsignificantly poorer resolution of depressive symptoms. In the second study, Clarkin, Haas, and Glick (1988) examined the effectiveness of a brief psychoeducational and problem-focused intervention aimed at helping spouses of hospitalized patients cope with the hospitalization. Fifty inpatients with either unipolar or bipolar depression were randomly assigned to either the conjoint treatment (inpatient family intervention, IFI) or standard hospital treatment. There was no overall main effect of IFI on global functioning. However, a trend emerged at six months and reached significance ($p < .05$) at 18 months, indicating an interaction between treatment condition and diagnosis. For bipolar patients there was better outcome with IFI, while for unipolars there was better outcome with the comparison treatment. Thus, spousal involvement was not shown to be helpful for patients with unipolar depression. In both studies, inpatient unipolar depressives fared more poorly when spouses were involved in

treatment than when they were excluded. It is not clear in either case that the patients were complaining of prominent marital concerns. Nor was behavioral marital therapy used as the intervention approach. Perhaps an inpatient sample selected for discord might have responded favorably to conjoint BMT. Alternatively, it may be that marital approaches are more difficult to implement with severely depressed patients (compare with Foley et al., 1989) and so should be used in hospital settings with more severely depressed patients only after symptomatic recovery is already under way (compare with O'Leary, Sandeen, & Beach, 1987). Accordingly, the use of conjoint and marital approaches with inpatient populations requires additional study before it can be recommended.

VII. Can Depression Be Prevented?

Several cognitive behavioral–type programs have been designed to help engaged and newlywed couples learn skills to decrease future marital discord. These programs include Guerney's Relationship Enhancement Program (see Guerney, 1977), the Minnesota Couples Communication Program (see Miller, Nunally, & Wackman, 1975), and the Premarital Relationship Enhancement Program (PREP) (see Markman, Floyd, Stanley, & Jamieson, 1984). The focus of all three programs is teaching communication, problem solving, and other skills important in decreasing long-term relationship stress and enhancing support within the marriage. Each program targets areas of relationship functioning identified in the marital discord model of depression; therefore, to the extent the programs are effective, the logic of the model implies that they should also confer some level of protection from episodes of depression.

Hahlweg and Markman (1988) did an effect-size (ES) analysis of the empirical work on behavioral premarital intervention (BPI). In the BPI versus control (pre-post), the seven studies used had a mean of the averaged effect sizes of 0.79. Accordingly, it can be said that the average couple in the BPI group was better off at the end of intervention than 79% of the control participants (p. 443). For BPI versus different control groups, the three studies had an attention-placebo control group, and four studies compared BPI with waiting list control groups. The effect size was 0.55 for nontreatment controls and 1.12 for attention-placebo controls (p. 444). When Hahlweg and Markman compared BPI on observational versus self-report measures, they found greater effect sizes for observational measures, 1.51 versus 0.52 (p. 444). Accordingly, couple behavior change may be more robust than changes in perceptions of the relationship. Alternatively, there may be a "ceiling effect" on the self-report measures because couples are already happy in their relationships at premarital assessment.

Hahlweg and Markman (1988) also computed effect sizes for the stability of treatment gains. The analysis of follow-up data from 9 and 18 months after participation showed that effect sizes decreased over time. The Markman group (Renick, Blumber, & Markman, 1992) has five-year follow-up data of 42 PREP couples and 50 control couples. They found that at five years PREP husbands had significantly less negative escalation in interactions with their wives, whereas PREP wives showed no difference in communication skills compared to controls. As far as marital satisfaction goes, Markman et al. (1987) found PREP husbands to have greater relationship satisfaction than control husbands at five-year follow-up. PREP wives showed similar levels of marital satisfaction to control wives. Markman suggests that attenuation effects for wives points to the need for booster sessions as part of prevention. Caution must still be exercised, however, in suggesting premarital prevention programs as a cost-effective means of reducing depressive symptoms and perhaps episodes of depression. Replication research is required before confidence is placed in the ability of prevention programs to enhance long-term marital adjustment. The findings to date are sufficiently encouraging, however, to spur additional research in this area with the goal of developing premarital interventions targeted at the specific areas of marriage most relevant to depression.

erbates, maintains, or increases the probability of relapse of depressive episodes. While practical considerations will sometimes lead the clinician to use individual social skills training, cognitive therapy, or interpersonal therapy, it is often possible to initiate a course of marital therapy. Currently, available data suggest that behavioral marital therapy for depression is an effective means of addressing depression occurring in the context of marital discord. Behavioral marital therapy is well accepted by many couples in which one partner is depressed and is capable of reducing both marital difficulties and depressive symptomatology simultaneously. Although additional work is necessary to specify more exactly the parameters that predict better and worse response, it currently appears that behavioral marital therapy is most appropriate for couples whose marital problems are relatively more severe and longer standing than is the episode of depression. When marital problems are relatively mild or are reported to have started only after the onset of the depressive episode, individual approaches appear to be equally or more appropriate. The success of behavioral marital therapy for depression in conjunction with the large body of data linking marital discord and depression highlights the potential for prevention of some cases of depression through premarital programs aimed at enhancing long-term marital functioning.

At a minimum, the marital relationship is an important aspect of the interpersonal environment of depressed individuals. Early behavioral insights into the importance of enhancing this aspect of the depressed person's interpersonal environment (Lewinsohn, 1974) appear to have been well founded. Now that we can draw on the strength of 20 years of research on behavioral marital therapy, perhaps it is time for behavior therapists dealing with depression occurring in the context of marital discord to incorporate behavioral marital therapy into their clinical armamentarium.

VIII. Conclusion

Depression often occurs in the context of ongoing marital discord. In many cases, marital conflict exac-

References

ARKOWITZ, H., Holliday, S., & Hutter, M. (1982). *Depressed women and their husbands: A study of marital interaction and adjustment.* Paper presented at the annual meeting of the Association for the Advancement of Behavior Therapy, Los Angeles, CA.

BARLING, J., MacEwen, K. E., & Kelloway, E. K. (1991, November). *Effects of short term role overload on marital interactions.* Paper presented to the 25th annual convention of the Association for the Advancement of Behavior Therapy, New York, NY.

BAUCOM, D. H., & Epstein, N. (1990). *Cognitive-behavioral marital therapy.* New York: Brunner/Mazel.

BEACH, S. R. H., Abramson, L. Y., & Levine, F. M. (1981). Attributional reformulation of learned helplessness and depression: Therapeutic implications. In J. F. Clarkin & H. I. Glazer (Eds.), *Depression: Behavioral and directive intervention strategies* (pp. 131–165). New York: Garland.

BEACH, S. R. H., & Bauserman, S. A. K. (1990). Enhancing the effectiveness of marital therapy. In F. O. Fincham & T. N. Bradbury (Eds.), *The psychology of marriages* (pp. 349–374). New York: Guilford Press.

BEACH, S. R. H., & Fincham, F. D. (1994). Towards an integrated model of negative affectivity in marriage. In S. M. Johnson & L. S. Greenberg (Eds.), *Emotion in marriage and marital therapy* (pp. 227–255). New York: Brunner/Mazel.

BEACH, S. R. H., Jouriles, E. N., & O'Leary, K. D. (1985). Extramarital sex: Impact on depression and commitment in couples seeking marital therapy. *Journal of Sex and Marital Therapy, 11,* 99–108.

BEACH, S. R. H., Martin, J. D., Blum, T. C., & Roman, P. M. (1993). Effects of coworker and marital relationships on negative affect: Testing the central role of marriage. *American Journal of Family Therapy, 21,* 312–322.

BEACH, S. R. H., & Nelson, G. M. (1990). Pursuing research on major psychopathology from a contextual perspective: The example of depression and marital discord. In G. Brody & I. E. Sigel (Eds.), *Family research: Volume II* (pp. 227–259). Hillsdale, NJ: Erlbaum.

BEACH, S. R. H., Nelson, G. M., & O'Leary, K. D. (1988). Cognitive and marital factors in depression. *Journal of Psychopathology and Behavioral Assessment, 10,* 93–105.

BEACH, S. R. H., & O'Leary, K. D. (1986). The treatment of depression occurring in the context of marital discord. *Behavior Therapy, 17,* 43–49.

BEACH, S. R. H., & O'Leary, K. D. (1992). Treating depression in the context of marital discord: Outcome and predictors of response for marital therapy versus cognitive therapy. *Behavior Therapy, 23,* 507–528.

BEACH, S. R. H., Sandeen, E. E., & O'Leary, K. D. (1990). *Depression in marriage: A model for etiology and treatment.* New York: Guilford Press.

BECK, A. T., Rush, A. J., Shaw, B. F., & Emery, G. (1979). *Cognitive therapy of depression.* New York: Guilford Press.

BECKER, R. E., & Heimberg, R. G. (1985). Social skills training approaches. In M. Hersen & A. S. Bellack (Eds.),

Handbook of clinical behavior therapy with adults (pp. 365–395). New York: Plenum.

BECKER, R. E., Heimberg, R. G., & Bellack, A. S. (1987). *Social skills training treatment for depression.* New York: Pergamon Press.

BELLACK, A. S., Hersen, M., & Himmelhoch, J. M. (1983). A comparison of social skills training, pharmacotherapy and psychotherapy for depression. *Behaviour Research and Therapy, 21,* 101–107.

BIGLAN, A., Hops, H., Sherman, L., Friedman, L. S., Arthur, J., & Osteen, V. (1985). Problem solving interactions of depressed women and their spouses. *Behavior Therapy, 16,* 431–451.

BIGLAN, A., Lewin, L., & Hops, H. (1990). A contextual approach to the problem of aversive practices in families. In G. R. Patterson (Ed.), *Depression and aggression in family interaction* (pp. 103–129). Hilsdale, NJ: Erlbaum.

BLANEY, P. H. (1986). Affect and memory: A review. *Psychological Bulletin, 99,* 229–246.

BOWER, G. H. (1981). Mood and memory. *American Psychologist, 36,* 129–148.

BOWER, G. H. (1991). Mood congruity of social judgements. In J. P. Forgas (Ed.), *Affect emotion and social judgements* (pp. 31–53). Oxford: Pergamon Press.

BRODERICK, J. E., & O'Leary, K. D. (1986). Contributions of affect, attitudes and behavior to marital satisfaction. *Journal of Consulting and Clinical Psychology, 54,* 514–517.

BROWN, G. W., & Harris, T. (1978). *Social origins of depression: A study of psychiatric disorders in women.* New York: Free Press.

CHRISTIAN, J. L., O'Leary, K. D., & Vivian, D. (1991, November). *Discriminating between depressed and nondepressed maritally discordant spouses.* Paper presented to the 25th annual convention of the Association for the Advancement of Behavior Therapy, New York, NY.

CLARK, M. S., Milberg, S., & Ross, J. (1983). Arousal cues arousal-related material in memory: Implications for understanding effects of mood on memory. *Journal of Verbal Learning and Verbal Behavior, 22,* 633–649.

CLARKIN, J. F., Haas, G. L., & Glick, I. D. (1988). Inpatient family intervention. In J. F. Clarkin, G. L. Haas, & I. D. Glick (Eds.), *Affective disorders and the family* (pp. 134–152). New York: Guilford Press.

COYNE, J. C. (1976). Depression and the response of others. *Journal of Abnormal Psychology, 85,* 186–193.

COYNE, J. C., Kessler, R. C., Tal, M., Turnbull, J., Wortman, C. B., & Greden, J. F. (1987). Living with a depressed person. *Journal of Consulting and Clinical Psychology, 55,* 347–352.

DENT, J., & Teasdale, J. D. (1988). Negative cognition and the persistence of depression. *Journal of Abnormal Psychology, 97,* 29–34.

DERRY, P. A., & Kuiper, N. A. (1981). Schematic processing and self-reference in clinical depression. *Journal of Abnormal Psychology, 90,* 286–297.

DIENER, E. (1984). Subjective well-being. *Psychological Bulletin, 95*, 542–575.

D'ZURILLA, T. J. (1988). *Problem-solving therapy: A social competence approach to clinical intervention.* New York: Springer.

D'ZURILLA, T. J., & Goldfried, M. R. (1971). Problem solving and behavior modification. *Journal of Abnormal Psychology, 78*, 107–126.

EGAN, G. (1986). *The skilled helper: A systematic approach to effective helping.* Pacific Grove, CA: Brooks/Cole.

FINCHAM, F. D., Beach, S. R. H., & Nelson, G. M. (1987). Attribution processes in distressed and non-distressed couples: 4. Self-partner attribution differences. *Journal of Personality and Social Psychology, 52*, 739–748.

FINCHAM, F. D., & Bradbury, T. N. (1988a). The impact of attributions in marriage: Empirical and conceptual foundations. *British Journal of Clinical Psychology, 27*, 77–90.

FINCHAM, F. D., & Bradbury, T. N. (1988b). The impact of attributions in marriage: An experimental analysis. *Journal of Social and Clinical Psychology 7*, 147–162.

FOLEY, S. H., Rounsaville, B. J., Weissman, M. M., Sholomaskas, D., & Chevron, E. (1989). Individual versus conjoint interpersonal therapy for depressed patients with marital disputes. *International Journal of Family Psychiatry, 10*, 29–42.

FORGAS, J., Bower, G., & Moylan, S. (1990). Praise or blame? Affective influences on attributions for achievement. *Journal of Personality and Social Psychology, 59*, 809–819.

FRIEDMAN, A. (1975). Interaction of drug therapy with marital therapy in depressive patients. *Archives of General Psychiatry, 32*, 619–637.

GOTLIB, I. H. (1981). Self-reinforcement and recall: Differential deficits in depressed and non-depressed psychiatric inpatients. *Journal of Abnormal Psychology, 90*, 521–530.

GOTLIB, I. H. (1983). Perception and recall of interpersonal feedback: Negative bias in depression. *Cognitive Therapy and Research, 7*, 399–412.

GOTTMAN, J. M., & Krokoff, L. J. (1989). Marital interaction and satisfaction: A longitudinal view. *Journal of Consulting and Clinical Psychology, 57*, 47–52.

GUERNEY, B. G. (1977). *Relationship enhancement.* San Francisco, CA: Jossey-Bass.

GUTHRIE, D. M. (1988). *Husbands' and wives' expressiveness: An analysis of self-evaluations, perceptions of expressiveness and emotional cues.* Unpublished doctoral dissertation, University of Queensland, St. Lucia, Australia. Cited in Weiss & Heyman (1990).

HAFNER, R. J., Badenoch, A., Fisher, J., & Swift, H. (1983). Spouse-aided versus individual therapy in persisting psychiatric disorders: A systematic comparison. *Family Process, 22*, 385–399.

HAHLWEG, K., Baucom, D. H., & Markman, H. J. (1988). Recent advances in therapy and prevention. In I. R. H. Falloon (Ed.), *Handbook of behavioral family therapy* (pp. 413–448). New York: Guilford Press.

HAHLWEG, K., & Markman, H. J. (1988). Effectiveness of behavioral marital therapy: Empirical status of behavioral techniques in preventing and alleviating marital distress. *Journal of Consulting and Clinical Psychology, 56*, 440–447.

HAUTZINGER, M., Linden, M., & Hoffman, N. (1982). Distressed couples with and without a depressed partner: An analysis of their verbal interaction. *Journal of Behaviour Therapy and Experimental Psychology, 13*, 307–314.

HERSEN, M., Bellack, A. S., Himmelhoch, J. M., & Thase, M. E. (1984). Effects of social skills training, amitriptyline, and psychotherapy in unipolar depressed women. *Behavior Therapy, 15*, 21–40.

HINCHLIFFE, M., Hooper, D., & Roberts, F. J. (1978). *The melancholy marriage.* New York: Wiley.

HOOLEY, J. M. (1986). Expressed emotion and depression: Interactions between patients and high vs. low expressed-emotion spouses. *Journal of Abnormal Psychology, 95*, 237–246.

HOOLEY, J. M. (1990). Expressed emotion and depression. In G. I. Keitner (Ed.), *Depression and families* (pp. 64–94). Washington, DC: American Psychiatric Press.

HOOLEY, J. M., & Hahlweg, K. (1986). The marriages and interaction patterns of depressed patients and their spouses: Comparison of high and low EE dyads. In M. J. Goldstein, I. Hand, & K. Hahlweg (Eds.), *Treatment of schizophrenia: Family assessment and intervention* (pp. 157–178). Berlin: Springer-Verlag.

HOOLEY, J. M., Orley, J., & Teasdale, J. D. (1986). Levels of expressed emotion and relapse in depressed patients. *British Journal of Psychiatry, 148*, 642–647.

HOOLEY, J. M., & Teasdale, J. D. (1989). Predictors of relapse in unipolar depressives: Expressed emotion, marital distress, and perceived criticism. *Journal of Abnormal Psychology, 98*, 229–237.

ILFELD, F. W. (1976). Methodological issues in resulting psychiatric symptoms to social stressors. *Psychological Reports, 39*, 1251–1258.

JACOBSON, N. S. (1989). The maintenance of treatment gains following social learning-based marital therapy. *Behavior Therapy, 20*, 325–336.

JACOBSON, N. S., Dobson, K., Fruzzetti, A. E., Schmaling, K. B., & Salusky, S. (1991). Marital therapy as a treatment for depression. *Journal of Consulting and Clinical Psychology, 59*, 547–557.

JACOBSON, N. S., & Margolin, G. (1979). *Marital therapy: Strategies based on social learning and behavior exchange principles.* New York: Brunner/Mazel.

JACOBSON, N. S., Schmaling, K. B., & Holtzworth-Munroe, A. (1987). Component analysis of behavioral marital therapy: 2-year follow-up and prediction of relapse. *Journal of Marital and Family Therapy, 13*, 187–195.

JOHNSON, M. H., & Magaro, P. A. (1987). Effects of mood and severity on memory processes in depression and mania. *Psychological Bulletin, 101*, 28–40.

KAHN, J., Coyne, J. C., & Margolin, G. (1985). Depression and marital disagreement: The social construction of despair. *Journal of Social and Personal Relationships, 2*, 447–461.

KLERMAN, G. L., Weissman, M. M., Rounsaville, B. J., & Chevron, E. S. (1984). *Interpersonal psychotherapy of depression*. New York: Basic Books.

KOWALIK, D. L., & Gotlib, I. H. (1987). Depression and marital interaction: Concordance between intent and perception of communication. *Journal of Abnormal Psychology, 96*, 127–134.

LEWINSOHN, P. M. (1974). A behavioral approach to depression. In R. J. Friedman & M. M. Katz (Eds.), *The psychology of depression: Contemporary theory and research* (pp. 157–185). Washington, DC: Winston.

LEWINSOHN, P. M., & Arconad, M. (1981). Behavioral treatment of depression: A social learning approach. In J. F. Clarkin & H. I. Glazer (Eds.), *Depression: Behavioral and directive intervention strategies* (pp. 33–67). New York: Garland.

LEWINSOHN, P. M., & Atwood, G. E. (1969). Depression: A clinical research approach. *Psychotherapy: Theory, Research, and Practice, 6*, 166–171.

LEWINSOHN, P. M., & Shaffer, M. (1971). Use of home observations as an integral part of the treatment of depression: Preliminary report and case studies. *Journal of Consulting and Clinical Psychology, 37*, 87–94.

LUBIN, G. (1965). Adjective checklist for the measurement of depression. *Archives of General Psychiatry, 12*, 57–62.

MANDLER, G. (1984). *Mind and body: Psychology of emotion and stress*. New York: Norton.

MARKMAN, H. J., Duncan, S. W., Storaasli, R. D., & Howes, P. W. (1987). The prediction of marital distress: A longitudinal investigation. In K. Hahlweg & M. Goldstein (Eds.), *Understanding major mental disorder: The contribution of family interaction research* (pp. 266–289). New York: Family Process Press.

MARKMAN, H. J., Floyd, F. J., Stanley, S. M., & Jamieson, K. (1984). A cognitive-behavioral program for the prevention of marital and family distress: Issues in program development and delivery. In K. Hahlweg & N. S. Jacobson (Eds.), *Marital interaction* (pp. 253–281). New York: Guilford Press.

McLEAN, P. D., Ogston, K., & Grauer, L. (1973). A behavioral approach to the treatment of depression. *Journal of Behavior Therapy and Experimental Psychiatry, 4*, 323–330.

MERIKANGAS, K. R. (1984). Divorce and assortative mating among depressed. *American Journal of Psychiatry, 141*, 74–76.

MILLER, S., Nunally, E. W., & Wackman, D. B. (1975). *Alive and aware: Improving communication in relationships*. Minneapolis, MN: Interpersonal Communication Program.

MONROE, S. M., Bromet, E. J., Connell, M. M., & Steiner, S. C. (1986). Social support, life events, and depressive symptoms: A one year prospective study. *Journal of Consulting and Clinical Psychology, 54*, 424–431.

NELSON, G. M., & Beach, S. R. H. (1990). Sequential interaction in depression: Effects of depressive behavior on spousal aggression. *Behavior Therapy, 12*, 167–182.

NEZU, A. M., Nezu, C. M., & Perri, M. G. (1989). *Problem-solving therapy for depression: Theory, research and clinical guidelines*. New York: Wiley.

O'HARA, M. W., Rehm, L. P., & Campbell, S. B. (1982). Predicting depressive symptomatology: Cognitive-behavioral models and post-partum depression. *Journal of Abnormal Psychology, 91*, 457–461.

O'LEARY, K. D., & Beach, S. R. H. (1990). Marital therapy: A viable treatment for depression and marital discord. *American Journal of Psychiatry, 147*, 183–186.

O'LEARY, K. D., Risso, L. P., & Beach, S. R. H. (1990). Attributions about the marital discord/depression link and therapy outcome. *Behavior Therapy, 21*, 413–422.

O'LEARY, K. D., Sandeen, E., & Beach, S. R. H. (1987, November). *Treatment of suicidal, maritally discordant clients by marital therapy or cognitive therapy*. Paper presented at the 21st annual meeting of the Association for Advancement of Behavior Therapy, Boston, MA.

PATTERSON, G. R., & Reid, J. B. (1970). Reciprocity and coercion: Two facets of social systems. In C. Neuringer & J. L. Michael (Eds.), *Behavior modification in clinical psychology* (pp. 133–177). New York: Appleton-Century-Crofts.

PAYKEL, E. S. (1979). Recent life events in the development of the depressive disorders. In R. A. Depue (Ed.), *The psychology of the depressive disorders: Implications for the effects of the stress* (pp. 245–262). New York: Academic Press.

PAYKEL, E. S., Myers, J. K., Dienelt, M. N., Kierman, G. L., Lindenthal, J. J., & Peper, M. P. (1969). Life events and depression: A controlled study. *Archives of General Psychiatry, 21*, 753–760.

PAYKEL, E. S., & Tanner, J. (1976). Life events, depressive relapse, and maintenance treatment. *Psychological Medicine, 6*, 481–485.

PIETROMONACO, P. R., & Rook, K. S. (1987). Decision style in depression: The contribution of perceived risks and benefits. *Journal of Personality and Social Psychology, 52*, 399–408.

RENICK, M. J., Blumber, S. L., & Markman, H. J. (1992). The prevention and relationship enhancement program (PREP): An empirically based preventive intervention program for couples. Unpublished manuscript. University of Denver, Denver, CO.

ROUNSAVILLE, B. J., Weissman, M. M., Prusoff, B. A., & Herceg–Baron, R. L. (1979). Marital disputes and treatment outcome in depressed women. *Comprehensive Psychiatry, 20,* 483–490.

RUSCHER, S. M., & Gotlib, I. H. (1988). Marital interaction patterns of couples with and without a depressed partner. *Behavior Therapy, 19,* 455–470.

RUTTER, M., & Quinton, D. (1984). Parental psychiatric disorder: Effects on children. *Psychological Medicine, 14,* 891–898.

SCHAEFER, E. S., & Burnett, C. K. (1987). Stability and predictability of quality of women's marital relationships and demoralization. *Journal of Personality and Social Psychology, 53,* 1129–1136.

SCHLESS, A. P., Schwartz, L., Goetz, C., & Mendels, J. (1974). How depressives view the significance of life events. *British Journal of Psychiatry, 125,* 406–410.

SCHMALING, K. B., & Jacobson, N. S. (1990). Marital interaction and depression. *Journal of Abnormal Psychology, 99,* 229–236.

SCHMALING, K. B., Whisman, M. A., Fruzzetti, A. E., & Truax, P. (1991). Identifying areas of marital conflict: Interactional behaviors associated with depression. *Journal of Family Psychology, 5,* 145–157.

SPANIER, G. B. (1976). Measuring dyadic adjustment: New scales for assessing the quality of marriage and similar dyads. *Journal of Marriage and the Family, 38,* 15–28.

STEPHENS, R. S., Hokanson, J. E., & Welker, R. (1987). Responses to depressed interpersonal behavior: Mixed reactions in a helping role. *Journal of Personality and Social Psychology, 52,* 1274–1282.

STUART, R. B. (1980). *Helping couples change: A social learning approach to marital therapy.* New York: Guilford Press.

SWINDLE, R. W., Cronkite, R. C., & Moos, R. H. (1989). Life stressors, social resources, coping, and the 4-year course of unipolar depression. *Journal of Abnormal Psychology, 98,* 468–477.

VAUGHN, C. E., & Leff, J. P. (1976). The influence of family and social factors on the course of psychiatric illness: A comparison of schizophrenic and depressed neurotic patients. *British Journal of Psychiatry, 129,* 125–137.

WARING, E. M. (1988). *Enhancing marital intimacy through cognitive self-disclosure.* New York: Brunner/Mazel.

WEISS, R. L. (1978). The conceptualization of marriage from a behavioral perspective. In T. Paolino, Jr., & B. McCrady (Eds.), *Marriage and marital therapy: Psychoanalytic, behavioral, and systems theory perspectives* (pp. 165–239). New York: Brunner/Mazel.

WEISS, R. L., & Birchler, G. R. (1978). Adults with marital dysfunction. In M. Hersen & A. S. Bellack (Eds.), *Behavior therapy in the psychiatric setting* (pp. 331–364). Baltimore: Williams & Wilkins.

WEISS, R. L., & Heyman, R. E. (1990). Marital distress and therapy. In A. S. Bellack, M. Hersen, & A. Kazdin (Eds.), *International handbook of behavior modification* (2nd ed., pp. 475–503). New York: Plenum.

WEISSMAN, M. M. (1987). Advances in psychiatric epidemiology: Rates and risks for major depression. *American Journal of Public Health, 77,* 445–451.

CHAPTER 5

Behavior Therapy with Lesbian and Gay Individuals

Gail S. Bernstein
Megan E. Miller

I. Introduction
II. History of Behavior Therapy with Lesbians
   and Gay Men
   A. Articles and Papers
   B. Clinical Practice
   C. Books
   D. Professional Organizations
   E. Summary
III. Case Formulation and Treatment
   A. Cultural and Institutional Contextual Variables
   B. Assessment and Case Formulation
      1. Assessing Contextual Variables
      2. Assessing Client Interpersonal and
         Intrapersonal Variables
      3. Selecting Treatment Goals
   C. Treatment
IV. Recommendations
   A. Research
   B. Training
   C. Professional Development
V. Conclusion
   References

I. Introduction

All mental health professionals, whether they know it or not, work with lesbian and gay clients. Further, gay men and lesbians are a significant minority of the population, usually estimated to be 10%.[1] There are nearly as many gay men and lesbians in the United States as there are African Americans, half again as many as Latinos, and more than three times as many as Jews (Kirk & Madsen, 1989). It is therefore essential that behavior therapists know how to apply their skills in ways that will be effective and useful with the 10% of their clients who are lesbian or gay.[2]

The topic of this chapter clearly resides at the intersection of science and values. Segal (1982) observed, "though nature is impersonal, data may be impersonal, science is not impersonal, nor is it value-free. Science is a human enterprise carried on by real people" (p. 2). Therapy, too, is always influenced by values based on the social and political context in which it occurs. For instance, during the 1800s clinicians theorized that freedom resulted in psychopathology for African Americans. One 19th-century physician argued for the existence of a form of psychopathology called "dysathesia aethiopica," also known as rascality. The symptoms were destroying plantation property, talking back, fighting with masters, and refusing to work (Landrine, 1988). This is a clear example of how self-protective and assertive behavior becomes pathologized when it is not consistent with existing

Preparation of this chapter was facilitated by Grant R01MH4419 from the National Institute of Mental Health to Richard G. Heimberg.

Correspondence concerning this article should be addressed to Richard G. Heimberg, Center for Stress and Anxiety Disorders, University at Albany, State University of New York, Pine West Plaza, Building 4, Washington Avenue Extension, Albany, New York 12205.

[1]Sexual orientation and sexual behavior are complex phenomena, and many people experience some combination of attraction toward, fantasies about, and sexual experience with members of both genders (Kinsey, Pomeroy, & Martin, 1948; Kinsey, Pomeroy, Martin, & Gebhard, 1953). Our focus in this chapter is on people who identify themselves as primarily or exclusively lesbian or gay and must therefore deal with the cultural meanings attached to same-gender orientations.

[2]Omission of the unique clinical issues relevant to bisexual individuals is deliberate. Those issues are, at least in part, distinct from the unique issues relevant to therapy with lesbian and gay individuals and therefore outside the scope of this chapter.

social biases. Confrontation of the oppressive behavior of members of the dominant culture by African Americans (or any other disenfranchised group) is trivialized by applying a label of psychopathology.

Social and cultural contexts continue to influence our work. "Both in our choice of goals and techniques, we make statements, often unwittingly, about how people should lead their lives" (Davison, 1991, p. 199). The ways in which lesbians and gay men are viewed and treated in this country, and the controversy over those views and behaviors, are directly reflected in the mental health literature in general, and the behavioral literature in particular, over the last 40 years. The primary purpose of this chapter is to provide behavior therapists with useful information about and a framework for addressing clinical issues unique to gay men and lesbians. The literature on this topic has changed dramatically since the early days of behavior therapy and is still evolving. Thus, the clinical section of this chapter is preceded by a brief history of behavior therapy with lesbians and gays.

II. History of Behavior Therapy with Lesbians and Gay Men

The applied behavioral literature of the 1950s and 1960s had very little to say about how behavior therapy might be used with gay men and lesbians. There was considerable literature generated by nonbehavioral therapists, and most of it was based on the assumption that to be lesbian or gay was to be inherently mentally ill. Given this assumption, it is not surprising that graduate students in psychology could be expelled for being gay or lesbian; these students found it necessary to pretend to be heterosexual to complete their degrees (Segal, 1982). A few exceptions to the view of lesbians and gay men as inherently ill did appear, such as Hooker's (1957) demonstration that evaluators who were blind to the sexual orientation of the participants could not discriminate Rorschach responses generated by gay men from responses generated by heterosexual men. Hooker's research foreshadowed the changes that were to follow.

The 1960s and 1970s were a time of social turmoil and emerging demands for increased civil rights and respect from a variety of disenfranchised groups, including people of color, women, people with disabilities, and lesbians and gay men. One impact of these civil rights movements was to influence mental health policy and services. The behavior therapy literature of that period reflected the broader social debate about sexual orientation.

A. Articles and Papers

Two main themes dominated the behavior therapy literature during the 1970s. One theme was conversion, pro and con. Specifically, numerous articles reported on the use of behavior therapy, usually aversive therapy, to reduce the sexual response of gay men to men and also often to increase the sexual response of gay men to female sexual stimuli. We found 21 published reports of this nature. All but two were published during the 1970s, and 20 of them reported on work with males, with one report on work with both males and females (Barlow & Agras, 1973; Canton-Dutari, 1976; Conrad & Wincze, 1976; Feldman & MacCulloch, 1965; Freeman & Meyer, 1975; Herman, Barlow, & Agras, 1974; Ince, 1973; James, 1978; James, Orwin, & Turner, 1977; LoPiccolo, 1971; Mac-Culloch, Burtles, & Feldman, 1971; Maletzky, 1977; Marshall, 1975; McConaghy, 1970; McConaghy, Armstrong, & Blaszczynski, 1981; McCrady, 1973; Rehm & Rozensky, 1974; Sambrooks, MacCulloch, & Waddington, 1978; Sandford, Tustin, & Priest, 1975; Tanner, 1974, 1975).

Meanwhile, Davison and his colleagues were questioning whether behavioral attempts at conversion therapy were an acceptable way to treat gay men and lesbians (for example, Davison, 1976, 1978; Davison & Friedman, 1982; Davison & Wilson, 1973; Wilson & Davison, 1974). Davison's (1976) presidential address at the meeting of the Association for the Advancement of Behavior Therapy in 1974 addressed suggestions that it was acceptable to try to change an individual's sexual orientation if the client chose to change (for example, Phillips, Fischer, Groves, & Singh, 1976). Davison (1976), in considering that argument, pointed out:

> If we are to take the basic deterministic dictum of science seriously, however, we must come to grips with the conditions surrounding even those decisions in therapy that have hitherto been termed voluntary or free. (p. 162)

He pointed out that those who asked therapists to help them become heterosexual were not making a free choice but rather were reacting to a lifetime of cultural messages that they were sick, sinful, and ill. Further, he noted that therapist participation in conversion therapy condoned current societal prejudice. He concluded that behavior therapists should not be engaged in any attempt—regardless of the type of procedure used—to convert clients to heterosexuality.

During the same period, a small number of studies were conducted that offered positive alternatives to conversion therapy. We found three studies in which gay men were taught assertiveness skills (Duehn & Mayadas, 1976; McKinlay, Kelly, & Patterson, 1977; Russell & Winkler, 1977). These papers were examples of the vision Davison (1978) offered of alternatives to conversion therapy:

> It is one thing to say that one should not treat homosexuality: it is quite another to suggest that one should not treat homosexuals. Indeed, I have urged that therapists do finally consider the problems in living that homosexuals really have. Such problems are perhaps especially severe, given the prejudice against their sexual orientation. It would be nice if an alcoholic homosexual, for example, could be helped to reduce his/her drinking without having his/her sexual orientation questioned. It would be nice if a homosexual fearful of interpersonal relationships, or incompetent in them, could be helped without the therapist assuming that homosexuality lies at the root of the problem. It would be nice if a nonorgasmic or impotent homosexual could be helped as a heterosexual would be rather than guiding his/her wishes to change-of-orientation regimens. (p. 171)

During most of the 1980s, lesbian and gay men were, at least in print, almost invisible to behavior therapists. That situation is just beginning to change. Our literature search found a description of how stress inoculation training could be useful to lesbians and gay men (Hunter & Kelso, 1983), suggestions for using cognitive therapy with lesbians (Padesky, 1989), a description of the skills needed to use behavior therapy with lesbians (Miller & Bernstein, 1989), and a report on the treatment of retarded ejaculation in gay men (Wilensky & Myers, 1987). The remainder of the existing behavioral work with gays and lesbians is HIV-related.

Kelly and his colleagues have generated a series of papers related to the reduction of high-risk sexual behavior with gay men. Their work began with a discussion paper on how behavior therapists could contribute to the replacement of high-risk sexual behavior with safer alternatives (Kelly & St. Lawrence, 1986) and continued with data-based papers that include a report on a behavioral intervention intended to reduce the occurrence of high-risk sexual behavior (Kelly, St. Lawrence, Hood, & Brasfield, 1989a), a study designed to identify predictors of vulnerability to AIDS risk behavior relapse (Kelly, St. Lawrence, & Brasfield, 1991), a report on the development of an objective test of AIDS risk behavior knowledge (Kelly, St. Lawrence, Hood, & Brasfield, 1989b), and a study of psychological factors that predict AIDS high-risk versus AIDS precautionary behavior (Kelly et al., 1990). In addition, Coates, McKusick, Stites, and Kuno (1989) described a stress management training program aimed at improving immune function. The other HIV-related literature we found is not specific to gay men (for example, Schinke, Gordon, & Weston, 1990; Schmaling & DiClementi, 1991).

B. Clinical Practice

The reader of current behavior therapy literature might conclude that behavior therapists are no longer attempting to convert gay men and lesbians to heterosexuality. However, a careful reading of the recent American Psychological Association report, *Bias in Psychotherapy with Lesbians and Gay Men* (Committee on Lesbian and Gay Concerns, 1990), suggests otherwise. That report includes examples from a survey of 6580 psychologists, of whom 2544 responded. The survey included a request for descriptions of incidents where therapy was biased, inadequate, or inappropriate for a gay or lesbian client, as well as a request for descriptions of incidents where a therapist demonstrated special sensitivity to a lesbian or gay client. Examples of biased or inadequate treatment included the following:

> A friend told me a therapist insisted a gay man participate in aversive shock therapy to "overcome his problem." (p. 13)

I once heard a lecture by a man who used cognitive behavioral techniques to "help" homosexual men become heterosexual, and who stated that he would not work with a gay client who wanted to improve aspects of his life without giving up gayness. (p. 21)

> A [gay] clinical psychology student was required to get aversion therapy from a professor as a condition of his remaining in the program once he was discovered. (p. 21)

C. Books

Although most current behavioral literature does not advocate conversion therapy, there are exceptions. Some texts still refer to behavioral conversion therapy research without mentioning that such therapy is no longer considered ethically acceptable by the mental health professions. For instance, a popular text by one of the founders of behavior therapy discusses aversive conversion therapy for gay men and lesbians as if it were an acceptable therapeutic intervention (Wolpe, 1982).

The AABT Special Interest Group for the Study of Gay and Lesbian Issues was sufficiently concerned about continued references in the professional literature to behavioral conversion therapy that it recently passed a policy that states, in part:

> Any published reference to behavioral conversion therapy should *always* be accompanied by an acknowledgement that such treatment is inconsistent with current professional and ethical standards for clinical work with gays and lesbians. (Group for the Study of Gay and Lesbian Issues, 1991, p. 4)

The omission of important lesbian- and gay-related information from publications is yet another, less obvious form of bias. For example, the recent book *Suicide Risk: Assessment and Response Guidelines* (Fremouw, de Perczel, & Ellis, 1990) contains no mention of sexual orientation as a demographic risk indicator even though the U.S. Department of Health and Human Services Report of the Secretary's Task Force on Youth Suicide indicates that as many as 30% of all teen suicides in this country are committed by gay and lesbian youth and that lesbian and gay youth are two to three times more likely to attempt suicide than their heterosexual counterparts (Some Facts on Suicide and Gay Youth, 1990).

D. Professional Organizations

During the 1970s, nearly all the national professional organizations concerned with mental health made changes in organizational policies regarding lesbians and gay men. Both the American Psychological Association and the American Psychiatric Association acknowledged that homosexuality was not a mental disorder, and, in the spring of 1974, the Association for Advancement of Behavior Therapy (AABT) adopted the following resolution:

> The AABT believes that homosexuality is not in itself a sign of behavioral pathology. The Association urges all mental health professionals to take the lead in removing the stigma of mental illness that has long been attributed to these patterns of emotion and behavior. While we recognize that this long-standing prejudice will not be easily changed, there is no justification for a delay in formally according these people the basic civil and human rights that other citizens enjoy. (Davison, 1991, p. 199)

In spite of these changes, bias with respect to sexual orientation can still be a problem within our professional cultures. In 1979, Evelyn Segal put a notice in the Division 25 Recorder [3] asking who wanted to join her in forming a gay behaviorists support group. She received only two replies, one from a man and one from a woman. According to Segal, "The woman said in her letter that, as much as she'd like to join such a support group, she feared that joining such a group would be risking exposure and might cost her her career" (Segal, 1982, p. 7). (The first author of this chapter wrote that letter in 1979.) To the best of our knowledge, there has never been a group interested in studying gay and lesbian issues or a group for lesbian and gay behaviorists within either Division 25 or the AABT. There is, however, a Special Interest Group for the Study of Gay and Lesbian Issues within the AABT. It was first discussed at the 1979 AABT convention by several people who had attended a workshop on sex therapy with gay men and lesbians and was formally organized in 1980 by Charles Silverstein and Violet Franks.

At the 1989 AABT convention, we presented a poster on the competencies behavior therapists need to work effectively with lesbian clients (Miller & Bernstein, 1989). That poster was placed in the middle of a series of posters on sexual dysfunctions. Unfortunately, the inclusion of lesbians and gay men with sexual dysfunctions is a typical example of how the unfounded stereotype of gay men and lesbians as mentally ill is perpetuated. When both the Special Interest Group for the Study of Gay and Lesbian Issues and the Special Interest Group on Women's Issues in Behavior Therapy protested this action, they were assured that the placement of the poster was "not intended to offend or discriminate." Good intentions, however, do not repair the damage done by behaviors that perpetuate stereotypes.

E. Summary

The current status of behavioral literature regarding gay men and lesbians is mixed. On one hand, both data-based reports and discussion articles are starting to appear that are useful to behavior therapists seeking to provide effective services to their lesbian and gay clients. On the other hand, there is still considerable negative bias appearing in the literature and within professional organizations. This is a most unfortunate state of affairs for a variety of reasons. Behavior therapy has a great deal to offer the therapist who wants to serve gay men and lesbians effectively. While there is a large body of lesbian and gay affirmative clinical literature available elsewhere (for example, Eldridge, 1987; Gonsiorek, 1988; Martin, 1982; Roth & Murphy, 1986), much of it is not data-based. The remainder of this chapter addresses ways behavior analysis and therapy could make a positive contribution to the lives of gay men and lesbians.

III. Case Formulation and Treatment

The purpose of this section is to describe the unique clinical needs of lesbians and gay men, to propose a conceptual framework for functional analysis and case formulation specific to those needs, and to suggest ways behavior therapists can meet those needs. While the gay or lesbian client often presents with complaints similar to the presenting complaints of heterosexual clients (for example, depression, anxi-

---

[3]Division 25 of the American Psychological Association is the Division for the Experimental Analysis of Behavior.

ety), the origin of those complaints may be, at least in part, rooted in the following:

1. Coming-out issues: that is, issues around identifying oneself as gay or lesbian to oneself, friends, coworkers, and relatives

2. Internalized homophobia: negatively valued beliefs and thoughts about lesbians or gays, negative self-perceptions

3. External homophobia: the client's responses to external expressions of negative values about gay and lesbian individuals (for example, verbal censure, employment discrimination, verbal harassment, physical violence) from friends, relatives, coworkers, and the general public

4. Lesbian or gay social and sexual functioning: lack of skills in meeting, socializing with, and dating members of the same gender, lack of or incorrect knowledge about sexual functioning, erotophobia that functions as a survival mechanism

5. Relationship concerns: how to create successful relationships, how to manage problems unique to same-gender couples, how to maintain a relationship in the absence of social support or validation (Brown, 1988)

A comprehensive case formulation for a gay or lesbian client will include consideration of these issues and the contexts in which they arise; in addition, consideration of race, class, culture, ethnicity, gender, age, and all standard questions asked during case formulation for any client are essential. Our approach to case formulation has been influenced strongly by Rainwater's (1989) model, which defined cultural, institutional, interpersonal, and intrapersonal analyses as fundamental to a comprehensive functional analysis.

In one of the first texts on behavior analysis and therapy with women, Blechman (1984) noted that while the same basic mechanisms of behavior might occur in both genders, those mechanisms "operate in two different social environments, one male, one female" (p. xii). Similarly, while the principles of behavior apply regardless of sexual orientation, our lesbian and gay clients are treated very differently by the world in which they live than are their heterosexual counterparts. They may experience the world very differently. "When straight therapists do treat gays and lesbians, they often ignore or underestimate the

experiential gulf that separates therapist and client" (Markowitz, 1991, p. 28). One of the purposes of this chapter is to help behavior therapists, particularly heterosexual behavior therapists, attend to the contextual variables relevant to their lesbian and gay clients.

A. Cultural and Institutional Contextual Variables

Our basic premise is that the unique clinical issues gay men and lesbians present in therapy are the direct result of the negative value placed on their sexual orientation by the dominant culture in this country. Culture is "the totality of socially transmitted behavior patterns, arts, beliefs, institutions, and all of the products of human work and thought characteristic of a community or population" (Morris, 1979). One significant characteristic of the dominant culture in the United States is that heterosexuality is positively valued. Heterosexual marriage and bearing and rearing children in heterosexual families are encouraged, and lesbian and gay relationships and child-rearing are actively discouraged. Gay men and lesbians are usually portrayed negatively in popular movies, music, television, and books. Negative stereotypes abound, and false myths are perpetuated regularly. The following are some of those myths and stereotypes:

- People become lesbian and gay by being "recruited."
- All gay men are swishy hairdressers and interior decorators.
- All lesbians hate men, all gays and lesbians are pedophiles.
- Lesbians and gay men are perverted killers.
- All gay men and lesbians have AIDS.
- All lesbians wear leather and ride motorcycles.
- Gay men and lesbians only meet in dimly lit, seedy bars.
- To be lesbian or gay is to grow old lonely.
- All gay men and lesbians eventually commit suicide.

Same-gender sexual orientation is rarely discussed openly, and children learn at an early age to use negatively laden descriptors of gay men and lesbians (for example, queer, faggot, dyke) as insults.

Institutions are structures that implement cultural values and goals. Nearly all of the institutions lesbian women and gay men encounter emphasize the positive cultural values placed on heterosexuality and the negative value placed on same-gender orientation. These institutions include most aspects of the government at all levels, all branches of the military, nearly all spiritual and religious organizations, most places of employment, most schools, and virtually all financial institutions.

Marriage as an institution has been exclusively heterosexual and is supported by most other institutions in this country. It affords married couples elevated social status as well as positive financial rewards. The clear cultural message is that long-term couples are valued, but only if they are heterosexual. Gay male and lesbian couples do not have access to any of the financial, legal, or social benefits available to heterosexual couples and do not have widely recognized ways of creating, maintaining, or dissolving intimate relationships. Lesbians and gay men also are denied formal recognition of the nature of their loss when a partner dies; if the surviving partner is mentioned in a newspaper obituary, it is often at the end of a list of blood relatives. Given limited recognition and support, it is not surprising that lesbian and gay relationships tend to be shorter in duration than heterosexual relationships (Blumstein & Schwartz, 1983).

Governments have a variety of powerful means for transmitting cultural messages about gay men and lesbians. For instance, sodomy laws that criminalize anal and sometimes oral sex are often selectively enforced only against same-gender couples. Until 1961, all 50 states had antisodomy laws, and sodomy is currently prohibited between any two adults in 17 states and prohibited only when practiced by same-gender couples in five states (The Sodomy Laws, State by State, 1990). To date, there is no statewide protection from discrimination based on sexual orientation in 43 of the 50 states in the United States.

The contribution the mental health professions have made to perpetuating negative views of gay men and lesbians was described earlier. While the assumption that same-gender sexual orientation is inherently pathological is no longer officially sanctioned, bias against lesbians and gay men is still common (Committee on Lesbian and Gay Concerns, 1991). Garfinkle and Morin (1978) found, for instance, that psychotherapists rated the same hypothetical therapy client differently depending on the client's sexual orientation, with both gay and lesbian clients rated as less psychologically healthy than their heterosexual counterparts.

B. Assessment and Case Formulation

1. Assessing Contextual Variables

The cultural and institutional context described previously shapes the environments within which our lesbian and gay clients function. However, the effects of that context vary among individuals. Our working hypothesis is that the intensity, frequency, and duration of exposure to cultural, institutional, and interpersonal expressions of negative values experienced by lesbian and gay individuals are directly related to the type and severity of clinical problems, such as internalized homophobia. For instance, gay men and lesbians raised in families where there is frequent involvement in and commitment to religions holding rigid negative views of lesbians and gay men (that is, as sinful and condemned to burn in hell) appear to have more severe internalized homophobia than those raised in spiritual traditions with less rigidly held negative views. We do not have nearly as much data regarding these hypotheses as we need, but the data that do exist are consistent with our hypothesis. Schneider, Faberow, and Kroks (1989), for instance, found that gay men who had been suicidal had more rejecting social supports, were more closeted, and depended more on rejecting social supports than gay men who had not been suicidal.

The interaction between exposure to negative cultural values and the client's other belief systems is also important. Women and men who view themselves as intensely patriotic and who join a branch of the military are at risk for psychological suffering through exposure to acts of military homophobia (for example, experiencing or observing involuntary discharge, based solely on sexual orientation, of otherwise successful military personnel) (Salholz, Glick, & Gordon, 1992).

The values conveyed by the client's family of origin also appear to play a significant role in the creation of internalized homophobia. These values may include religious condemnation, considerable concern about what others will think if there is a lesbian or gay family member, devaluation of same-gender relationships, expressions of repulsion, and rejection.

If the client is a member of an ethnic culture that is different from the majority culture, a comprehensive case formulation must consider the values that the minority culture conveys about same-gender sexual orientation as well as the values conveyed by the majority culture. The potential for isolation and increased discrimination is of particular concern for a client who comes out as gay or lesbian and then feels unwelcome in her or his home culture by virtue of sexual orientation and unwelcome in lesbian and gay communities due to racism (Lukes & Land, 1990). Another form of isolation may occur when individuals decide to stay hidden to avoid ostracism in both their home cultures and the gay and lesbian communities.

A further consideration is whether there are or have been significant sexual orientation-related current events that influence the client's life. The most well-known example is the AIDS epidemic. The Centers for Disease Control (1992) report a cumulative total of 209,171 adult and adolescent cases since data collection began. Of those, 64% are men who had sex with other men. For adults and adolescents more than two years postdiagnosis, the case fatality rate is greater than 50%; for those more than four years postdiagnosis, the case fatality rate is greater than 80%. The consequences of the epidemic for gay men and lesbians are overwhelming; most men have lost dozens of friends and acquaintances. The situation is similar for lesbians who interact regularly with gay men. Although there is somewhat less public hysteria than in the mid-1980s, the public reaction to the epidemic is still predominantly homophobic. For example, people with AIDS are often judged to be "innocent victims" and provided with social support only if they are not gay men. This is clearly prejudicial and specific to sexual orientation; people who engage in life-threatening behaviors such as smoking are not similarly condemned. It is important for the therapist to ask specific questions about the client's involvement with people with AIDS—questions such as how many lovers and friends have died or are currently sick, and how involved the client is in work, paid or volunteer, with people with AIDS. Specific questions are needed because many gay men and lesbians have become habituated to years of living in the midst of the epidemic and may not be aware of how it has affected them psychologically.

Another example of a current event that may significantly affect lesbians and gay men occurred recently in Colorado. In the November 1992 election, an amendment to the state constitution was passed that legalizes discrimination against gay men and lesbians in Colorado. The amendment not only eliminates all existing civil rights protection for lesbian and gay Coloradans but also prohibits any future legislation designed to protect basic civil rights based on sexual orientation. The frequency and intensity of harassment and assaults of gay men and lesbians has increased dramatically since the passage of this amendment. While hate crimes reported to the Gay and Lesbian Community Center of Colorado averaged 11 per month for the first nine months of 1992 (Castrone, 1992), 45 were reported in November of that year (S. Anderson, personal communication, December 11, 1992). Undoubtedly, there will be a profound effect on the mental health of lesbians and gay men as a result of the passage of the amendment.

Contextual assessment must also include questions about the client's involvement, if any, with gay and lesbian cultures. There are numerous possibilities, particularly in large metropolitan areas (for example, reading affirmative literature, having lesbian and gay friends, going to social events such as parties and concerts, volunteering, belonging to clubs, political action, patronizing gay and lesbian bookstores, and going to gay and lesbian bars, to name a few). This information is important for the therapist because it indicates whether the client may have positive models and support available as well as places to go where it is safe to be open about his or her sexual orientation. Few positive models are available outside the lesbian and gay community, because it is still too easy to be fired or evicted if you publicly acknowledge your same-gender sexual orientation. People with the most to lose (for example, income, prestige, or position) are often the most closeted.

In summary, one key aspect of a comprehensive evaluation with a lesbian or a gay client is consideration of the messages about sexual orientation conveyed by the cultural and institutional contexts in which the client functions as well as the historical contexts that have contributed to the client's current concerns.

2. Assessing Client Interpersonal and Intrapersonal Variables

One of the most important unique developmental tasks for gay men and lesbians is construction of a sophisticated decision-making process about disclosure of sexual orientation, including potential harm and potential benefits (Gonsiorek, 1988). A thorough assessment for a lesbian or gay client must include assessment of skills at managing complex and potentially dangerous interpersonal situations specific to sexual orientation. These include but are not limited to skills in coming out as gay or lesbian to oneself, to friends, to family, and to coworkers as well as the ability to respond to questions from strangers and casual acquaintances about relationship status, marital status, and living situation. Assessment should also ask whether the client has the skills needed to function effectively in gay and lesbian social settings. Most heterosexual socialization does not adequately teach lesbians and gay men the required skills. Lesbians, for example, may need to learn how to initiate nonsexual friendships with other women, as distinct from dating, a skill not usually emphasized for women in this society.

Assessment of the client's beliefs and attitudes about being lesbian or gay is also important. The client may subscribe, to a greater or lesser extent, to any of the negatively valued beliefs about gay men and lesbians that we are all taught. Such beliefs often interfere with effective functioning. People who believe they are destined to be lonely in old age by virtue of their sexual orientation, for example, may be quite depressed.

3. Selecting Treatment Goals

The selection of treatment goals poses a special challenge for the therapist working with a gay or lesbian client because certain behaviors that might be defined as pathological in a heterosexual individual can be functional for lesbians and gay men. Paranoid, anxious, and suspicious behaviors, for example, are often functional survival skills for gay men and lesbians. Members of the armed forces, gay or lesbian parents (whose former spouses might use information about sexual orientation in a custody battle), and lesbians and gay men employed in child care, teaching, and other occupations involving contact with children face a significant risk; an anxious response to this risk may be quite adaptive.

Similarly, erotophobia may serve to protect the individual from negative external consequences such as loss of employment or from facing his or her own internalized homophobia. The more likely the external danger or the more severe the client's internalized homophobia, the more functional it may be to avoid becoming sexually aroused. That is why erotophobia should not be assumed to be evidence that the client is really heterosexual.

Another way in which therapists sometimes mistakenly assume a client is not really same-gender oriented is by confusing capacity for heterosexual arousal with a predominantly heterosexual orientation. Many individuals identify as primarily heterosexual but have occasional erotic thoughts or actual sexual interactions with members of the same gender. The converse is true for many people who identify as lesbian or gay.

C. Treatment

We noted earlier that there is little research available on the constructive use of behavior therapy with gay men and lesbians. Current practice, therefore, involves application of behavior therapies developed for other purposes to the treatment of the clinical problems we have described. Cognitive approaches, for instance, are the obvious choice for work on negative beliefs and thoughts about being lesbian or gay (Padesky, 1989). Social skills and assertiveness training procedures, such as direct instruction, rehearsal, feedback, and homework, can be used to remediate social skills deficits (for example, Duehn & Mayadas, 1976; Hunter & Kelso, 1983; McKinlay, Kelly, & Patterson, 1977). Stress inoculation may be of assistance to those who need skills in managing the stress of living in a society that devalues and discriminates against them (Hunter & Kelso, 1983). Sex therapy procedures can be easily adapted (for example, Loulan, 1984; Wilensky & Myers, 1987). Bibliotherapy and psychoeducational interventions are useful for clients who do not have accurate or practical information. Resources and assistance in entering lesbian and gay cultures are often indicated, sometimes in combination with anxiety reduction strategies. The more isolated the client, the more important it is to help the person make contact with social supports and healthy models. Sometimes information is all that is needed, while at other times a complex shaping process may be required (for example, start with readings or videos, then calls to a community center for information, then contact with nonthreatening groups such as Parents and Friends of Lesbians and Gays).

IV. Recommendations

Behavior therapy is clearly in the midst of a transition from a view of lesbians and gay men as inherently pathological to a stance that assumes there is nothing inherently pathological about same-gender sexual orientation. However, gay and lesbian clients may have specialized clinical needs related to their sexual orientation and relationships. We have described a conceptual model for case formulation and provided current knowledge about meeting those clinical needs. This section addresses strategies and goals for the continuing evolution of behavior therapy. This section may serve as a guide for behavior therapists to integrate research, training, and professional development to provide competent ethical therapy and to expand our knowledge base.

A. Research

Research is needed that investigates applications of existing behavior therapy and behavioral assessment strategies and procedures to clinical work with gay men and lesbians. There is a wealth of behavior therapy research available that is being applied clinically in work with lesbians and gay men. However, no research has been conducted that asks what, if any, modifications are needed in existing practices if they are to be maximally effective with gay men and lesbians. For instance, we do not know how well and under what conditions existing behavioral marital therapy procedures work with same-gender couples. Numerous behavioral assessment tools exist, such as forms and coding systems, but many of these tools were designed for heterosexual individuals and couples. We do not know which behavioral assessment procedures require modification, linguistic or otherwise, if they are to be used effectively with lesbians and gay men.

Research is needed on how behavior therapy can most effectively address problems unique to gay men and lesbians. For instance, are existing cognitive approaches to changing dysfunctional thoughts equally effective with internalized homophobic thoughts? Do our usual methods of teaching new social skills work well when we are teaching people how to function successfully in lesbian and gay communities? Do existing problem-solving strategies work for deciding how to tell one's parents that he or she is gay or lesbian?

Behavior therapy research should be designed to avoid heterosexual bias. Research questions should acknowledge the existence of lesbians and gay men (for example, as therapists and clients in clinical research) and avoid stereotypes that devalue or stigmatize. The difficult question of whether a sample of gay men or lesbians is representative enough to justify any sort of generalization must be addressed. Sexual orientation should be assessed in a manner appropriate to the sample and to the research question. Forms, interview questions, and experimental manipulations that assume all participants are heterosexual should not be used unless only heterosexual participants are explicitly recruited (and that recruitment strategy may attract closeted lesbian and gay participants). Issues related to confidentiality of participants must be carefully addressed given the lack of protection lesbian and gay individuals have from discrimination and prejudice. For a more detailed discussion of these issues, see Herek, Kimmel, Amaro, and Melton (1991).

Behavior therapy research is needed that addresses the different needs of lesbians and gay men. Gonsiorek (1988) suggests that gay men tend to be sexually active with men before developing a gay identity, whereas lesbians tend to develop emotional relationships and then a lesbian identity before becoming sexually active with women. Some clinicians have suggested that lesbian couples who seek therapy often have become overly enmeshed, whereas gay male couples who seek help are more likely to present with power and competition issues (Berzon, 1979; Kaufman, Harrison, & Hyde, 1984). If these observations are accurate (another empirical question), then research is needed to evaluate how, if at all, treatment of clinical issues unique to lesbians and gay men should vary according to the gender of the client.

B. Training

Behavior therapists need training about issues unique to gay men and lesbians as well as training in the application of behavior therapy to work with these issues. Behavior therapists need to know about unique clinical issues, such as those described earlier, even though there is a limited amount of research available on treatment. Training should include data about the social and legal context in which lesbians and gay men exist. For instance, any therapist who is helping a lesbian decide whether to come out to the ex-husband who fathered her minor children needs to know that lesbian mothers almost always lose custody of their children when the mother's sexual orientation becomes an issue in court.

Behavior therapists of all sexual orientations need ongoing training in assessment and reduction of their own discomfort with lesbian and gay clients and the issues these clients bring to therapy. All of us, clients and therapists alike, were raised and live in a society that taught us to devalue, fear, and label as sick or sinful, people with same-gender sexual orientations. In behavioral terms, we were taught a conditioned negative response to gay men and lesbians at a time when we were too young to critically evaluate the lesson being learned. Because anxiety reduction has been the goal of considerable research, we should be able to draw on the findings of that body of literature to design training programs that help behavior therapists to increase their comfort levels during work with lesbian and gay clients. Given how thoroughly our culture teaches negative lessons about gay men and lesbians, it is reasonable to assume that therapists need ongoing education intended to strengthen and maintain newly learned skills in relating to lesbian and gay clients.

This type of training is necessary because clients are able to identify discomfort on the part of the therapist. Therapist discomfort is problematic because it can result in nonverbal messages that the client's sexual orientation is negatively valued. It may also result in avoidance of topics important to the client. For instance, Davison and Wilson (1973) found that less than one-third of the behavior therapists they surveyed had asked their gay clients about specific sexual practices—even though the focus of treatment was on changing sexual orientation. Therapist discomfort can also take more subtle forms. We are aware of one situation in which a male client was confused about his sexual orientation and was dating both men and women. When his therapist knew this man would be spending a weekend with a woman, the therapist said, "Have a nice weekend." When the therapist knew the client would be spending the weekend with a man, the therapist said, "Call me if you need to."

C. Professional Development

It seems reasonable to suggest that we cannot teach our students to create safe environments for their lesbian and gay clients unless we provide them with good models. It therefore behooves us to put our professional house in order, and here are some ways to get started.

Identify and change professional practices that assume everyone is heterosexual. One of the constant stresses faced by gay men and lesbians is what Riddle and Sang (1978) call the "pain of invisibility." Every time a lesbian or gay client is handed a form asking for marital (instead of relationship) status, a list of support groups for spouses (not partners) of abuse survivors or substance abusers, a self-help book that does not mention lesbians and gay men, or a life history questionnaire that asks what form of birth control the client uses (but does not ask with whom the client is sexually active), a major part of the client's identity has been discounted. The society in which we live routinely commits these acts of omission. It is unreasonable to expect lesbian or gay clients to feel safe with therapists who behave as if all their clients are heterosexual.

Use and support the use of language that is inclusive and positively valued. Heterosexually biased language results in unclear communication and perpetuates old stereotypes and exclusionary practices (Bernstein, 1992; Committee on Lesbian and Gay Concerns, 1991). Instead, we recommend these changes:

- Use sexual *orientation*, not sexual *preference.*
- Use *lesbian, gay,* and *bisexual,* not *homosexual.*

- Distinguish between sexual *orientation* and sexual *behavior.*
- Use *lesbian, gay, and bisexual* rather than *gay* when you intend to be inclusive.
- Use *gender* rather than *sex.*
- Choose inclusive terms, such as *relationship status,* instead of exclusive phrases, such as *marital status.*
- Avoid using lists or groupings that marginalize or stigmatize. (Bernstein, 1992)

Use our professional institutions and publications to support the implementation of these recommendations. For instance, require the use of nonheterosexist language in all papers submitted to behavioral journals, newsletters, and conventions. Encourage publication of papers that report on needed research or describe practical ways to approach lesbian and gay issues clinically.

Identify and take issue with behavioral publications and presentations that promote a pathological view of gay men and lesbians. Any publication that promotes the view that to be gay or lesbian is to be inherently pathological (a) ignores the fact that there is no empirical support for that position (for example, Thompson, McCandless, & Strickland, 1971), and (b) is in direct opposition to the position of the American Psychological Association, the American Psychiatric Association, the National Association of Social Workers, and the Association for the Advancement of Behavior Therapy. The perpetuation, in print, of old stereotypes unsupported by data is bad science and bad practice.

V. Conclusion

As we noted earlier, our working hypothesis is that the unique clinical needs of lesbians and gay men are the direct result of the negative value our culture and institutions place on same-gender sexual orientation. That negative valuation leads to clinical problems such as internalized homophobia, which then require treatment. This puts the behavior therapist in a role similar to the circus worker who shovels up the droppings of the beasts under the big top. In other words, we clean up after the cultural and institutional mess has been made. That is an important task, and it has been the subject of this chapter.

However, the ultimate solution to the clinical problems created for lesbians and gay men by a prejudiced society is prevention. Prevention can occur only if we find answers to the question of how to effectively decrease prejudice against gay men and lesbians. Our colleagues in behavioral community psychology have demonstrated the ability to develop useful solutions to other large scale social problems (for example, Jason, 1991); we urge them to lend their skills to the quest for ways to reduce and ultimately eliminate prejudice based on sexual orientation.

References

BARLOW, D. H., & Agras, W. S. (1973). Fading to increase heterosexual responsiveness in homosexuals. *Journal of Applied Behavior Analysis, 6,* 355–366.

BERNSTEIN, G. S. (1992). How to avoid heterosexual bias in language. *The Behavior Therapist, 15,* 161.

BERZON, B. (1979). *Positively gay.* Los Angeles: Mediamix Associates.

BLECHMAN, E. A. (1984). *Behavior modification with women.* New York: Guilford Press.

BLUMSTEIN, P., & Schwartz, P. (1983). *American couples.* New York: Morrow.

BROWN, L. A. (1988). Feminist therapy with lesbians and gay men. In M. A. Dutton-Douglas & L. E. A. Walker, (Eds.), *Feminist psychotherapies: Integration of therapeutic and feminist systems* (pp. 206–227). Norwood, NJ: Ablex Publishing Corporation.

CANTON-DUTARI, A. (1976). Combined intervention for controlling unwanted homosexual behavior: An extended follow-up. *Archives of Sexual Behavior, 5,* 323–325.

CASTRONE, L. (1992, November 11). Amendment 2 aftermath. *Rocky Mountain News,* Denver, CO.

CENTERS for Disease Control. (1992, February). *HIV/AIDS surveillance.* Atlanta, GA.

COATES, T. J., McKusick, L., Stites, D. P., & Kuno, R. (1989). Stress management training reduced number of sexual partners but did not improve immune function in men infected with HIV. *American Journal of Public Health, 79,* 885–887.

COMMITTEE on Lesbian and Gay Concerns. (1990). *Bias in psychotherapy with lesbians and gay men.* Washington, DC: American Psychological Association.

COMMITTEE on Lesbian and Gay Concerns. (1991). Avoiding heterosexual bias in language. *American Psychologist, 46,* 973–974.

CONRAD, S. R., & Wincze, J. P. (1976). Orgasmic reconditioning: A controlled study of the effects upon the sexual arousal and behavior of adult male homosexuals. *Behavior Therapy, 7,* 155–166.

DAVISON, G. C. (1976). Homosexuality: The ethical challenge. *Journal of Consulting and Clinical Psychology, 44,* 157–162.

DAVISON, G. C. (1978). Not can but ought: The treatment of homosexuality. *Journal of Consulting and Clinical Psychology, 46,* 170–172.

DAVISON, G. C. (1991). The shaping of behavior therapy: Reflections on my AABT presidency. *The Behavior Therapist, 14,* 198–200.

DAVISON, G. C., & Friedman, S. (1982). Sexual orientation stereotypy in the distortion of clinical judgement. *Journal of Homosexuality, 6,* 37–44.

DAVISON, G. C., & Wilson, G. T. (1973). Attitudes of behavior therapists toward homosexuality. *Behavior Therapy, 4,* 686–696.

DUEHN, W. D., & Mayadas, N. S. (1976). The use of stimulus/modeling videotapes in assertive training for homosexuals. *Journal of Homosexuality, 1,* 373–381.

ELDRIDGE, N. S. (1987). Gender issues in counseling same-sex couples. *Professional Psychology: Research and Practice, 18,* 567–572.

FELDMAN, M. P., & MacCulloch, J. (1965). The application of anticipatory avoidance learning to the treatment of homosexuality. *Behaviour Research & Therapy, 2,* 165–183.

FREEMAN, W., & Meyer, R. G. (1975). A behavioral alteration of sexual preferences in the human male. *Behavior Therapy, 6,* 206–212.

FREMOUW, W. J., de Perczel, M., & Ellis, T. E. (1990). *Suicide risk: Assessment and response guidelines.* Elmsford, NY: Pergamon Press.

GARFINKLE, E. M., & Morin, S. F. (1978). Psychologists' attitudes toward homosexual psychotherapy clients. *Journal of Social Issues, 34,* 101–112.

GONSIOREK, J. C. (1988). Mental health issues of gay and lesbian adolescents. *Journal of Adolescent Health Care, 9,* 114–122.

GROUP for the Study of Gay and Lesbian Issues. (1991). *Spring 1991 Newsletter.*

HEREK, G. M., Kimmel, D. C., Amaro, H., & Melton, G. B. (1991). Avoiding heterosexist bias in psychological research. *American Psychologist, 46,* 957–963.

HERMAN, S. H., Barlow, D. H., & Agras, W. S. (1974). An experimental analysis of classical conditioning as a method of increasing heterosexual arousal in homosexuals. *Behavior Therapy, 5,* 33–47.

HOOKER, E. (1957). Male homosexuality in the Rorschach. *Journal of Projective Techniques, 22,* 33–54.

HUNTER, P., & Kelso, E. (1983, December). *Stress inoculation as a component of assertiveness training for gay and lesbian clients.* Poster presented at the Association for Advancement of Behavior Therapy, 7th Annual Convention & World Congress on Behavior Therapy, Washington, DC.

INCE, L. P. (1973). Behavior modification of sexual disorders. *American Journal of Psychotherapy, 27,* 445–446.

JAMES, S. (1978). Treatment of homosexuality II. Superiority of desensitization/arousal as compared with anticipatory avoidance conditioning: Results of a controlled trial. *Behavior Therapy, 9,* 28–36.

JAMES, S., Orwin, A., & Turner, R. K. (1977). Analysis of failure following a trial of anticipatory avoidance conditioning and the development of an alternative treatment system. *Behavior Therapy, 8,* 840–848.

JASON, L. A. (1991). Participating in social change: A fundamental value for our discipline. *American Journal of Community Psychology, 19,* 1–16.

KAUFMAN, P. A., Harrison, E., & Hyde, M. L. (1984). Distancing for intimacy in lesbian relationships. *American Journal of Psychiatry, 141*(4), 530–533.

KELLY, J. A., & St. Lawrence, J. S. (1986). Behavioral intervention and AIDS. *The Behavior Therapist, 9,* 121–125.

KELLY, J. A., St. Lawrence, J. S., & Brasfield, T. L. (1991). Predictors of vulnerability to AIDS risk behavior relapse. *Journal of Consulting and Clinical Psychology, 59,* 163–166.

KELLY, J. A., St. Lawrence, J. S., Brasfield, T. L., Lemke, A., Amidei, T., Roffman, R. E., Hood, H. V., Smith, J. E., Kilgore, H., & McNeill, C., Jr. (1990). Psychological factors that predict AIDS high-risk versus AIDS precautionary behavior. *Journal of Consulting and Clinical Psychology, 58,* 117–120.

KELLY, J. A., St. Lawrence, J. S., Hood, H. V., & Brasfield, T. L. (1989a). Behavioral intervention to reduce AIDS risk activities. *Journal of Consulting and Clinical Psychology, 57,* 60–67.

KELLY, J. A., St. Lawrence, J. S., Hood, H. V., & Brasfield, T. L. (1989b). An objective test of AIDS risk behavior knowledge: Scale development, validation, and norms. *Journal of Behaviour Therapy and Experimental Psychiatry, 20,* 227–234.

KINSEY, A., Pomeroy, W., & Martin, C. (1948). *Sexual behavior in the human male.* Philadelphia: Saunders.

KINSEY, A., Pomeroy, W., Martin, C., & Gebhard, P. (1953). *Sexual behavior in the human female.* Philadelphia: Saunders.

KIRK, M., & Madsen, H. (1989). *After the ball: How America will conquer its fear & hatred of gays in the 90's.* New York: Plume.

LANDRINE, H. (1988). Revising the framework of abnormal psychology. In P. Bronstein & K. Quina (Eds.), *Teaching a psychology of people* (pp. 37–64). Washington, DC: American Psychological Association.

LoPICCOLO, J. (1971). Case study: Systematic desensitization of homosexuality. *Behavior Therapy, 2,* 394–399.

LOULAN, J. (1984). *Lesbian sex.* San Francisco: Spinsters/Aunt Lute.

LUKES, C. A., & Land, H. (1990, March). Biculturality and homosexuality. *Social Work, 35,* 155–161.

MacCULLOCH, M. J., Burtles, C. J., & Feldman, M. P. (1971). Anticipatory avoidance learning for the treatment of homosexuality: Recent developments and an automatic aversive therapy system. *Behavior Therapy, 2,* 151–169.

MALETZKY, B. M. (1977). "Booster" sessions in aversion therapy: The permanency of treatment. *Behavior Therapy, 8,* 460–463.

MARKOWITZ, L. M. (1991). Homosexuality: Are we still in the dark? *The Family Therapy Networker,* 27–35.

MARSHALL, W. L. (1975). Reducing masturbatory guilt. *Journal of Behaviour Therapy & Experimental Psychiatry, 6,* 260–261.

MARTIN, A. (1982). Some issues in the treatment of gay and lesbian patients. *Psychotherapy: Theory, Research, and Practice, 19,* 341–348.

McCONAGHY, N. (1970). Penile response conditioning and its relationship to aversion therapy in homosexuals. *Behavior Therapy, 1,* 213–221.

McCONAGHY, N., Armstrong, M.S., & Blaszczynski, A. (1981). Controlled comparison of aversive therapy and covert sensitization in compulsive homosexuality. *Behaviour Research & Therapy, 19,* 425–434.

McCRADY, R. E. (1973). A forward-fading technique for increasing heterosexual responsiveness in male homosexuals. *Journal of Behaviour Therapy and Experimental Psychiatry, 4,* 257–261.

McKINLAY, T., Kelly, J., A., & Patterson, J. (1977). Teaching assertive skills to a passive homosexual adolescent: An illustrative case study. *Journal of Homosexuality, 3,* 163–170.

MILLER, M. E., & Bernstein, G. S. (1989). *Cognitive behavior therapy with lesbians: Current wasteland, future opportunity.* Poster presented at the meeting of the Association for the Advancement of Behavior Therapy, Washington, DC.

MORRIS, W. (Ed.). (1979). *American heritage dictionary, new college edition.* Boston: Houghton Mifflin.

PADESKY, C. A. (1989). Attaining and maintaining positive lesbian self-identity: A cognitive therapy approach. *Women & Therapy, 8,* 145–156.

PHILLIPS, D., Fischer, S. C., Groves, G. A., & Singh, R. (1976). Alternative behavioral approaches to the treatment of homosexuality. *Archives of Sexual Behavior, 5,* 223–228.

RAINWATER, N. (1989). An expanded conceptual model for behavior therapists. In G. S. Bernstein (Chair), *Behavior therapy with women: Contemporary issues and applications.* Symposium presented at the meeting of the Colorado Society for Behavior Analysis and Therapy, Denver, CO.

REHM, L. P., & Rozensky, R. H. (1974). Multiple behavior therapy techniques with a homosexual client: A case study. *Journal of Behaviour Therapy & Experimental Psychiatry, 5,* 53–57.

RIDDLE, D. I., & Sang, B. (1978). Psychotherapy with lesbians. *Journal of Social Issues, 34,* 84–100.

ROTH, S., & Murphy, B. C. (1986). Therapeutic work with lesbian clients: A systemic therapy view. In Ault-Richie

(Ed.), *Women and family therapy: The family therapy connections* (pp. 78–89). Rockville, MD: Aspen Systems Corporation.

RUSSELL, A., & Winkler, R. (1977). Evaluation of assertive training and homosexual guidance service groups designed to improve homosexual functioning. *Journal of Consulting and Clinical Psychology,* 1–13.

SALHOLZ, E., Glick, D., & Gordon, R. (1992, June 1). Gunning for gays. *Newsweek,* pp. 44–45.

SAMBROOKS, J. E., MacCulloch, M. J., & Waddington, J. L. (1978). Incubation of sexual attitude change between sessions of instrumental aversion therapy. *Behavior Therapy, 9,* 477–485.

SANDFORD, D. A., Tustin, R. D., & Priest, P. N. (1975). Increasing heterosexual arousal in two adult male homosexuals using a differential reinforcement procedure. *Behavior Therapy, 6,* 689–693.

SCHINKE, S. P., Gordon, A. N., & Weston, R. E. (1990). Self-instruction to prevent HIV infection among African-American and Hispanic-American adolescents. *Journal of Consulting and Clinical Psychology, 58,* 432–436.

SCHMALING, K. B., & DiClementi, J. D. (1991). Cognitive therapy with the HIV seropositive patient. *The Behavior Therapist, 14,* 221–224.

SCHNEIDER, S. G., Faberow, N., & Kroks, G. N. (1989). Suicidal behavior in adolescent and young adult gay men. *Suicidal and Life-Threatening Behavior, 19,* 381–394.

SEGAL, E. (1982). *Women, borscht, gays, laboratory animals, and nuclear extinction.* Invited address at the meeting of the American Psychological Association, Washington, DC.

SOME facts on suicide and gay youth. (1990, Winter). *Momentum: A news publication of the Human Rights Campaign Fund,* p. 1.

TANNER, B. A. (1974). A comparison of automated aversive conditioning and a waiting list control in the modification of homosexual behavior in males. *Behavior Therapy, 5,* 29–32.

TANNER, B. A. (1975). Avoidance training with and without booster sessions to modify homosexual behavior in males. *Behavior Therapy, 6,* 649–653.

THE sodomy laws, state by state. (1990, December 21). *The New York Times.*

THOMPSON, N. L., Jr., McCandless, B. R., & Strickland, B. R. (1971). Personal adjustment of male and female homosexuals and heterosexuals. *Journal of Abnormal Psychology, 78,* 237–240.

WILENSKY, M., & Myers, M. F. (1987). Retarded ejaculation in homosexual patients: A report of nine cases. *The Journal of Sex Research, 23,* 85–105.

WILSON, G. T., & Davison, G. C. (1974). Behavior therapy and homosexuality: A critical perspective. *Behavior Therapy, 5,* 16–28.

WOLPE, J. (1982). *The practice of behavior therapy.* New York: Pergamon Press.

CHAPTER 6

Cognitive Behavioral Strategies in Athletic Performance Enhancement

Andrew W. Meyers
James P. Whelan
Shane M. Murphy

I. Introduction
II. Scope and History
  A. Scope of Sport Psychology
  B. History of Sport Psychology
III. Cognitive Behavioral Interventions
  A. A Cautionary Note on Adopting a Model
  B. Goal Setting
  C. Imagery and Mental Rehearsal
  D. Arousal Management
  E. Cognitive Self-Regulation
  F. Multicomponent Interventions
IV. Quantitative Review
  A. Existing Reviews
  B. Execution of the Meta-Analysis
  C. The Database
  D. Overall Effectiveness of Psychological
     Interventions
  E. Reliability of Treatment Effectiveness
    1. Type of Control Group
    2. Type of Dependent Measure
    3. Components of Treatment
    4. Goal Setting Interventions
    5. Mental Rehearsal Interventions
    6. Anxiety Management Interventions
    7. Cognitive Self-Regulation Interventions
    8. Multicomponent Interventions
  F. Design Issues

G. Generalizability
    1. Task Characteristics
    2. Context Characteristics
    3. Participant Characteristics
V. Applications to Elite Athletes
VI. Summary and Conclusions
    References

I. Introduction

George Will (1990), in his best-selling book on base-ball, *Men at Work*, tells us that "the day Custer lost at Little Bighorn, the Chicago White Sox beat the Cincinnati Red Legs, 3–2" (p. 293). It is clear that sport has woven a thread throughout hundreds, if not thousands, of years, and athletic achievement and competition play significant roles in modern American culture (Michener, 1976). Sport has a place in our history, and as we hope to demonstrate, in our psychology in general and cognitive behavioral psychology in particular. We begin this chapter by presenting a brief justification of applied sport psychology and follow this with an introduction to the history of the field. We then describe contemporary cognitive behavioral interventions for athletic performance enhancement. This work is summarized first in a descriptive fashion and then in a meta-analytic review. This is followed by a brief discussion of work with elite athletes. In closing, we highlight the major issues in the area and attempt to guide future application and evaluative efforts.

II. Scope and History

A. Scope of Sport Psychology

The most dramatic applications of sport psychology occur with Olympic or professional athletes. While we are well aware of the numbers of these elite amateur and professional competitors, there are also legions of competitive recreational athletes, weekend athletes, and children involved in organized sport (Whelan, Meyers, & Donovan, 1995). Nearly all sports boast their share of loyal participants. The Athletic Congress (Honikman & Honikman, 1991), the governing body of track and field in the United States, estimated that over 4 million people participate in sanctioned road races each year. A survey by the National Sporting Goods Association (1990) found

Partial support for this paper was provided by a Centers of Excellence grant from the State of Tennessee to the Department of Psychology at Memphis State University. Thanks to Charlene Donovan and Sean C. McCann for their help in the preparation of this manuscript.

that more than 3 million men and women over the age of 18 years consider themselves to be very frequent tennis players, playing more than 30 days every year, while the United States Tennis Association (1990) claims approximately 150,000 people currently playing in adult recreational leagues. According to the National Golf Foundation (1991) about 10% of adult males and 2% of adult females in the United States play golf. The National Bowling Council (1990) reported that there are 6 million adult men and women league bowlers in the United States. United States Masters Swimming, Inc. (1991) records indicated that 25,000 people participated in Masters swim meets last year, while the United States Cycling Federation (1990) licensed over 30,000 competitive cyclists in 1990. Sport participation among children and adolescents may be even more impressive. Little League baseball alone boasts over 2.5 million children participating in its affiliated organizations, and youth sport groups in soccer, swimming, basketball, and football are active nationwide (LeUnes & Nation, 1989). Organized junior and senior high school athletic programs account for several million more participants.

It is apparent that a substantial number of Americans are engaged in sporting activities and other regular, organized physical activity. And for a considerable segment of these athletes, competition and development and demonstration of competence are quite important. Given the high level of participatory and competitive involvement and the meaning of sport in our culture, it is not surprising that social scientists have adopted sport as a valid area of inquiry and that applied sport psychologists have found fertile ground for their intervention programs.

B. History of Sport Psychology

While it may appear that sport psychology exploded into Western Europe and the Americas out of Eastern Europe in the early 1980s, of course, this is not true. Mahoney (1989) has argued that the study of play, competition, and exercise in our lives is as old as the study of human behavior itself. The first research project that fits neatly into our contemporary notion of sport psychology was Triplett's investigation in 1897 of the effects of competition on motor performance. Triplett compared cyclists performing against the clock, against a standard or goal, or against other cyclists in competition. As might be expected, cyclists in competition performed best, and Triplett concluded that the presence of a competitor served to "liberate latent energy not ordinarily available" (p. 532).

Participants in virtually every area of study can trace their roots back to a "parent," and for North American sport psychology that parent figure is undoubtedly Coleman Roberts Griffith. Griffith is often credited with founding the first sport psychology laboratory in 1925 at the University of Illinois, although Diem in Berlin and Puni in Leningrad likely preceded him (Wiggins, 1984). Griffith is not only known for his relatively rigorous experimental work in psychomotor skill development, learning theory applied to sport, and the role of personality in athletic performance but also for his interviews and field observations with elite athletes. Griffith's interview with Red Grange, the great American football player, immediately after his spectacular six-touchdown performance in a major college game, produced the first report of the "automatic" or "flow" performance that elite competitors now frequently report (Csikszentmihalyi, 1990). The concept of flow is similar to, but perhaps more dramatic than, Meichenbaum's (1977) concept of "automaticity." In the early 1930s Griffith left academia to serve as sport psychologist for the Chicago Cubs; this was the first example of the psychologist in professional sports—and, some have argued, the only example of the Cubs being first at anything.

Development in sport psychology proceeded slowly until the 1960s when the First International Congress of Sport Psychology was held in Rome in 1965, and two years later the North American Society for the Psychology of Sport and Physical Activity was founded. Among applied sport psychologists, this period may best be known for Ogilvie and Tutko's (1966) attempt to integrate psychological assessment and personality theory in sport psychology. Their work marked the first contemporary melding of clinical psychology and the study of athletic performance. Ogilvie and Tutko concentrated on the development of a personality test that they hoped would allow them to predict the performance of athletes. This work was based on the assumption that elite athletes possess unique and definable personality attributes different from nonathletes, from athletes in other sports, and from athletes of different skill levels. If this assumption was supported, personality testing would facilitate athlete selection, coach-player interaction, and the design of training programs. Unfortunately, this work fell victim to the same problems and criticisms that general personality theory was receiving in the 1960s and 1970s. As Mischel (1968) argued, global personality traits had been poor predictors of behavior, in large part due to their failure to consider situational contributions to behavior and the interaction between those situational demands and the individual's behavioral and psychological skills. The search for an "athletic personality" has been extremely disappointing (Meyers, 1980; Morgan, 1980; Rushall, 1972; Silva, 1984).

Coincidentally, studies appearing in the motor learning literature provided evidence supporting the efficacy of "mental practice" or covert rehearsal on acquisition and retention of complex motor skills (Corbin, 1972; Richardson, 1967a, 1967b). Covert rehearsal, when compared to no practice, significantly improved skilled motor performance by approximately one-half standard deviation (Feltz & Landers, 1983). Then in 1972, Richard Suinn, in *Behavior Therapy*, the journal of the Association for Advancement of Behavior Therapy, applied a set of cognitive and behavioral interventions to sport performance. He reported that training in relaxation and imagery skills, combined with a behavioral rehearsal technique, improved race performances in a group of skilled skiers. Based on Suinn's work, simple imagery-based "mental practice" interventions for performance enhancement became more intricate (compare with Meyers, Schleser, & Okwumabua, 1982) and began to resemble the growing body of cognitive-oriented clinical interventions that had gained favor in the late 1960s and early 1970s (Bandura, 1969, 1977; Beck, 1976; Meichenbaum, 1977).

Over the last 15 years, interest in an increasingly sophisticated psychology of sport and athletic performance enhancement has been evidenced by the development of several new journals, including the *Journal of Sport and Exercise Psychology*, *The Sport Psychologist*, and the *Journal of Applied Sport Psy-*

chology, and the birth of two new sport psychology organizations. The Association for the Advancement of Applied Sport Psychology (AAASP) held its first annual meeting in 1986. This group has grown to over 800 members in just six years and is relatively unique in that the membership is almost equally divided between psychologists and physical educators. The American Psychological Association's (APA) Division of Exercise and Sport Psychology (Division 47) was founded in 1986 and, with over 1000 members, is the fastest growing division in APA. Both AAASP and APA's Division 47 have specified ethical guidelines for sport psychologists, and both organizations are discussing criteria for consultation activities in sport settings.

This brief history, the evidence of tremendous growth in recreational sports (Whelan et al., 1995), the importance of elite competitive sports in our culture (Michener, 1976), and the expanding professional and scientific interest in athletic performance enhancement have generated an increasingly rich descriptive and investigative body of research. In the next sections we report qualitative and quantitative reviews of this literature.

III. Cognitive Behavioral Interventions

A. A Cautionary Note on Adopting a Model

In this section we describe the common components of cognitive behavioral-based athletic performance enhancement programs. While we do this in an acritical manner, it is important to acknowledge that packaged psychological interventions in sport suffer the same difficulties that such nonideographic programs do in other areas of clinical work (Kirschenbaum, 1992). The failure to tie specific assessment strategies and information to treatment must surely reduce the efficacy of the intervention. Furthermore, athletes seeking performance enhancement also typically present with a range of psychological complaints (for example, marital or family discord, a history of abuse as a child, stress from financial difficulties) common to the broad population of clinical clients or to any career, profession, or employment group (for example, stockbrokers, construction workers, or university professors). These presenting problems obvi-

ously require appropriate psychosocial or biological treatments that would be extended to any nonathlete clients. In a recent book chapter we have made the argument that athletes' problems, broadly defined, might be most beneficially managed within a comprehensive cognitive behavioral-oriented, systemic model (Whelan et al., 1995). However, the athletic performance enhancement literature has not adopted such a broad perspective. Intervention efforts have instead been largely limited to cognitive behavioral-oriented programs to improve the psychological skills of athletes and sport participants.

Contemporary sport performance enhancement programs have included a broad sample of cognitive behavioral intervention strategies. Common intervention components include goal setting (Miller & McAuley, 1987), imagery or mental rehearsal (Woolfolk, Murphy, Gottesfeld, & Aitken, 1985), relaxation training (Greer & Engs, 1986), stress management (Smith, 1980), self-monitoring (Kirschenbaum, Ordman, Tomarken, & Holtzbauer, 1982), self-instruction (Meyers, Schleser, Cooke, & Cuvillier, 1979), cognitive restructuring (DeWitt, 1980), and modeling (McCullagh, 1986). While many sport scientists have attempted to identify the potency of particular intervention strategies, many investigators have followed Suinn's (1972) lead and packaged a series of intervention strategies hypothesized to create performance gain. Before providing a meta-analytic overview of the research findings, we briefly describe these intervention strategies and their use (see also, Whelan, Mahoney, & Meyers, 1991).

B. Goal Setting

Goal setting strategies for behavior change have been examined primarily within the field of industrial and organizational psychology (Locke & Latham, 1990). Locke and Latham (1985) speculated that the effectiveness of goal setting in the workplace would generalize well to athletic contexts, and this assumption has inspired a number of applied and research efforts.

Typically, goal setting interventions in sport are designed to instruct and encourage the athlete to adopt specific and measurable goals for both the practice and competitive environments. Both proximal and distal goals are generated, often in a hierarchical manner, so the athlete has a planned path to the end goal. Recommendations typically emphasize positive rather than negative goals, challenging but realistic goals, and goals that require the athlete to focus on task mastery rather than outcome. Based on these applications, investigators of goal setting in sport performance have examined two fundamental questions.

The hypothesis that specific, difficult, and realistic goals compared with nonspecific ("do your best") goals, lenient goals, or no goals, leads to improved task performance (Locke, 1968) has received a good deal of research attention. Evaluations of this proposition have been equivocal. Barnett and Stanicek (1979) found that novice athletes given specific goals, compared with no goals, significantly improved archery performance over a ten-week training period. In contrast, several studies have failed to document the facilitative effects of specific, realistically difficult goals on the performance of gross motor tasks. Hollingsworth (1975) did not detect performance differences between no goal, general goal, and specific goal conditions in the development of juggling skills. Weinberg, Bruya, and Jackson (1985) found no performance differences between specific goal, "do your best" goal, and no goal groups on an endurance sit-up task for students enrolled in a fitness class. Consistent with Locke's hypotheses, Hall, Weinberg, and Jackson (1987) found that nonathletes using specific goals performed better than individuals using "do your best" goals in an endurance hand strength task. However, there was no support for the predicted relationship between goal difficulty and performance. Similarly, Weinberg, Bruya, Jackson, and Garland (1987) assigned students easy, difficult, and very difficult goals for a three-minute sit-up task. No between-group differences were identified, although individuals in the very difficult goal condition showed the greatest improvement. Finally, Weinberg, Bruya, Garland, and Jackson (1990) conducted a series of laboratory and field studies and found that performance of hand strength and sit-up tasks was unrelated to goal difficulty and goal specificity.

The examination of the motivational influence of learning or mastery goals versus competitive or outcome goals (Orlick, 1986) has served as a second focus of goal setting research. Several authors (Csik-

szentmihalyi, 1990; Nicholls, 1984; Orlick, 1986) have argued that individuals who aspire to demonstrate task mastery cope more effectively with task demands than individuals whose motive is competitive superiority (see also Sternberg & Kolligian, 1990, for a collection of essays on this issue). Individuals who adopt mastery-oriented achievement goals are assumed to seek out challenging tasks that encourage skill development. Obversely, at least for those who do not perceive high ability on the relevant task, adoption of outcome-oriented achievement goals leads individuals to avoid threats to self-efficacy. They can do this by selecting nonchallenging tasks that serve to validate their capabilities (Nichols, Whelan, & Meyers, 1991). That is, outcome-oriented individuals are more likely to select easy tasks where success is likely or extremely difficult tasks where failure is almost surely guaranteed. The correlational relationship between goal perspective and participation and persistence in sport lends empirical support to this hypothesis. Adolescents who participated in and persisted on athletic tasks tended to be more task mastery–oriented than outcome-oriented (Duda, 1989; Vealey & Campbell, 1988).

Manipulation of achievement goal orientation in sport situations has not been thoroughly evaluated. Wraith and Biddle (1989) assigned children to either learning or competitive performance goals and varied their participation in the goal setting process. While no differences in goal participation were identified, greater improvement in ball throwing distance was found for children with learning goals compared to those with competitive goals.

Several studies have evaluated the potency of training athletes to use mastery-oriented goal setting with specific, realistically difficult goals versus no goal setting. Miller and McAuley (1987) matched college students in a basketball physical education class on free-throw shooting ability, then assigned them to receive either mastery goal training or no goal training. After five weeks, no performance differences were evident; however, the goal training group reported higher ratings of self-efficacy. Burton (1989) reported similar results in a season-long evaluation of a goal setting training program with collegiate swimmers. Swimmers trained to set and use mastery performance goals compared to those who did not use goal training reported a more favorable view of their abilities, and greater confidence, satisfaction, and concentration. However, they did not experience any clear performance change.

The predicted impact of goal setting on physical performance has not been verified. Nevertheless, evidence does suggest that under certain conditions goal setting may enhance the motivation for involvement and promote more positive self-evaluation of training and competitive performance. Such changes may facilitate task persistence and therefore indirectly lead to performance improvements.

C. Imagery and Mental Rehearsal

The use of imagery, or the covert practice of a physical task in the absence of gross muscular movement (Corbin, 1972), is the most prevalent form of mental rehearsal strategy. However, other forms of rehearsal, such as modeling, have also been evaluated (Weinberg, 1982). Athletes often report using imagery in the process of athletic task rehearsal, and they typically judge this imagery to be a valuable preparatory strategy (Mahoney & Avener, 1977; Meaney, 1984). These anecdotal and descriptive reports have led scientists and practitioners to employ imagery as a major component of cognitive behavioral interventions for performance enhancement (Kirschenbaum & Bale, 1980; Suinn, 1983). These strategies have also been heavily emphasized in self-help books for athletes (Vealey, 1988).

Application of imagery to sport performance has been a logical extension of the research on imagery's utility in complex motor learning. An examination of the motor skill acquisition and execution literature has produced cautious optimism on the benefits of mental practice (Corbin, 1972; Feltz & Landers, 1983; Weinberg, 1982). While some investigations have not supported the use of imaginal rehearsal in sport (Epstein, 1980; Mumford & Hall, 1985), imagery has been used successfully to improve the performances of ski racers (Suinn, 1972, 1977), basketball players (Meyers et al., 1982), gymnasts (Start & Richardson, 1964), dart throwers (Mendoza & Wichman, 1978; Wichman & Lizotte, 1983), golfers (Woolfolk, Murphy, Gottesfeld, & Aitken, 1985; Woolfolk, Parrish, & Murphy, 1985), volleyball players (Shick, 1970), and swimmers (White, Ashton, & Lewis, 1979).

Much of the research on the utility of imagery has focused on evaluating the parameters that mediate efficacy of mental rehearsal. One potential mediator of imagery effects is whether the individual adopts an internal or external imagery perspective. Internal imagery consists of visualization from the first-person or the performer's perspective. Hence, the imager's view replicates the actual perceptual information, visual and possibly kinesthetic, that the athlete experiences during task execution. An external image involves witnessing the athlete perform from a third-person perspective.

Unfortunately, research on the benefits of imaginal rehearsal across different imagery perspectives has been equivocal. Some athletes' reports suggested that highly successful competitors were more likely to rely on internal imagery, whereas less successful athletes used more external imagery (Harris & Robinson, 1986; Mahoney & Avener, 1977). However, other experimental work has not supported the proposed importance of imagery perspective. Imagery perspective was not related to performance in dart throwing (Epstein, 1980), figure skating (Mumford & Hall, 1985), or racquetball (Meyers, Cooke, Cullen, & Liles, 1979). One interpretation of these conflicting findings is that different imagery perspectives are beneficial for different types of tasks at different levels of task mastery (D. Smith, 1989).

The specific performance outcome of the imagery work may serve as a second possible mediator of imagery effects. There is convincing evidence of the beneficial consequences of imagining successful athletic performances (Caudill, Weinberg, & Jackson, 1983; White et al., 1979) and the detrimental effects of imagining athletic failure (Powell, 1973; Woolfolk, Murphy, et al., 1985; Woolfolk, Parrish, & Murphy, 1985). For example, Woolfolk, Murphy, et al. (1985) blocked college students on their ability to putt a golf ball, then randomly assigned students to success imagery, failure imagery, or no imagery conditions. Performance following a positive image was superior to performance without imagery, and performance without imagery was reliably superior to performance following a negative image. Suinn (1985) suggests that skilled athletes, with experience in imagery use, may benefit from coping-oriented imagery. Coping imagery involves presentation of a model who manages performance difficulties and corrects performance mistakes. Although untested, Suinn's proposal is supported by intervention research demonstrating that highly skilled athletes benefit from corrective attention to performance mistakes (Kirschenbaum & Smith, 1983).

Several potential mediators of imagery effects have received experimental support. This research has shown that the effects of imagery are enhanced when clarity or vividness of the image is increased (D. Smith, 1989), relaxation skills are present (Lanning & Hisanga, 1983), and specific, personally meaningful images are used (Hecker & Kaczor, 1988; Lee, 1990). The role of other potential imagery mediators, such as experience and familiarity with the task (Shick, 1970), the amount and type of imagery training (Epstein, 1980), the distribution of imagery practice trials (Suinn, 1985), and the type of physical task (Weinberg, 1982), remains to be determined. An understanding of the possible interactions among mediators of the educational and therapeutic effects of imagery also awaits further systematic evaluation.

D. Arousal Management

Interest in the relationship between performance and arousal has existed throughout the 20th century (Yerkes & Dodson, 1908). Unfortunately, the Yerkes-Dodson Law (Yerkes & Dodson, 1908), Drive Theory (Hull, 1943; Spence & Spence, 1966), state-trait conceptions (Spielberger, 1972), and other theoretical explanations of the anxiety-performance relationship have failed to account fully for the available research findings (Mahoney & Meyers, 1989; Martens, 1972). But we do know that athletes across sports and at a wide variety of skill levels typically report arousal and other somatic and emotional changes prior to and during competition (Gould, Horn, & Spreemann, 1983; Mahoney & Avener, 1977). While often uncomfortable, and in some cases debilitating, such arousal appears to be essential for optimal response to competitive demands (Landers, 1980; Mahoney & Meyers, 1989). Contemporary investigations of the performance-arousal relationship have focused on identification of mediating variables, such as atten-

tional focus, coping skills, task complexity, task familiarity, and athlete skill level that may dictate the influence of arousal on performance.

Given the universal nature of arousal during stress and the possible facilitating effects of that arousal, it is somewhat surprising that most performance enhancement interventions include a component to reduce the athlete's arousal level (Orlick, 1986; Suinn, 1983). These efforts to attenuate "over-arousal" mirror anxiety reduction and stress management efforts prevalent in clinical psychology (Smith, 1985). Progressive relaxation training, biofeedback, and stress inoculation training (Meichenbaum, 1977; Woolfolk & Lehrer, 1984) have been employed effectively to lower athletes' arousal and anxiety (DeWitt, 1980; Murphy & Woolfolk, 1987; Smith, 1985; Ziegler, Klinzing, & Williamson, 1982). For example, Costa, Bonaccorsi, and Scrimali (1984) evaluated the effectiveness of biofeedback training for reducing precompetitive anxiety among highly skilled handball players. During two weeks of training, the biofeedback program yielded lower state anxiety and improved athletic performance when compared to a no-treatment control.

In contrast to structured arousal reduction interventions, efforts to increase arousal or to "psych up" have relied on athletes' ability to ready themselves psychologically or employ arousing contextual demands. Typical arousal instructions involve telling the participant "to get yourself emotionally prepared . . . psych yourself up by getting mad, aroused, pumped-up or charged up" (Gould, Weinberg, & Jackson, 1980, p. 331). These "psyching-up" efforts are buttressed by the assumption that mental preparation heightens arousal, thereby preparing the athlete to meet performance demands (Weinberg, Gould, & Jackson, 1980). Shelton and Mahoney (1978) illustrated this by having weightlifters perform a handgrip strength task following each of three preparation intervals. Performance improved reliably following the psych-up period when compared to two control conditions. While there was great variability in the athletes' descriptions of their arousal strategies, most reported the use of preparatory cognitive strategies such as imaginal rehearsal, attentional focus, self-efficacy statements, or simply focusing on the arousal.

Replications of this psych-up effect with athletes and nonathletes have found strength performance after mental preparation to be reliably superior to strength performance following cognitive distraction for a variety of tasks, including leg strength (Gould et al., 1980; Tynes & McFatter, 1987), muscular endurance (Caudill & Weinberg, 1983), and sprinting (Caudill et al., 1983). Performance improvements have not been found following such mental preparation when the task involved speed or balance skills rather than strength (Weinberg et al., 1980; Whelan, Epkins, & Meyers, 1990). Whelan et al. (1990) hypothesized that novel, complex coordination and speed tasks may require either a low level of arousal or a high level of arousal coupled with high task mastery for maximal performance.

Unfortunately, support for the possible instrumental role of increased arousal in athletic performance improvement has remained tentative. One reason for this is that no study has documented that these strategies produce physiological arousal. Most intervention evaluations have relied on change in measures of state anxiety to demonstrate arousal effects (compare with Gould et al., 1980; Weinberg, Jackson, & Seabourne, 1985). Recently, Whelan et al. (1990) reported that heart rate changes during a psych-up period were not related to performance on a gross motor skill task.

The inadequacy of the available theoretical explanations and our limited ability to reliably modify arousal in the field setting have fueled speculation about the arousal-anxiety-performance relationship (Mahoney & Meyers, 1989). Level of arousal is surely not the only consequential variable mediating the impact of anxiety on performance. Athletes' perceptions of the anxiety-arousal context, their previous experience with arousal changes, and their perceived ability to manage or control arousal may play pivotal roles in the relationship. The role of other variables, such as experience with the task, presence of observers or other competitors, and importance of the performance in the particular context, may also be central to understanding the influence of anxiety and arousal level on performance. While arousal, and perhaps anxiety itself, appears necessary for exceptional athletic performance, the athlete's perception of that anxiety and his or her ability to manage it may be the variables most highly related to performance.

E. Cognitive Self-Regulation

Kirschenbaum (Kirschenbaum & Bale, 1980; Kirschenbaum & Wittrock; 1984) has proposed a self-regulatory model of athletic skill development. He argued that an athlete's performance is, at least in part, a test of that individual's skill in self-directed cognition and action. The individual must successfully execute the physical skill, monitor his or her performance, evaluate that performance against some standard or goal, and then alter the execution of the physical skills. Bandura (1977) has extended this argument to suggest that both the individual's initiation of and persistence on a task is dependent on his or her sense of self-efficacy or belief in his or her own ability to perform a task successfully. Targets of interventions central to these processes include self-monitoring and self-instruction. Specific attempts to influence athletes' core cognitive constructs (for example, the athlete's world view or cognitive belief system; compare with Beck, 1976) through cognitive restructuring interventions have not been exposed to controlled experimental evaluation. Such change may be the implicit targets of the multicomponent interventions that have been applied recently.

Several studies have examined the use of differential self-monitoring in physical skill development. Differential self-monitoring is the process of systematically observing and recording successful (positive self-monitoring) or unsuccessful (negative self-monitoring) behaviors. Tomarken and Kirschenbaum (1982) hypothesized that on tasks where participants display low task mastery, positive self-monitoring, compared to negative self-monitoring, should enhance performance. However, when participants are highly skilled, the addition of negative self-monitoring may provide information for further refinement of the self-regulated behavior. To test this proposition, Kirschenbaum et al. (1982) exposed novice and experienced bowlers to either positive self-monitoring, negative self-monitoring, traditional bowling instruction, or no instruction. Only novice bowlers using positive self-monitoring demonstrated a performance gain five weeks after treatment. Counter to expectations, inclusion of negative self-monitoring did not influence high skill bowlers. In a subsequent study, Johnston-O'Conner and Kirschenbaum (1986) had moderately skilled golfers use positive self-monitoring, neutral self-monitoring, or no self-monitoring with or without videotaped feedback. The purpose of the video feedback variable was to induce an increased self-awareness (Carver & Scheier, 1981) of the performance. Both observer and self-report ratings of golf skill indicated improvement following positive self-monitoring only. Use of videotape feedback slightly exaggerated this treatment effect.

While imagery and mental rehearsal strategies may be viewed as forms of self-instruction, few controlled outcome studies have examined the potency of traditional self-instruction in athletic skill development. Meyers, Schleser, et al. (1979) conducted two experiments that compared the effectiveness of positive, coping, and negative self-instruction on elementary school students' acquisition of gymnastics skills. Self-instruction involved training participants to use a verbal script to guide and structure the performance skill. Both studies failed to support the effectiveness of self-instructional training in physical skill acquisition.

Cognitive self-regulation strategies are potentially promising interventions for the development of athletic skills. As is true for the other intervention strategies presented here, efficacy of self-regulation strategies may only be fully realized when the influence of person, task, and situational mediators under actual competitive conditions are thoroughly explored. One avenue for assessing and effecting these multiple targets of change are programs that include a variety of intervention components.

F. Multicomponent Interventions

Recognizing early on that athletes across a range of skills and sports present with a wide variety of psychological needs, Suinn (1972) and others designed intervention packages containing several behavior change strategies. However, these performance enhancement efforts typically included a core set of behavioral and cognitive approaches (Orlick, 1986; Suinn, 1983). Imaginal rehearsal and arousal management techniques usually served as cornerstones of these programs.

A number of multicomponent interventions have received nonexperimental attention, but Suinn's (1972, 1977, 1983) visuo-motor behavior rehearsal

(VMBR) is the only program that has been subject to considerable experimental evaluation. VMBR was designed to assist competent athletes to cope with competitive stress and performance errors (Suinn, 1972). In Suinn's seven-step treatment program, athletes are first taught to master relaxation and imagery skills. Then, using simple, slow-motion images, athletes are taught to apply positive thought control, stress management, and energy control strategies to the athletic task. The difficulty and speed of the images increases as the athlete becomes more able. Then the athletes are taught to apply cognitive coping strategies in response to performance errors. Finally, imaginal rehearsal is replaced by in vivo application of cognitive strategies (Suinn, 1983).

Suinn's (1972) initial attempt to experimentally evaluate VMBR with a team of 12 ski racers was unsuccessful. Unfortunately, performance data for the no-treatment control group were not available. Suinn did note that the performance gains of the VMBR group members led the coach to enter in competition racers from that group only.

Suinn's commitment to VMBR has been supported with other athlete groups (compare with Gravel, Lemieux, & Ladouceur, 1980). Hall and Erffmeyer (1983) used VMBR to improve the free-throw shooting performance of ten female collegiate basketball players. Half the players were given a combination of VMBR and videotape modeling, while the other five used relaxation alone. Only the group that received VMBR improved over baseline. Noel (1980) used a variation of VMBR to effect the competitive performance of high- and low-ability tennis players. The effectiveness of the ten-session VMBR intervention was mediated by ability level. Only the high-skill group demonstrated performance improvements. Meacci and Price (1985) found a variation of VMBR with physical practice improved putting performance of above average golfers when compared to VMBR without practice, a practice only group, and no training. Unfortunately, no differences were found at a three-month follow-up. In perhaps the strongest test of VMBR, Weinberg, Seabourne, and Jackson (1981) provided six weeks of daily exercises of VMBR, relaxation training, imagery training, or a placebo to members of a karate club. The VMBR and the relaxation groups subsequently exhibited reliably lower pre-competition state anxiety when compared with placebo and imagery groups. In addition, the VMBR group displayed significantly better performance during competitive sparring than the other groups. Two other performance measures showed no reliable differences.

Suinn's VMBR has received some interesting empirical support. This conclusion can be extended to research on the effectiveness of various individualized and packaged multicomponent intervention efforts to enhance sport performance (for example, DeWitt, 1980; Silva, 1982; Wrisberg & Anshel, 1989).

IV. Quantitative Review

A. Existing Reviews

The qualitative review we have presented here is largely supportive of cognitive behavioral athletic performance enhancement efforts. However, several distinguished authors have adopted a much more conservative interpretation of the state of the field. Morgan argued that there is little evidence to support the efficacy of psychological intervention efforts for athletic performance enhancement (Gould, 1988). He strongly advised that until a supportive scientific database has been clearly established, these interventions should not be used.

R. Smith (1989) and Greenspan and Feltz (1989) have adopted a more moderate but still cautious position. R. Smith expressed concerns about the rapid growth in applied sport psychology. He stressed the need for greater accountability and added that "much additional research is needed to fully evaluate the efficacy of our [intervention] programs" (1989, p. 174). Greenspan and Feltz (1989), in a review of experimental and descriptive performance enhancement efforts with athletes, concluded that the research was promising but questioned its generalizability to competitive athletes in competitive field settings. These authors were also extremely critical of the methodological sophistication of this literature.

To further confuse the picture, other sport scientists and psychologists have offered indirect evidence in support of psychological interventions with athletes. First, as we noted earlier, narrative (for example,

Corbin, 1972; Ryan & Simons, 1981; Weinberg, 1982) and quantitative (Feltz & Landers, 1983) reviews of the motor learning and mental practice literature reliably endorse mental rehearsal strategies. Techniques based on these rehearsal strategies, particularly imagery, are central to many athletic performance enhancement treatment programs (Vealey, 1988).

Second, the clinical efficacy of cognitive behavioral interventions (Lambert, Shapiro, & Bergin, 1986) has been viewed as support for sport performance enhancement work. A majority of interventions used with athletes can be directly linked to established cognitive behavioral strategies (Whelan et al., 1991). The effectiveness of these strategies in clinical situations, therefore, has been interpreted as indirect support for similar efficacy with athletes.

Third, a body of clinical case reports have been used to support performance enhancement work. Many descriptive and anecdotal evaluations by practitioners and athletes have endorsed the value of psychological interventions (for example, Fenker & Lamiotte, 1987; Heishman & Bunker, 1989; Roberts, 1989; Roberts & Halliwell, 1990; Suinn, 1972). Indeed, Martens (1987) has argued that practitioners' experience of treatment success and athletes' reports of treatment gains are the only meaningful data for judging clinically significant treatment effectiveness.

Finally, narrative reviews of interventions for athletic performance typically assume intervention effectiveness. Consequently, these authors primarily describe the field and speculate about the promise of enhancing performance (Browne & Mahoney, 1984; Donahue, Gillis, & King, 1980; Epstein & Wing, 1980; Kirschenbaum & Wittrock, 1984; Whelan et al., 1991).

B. Execution of the Meta-Analysis

Given the contradictory claims for the effectiveness of cognitive behavioral performance enhancement interventions, a more conclusive consideration of this literature was necessary. Through 1989, more than 100 empirical evaluations of performance enhancement were published (Greenspan & Feltz, 1989; Whelan, Meyers, & Berman, 1989). Unfortunately, several of these evaluations were case study or pre-post single group designs. Without clear comparison groups, these studies failed to provide evidence that psychological interventions were responsible for performance change. A second group of studies employed laboratory performance tasks rather than sport performance tasks. The generalizability of findings from the laboratory to the competitive arena is unknown. Fortunately, a number of these publications did conform to more rigorous experimental standards, used sport tasks, and allowed a direct examination of intervention effectiveness.

Consequently, in 1989 we (Whelan et al., 1989) focused on this latter group of studies and presented a preliminary quantitative review to evaluate the effectiveness of interventions with athletes. Interventions in these studies were all variations on cognitive behavioral strategies found in the clinical psychology literature, and the target tasks were an accepted sport performance or a component of that performance. In addition, each experiment provided a clear statistical indication of the direction and magnitude of the intervention efforts.

This review was specifically designed to answer three questions. First, what is the overall effectiveness of these cognitive behavioral interventions for athletic performance enhancement? Second, what is the strength or reliability of these interventions? Specifically, how effective are the treatments considering methodological issues such as type of control group, type of dependent measure, and type of intervention? Finally, how generalizable, or ecologically valid, is this estimate of overall effectiveness?

C. The Database

Since this intervention literature first began appearing approximately 20 years ago, the present review considered treatment evaluation studies published since 1970 and before 1989. The search for these articles began by identifying all psychology intervention studies that contained random assignment of participants to treatment or treatment to haphazardly formed groups, at least one treatment group that received a cognitive behavioral intervention, at least one control group, a direct comparison between treatment and control groups, a sport performance task, an assessment of treatment outcome, and

descriptive or inferential statistics from which an effect size could be determined. Cognitive behavioral intervention was broadly defined to include strategies designed to directly change behavior or that emphasized mental activities as a mediational process in behavior change (Dobson, 1988). Similarly, sport was considered broadly to include institutionalized game activity characterized by physical prowess, strategy, and chance (Loy, 1968).

Identification of articles that met these criteria involved several steps. First, the sport science journals were searched. Specifically, abstracts and method sections were examined to discern whether the evaluation met all the criteria for inclusion. Each potential article was examined by two raters. Inclusion or exclusion from this review was based on the consensus of these raters. The journals that were searched included *The Australian Journal of Science and Medicine in Sport, The Canadian Journal of Applied Sport Sciences, The International Journal of Sport Psychology, Journal of Exercise and Sport Psychology, Journal of Sport Behavior, Physician and Sportmedicine, Quest, Research Quarterly*, and *The Sport Psychologist*. Second, *Psychological Abstracts* was used to identify other potential articles. Once identified, the study was reviewed for possible inclusion. Finally, reference sections from the studies collected in steps one and two were used to reveal other published presentations of performance enhancement evaluations. Interestingly, this final step yielded only one study, presented in an edited book, that had not been identified in the previous two steps.

To address the primary questions of interest in this review, several characteristics of each study were quantified and coded (Wolf, 1986). To evaluate the reliability of the treatment effect, each study was coded to distinguish the different types of control groups, the different types of dependent measures (for example, performance versus self-report), the specific components of the independent measure or intervention (for example, imagery), and certain design characteristics (for example, use of a manual). To judge generalizability of the conclusions on intervention effectiveness, the studies were coded for characteristics of the sport task (for example, team versus individual), the context of assessment (for example, competition versus practice), and subject characteristics (for example, skill level).

Finally, the effect size calculations and subsequent comparisons were completed based on the meta-analytic techniques of Glass, McGraw, and Smith (1981) and Mansfield and Busse (1987). Effect size is an index indicating the degree of departure from the null hypothesis of the alternative hypothesis (Wolf, 1986). Or, in this case, it is the degree to which we can say that the experience of receiving the cognitive behavioral intervention departs from the experience of receiving some alternate control experience. The effect size, a variation of Cohen's d (Cohen, 1988), divides the difference between treatment and control means by the pooled standard deviation of these two groups. In this review, a positive effect size reflects the superiority of the treatment group over the control group.

Our literature search yielded 56 independent studies published in 47 journal articles and one book chapter. Since a number of the studies included more than one treatment or control group, a total of 121 treatment versus control group comparisons were made. The average number of participants per group was 26.6, with the smallest study having a sample size of four participants per condition and the largest having a sample size of 72 participants per condition. Although many of the studies failed to provide details of how treatments were delivered, the average intervention involved 11.1 treatment sessions lasting an average of 27.7 minutes per session. Furthermore, the studies were found to average 2.7 outcome measures (range = 1 to 10) per comparison. Thirty-five of the studies included an objective measure of performance on the athletic task.

D. Overall Effectiveness of Psychological Interventions

A preliminary question in meta-analytic reviews concerns the unit of analysis. Should each outcome measure be considered an independent assessment of intervention effectiveness? If each measure is considered independent, then a study with ten dependent variables will contribute ten estimates of the effect size and a study that used one dependent variable would contribute only one effect size. Similarly, should each treatment-control comparison be considered independent from every other treatment-control comparison, or should the study be considered as the unit of analysis? If the outcome measures are considered independent, then n in our review would be 333. If treatment-control comparisons are each considered independent, then the sample size would be 121. If, instead, the study was the unit of analysis, then n would equal 56. Logic would suggest that outcome measures within the same comparison are correlated and, therefore, interdependent. Similarly, comparisons within studies would typically be interdependent (Bangert-Drowns, 1992). If this assumption is correct, then the study is the appropriate unit of analysis.

To address this issue empirically, intraclass correlations were calculated and found to support the conclusion that the study should be the unit analysis for this review. The first of these analyses revealed that the variation in effect sizes derived from different treatment comparisons was greater than the variation of effect sizes within a single treatment comparison ($R = .29, p < .001$). This suggested that the relationship between all outcome measures used to compare a treatment and a control group was greater than the relationship between different treatment-control comparisons. This finding supported the assumption that the outcome effect sizes within comparisons should not be considered independent. The second intraclass correlation revealed that the variance between studies was greater than the variance between comparisons within studies ($R = .31, p < .01$). This finding indicated that the comparisons within studies were nonindependent. Consequently, these preliminary analyses supported the study as the appropriate unit of analysis.

With this issue resolved, we turned to the question of the overall effectiveness of the interventions for athletic performance. Across the 56 studies, the average effect size for cognitive behavioral interventions compared to the control group experience was .62 (SD = .85). Several methods can be used to interpret the meaning of this effect size. According to Cohen's (1988) guidelines for interpreting effect sizes in the social sciences, the effect size found in this review should be considered in the moderate to large range. A more refined method to understanding the strength of the effect is to use evaluations from a similar literature; for example, psychotherapy outcome research. Lambert et al. (1986) noted that the average effect size found in meta-analytic reviews of psychotherapy outcome, where treatment is compared to control experiences, ranged from .43 to 1.20. Clearly, the .62 effect size reported here for the outcome of athletic performance enhancement efforts compares favorably with the psychotherapy effectiveness literature. A third method of interpreting effect size results is to determine the confidence interval for this value of the average effect size. In this case the 95% confidence interval ranges from .40 to .84. Since this confidence interval does not encompass zero, the interpretation is that cognitive behavioral interventions for athletic performance enhancement are reliably and significantly superior to control experiences.

E. Reliability of Treatment Effectiveness

Since the type of control group, the type of dependent measure, the type of intervention, and methodological issues have been suggested to moderate the effectiveness of performance enhancing interventions (Feltz & Landers, 1983; Greenspan & Feltz, 1989; Whelan et al., 1989, 1991), the influence of variations in each of these study characteristics on the overall estimate of treatment effectiveness was considered separately. Such variations may have effects on the reliability of the conclusion that psychological interventions for performance enhancement are generally effective.

1. TYPE OF CONTROL GROUP

The studies included in the Whelan et al. (1989) review encompassed five varieties of control conditions, with several studies including more than one control condition. The most frequently used control condition, found in 28 of the studies (50% of the sample), was a no treatment control group. In these groups, participants sometimes received the same physical practice or coaching instruction as the treatment group but did not receive any form of psychological intervention. The second largest group of studies (36%) included attention control groups where participants did not receive the cognitive behavioral intervention but did receive equal time with an additional instructor who typically provided noncoaching didactic information about the sport task in addition to equal amounts of physical practice. Five studies (9%) included a placebo control group, where an

experience was provided that participants might believe would be performance enhancing. An additional six studies (11%) contained negative alternative treatment control groups, where the participants were presented with an experience that the experimenter predicted would interfere with performance execution. Finally, the comparison condition in five studies (9%) was a positive alternative treatment control group. These groups were designed to be a less potent variation of the intervention being evaluated. As shown in Table 6.1, effect sizes related to differences in control condition varied from .40 to .85.

To interpret the effect size estimates for type of control group two steps were completed. First, the 95% confidence intervals of these mean estimates were calculated. As shown in Table 6.1, only the effect sizes found in studies that contained negative alternative treatment control groups failed to reliably differentiate the outcome of the control and treatment groups. Second, an analysis of variance (ANOVA) was completed to compare the effect sizes across the different control group subtypes. This analysis re-

Table 6.1 Differences between cognitive behavioral intervention groups and control groups at posttreatment for different types of control groups and dependent measures

| | | Effect Size[a][b] | | |
	N of Studies	M	SD	95% Confidence Interval
Type of Control Group				
No treatment	28	.47*	.69	.21 to .83
With physical practice	21	.40*	.88	.01 to .79
No physical practice	12	.64*	.84	.15 to 1.03
Attentional	20	.62*	1.12	.12 to 1.12
Placebo	5	.79*	.47	.33 to 1.25
Alternate treatment	6	.61	.78	−.07 to 1.29
Negative treatment	5	.85*	.63	.23 to 1.47
Type of Dependent Measure				
Objective	38	.64***	.68	.42 to .86
Physiological	14	.49*	.84	.03 to .95
Subject self-report	24	.51*	1.20	.02 to 1.00
Judge ratings	17	.29	.58	.00 to .67

[a]Positive effect size indicates that the cognitive behavioral intervention was more effective.
[b]Asterisks indicate comparisons in which the mean effect size differed reliably from zero: *p < .05; **p < .01; ***p < .001.

vealed that the estimate of treatment effectiveness did not vary with type of control group. In general, these findings provide clear support for the conclusion that cognitive behavioral interventions effectively enhance athletic performance.

2. TYPE OF DEPENDENT MEASURE

The type of dependent measure used in each study is another study characteristic central to discussing the reliability of the treatment effect. As with the psychotherapy outcome literature (Lambert, Shapiro, & Bergin, 1986), this research included an array of dependent variables, including objective, physiological, self-report, and observer rating measures. A majority of the reports, 34 studies (61%), included an objective measure of performance change. The frequent use of objective measures has been considered a hallmark of the sport psychology research (Shelton & Mahoney, 1978). Due to the nature of sport performance, objective measures—such as time, weight, distance, or success/failure—can be assessed easily and accurately. The average effect size across studies with objective measures was .64 (SD = .68). The 95% confidence interval of this estimate supports the interpretation that objective performance gains for the treatment groups were greater than the gains for the control groups (see Table 6.1).

The average effect sizes for the other types of dependent variables also clearly supported the conclusion that psychological interventions for athletic performance enhancement were reliably effective. Twenty-four studies (43%) reported self-report measures, and the average effect size of these studies was .49. Fourteen studies (25%) used physiological measures, and the average effect size was .51. Observer ratings included both official competition judges and trained observers and were reported in 17 studies (30%). The average effect size was .29 and, while significant, was significantly lower than the effect size revealed with any of the other types of dependent variables.

3. COMPONENTS OF TREATMENT

Effectiveness of cognitive behavioral interventions for sport performance was shown to be reliable across the different types of intervention strategies discussed earlier in this chapter—goal setting, mental

rehearsal, arousal management, cognitive restructuring, and multicomponent treatments. (See Table 6.2 for a summary.)

4. GOAL SETTING INTERVENTIONS

Three of the 56 studies (2%) evaluated the effectiveness of goal setting interventions and the average effect size for these three studies was .54 (SD = .15). This finding suggests that goal setting interventions produce a statistically significant moderate effect over the no treatment experiences. The interventions evaluated in these studies focused on whether goal setting had an impact on performance and did not evaluate the type of achievement goals or issues such as goal difficulty or goal specificity.

For example, Barnett and Stanicek (1979) questioned the effect of specific, personal performance goals on achievement in archery. The initial pool of participants included 60 undergraduates enrolled in beginner archery classes. Students were randomly assigned to receive the typical didactic instruction plus physical practice or didactic instruction with goal setting plus physical practice. Unfortunately, only 30 (50%) participants completed the ten-week class, which

Table 6.2 Differences between cognitive behavioral intervention groups and control groups for specific types of interventions

Types of Interventions	N of Studies	Effect Size[ab] M	SD	95% Confidence Interval
Goal setting	3	.54**	.15	.44 to .56
Mental rehearsal	28	.57**	.75	.29 to .85
Anxiety management				
Relaxation	25	.73**	1.64	.07 to 1.39
Psych-up	5	1.23**	.73	.52 to 1.94
Cognitive self-management				
Attentional focus	7	1.21	1.61	⁻.07 to 2.49
Self-instruction	6	.76	1.17	–.26 to 1.78
Self-monitoring	3	.66**	.45	.38 to .94
Cognitive restructure	4	.79**	.36	.38 to 1.10
Multicomponent	9	1.01***	.65	.56 to 1.46

[a]Positive effect size indicates that the cognitive behavioral intervention was more effective.
[b]Asterisks indicate comparisons in which the mean effect size differed reliably from zero: *p < .05; **p < .01; ***p < .001.

met for two 50-minute sessions per week. Assessment of archery performance occurred during the first and tenth weeks of the class. During the first five-weeks, students in the goal setting condition were instructed to establish a list of specific goals related to the execution of an archery shot, such as aspects of the aim, release, or follow-through. During the second five-weeks, the students were directed to add goals related to improving their archery score. This goal setting was completed during a ten-minute meeting between the archery instructor and the group. The instructor provided examples but encouraged students to use goal sheets to establish personally meaningful goals. Students who were not instructed in goal setting also met for a group meeting where similar content was discussed but goal setting was not encouraged. While both groups experienced performance gains in the class, Barnett and Stanicek (1979) reported significantly superior performances for participants who received goal setting when compared with participants who did not.

5. MENTAL REHEARSAL INTERVENTIONS

Of the 28 studies (50%) where the intervention included some form of mental rehearsal, typically imagery, the average effect size was .57 (SD = .75). This effect size indicated that participants using mental rehearsal strategies reliably outperformed participants not directed to use imagery. This result is consistent with the findings of Feltz and Landers's (1983) quantitative review of the effects of mental rehearsal on motor skill performance, where the average effect size was .48 (SD = .67). The primary difference between the two samples of studies was that Feltz and Landers's (1983) review focused on laboratory motor learning tasks while the Whelan et al. (1989) summary flagged sport performance tasks. A second difference was that, unlike the laboratory motor learning studies, some sport performance studies paired imagery with other intervention techniques (for example, Meacci & Price, 1985; Weinberg, Seabourne, & Jackson, 1982). Considering the 95% confidence interval for each effect size estimate, the slightly larger average effect size in the Whelan et al. (1989) review is not reliably different from the average effect size in the Feltz and Landers (1983) review.

An example of mental rehearsal interventions is the White et al. (1979) examination of the utility of imagery, with or without physical practice, on learning diving starts used in competitive swimming. Twenty high school and college age novice swimmers were matched on age and imagery skills and then assigned to receive either imagery only, imagery plus physical practice, physical practice only, or no practice. Participants in the imagery condition received a list of 15 steps with illustrative drawings that detailed correct technique and were directed to mentally rehearse for five-minute periods on each of eight consecutive nights. No specific training in imagery or verification of intervention compliance was described. Physical training included four ten-minute individual instruction sessions evenly distributed across the eight days. The combined physical and mental rehearsal condition received both experiences. The no practice group received no instruction and no directions to rehearse. Qualified judges, who were blind to the manipulation and were found to have high inter-rater reliability, rated the participants' start performance on both the first and eighth day. Start performances significantly improved for participants assigned to imagery, physical practice, and combined imagery and physical practice, but not for participants in the no practice group. The small sample size prevented conclusions concerning potential differences among the practice conditions.

In an experiment that is somewhat more representative of contemporary imagery interventions, Mumford and Hall (1985) examined the efficacy of different imagery perspectives—internal visual imagery, external visual imagery, internal kinesthetic imagery, or no imagery—on the performance of ice-skating skills. Fifty-nine moderate to highly skilled competitive skaters were randomly assigned to conditions. The imagery training included four one-hour group treatment sessions. Specifics of these training sessions were not reported. The control group spent an equal amount of time viewing skating films. The performance task was to skate a senior-level figure that included skating elements familiar to all participants. Performance was rated by three certified, experienced judges. Results failed to reveal differences between imagery type; however, all imagery groups realized performance gains when compared with a control group.

6. ANXIETY MANAGEMENT INTERVENTIONS

While no single study examined the ability to both increase or decrease arousal level, 25 studies (45%) reported using relaxation training to decrease arousal level and five other studies (9%) focused on mental preparation for arousal increase. Both relaxation ($d = .73$, SD = 1.64) and arousal increase interventions ($d = 1.23$, SD = .73) were found to be reliably effective when compared with a variety of control groups. Several different relaxation strategies have been evaluated, including abbreviated Jacobson progressive relaxation (for example, Chaney & Andreasen, 1973; Lanning & Hisanga, 1983), imagery-based relaxation (for example, Murphy & Woolfolk, 1987), hypnosis (Albert & Williams, 1975), and biofeedback (for example, Costa, Bonaccorsi, & Scrimali, 1984). The targeted effect of the interventions included facilitation of physical skill development (for example, Weinberg et al., 1982), enhancement of concentration (for example, Murphy & Woolfolk, 1987), and management of precompetitive anxiety (for example, Costa et al., 1984).

Lanning and Hisanga (1983) examined the effect of a variation of Jacobson's progressive relaxation training on competitive anxiety and performance in female high school volleyball players. They randomly assigned 24 players to receive relaxation training or no treatment. During an 18-day period, participants who received the relaxation training met with a masters-level counselor for seven 30-minute sessions. The specifics of the intervention were not described. Self-report experience of anxiety and serving performance in game situations were assessed immediately before and immediately after the training period and again at a two-week follow-up. A significant decrease in anxiety and a significant increase in performance were found for those athletes who received the relaxation training but not for those who were untreated. Although treatment effects were evident at the follow-up assessment, they were not as strong as those reported immediately after treatment.

Caudill et al. (1983) reported two examples of attempts to influence psyching-up. Sixteen collegiate sprinters and hurdlers ran 60-yard time trials under different race preparation conditions. In one condition, runners were cued to "mentally psych-up" for one minute. In a second condition, the experimenter conversed with runners to distract them from any possible focus on the race. The third condition was a placebo in which runners were asked to assess their heart rate to achieve better body awareness. These preparation conditions were counterbalanced to control for order effects. Results revealed that the psych-up condition yielded significantly faster 60-yard times than the other conditions. Runners reported combinations of strategies during the psych-up period, including narrowing attentional focus, self-efficacy statements, relaxation efforts, preparatory arousal, imagery, and religious thoughts.

7. COGNITIVE SELF-REGULATION INTERVENTIONS

Cognitive self-management studies included in the quantitative review evaluated interventions such as altering attentional focus (Okwumabua, Meyers, Schleser, & Cooke, 1983), self-instruction (Meyers, Schleser, et al., 1979), self-monitoring (Kirschenbaum et al., 1982), and variations of cognitive restructuring (Ziegler et al., 1982). As shown in Table 6.2, this review did not support the effectiveness of either attentional focus or self-instruction interventions. Experiments using these interventions had widely varying outcomes. In contrast, self-monitoring and cognitive restructuring interventions were found to facilitate positive performance changes.

One example from this literature is the demonstration by Kirschenbaum et al. (1982) of the utility of self-monitoring strategies and the moderating effects of athlete skill level. The authors predicted that low-skilled bowlers would benefit from positive self-monitoring and high-skilled bowlers would benefit from negative self-monitoring. To test these hypotheses, high- and low-skilled bowlers were assigned to either positive self-monitoring, negative self-monitoring, skill instructions, or no treatment. In one 30-minute session, participants in the self-monitoring conditions or in the skill instruction condition were instructed on seven components of effective bowling. In addition, positive self-monitoring participants were told to follow each frame bowled by identifying the components they executed well. They then rated their performance of these components as good, very good, or excellent. Negative self-monitoring participants were told to follow each frame bowled with a review of possible errors made across the seven components. They were also told to rate their performance as poor, very poor, or terrible. Postintervention outcome was assessed by averaging the next 15 games bowled. The results revealed that positive self-monitoring benefited low-skilled bowlers, but neither intervention was effective with high-skilled bowlers.

8. MULTICOMPONENT INTERVENTIONS

Nine studies evaluated variations of multicomponent interventions, including eight evaluations of Suinn's (1972) VMBR. The average effect size across these studies was large, $d = 1.01$ (SD = .65). This evidence suggests that multicomponent intervention packages lead to reliably superior performance when compared with a variety of control conditions.

A study by Ziegler et al. (1982) illustrates the multicomponent intervention literature. These investigators compared two variations of stress management training with a no treatment control condition on the cardiorespiratory efficiency of collegiate cross-country runners. Nine male runners were matched on preintervention cardiorespiratory efficiency and assigned to one of the three groups. One treatment group received a variation of Stress Inoculation Training (Meichenbaum, 1977) and the other treatment group received Stress Management Training (Smith, 1980). Components of both interventions are similar and include relaxation training, cognitive coping strategies, and imagery. Each group met twice weekly for 5.5 weeks. Postintervention evaluations of cardiovascular efficiency, as assessed using a maximal oxygen consumption treadmill run, found significant differences between the two treatment groups and the control group.

As noted previously, VMBR has been shown to be effective across several sport performance tasks. The Seabourne, Weinberg, Jackson, and Suinn (1985) study was particularly informative because, in addition to demonstrating the effectiveness of VMBR, it also examined the efficacy of individually tailored versus packaged intervention programs. The 43 volunteer participants were enrolled in beginner karate classes, and the targeted performance tasks were specific karate skills, execution of skill combinations, and sparring. Participants were randomly assigned to receive either an individualized VMBR treatment, treatment yoked to another athlete's individualized VMBR treatment, packaged VMBR treatment, placebo control experience, or no treatment. Procedurally, a detailed needs assessment was completed with all participants. For the individually tailored group, this needs assessment was used to develop a specific intervention program. Each participant in the yoked group was given an intervention program specifically developed for a participant in the individualized treatment. The third group received the standard VMBR program, and the placebo group discussed quotations from Chinese writings. Across the 15 weeks of treatment, all participants received 17 hours of intervention, including time for homework exercises. The authors used homework to check compliance with treatment and as verification that participants understood the intervention. In addition, ten weeks into the study participants' performance was assessed and interviews were repeated to ensure compliance. Results indicated that after 15 weeks of intervention both the individualized and packaged interventions groups realized significant performance improvements compared with the other conditions on the performance of skill combinations and sparring.

F. Design Issues

Conclusions about this intervention literature must be tempered in the face of several critical design issues (Greenspan & Feltz, 1989; Whelan et al., 1989, 1991). One primary criticism of the studies reviewed here is the lack of attention to the integrity of treatment delivery. Treatment integrity refers to the degree to which the treatment was delivered as intended (Yeaton & Sechrest, 1992). While our criticism is not unique to this literature (Kazdin, 1986; Yeaton & Sechrest, 1992), few of the studies included in this review attended to this concern. In fact, method sections only rarely included detailed descriptions of treatment components or treatment delivery, descriptions of the training of the treatment providers, or systemic verification that these providers implemented the planned intervention. An example of a study that did attend to these issues was the Seabourne et al. (1985) evaluation of VMBR with beginner karate classes. Although no information about the training of the experimenters was provided, a manual was made available to the experimenters. The authors also assessed psychological skills during treatment to verify that the appropriate skills were being addressed in the training exercises.

A corollary design issue is treatment reception. Treatment cannot be delivered with integrity if the designed treatment is not received by the targeted participants (Smith & Sechrest, 1992). Interference with reception may occur from a variety of sources, including the complexity, brevity, believability, applicability, or monotony of the treatment. Characteristics of the client, such as intelligence, expectations about the treatment, or reactions to the experimenter, may influence the way treatment is received. Since all the studies in this review described skill-building interventions, treatment reception could have been easily monitored. While many studies in this review (31, or 55%) included manipulation checks, few provided clear indication that the training for targeted psychological skill was actually received by the participants. One study that included a check on treatment reception was the evaluation by Kirschenbaum et al. (1982) of self-monitoring on bowling performance. Collection of self-monitoring forms from the participants provided an indication of their competence at self-monitoring. Use of deposits from the self-monitors to ensure completion of the forms further assisted in this check. Unfortunately, the authors did not provide a report of treatment compliance. Only with consideration of treatment integrity and certainty about treatment reception can the efficacy of the specific intervention be fully evaluated.

A second significant design criticism is the general failure to assess the maintenance of treatment effects. Only 2 of the 56 studies (4%) included a follow-up evaluation of intervention effectiveness beyond treatment termination. Greenspan and Feltz (1989) reported that follow-up assessments were also infrequently used in studies with single-subject designs or uncontrolled descriptive evaluations. While gains at the end of an intervention appear to be a necessary

condition to endorse treatment effectiveness, maintenance of those gains is also necessary to validate the long-term efficacy of intervention. This should be particularly true in evaluations of skill development interventions, where performance changes are assumed to be enduring. Reviews of the psychotherapy literature have concluded that treatment maintenance remains an important question (Lambert et al., 1986). Follow-up evaluations of behavioral skill-building interventions typically reveal that treatment gains are maintained (Nicholson & Berman, 1983). However, some reviewers have noted that treatment gains often decrease over a follow-up period of six to eight months (Lambert et al., 1986), and investigators typically recommend follow-up assessments at least six months posttreatment (Galassi & Galassi, 1984).

The athletic performance enhancement intervention studies that included a follow-up assessment supported maintenance of treatment effects. Lanning and Hisanga (1983) included a two-week follow-up period in their evaluation of relaxation training with high school volleyball players. They noted that the treatment group's self-report of anxiety and serve accuracy continued to be statistically superior to that of the no treatment control group; however, the absolute differences between these groups decreased over the brief follow-up period. Three weeks after treatment, Gravel et al. (1980) assessed self-reported evaluations of performance and cognitive ruminations in cross-country skiers who did or did not receive VMBR training. Self-reports revealed that treatment differences were maintained, and the frequency of cognitive ruminations continued to significantly decrease for participants in the VMBR group. The evaluation by Kirschenbaum et al. (1982) of self-monitoring with bowlers did not include a follow-up but did reveal information about treatment maintenance. Posttreatment assessment was five weeks long, with an average of three games bowled per week. Performance changes during these five weeks were not discussed; however, intervention effectiveness over a relatively long assessment period does suggest stability of the treatment effect.

A third critical issue in this literature is the restricted range of treatment evaluation strategies. Little attention has been given to evaluations involving dismantling, constructive, parametric, or comparative treatment strategies. Such variation in research design can address a variety of issues, including potency of components within a treatment package, the value of aspects of particular strategies, and dosage effects (Kazdin, 1986). The series of evaluations of VMBR with karate classes (Seabourne et al., 1985; Weinberg et al., 1981, 1982) provided an example of using alternative designs to clarify the parameters of an intervention package. Other investigators (Ziegler et al., 1982) have attempted to evaluate the relative contribution of slightly different intervention programs, but typically these efforts did not employ sufficiently large sample sizes to detect small treatment effects. Investigators working in this literature would do well to focus less on isolated demonstrations of cognitive behavioral intervention effectiveness and more on studies designed to answer questions on the interaction among types of interventions, athlete characteristics, and situational demands.

A final design issue concerns the lack of attention to treatment characteristics not necessarily related to the intervention strategies. These factors include participant characteristics, service provider characteristics, aspects about participant-provider dyads, process variables, and influence of external events. These extra-strategy variables have had an effect on psychotherapy outcome (Garfield, 1986) and consequently might have an impact on interventions for athletic performance. As evident in the next section, the athletic performance enhancement literature has considered several participant variables (for example, sex, age, and skill level). Unfortunately, variables such as education, socioeconomic status, motivation, treatment expectations, and value of performance improvement have not been addressed. Similarly, characteristics of the service provider and the intervention situation have not been examined.

G. Generalizability

Generalizability, or ecological or external validity, concerns how well the existing research simulates and predicts "real" behaviors in "real" contexts (Kazdin, 1978). Its importance depends on the research question and the type of inferences the experimenter wishes to draw (Berkowitz & Donnerstein, 1982). In athletic performance enhancement research, the ability to draw inferences from experimental settings to effective application in sport settings is crucial. The goal of this research is to identify psychological skills and develop cognitive behavioral interventions that effectively improve the performance of athletes in competitive situations. Consequently, generalizability of the research findings becomes a vital question.

Unfortunately, the process of securing controls necessary to guarantee internal validity often induces a degree of artificiality in the research setting that limits external validity (Mook, 1992). Aspects of the tasks, the contexts, and the subjects are often compromised so that the hypothetico-deductive method can lead to clear causal inference. Descriptive information produced from qualitative methods and practical experiences (Martens, 1987) can help generate hypotheses and build theories, but only experimental data can lead to an understanding of causality. The experimental method cannot be discarded because of inherent artificiality. Instead, an empirical consideration of generalizability must be mounted. The process of replication and extension of research findings can provide information about how much cognitive behavioral interventions affect athletic performance. The Whelan et al. (1989) review attended to the characteristics of the participants, the tasks, and the contexts to address the ecological validity of this body of research.

1. Task Characteristics

Three task characteristics were considered in this review: team versus individual sports, open versus closed sports, and type of physical skill. Of the studies included in this review, 51 (91%) focused on individual performance tasks and included representatives from a wide variety of sports, including dart throwing, swimming, running, tennis, and archery. The mean effect size across these studies was found to be significantly different from zero (see Table 6.3). Team sports were underrepresented, with two studies using volleyball players and three studies on basketball players. In all these studies, the focus of the intervention was an individual performance task. Price and Braun (1983) focused on basketball free-throw shooting. Lanning and Hisanga (1983) targeted volleyball serves, while

Table 6.3 Posttreatment differences between cognitive behavioral intervention groups and control groups for different performance tasks characteristics

	N of Studies	Effect Size[a][b]		
		M	SD	95% Confidence Interval
Individual versus Team Sports				
Individual	51	.65***	.88	.40 to .90
Team	5	.63**	.30	.33 to .93
Closed versus Open Sport				
Closed	47	.65*	.90	.39 to .91
Open	8	.50*	.56	.11 to .89
Performance Skills				
Accuracy	24	.72***	.98	.33 to 1.11
Balance	2	−.07	.10	−.26 to .12
Endurance	12	.59*	.78	.35 to .83
Speed	3	1.18	1.09	−.33 to 2.69
Strength	3	.70*	.17	.46 to .94
Combination of skills	12	.25	.47	−.02 to .52

[a]Positive effect size indicates that the cognitive behavioral intervention was more effective.
[b]Asterisks indicate comparisons in which the mean effect size differed reliably from zero: *$p < .05$; **$p < .01$; ***$p < .001$.

Shick (1970) included both serving and volleying skills. The volleying skills did not focus on hitting with other players but rather hitting against a wall. On average, the effect size associated with these interventions was significant. Consequently, this review provides little evidence about strategies for improving team performance, although the evidence does support the use of interventions to enhance individual team members' physical performance skills.

A second task characteristic was whether the sport was considered a closed skill or an open skill. Closed skill tasks embody self-paced performance, where participants execute a specific, predetermined action. Examples would include firing a rifle at a target, running a marathon, and shooting free-throws. In contrast, open skill tasks involve performance in which the participant must respond to action by other competitors or teammates. Examples would include tennis service returns and goal keeping in soccer or ice hockey. A majority of the experiments included in this review examined the performance of closed skill tasks

($n = 47$, 84%). The average effect sizes associated with interventions on both closed skill and open skill tasks were found to be significant. This suggests that while the literature focuses on self-paced tasks there is empirical support for interventions on both types of performance tasks.

The experiments were also coded to examine the primary type of physical skill targeted by each intervention. Sport tasks were divided into categories of accuracy, balance, endurance, strength, speed, or combinations of these skills. As can be seen in Table 6.3, studies most frequently targeted accuracy skills, followed by endurance skills, and then a combination of skills. An examination of the average effect size for each category revealed that interventions effectively enhanced athletic performances that required accuracy, endurance, or strength skills. There were simply too few studies to draw conclusions about the efficacy of interventions for balance or speed skills.

2. Context Characteristics

The primary task characteristic relevant to the issue of generalization is the assessment of performance in the competitive setting. Although the goal of athletic performance enhancement does not necessitate competition, the goal of cognitive behavioral interventions is typically to improve performance in competition (Roberts, 1989; Roberts & Halliwell, 1990). Twenty-two (39%) of the studies in this review did assess competitive performance, and 12 of these 22 studies included assessment of performance while in direct competition against others. The remaining 34 (61%) studies assessed performance under noncompetitive conditions. The mean effect size for both competition and noncompetition assessments was found to be significantly different from zero. A direct comparison, using a *t*-test, revealed that the strength of the effect was significantly greater when performance was assessed in noncompetitive situations. Noncompetitive performance assessments, therefore, appear to overestimate the effectiveness of the treatment. Despite the overestimation, this pattern of results indicates that cognitive behavioral interventions are effective in enhancing competitive performance.

3. Participant Characteristics

The participant characteristic of greatest relevance to generalization is the participant's skill level. The most easily obtained group of participants in sport psychology research, as in other areas of human research, is the undergraduate college student (Owen & Lee, 1987). These student participants typically have been novices at the assessed sport task; often they are enrolled in an introductory physical education course. In contrast, applied cognitive behavioral interventions for sport performance is most often aimed at highly skilled and elite competitors (Murphy, 1988; Orlick & Partington, 1988; Suinn, 1972). The literature contrasting the cognitive strategies of successful versus less successful athletes has found these groups to be quite different (Gould, Weiss, & Weinberg, 1981; Mahoney, Gabriel, & Perkins, 1987; Meyers, Cooke, et al., 1979). As a consequence, we must determine whether intervention research with novices or nonathletes will allow us to draw conclusions about treatment effectiveness with competent and elite athletes.

To address this concern, participants in each of the studies included in the Whelan et al. (1989) review were rated for level of skill proficiency by two trained research assistants. Since a few studies used participants from more than one skill level, each group of participants was rated, and 58 separate effect sizes were calculated. A check on the reliability of the raters was found to be quite high (Cohen's Kappa = .86).

As shown in Figure 6.1, 37 (64%) of the 58 comparisons involved participants with little or no proficiency with the sport task, and most disappointing, no controlled outcome study addressed the efficacy of cognitive behavioral interventions with elite athletes. An examination of the average effect size for the various levels of skill proficiency suggests that interventions to enhance sport performance were reliably effective for both minimally proficient and proficient groups of participants. Interventions with high school and college varsity athletes were also found to be reliably effective. Finally, there is no statement about the effectiveness of these interventions with elite athletes. The two studies that focused on nationally ranked or pre-elite athletes both included small samples that may have prohibited a clear evaluation of treatment effectiveness.

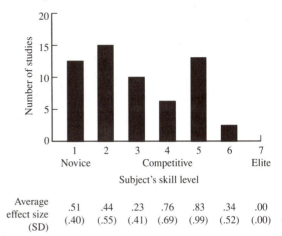

| Average effect size (SD) | .51 (.40) | .44 (.55) | .23 (.41) | .76 (.69) | .83 (.99) | .34 (.52) | .00 (.00) |

Figure 6.1 Frequency and average effect sizes of studies with varying levels of skill with sport performance tasks

The evidence presented in this review supports the efficacy of a wide range of cognitive behavioral performance enhancement interventions with athletes at a variety of skill levels. Unfortunately, we do not have evidence to address whether these interventions work with elite athletes.

V. Applications to Elite Athletes

Psychological interventions with elite athletes have come to be heavily influenced by cognitive behavioral models and the intervention strategies we have described here (see Roberts, 1989; Roberts & Halliwell, 1990). Indeed, most athletic performance enhancement programs were originally designed for the elite athlete (Bennett & Pravitz, 1987; Loehr & Kahn, 1987; Nideffer & Sharpe, 1978; Orlick, 1986; Porter & Foster, 1986; Ungerleider & Golding, 1992). These programs have typically adopted a packaged or technique-driven, mental skills training approach to performance enhancement. As we warned earlier in this chapter, the failure to engage in assessment or the poor fit between assessment strategies and intervention raises serious concerns about this applied work.

One reason that assessment and the resulting tailoring of interventions have not received sufficient attention is an underlying assumption in applied sport psychology that elite athletes have few, if any, problems and that their primary concern is better performance. Perhaps the most impressive statement of this position is Morgan's (1985) mental health model of athletic performance. Morgan has asserted both that exercise contributes to emotional well-being and that the achievement of elite athletic status requires a stable, healthy psychological system. We believe that this assumption is difficult to defend and may lead practitioners to hold complacent attitudes about elite athletes' emotional health.

Obviously, elite athletes operate in an extremely stressful world. Consider the different concerns and pressures faced by very young sports stars (for example, the 14-year-old gymnast), minority athletes in collegiate sports, collegiate athletes in revenue-producing sports, or athletes preparing for the Olympics or professional careers. At the Olympic Training Center (OTC) in Colorado Springs, Colorado, records have been maintained for over six years on more than 1000 athletes who have sought consultation with OTC sport psychology staff. More than 60% of the identified issues leading to consultation involved performance concerns. Examples of typical concerns included anxiety at competition, concentration deficits during performance, lack of motivation in the face of grueling training schedules, worry over success and failure, and communications difficulties with a coach or fellow athlete.

However, an interesting finding from this database was that despite the common initial focus on performance, 85% of all cases seen by the staff involved personal counseling with the athlete. Even seemingly simple performance-related issues often touched—or were touched by—many other areas of the athlete's life. For example, an athlete sought consultation complaining of an inability to concentrate during competition. Assessment indicated that the athlete's father attended all competitions (but not practices) and that the athlete was very nervous when performing in the presence of her father. Further analysis indicated that the father had undertaken a significant financial commitment to the athlete's training, that father-daughter communication was ineffective, and that the athlete's mother was concerned that the daughter's sports involvement would delay her educational advancement.

What began as a simple performance issue actually required substantial personal counseling or even a form of family therapy to address all the issues that affected the athlete's performance.

A crucial problem in evaluating either traditional cognitive behavioral skill development programs for the performance enhancement of elite athletes or more broadly defined clinical or counseling interventions is the scarcity of controlled research in the area. Both practical and ethical concerns have impeded this research. A team of a dozen athletes does not easily lend itself to comparisons of treatment and necessary control conditions. Small sample sizes create statistical power problems that negatively affect our ability to draw conclusions about our work. And who receives the hypothesized active intervention, and who receives the control experience? At the elite level, no athlete or coach willingly bypasses any possible (and hopefully legal) aid to performance. While controlled group research can be run in some elite settings, investigators will have to seek creative and palatable strategies to evaluate these interventions. Quasi-experimental and intrasubject research designs have already been put to good use (compare with Meyers et al., 1982). Unfortunately, as documented in both our qualitative and quantitative reviews, we have yet to document the performance enhancement benefits of cognitive behavioral interventions with elite athletes.

VI. Summary and Conclusions

While we might debate the role of sport in our culture, its influence is certainly pervasive. Each day millions of Americans engage in some form of competition, training, or physical exercise. Such popularity and the value our culture places on competition have made sport a valid area of psychological inquiry. Within the cognitive behavioral model, sport psychology and, specifically, athletic performance enhancement have experienced vigorous growth over the past two decades. Behavior change strategies familiar to most cognitive behaviorists form the core of virtually all athletic performance enhancement interventions. Goal setting, imagery or mental rehearsal, relaxation training, stress management, self-monitoring, self-instruction, cognitive restructuring, and modeling interventions dominate this literature.

Our examination of these performance enhancement programs, both through a qualitative review and the Whelan et al. (1989) meta-analysis, supports the efficacy of cognitive behavioral interventions for the enhancement of sport performance. First, the average effect size across the empirical literature indicates that these interventions are reliably effective. Furthermore, this positive result is observed across variations in treatment conditions, control conditions, and across different types of dependent measures. Evidence on goal setting, imagery, arousal management, cognitive self-regulation, and packaged programs specifically support the behavior change efficacy of these interventions.

These findings are encouraging, but much work needs to be done. Few investigators cited in this review attend to crucial internal and external validity issues. Attention to treatment integrity, including training of behavior change agents, verification of intervention implementation, and verification of reception of the treatment, is sorely lacking. Psychological skill development and its relationship to performance improvements are rarely checked.

Now that cognitive behavioral interventions appear to be reliably effective at posttreatment, we must have meaningful evaluation of maintenance of psychological skill and performance changes. Six-month, 12-month, and longer follow-up evaluations are necessary. We must also begin more detailed evaluations of these effective interventions. What program components are responsible for performance enhancement? What combination of components are most effective? What participant and provider characteristics contribute to successful intervention? What additional process variables are important to athletic behavior change?

Finally, we must begin to extend the findings presented here to new domains. Few studies examine performance change in team sports. Open skill or interactive sports are also underrepresented in this literature. And we know less about balance or speed sports than we know about strength or endurance sports. These are all critical questions, but our most demanding task is the challenge of extending this

research to actual competitive situations and to elite athletes. Only then will the final verdict truly be in on cognitive behavioral interventions for athletic performance enhancement.

References

ALBERT, I., & Williams, M. H. (1975). Effects of post-hypnotic suggestions on muscular endurance. *Perceptual and Motor Skills, 40*, 131–139.

BANDURA, A. (1969). *Principles of behavior modification.* New York: Holt, Rinehart & Winston.

BANDURA, A. (1977). Self-efficacy: Toward a unifying theory of behavioral change. *Psychological Review, 84*, 919–215.

BANGERT-DROWNS, R. L. (1992). Review of the developments in meta-analytic method. In A. E. Kazdin (Ed.), *Methodological issues and strategies in clinical research* (pp. 439–467). Washington, DC: American Psychological Association.

BARNETT, M. L., & Stanicek, J. A. (1979). Effects of goal setting on achievement in archery. *Research Quarterly, 50*, 328–332.

BECK, A. (1976). *Cognitive therapy and emotional disorders.* New York: International Universities Press.

BENNETT, J. G., & Pravitz, J. E. (1987). *Profile of a winner: Advanced mental training for athletes.* Ithaca, NY: Sport Science International.

BERKOWITZ, L., & Donnerstein, E. (1982). External validity is more than skin deep. *American Psychologist, 37*, 245–257.

BROWNE, M. A., & Mahoney, M. J. (1984). Sport psychology. *Annual Review of Psychology, 35*, 605–625.

BURTON, D. (1989). Winning isn't everything: Examining the impact of performance goals on collegiate swimmers' cognitions and performance. *The Sport Psychologist, 2*, 105–132.

CARVER, C. S., & Scheier, M. F. (1981). *Attention and self-regulation: A control theory approach to human behavior.* New York: Springer-Verlag.

CAUDILL, D., & Weinberg, R. (1983). The effects of varying the length of the psych-up interval on motor performance. *Journal of Sport Behavior, 6*, 86–91.

CAUDILL, D., Weinberg, R., & Jackson, A. (1983). Psyching-up and track athletes: A preliminary investigation. *Journal of Sport Psychology, 5*, 231–235.

CHANEY, D. S., & Andreasen, L. (1973). Relaxation and neuromuscular tension control and changes in motor performance under induced tension. *Perceptual and Motor Skills, 36*, 185–186.

COHEN, J. (1988). *Statistical power analysis for the behavioral sciences* (2nd ed.). Hillsdale, NJ: Erlbaum.

CORBIN, C. B. (1972). Mental practice. In W. P. Morgan (Ed.), *Ergogenic acids and muscular performance* (pp. 94–118). New York: Academic Press.

COSTA, A., Bonaccorsi, M., & Scrimali, T. (1984). Biofeedback and control of anxiety preceding athletic competition. *International Journal of Sport Psychology, 15*, 98–109.

CSIKSZENTMIHALYI, M. (1990). *Flow: The psychology of optimal experience*. New York: Harper & Row.

DeWITT, D. J. (1980). Cognitive and biofeedback training for stress reduction with university athletes. *Journal of Sport Psychology, 2*, 288–294.

DOBSON, K. S. (Ed.). (1988). *Handbook of cognitive-behavioral therapies*. New York: Guilford Press.

DONAHUE, J. A., Gillis, J. H., & King, K. (1980). Behavior modification in sport and physical education: A review. *Journal of Sport Psychology, 2*, 311–328.

DUDA, J. L. (1989). Relationship between task and ego orientation and the perceived purpose of sport among high school athletes. *Journal of Sport and Exercise Psychology, 11*, 318–335.

EPSTEIN, L. H., & Wing, R. R. (1980). Behavioral approaches to exercise habits and athletic performance. In J. M. Ferguson & C. B. Taylor (Eds.), *The comprehensive handbook of behavioral medicine* (Vol. 1, pp. 125–137). New York: Spectrum.

EPSTEIN, M. L. (1980). The relationship of mental imagery and mental rehearsal to performance on a motor task. *Journal of Sport Psychology, 2*, 211–220.

FELTZ, D. L., & Landers, D. M. (1983). The effects of mental practice on motor skill learning and performance: A meta-analysis. *Journal of Sport Psychology, 5*, 25–27.

FENKER, R., & Lamiotte, J. (1987). A performance enhancement program for a college football team: One incredible season. *The Sport Psychologist, 1*, 224–236.

GALASSI, J. P., & Galassi, M. D. (1984). Promoting transfer and maintenance of counseling outcomes: How do we do it and how do we study it? In S. D. Brown & R. W. Lent (Eds.), *Handbook of counseling psychology* (pp. 397–431). New York: Wiley.

GARFIELD, S. L. (1986). Research on client variables in psychotherapy. In S. L. Garfield & A. E. Bergin (Eds.), *Handbook of psychotherapy and behavior change* (3rd ed., pp. 213–256). New York: Wiley.

GLASS, G., McGraw, B., & Smith, M. (1981). *Meta-analysis in social science*. London: Sage.

GOULD, D. (1988). Editorial—ABC *Nightline* news telecast focuses on sport psychology. *The Sport Psychologist, 2*, 95–96.

GOULD, D., Horn, T., & Spreemann, J. (1983). Sources of stress in junior elite wrestlers. *Journal of Sport Psychology, 5*, 159–171.

GOULD, D., Weinberg, R. S., & Jackson, A. (1980). Effects of mental preparation strategies on a muscular endurance task. *Journal of Sport Psychology, 2*, 329–339.

GOULD, D., Weiss, M., & Weinberg, R. (1981). Psychological characteristics of successful and nonsuccessful Big Ten wrestlers. *Journal of Sport Psychology, 3*, 69–81.

GRAVEL, R., Lemieux, G., & Ladouceur, R. (1980). Effectiveness of a cognitive behavioral treatment package for cross-country ski racers. *Cognitive Therapy and Research, 4*, 83–89.

GREENSPAN, M. J., & Feltz, D. L. (1989). Psychological interventions with athletes in competitive situations: A review. *The Sport Psychologist, 3*, 219–236.

GREER, H. S., & Engs, R. (1986). Use of progressive relaxation and hypnosis to increase tennis skill learning. *Perceptual and Motor Skills, 63*, 161–162.

HALL, E. G., & Erffmeyer, E. S. (1983). The effects of visuo-motor behavior rehearsal with videotaped modeling on free throw accuracy of intercollegiate female basketball players. *Journal of Sport Psychology, 5*, 343–346.

HALL, H. K., Weinberg, R. S., & Jackson, A. (1987). Effects of goal specificity, goal difficulty, and information feedback on endurance performance. *Journal of Sport Psychology, 9*, 43–54.

HARRIS, D. V., & Robinson, W. J. (1986). The effects of skill level of EMG activity during internal and external imagery. *Journal of Sport Psychology, 8*, 105–111.

HECKER, J. E., & Kaczor, L. M. (1988). Application of imagery theory to sport psychology: Some preliminary findings. *Journal of Sport and Exercise Psychology, 10*, 363–373.

HEISHMAN, M. F., & Bunker, L. (1989). Use of mental preparation strategies by international elite female lacrosse players from five countries. *The Sport Psychologist, 3*, 14–22.

HOLLINGSWORTH, B. (1975). Effects of performance goals and anxiety on learning a gross motor task. *The Research Quarterly, 46*, 162–168.

HONIKMAN, B., & Honikman, L. (Eds.). (1991, September-October). *TAC Times*. Santa Barbara, CA: The Athletic Congress.

HULL, C. L. (1943). *Principles of behavior*. New York: Appleton-Century-Crofts.

JOHNSTON-O'CONNER, E. J., & Kirschenbaum, D. S. (1986). Something succeeds like success: Positive self-monitoring in golf. *Cognitive Therapy and Research, 10*, 123–136.

KAZDIN, A. E. (1978). Evaluating the generality of findings in analogue therapy research. *Journal of Consulting and Clinical Psychology, 46*, 673–686.

KAZDIN, A. E. (1986). The evaluation of psychotherapy: Research design and methodology. In S. L. Garfield & A. E. Bergin (Eds.), *Handbook of psychotherapy and behavior change* (3rd ed., pp. 23–68). New York: Wiley.

KIRSCHENBAUM, D. S. (1992). Elements of effective weight control programs: Implications for exercise and sport psychology. *Journal of Applied Sport Psychology, 4*, 77–93.

KIRSCHENBAUM, D. S., & Bale, R. M. (1980). Cognitive behavioral skills in golf: Brain power golf. In R. M. Suinn (Ed.), *Psychology in sports: Methods and application* (pp. 334–343). Minneapolis: Burgess.

KIRSCHENBAUM, D. S., Ordman, A. M., Tomarken, A. J., & Holtzbauer, R. (1982). Effects of differential self-monitoring and level of mastery on sports performance: Brain power bowling. *Cognitive Therapy and Research, 6*, 335–342.

KIRSCHENBAUM, D. S., & Smith, R. J. (1983). Sequencing effects in simulated coach feedback: Continuous criticism, or praise, can debilitate performance. *Journal of Sport Psychology, 5*, 332–342.

KIRSCHENBAUM, D. S., & Wittrock, D. A. (1984). Cognitive behavioral interventions in sport: A self-regulatory perspective. In J. M. Silva & R. S. Weinberg (Eds.), *Psychological foundations of sport* (pp. 81–98). Champaign, IL: Human Kinetics.

LAMBERT, M. J., Shapiro, D. A., & Bergin, A. E. (1986). The effectiveness of psychotherapy. In S. L. Garfield & A. E. Bergin (Eds.), *Handbook of psychotherapy and behavior change* (3rd ed., pp. 157–212). New York: Wiley.

LANDERS, D. M. (1980). The arousal-performance relationship revisited. *Research Quarterly for Exercise and Sport, 51*, 77–90.

LANNING, W., & Hisanga, B. (1983). A study of the relationship between the reduction of competitive anxiety and an increase in athletic performance. *International Journal of Sport Psychology, 14*, 219–227.

LEE, C. (1990). Psyching up for a muscular endurance task: Effects of image content on performance and mood state. *Journal of Sport and Exercise Psychology, 12*, 66–73.

LeUNES, A. D., & Nation, J. R. (1989). *Sport psychology.* Chicago: Nelson-Hall.

LOCKE, E. A. (1968). Toward a theory of task motivation and incentives. *Organizational Behavior and Human Performance, 3*, 157–189.

LOCKE, E. A., & Latham, G. P. (1985). The application of goal setting to sport. *Journal of Sport Psychology, 7*, 205–222.

LOCKE, E. A., & Latham, G. P. (1990). *A theory of goal setting and task performance.* Englewood Cliffs, NJ: Prentice-Hall.

LOEHR, J. E., & Kahn, E. J. (1987). *Athletic excellence: Mental toughness training for sports.* Denver, CO: Forum Publishing.

LOY, J. W. (1968). The nature of sport: A definitional effort. *Quest, 10*, 1–15.

MAHONEY, M. J. (1989). Sport psychology. In I. S. Cohen (Ed.), *The G. Stanley Hall lectures series,* (Vol. 9, pp. 97–134). Washington, DC: American Psychological Association.

MAHONEY, M. J., & Avener, M. (1977). Psychology of the elite athlete: An exploratory study. *Cognitive Therapy and Research, 1*, 135–141.

MAHONEY, M. J., Gabriel, T. J., & Perkins, T. S. (1987). Psychological skills and exceptional athletic performance. *The Sport Psychologist, 1*, 181–199.

MAHONEY, M. J., & Meyers, A. W. (1989). Anxiety and athletic performance: Traditional and cognitive-developmental perspectives. In D. Hackfort & C. D. Spielberger (Eds.), *Anxiety in sports: An international perspective* (pp. 77–94). Washington, DC: Hemisphere.

MANSFIELD, R. S., & Busse, T. V. (1987). Meta-analysis of research: A rejoinder to Glass. *Educational Research, 6*, 3.

MARTENS, R. (1972). Trait and state anxiety. In W. P. Morgan (Ed.), *Ergogenic aids in muscular performance* (pp. 35–66). New York: Academic Press.

MARTENS, R. (1987). Science, knowledge, and sport psychology. *The Sport Psychologist, 1*, 29–55.

McCULLAGH, P. (1986). Model status as a determinant of observational learning and performance. *Journal of Sport Psychology, 8*, 319–331.

MEACCI, W. G., & Price, E. P. (1985). Acquisition and retention of golf putting skill through the relaxation, visualization, body rehearsal intervention. *Research Quarterly for Exercise and Sport, 56*, 176–179.

MEANEY, P. H. (1984). The use of mental rehearsal in sport. *Sport Coach, 8*, 3–6.

MEICHENBAUM, D. (1977). *Cognitive behavior modification.* New York: Plenum.

MENDOZA, D., & Wichman, H. (1978). "Inner" darts: Effects of mental practice on performance of dart throwing. *Perceptual and Motor Skills, 47*, 1195–1199.

MEYERS, A. W. (1980). Cognitive-behavior therapy and athletic performance. In C. H. Garcia Cadena (Ed.), *Proceedings of the first international sport psychology symposium* (pp. 131–161). Monterrey, Mexico: Editorial Trillas.

MEYERS, A. W., Cooke, C. J., Cullen, J., & Liles, L. (1979). Psychological aspects of athletic performance: A replication across sports. *Cognitive Therapy and Research, 36*, 361–366.

MEYERS, A. W., Schleser, R., Cooke, C. J., & Cuvillier, C. (1979). Cognitive contributions to the development of gymnastic skills. *Cognitive Therapy and Research, 3*, 75–85.

MEYERS, A. W., Schleser, R., & Okwumabua, T. M. (1982). A cognitive behavioral intervention for improving basketball performance. *Research Quarterly for Exercise and Sport, 53*, 344–347.

MICHENER, J. A. (1976). *Sports in America.* New York: Random House.

MILLER, J. T., & McAuley, E. (1987). Effects of a goal-setting training program on basketball free-throw, self-efficacy, and performance. *The Sport Psychologist, 1*, 103–113.

MISCHEL, W. (1968). *Personality and assessment.* New York: Wiley.

MOOK, D. G. (1992). In defense of external validity. In A. E. Kazdin (Ed.), *Methodological issues and strategies in clinical research* (pp. 119–136). Washington, DC: American Psychological Association.

MORGAN, W. P. (1980). The trait psychology controversy. *Research Quarterly for Exercise and Sport, 51,* 50–76.

MORGAN, W. P. (1985). Selected psychological factors limiting performance: A mental health model. In D. H. Clarke & H. M. Eckert (Eds.), *Limits of human performance* (pp. 70–80). Champaign, IL: Human Kinetics.

MUMFORD, B., & Hall, C. (1985). The effects of internal and external imagery on performing figures in figure skating. *Canadian Journal of Applied Sport Science, 10,* 171–177.

MURPHY, S. M. (1988). The on-site provision of sport psychology services at the 1987 U.S. Olympic Festival. *The Sport Psychologist, 2,* 337–350.

MURPHY, S. M., & Woolfolk, R. L. (1987). The effects of cognitive interventions on competitive anxiety and performance on a fine motor skill accuracy task. *International Journal of Sport Psychology, 18,* 152–166.

NATIONAL Bowling Council. (1990). *Profile of a dynamic market: Bowling.* Washington, DC: Author.

NATIONAL Golf Foundation. (1991). *Golf participation in the United States.* Jupiter, FL: Author.

NATIONAL Sporting Goods Association. (1990). *Sports participation in 1990.* Mt. Pleasant, IL: Author.

NICHOLLS, J. G. (1984). Achievement motivation: Conceptions of ability, subjective experience, task choice and performance. *Psychological Review, 91,* 328–346.

NICHOLS, A., Whelan, J. P., & Meyers, A. W. (1991). Assessing the effects of children's achievement goals on task performance, mood, and persistence. *Behavior Therapy, 22,* 491–503.

NICHOLSON, R. A., & Berman, J. S. (1983). Is follow-up necessary in evaluating psychotherapy? *Psychological Bulletin, 93,* 261–278.

NIDEFFER, R. M., & Sharpe, R.C. (1978). *Attention control training.* New York: Wyden Books.

NOEL, R. C. (1980). The effect of visuo-motor behavior rehearsal on tennis performance. *Journal of Sport Psychology, 2,* 221–226.

OGILVIE, B. C., & Tutko, T. A. (1966). *Problem athletes and how to handle them.* London: Pelham Books.

OKWUMABUA, T. M., Meyers, A. W., Schleser, R., & Cooke, C. J. (1983). Cognitive strategies and running performance: An exploratory study. *Cognitive Therapy and Research, 7,* 363–370.

ORLICK, T. (1986). *Psyching for sport: Mental training for sport.* Champaign, IL: Leisure Press.

ORLICK, T., & Partington, J. (1988). Mental links to excellence. *The Sport Psychologist, 2,* 105–130.

OWEN, N., & Lee, C. (1987). Current status of sport psychology. *Australian Psychologist, 22,* 62–76.

PORTER, K., & Foster, J. (1986). *The mental athlete: Inner training for peak performance.* Dubuque, IA: William C. Brown.

POWELL, G. E. (1973). Negative and positive mental practice in motor skill acquisition. *Perceptual and Motor Skills, 37,* 312.

PRICE, E., & Braun, T. (1983). Wake the sleeping giants: The science of cybernetics. *Athletic Journal, 10,* 42–44.

RICHARDSON, A. (1967a). Mental practice: A review and discussion. Part I. *Research Quarterly, 38,* 95–107.

RICHARDSON, A. (1967b). Mental practice: A review and discussion. Part II. *Research Quarterly, 38,* 263–273.

ROBERTS, G. (Ed.). (1989). Delivering sport psychology services to the 1988 Olympic athletes [Special issue]. *The Sport Psychologist, 3*(4).

ROBERTS, G., & Halliwell, W. (Eds.). (1990). Working with professional athletes [Special issue]. *The Sport Psychologist, 4*(4).

RUSHALL, B. (1972). Three studies relating personality variables to football performance. *International Journal of Sport Psychology, 3,* 12–24.

RYAN, D. E., & Simons, J. (1981). Cognitive demand, imagery, and frequency of mental rehearsal as factors influencing acquisition of motor skills. *Journal of Sport Psychology, 3,* 35–45.

SEABOURNE, T. G., Weinberg, R., Jackson, A., & Suinn, R. M. (1985). Effects of individualized, nonindividualized, and package intervention strategies on karate performance. *Journal of Sport Psychology, 7,* 40–50.

SHELTON, T. O., & Mahoney, M. J. (1978). The content and effect of "psyching-up" strategies in weight lifters. *Cognitive Therapy and Research, 2,* 275–284.

SHICK, J. (1970). Effects of mental practice on selected volleyball skills for college women. *Research Quarterly, 41,* 88–94.

SILVA, J. M. (1982). Competitive sport environments: Performance enhancement through cognitive intervention. *Behavior Modification, 6,* 443–463.

SILVA, J. M. (1984). Personality and sport performance: Controversy and challenge. In J. M. Silva & R. S. Weinberg (Eds.), *Psychological foundations of sport* (pp. 59–69). Champaign, IL: Human Kinetics.

SMITH, B., & Sechrest, L. (1992). Treatment of aptitude X treatment interactions. In A. E. Kazdin (Ed.), *Methodological issues and strategies in clinical research* (pp. 557–584). Washington, DC: American Psychological Association.

SMITH, D. (1989). Conditions that facilitate the development of sport imagery training. *The Sport Psychologist, 1,* 237–247.

SMITH, R. E. (1980). A cognitive-affective approach to stress management training for athletes. In C. H. Nadeau, W. R. Halliwell, K. M. Newell, & G. C. Roberts (Eds.), *Psychology of motor behavior and sport–1979* (pp. 54–72). Champaign, IL: Human Kinetics.

SMITH, R. E. (1985). A component analysis of athletic stress. In M. Weiss & D. Gould (Eds.), *Competitive sports for children and youths: Proceedings of Olympic Scientific Congress* (pp. 107–112). Champaign, IL: Human Kinetics.

SMITH, R. E. (1989). Applied sport psychology in an age of accountability. *Journal of Applied Sport Psychology, 1*, 166–180.

SPENCE, J. T., & Spence, K. W. (1966). The motivational components of manifest anxiety: Drive and drive stimuli. In C. D. Spielberger (Ed.), *Anxiety and behavior* (pp. 291–326). New York: Academic Press.

SPIELBERGER, C. D. (Ed.). (1972). *Anxiety: Current trends in theory and research* (Vol. 1). New York: Academic Press.

START, K. B., & Richardson, A. (1964). Imagery and mental practice. *British Journal of Educational Psychology, 34*, 280–284.

STERNBERG, R. J., & Kolligian, J. (Eds.). (1990). *Competence considered.* New Haven, CT: Yale University Press.

SUINN, R. M. (1972). Behavioral rehearsal training for ski racers. *Behavior Therapy, 3*, 519–520.

SUINN, R. (1977). Behavioral methods at the Winter Olympic Games. *Behavior Therapy, 8*, 283–284.

SUINN, R. (1983). *The seven steps to peak performance: Manual for mental training for athletes.* Fort Collins: Colorado State University.

SUINN, R. M. (1985). Imagery rehearsal applications to performance enhancement. *The Behavior Therapist, 8*, 155–159.

TOMARKEN, A. J., & Kirschenbaum, D. S. (1982). Self-regulatory failure: Accentuate the positive? *Journal of Personality and Social Psychology, 33*, 209–217.

TRIPLETT, N. (1897). The dynamogenic factors in pace-making and competition. *American Journal of Psychology, 9*, 507–553.

TYNES, L. L., & McFatter, R. M. (1987). The efficacy of "psyching" strategies on a weight lifting task. *Cognitive Therapy and Research, 11*, 327–336.

UNGERLEIDER, S., & Golding, J. M. (1992). *Beyond strength: Psychological profile of Olympic athletes.* Dubuque, IA: William C. Brown.

UNITED States Cycling Federation. (1990). *United States Cycling Federation rulebook.* Colorado Springs, CO: Author.

UNITED States Masters Swimming. (1991). *Masters swimming: What's it all about?* Rutland, MA: Author.

UNITED States Tennis Association. (1990). *USTA annual participation report for adult leagues.* Princeton, NJ: Author.

VEALEY, R. S. (1988). Future directions in psychological skills training. *The Sport Psychologist, 2*, 318–336.

VEALEY, R. S., & Campbell, J. L. (1988). Achievement goals of adolescent figure skaters: Impact on self-confidence, anxiety, and performance. *Journal of Adolescent Research, 3*, 227–243.

WEINBERG, R. S. (1982). The relationship between mental preparation strategies and motor performance: A review and critique. *Quest, 33*, 728–734.

WEINBERG, R. S., Bruya, L. D., Garland, H., & Jackson, A. (1990). Effects of goal difficulty and positive reinforcement on endurance performance. *Journal of Sport and Exercise Psychology, 12*, 144–156.

WEINBERG, R. S., Bruya, L. D., & Jackson, A. (1985). The effects of goal proximity and goal specificity on endurance performance. *Journal of Sport Psychology, 7*, 296–305.

WEINBERG, R. S., Bruya, L. D., Jackson, A., & Garland, H. (1987). Goal difficulty and endurance performance: A challenge to the goal attainability assumption. *Journal of Sport Behavior, 10*, 82–92.

WEINBERG, R., Gould, D., & Jackson, A. (1980). Cognition and motor performance: Effect of psyching-up strategies on three motor tasks. *Cognitive Therapy and Research, 4*, 239–245.

WEINBERG, R., Jackson, A., & Seabourne, T. (1985). The effects of specific versus nonspecific mental preparation strategies on strength and endurance performance. *Journal of Sport Behavior, 8*, 175–180.

WEINBERG, R., Seabourne, T. G., & Jackson, A. (1981). Effects of visuo-motor behavior rehearsal, relaxation, and imagery on karate performance. *Journal of Sport Psychology, 3*, 228–238.

WEINBERG, R., Seabourne, T. G., & Jackson, A. (1982). Effects of visuo-motor behavior rehearsal on state-trait anxiety and performance: Is practice important? *Journal of Sport Behavior, 5*, 209–219.

WHELAN, J. P., Epkins, C., & Meyers, A. W. (1990). Arousal interventions for athletic performance: Influence of mental preparation and competitive experience. *Anxiety Research, 2*, 293–307.

WHELAN, J. P., Mahoney, M. J., & Meyers, A. W. (1991). Performance enhancement in sport: A cognitive behavioral domain. *Behavior Therapy, 22*, 307–327.

WHELAN, J. P., Meyers, A. W., & Berman, J. S. (1989). Cognitive-behavioral interventions for athletic performance enhancement. In M. Greenspan (Chair), *Sport psychology intervention research: Reviews and issues.* Symposium presented at the American Psychological Association, New Orleans, LA.

WHELAN, J. P., Meyers, A. W., & Donovan, C. (1995). Interventions with competitive recreational athletes. In S. Murphy (Ed.), *Clinical sport psychology* (pp. 71–116). Champaign, IL: Human Kinetics.

WHITE, K. D., Ashton, R., & Lewis, S. (1979). Learning a complex skill: Effects of mental practice, physical practice, and imagery ability. *International Journal of Sport Psychology, 10*, 71–78.

WICHMAN, H., & Lizotte, P. (1983). Effects of mental practice and locus of control on performance of dart throwing. *Perceptual and Motor Skills, 56*, 807–812.

WIGGINS, D. K. (1984). The history of sport psychology in North America. In J. M. Silva & R. S. Weinberg (Eds.),

Psychological foundations of sport (pp. 9–22). Champaign, IL: Human Kinetics.

WILL, G. F. (1990). *Men at work*. New York: Macmillan.

WOLF, F. M. (1986). *Meta-analysis: Quantitative methods for research synthesis*. Beverly Hills, CA: Sage.

WOOLFOLK, R. L., & Lehrer, P. M. (Eds.). (1984). *Principles and practice of stress management*. New York: Guilford Press.

WOOLFOLK, R. L., Murphy, S. M., Gottesfeld, D., & Aitken, D. (1985). Effects of mental rehearsal of task motor activity and mental depiction of task outcome on motor skill performance. *Journal of Sport Psychology, 7*, 191–197.

WOOLFOLK, R. L., Parrish, M. W., & Murphy, S. M. (1985). The effects of positive and negative imagery on motor skill performance. *Cognitive Therapy and Research, 9*, 335–341.

WRAITH, S. C., & Biddle, S. J. (1989). Goal-setting in children's sports: An exploratory analysis of goal participation, ability and effort instructions, and post-event cognitions. *International Journal of Sport Psychology, 20*, 79–92.

WRISBERG, C. A., & Anshel, M. H. (1989). The effect of cognitive strategies on the free throw shooting performance of young athletes. *The Sport Psychologist, 3*, 95–104.

YEATON, W. H., & Sechrest, L. (1992). Critical dimensions in the choice and maintenance of successful treatments: Strength, integrity, and effectiveness. In A. E. Kazdin (Ed.), *Methodological issues and strategies in clinical research* (pp. 137–156). Washington, DC: American Psychological Association.

YERKES, R. M., & Dodson, J. D. (1908). The relation of strength of stimulus to rapidity of habit formation. *Journal of Comparative and Neurological Psychology, 18*, 459–482.

ZIEGLER, S. G., Klinzing, J., & Williamson, K. (1982). The effects of two stress management training programs on cardiorespiratory efficiency. *Journal of Sport Psychology, 4*, 280–289.

CHAPTER 7

Posttraumatic Stress Disorder: Conceptualization and Treatment

Patrick A. Boudewyns

I. Historical Overview: What's in a Name?
II. PTSD: Definition, Epidemiology, and Codiagnoses
III. Conceptual Models of PTSD and the Sequelae
of Trauma
   A. Horowitz's Psychodynamic and Information
      Processing Theory
   B. Conditioning and Learning Models
   C. Foa's Behavioral-Cognitive Model
   D. Biological Approaches
   E. A Comprehensive Model of PTSD
IV. Treatment Strategies
   A. Behavioral Strategies
   B. Case Demonstrations and Uncontrolled Outcome Studies
   C. Controlled Outcome Studies
V. PTSD in Children
VI. Conclusions Regarding Treatment of PTSD
VII. A Word about Pharmacotherapy for PTSD
VIII. Summary and Conclusions
   References

I. Historical Overview: What's in a Name?

Evidence that psychological and physical trauma can result in lasting emotional distress has been present in both lay and professional literature for centuries. Samuel Pepys's 17th-century diary account of his response to the great London fire several years after the event reveals that he suffered nightmares and flashbacks of the fire. He also appeared to have significant guilt over the fact that he survived while others did not (survivor guilt), experienced hyperarousal in response to stimuli that reminded him of the fire, avoided situations that involved fire, and may have suffered from numbing of emotions toward his family and friends (Daly, 1983).

A similar phenomenon, "war neurosis," has been observed by military physicians. Early terminology used to describe the long-term emotional response to combat seen in soldiers included "shell shock," "battle neurosis," and, somewhat later, "soldier's heart," "battle fatigue," and "combat exhaustion." Trimble (1985) points out that even the term *compensation neurosis*, implying a form of malingering, was used as early as 1879 to describe invalidism reported after railway accidents in Prussia.

During that same period, there was considerable discussion in the psychoanalytic literature as to whether war neurosis should be considered as distinct from peacetime psychoneurosis or as a subtype of traumatic neurosis. In 1919, Freud, at the Fifth Psycho-Analytical Congress in Budapest in September of 1918 and later in a paper with contributions by Ferenczi, Abraham, Simmel, and Jones, outlined the "official" psychoanalytic view on these issues (Freud, 1919/1953). Soon after the turn of the century, some military physicians began to hypothesize that the soldier's "neurotic" reactions to combat were evidence against Freud's contention that the origins of all neurotic conflict were in childhood. Many physicians in the late 19th and early 20th centuries, such as F. W. Mott, who coined the term *shell shock*, considered these traumatic reactions to have physical or neuro-

Appreciation is expressed to Dr. Suzanne Talbert for her valuable comments on an earlier draft of the manuscript and to Jennifer Touzé, Mark Roland, and Kimberly White for their assistance in preparation of the final draft.

logical causes (Trimble, 1985). Freud argued disdainfully:

> Now it is quite true, as Ernest Jones remarks in his contribution to this volume, that this (i.e. infantile sex) portion of the theory has not yet been proved to apply to the war neuroses. The work that might prove it has not yet been taken in hand. It may be that the war neuroses are altogether unsuitable material for the purpose. But the opponents of psycho-analysis, whose dislike of sexuality is evidently stronger than their logic, have been in a hurry to proclaim that the investigation of the war neuroses has finally disproved this portion of psychoanalytic theory. They have been guilty here of a slight confusion. If the investigation of the war neuroses (and a very superficial one at that) has *not shown* that the sexual theory of the neuroses is *correct*, that is something very different from its *showing* that the theory is *incorrect*. With the help of an impartial attitude and a little good will, it should not be hard to find the way to a further clarification of the subject. (Freud, 1919/1953, p. 85)

Freud goes on to summarize how the psychoanalytic theory of ego might incorporate the observations about combat neuroses:

> The conflict is between the soldier's old peaceful ego and his new warlike one, and it becomes acute as soon as the peace-ego realizes what danger it runs of losing its life owing to the rashness of its newly formed, parasitic double. It would be equally true to say that the old ego is protecting itself from a mortal danger by taking flight into a traumatic neurosis or that it is defending itself against the new ego which it sees is threatening its life. Thus the precondition of the war neuroses, the soil that nourishes them, would seem to be a national (conscript) army; there would be no possibility of their (i.e. War Neuroses) arising in an army of professional soldiers or mercenaries. (Freud, 1919/1953, p. 85)

Regardless of the apparent starting point (that is, peacetime trauma, transference, or combat), by 1918 Freud saw repression and its effect on the dynamic relationship between the ego, id, and superego as the basis of all neuroses and as the unifying theoretical construct that would explain the similarities among all neurotic conflicts.

For the first half of this century, Freud's dynamic theory of psychoneurosis strongly influenced abnormal psychology and psychiatry with regard to the long-term psychological sequelae of trauma. Indeed, by the time the American Psychiatric Association published its first *Diagnostic and Statistical Manual of Mental Disorders* (American Psychiatric Association, 1952), this influence (along with the influence of Adolph Myer's psychobiological model of mental disorders) was so strong that the section on psychoneurosis specifically forbade the use of terms such as *traumatic neurosis* or *traumatic reaction*.

White (1948/1956), who wrote one of the most widely used introductory abnormal psychology texts of that time, summed it up this way:

> These neuroses (traumatic, war) do not differ in their fundamental character from the more chronic neuroses that may build up quite slowly in the course of an outwardly uneventful life. Both are based on nuclear processes of anxiety and defense. Very often the symptoms are of a quite similar character. Neuroses of traumatic onset do not constitute, therefore, a separate class of neuroses, except in respect to the suddenness of onset. (pp. 223–224)

White went on to make an important point. He noted that this suddenness of onset offers some advantages to the researcher: "It is this very suddenness, and the transparency of the surrounding conditions, that gives them special value in the study of the neurotic process" (p. 224).

The two world wars offered ideal laboratories for the collection of data on both the long- and short-term effects of trauma. Near mid-century, researchers such as Kardiner (1941) and Grinker and Spiegel (1945) had objectively described the psychological sequelae of combat. These authors, especially, set the stage for present-day epidemiological studies of trauma effects (both war and otherwise) aimed at understanding the prevalence, incidence, and course of the disorder.

The Korean War created an opportunity to study this phenomenon again (for example, Dobbs & Wilson, 1960), but relatively little research was accomplished. In the years between the Korean and Vietnam wars, the notion that traumatic neurosis should be differentiated as a separate diagnostic entity was not accepted by the authors of DSM-II, either (American Psychiatric Association, 1968).

The long Vietnam experience again focused our attention on these issues. By this time, however, experimentally oriented "Boulder Model" psychologists, especially behaviorists, with backgrounds in learning and information processing as well as psychoanalytic theory, and psychiatrists with interests in epidemiology, unencumbered by theory, began to look at "post" traumatic behaviors without as many preconceived notions about etiology. Pressure for change was also driven by political and social motivation (compare with Williams, 1980). This combination of intellectual openness and political fervor is what finally led to the elevation of posttraumatic stress disorder (PTSD) from a "syndrome" to a full diagnostic entity in the neurosis-free DSM-III (American Psychiatric Association, 1980).

II. PTSD: Definition, Epidemiology, and Codiagnoses

DSM-III-R (American Psychiatric Association, 1987) defines PTSD under the anxiety disorders with five criteria:

1. That the patient has experienced an event that is outside the range of usual human experience and that would be markedly distressing to almost anyone
2. That the traumatic event is persistently reexperienced through one of the following:
   a. Intrusive recollections of the event
   b. Dreams
   c. Flashbacks
   d. Distress at exposure to events that resemble the trauma
3. That the patient avoids stimuli associated with the trauma or experiences numbing of general responsiveness in at least three of the following:
   a. Avoidance of thoughts and feelings associated with the trauma
   b. Avoidance of stimuli that arouse recollections of the trauma
   c. Incomplete memory for the trauma
   d. Markedly diminished interest in significant activities of life
   e. Feeling estranged or detached from people
   f. Experiencing restricted affect
   g. A sense that one will not live long or reap the usual benefits of life

4. That the patient experiences symptoms of increased arousal in at least two of the following ways:
   a. Difficulty falling or staying asleep
   b. Irritability or outbursts of anger
   c. Difficulty concentrating
   d. Hypervigilance
   e. Exaggerated startle response
   f. Physiologic reactivity when exposed to stimuli that resemble the traumatic event
5. That the duration of the disturbance is at least one month.

PTSD is considered to have a delayed onset if symptoms did not occur for at least six months after the disorder.

DSM-III-R differs in several ways from DSM-III in regard to the diagnosis of PTSD, generally reflecting advances in understanding the disorder that occurred during the late 1970s and early 1980s. These differences had to do primarily with increasing the specificity of the criteria, rearranging the specific symptoms more logically under the three symptom categories, combining avoidance with numbing in the second general category of symptoms, and requiring that the patient experience increased arousal in the third general symptom category. DSM-III-R also did away with the original subtypes of the disorder—acute versus chronic or delayed—leaving only the specification of "delayed onset," if applicable.

Because a standardized definition did not exist for PTSD prior to DSM-III in 1980, there were few studies of significance on the epidemiology (incidence and distribution of the disorder among populations) prior to that time. Epidemiologic research on PTSD has increased dramatically since then. Populations of interest have included the general population of adults, combat survivors, especially Vietnam veterans, clinical versus nontreatment-seeking individuals, children, men, women, twins, victims of sexual assault, and, more recently, victims of disasters and members of various racial and ethnic groups.

In a large epidemiological study on the prevalence of psychiatric disorders, Helzer, Robins, and McEvoy (1987) used the database of the NIMH Epidemiologic Catchment Area program to interview 2493 partici-

pants who would be representative of the population at large. From the general sample, Helzer et al. identified 18 individuals per 1000 sampled who had met DSM-III criteria for PTSD at anytime in their lives. Thus, from this study we might conclude that a diagnosis of PTSD occurs less than 2% of the time in the general population in this country. Helzer et al. go on to point out, however, that while the full diagnostic criteria for the disorder was unusual, experiencing some of these symptoms ("partial PTSD") after trauma was not. This occurred in about 15% of their sample.

Helzer et al. were satisfied that their data were generally representative of the population at large because it was developed from a large epidemiological database of individuals who did not know they were in a study of PTSD. Nevertheless, they pointed to some limitations of the study that could have resulted in an underestimate of the occurrence of PTSD in the population at large. For one thing, the number of Vietnam veterans in the sample was less than would be expected in the general population. Furthermore, we could speculate that even if Vietnam veterans had been representative, because of their disorder those with PTSD would have avoided involvement in the study. Many Vietnam veteran PTSD sufferers are homeless or have "dropped out" of society. Similarly, one would expect that anyone suffering from PTSD—or any other anxiety disorder where avoidance is a characteristic symptom—would be difficult to sample adequately in a general epidemiological study. Other procedural limitations of the study may also have contributed to an underestimation of PTSD in the general population. For example, the interviewers only asked if the participant had experienced a "frightening" event that was outside his or her usual experience, thus excluding events that may have been characterized by the respondent as "shocking," "disgraceful," or perhaps "disgusting," but not necessarily fear-provoking.

Helzer et al. also found that of the 1.8% of the general population that had suffered from PTSD at sometime in their lives, 1.3% were women and only 0.05% were men. Here again, such a large difference in gender rates makes the representativeness of the sample suspicious. Men, by and large, might be expected to underreport problems with "frightening" events because of their need to appear macho. In sum, we should probably consider the data in Helzer et al. to be a very conservative approximation of the occurrence of PTSD in the general population.

One specific population that experiences a traumatic event that would qualify for PTSD is victims of sexual assault. Estimates vary because of underreporting of sexual assault by women, but according to at least one large and highly respected program of research on the effects of sexual assault and other crimes against women, Kilpatrick and his colleagues at the Medical University of South Carolina found that nearly 5% of the female population have been raped, and another 4% have experienced attempted rape (Kilpatrick, Veronen, & Best 1985). Generalizing from their data, this would mean that at the present time almost 4 million adult women living in the United States have experienced rape at sometime in their lives.

Kilpatrick, Best, Veronen, Amick, Villeponteaux, and Ruff (1985) sampled over 2004 women about possibly having been assaulted or robbed. Of these, 100 had experienced rape, and 79 had experienced attempted rape. Although Kilpatrick et al. did not specifically diagnose PTSD, severe sustained emotional reactions occurred in over half the victims of completed rape, and 19% had made suicide attempts (compared to 2.2% in nonvictims). It could be assumed that a high percentage of these individuals suffered from PTSD. In a more recent study, Winfield, Swartz, and Blazer, 1990, using a large epidemiological data source, found that 3.7% of those women who had reported experiencing sexual assault suffered from PTSD (as compared to about 1% PTSD positive for nonvictims).

It should be pointed out that, although it is obvious from the literature that many people who have been raped suffer from PTSD, there is often resistance from professionals who work therapeutically with such individuals to apply this label (Burge, 1988). Burge uses "a sample of convenience" to show that people who have been raped do suffer from PTSD and offers a useful and interesting discussion on the implications and advantages of "reframing" the individual's experience as a response to traumatic stress, which sometimes results in full-blown PTSD.

Another area of epidemiological research that has shown an increase in activity lately is with people who have experienced civilian disasters. For example, Murphy (1986) compared controls to individuals who had experienced the Mt. St. Helens volcanic eruption. She concluded that at both one year and three years postdisaster, participants reported symptoms of both acute and chronic posttraumatic stress disorder at significantly greater rates than did controls. Other similar studies of the Buffalo Creek Dam collapse (Green, Grace, Lindy, Gleser, Leonard, & Kramer, 1990; Green, Lindy, Grace, Gleser, Leonard, Korol, & Winget, 1990), the Three Mile Island meltdown (Bromet, Parkinson, Schulberg, Dunn, & Gondek, 1982), and the 1984 crash landing of the East Tennessee State University basketball team aboard a commercial airplane (Sloan, 1988), to name only a few, produced similar results.

In a more sophisticated, albeit fortuitous, experimental investigation of the wake of disasters, Saigh (1984a, 1984b) studied the response of 88 Lebanese students to their country's long war. He was able to show pre- to postchange in psychological responding to bombardments and military activities. At the same time, he was able to compare groups of students from the same cultural background and living situation who had directly experienced trauma with those who were not as directly victimized. These latter students had been relocated during the most severe action but after Saigh's initial battery of psychological tests had been administered. Saigh's results were not as might be expected. He found no significant differences in self-report between the two groups or between pre- and postmeasures with regard to anxiety scores on several standardized measures. In a later study on a smaller sample of 12 students who were evaluated several times over a year, Saigh (1988) found only one student had developed PTSD with lasting symptoms.

Clearly, the most studied group of PTSD sufferers has been the Vietnam veteran. In the large epidemiological study by Helzer et al. (1987), even though they were underrepresented, 43 men in that sample had seen combat in Vietnam. Of these, 4 (9.3%) met the criteria for PTSD, compared to 1.8% in the general population. Helzer et al. also point out that the rate of PTSD was higher for Vietnam veterans who had been wounded (20%). It is interesting to compare these figures on combat-related PTSD to a form of civilian "combat" trauma. Twenty-nine members of the sample had been beaten or mugged in the 18 months prior to the study. Of these, 2 (3%) met the criteria for full PTSD.

In what is probably the most sophisticated and thorough epidemiological investigation of its kind, Kulka et al. (1988) carried out the four-year National Vietnam Veterans Readjustment Study (NVVRS), targeting the more than 8,238,000 veterans who had served during the Vietnam era (August 5, 1964, through May 7, 1975). Kulka et al. interviewed a representative sample of this population along with civilian counterparts. Over 3000 in-depth interviews were conducted in all 50 states and Puerto Rico. The NVVRS findings indicated that 15.2% of all male Vietnam combat veterans currently suffer from PTSD and that a total of 30.6% will eventually be diagnosed as having PTSD. By comparison, Vietnam-era male veterans (who served during the Vietnam era but were not stationed in Southeast Asia) evidenced a PTSD rate of 2.5%. Civilian controls had a 1.2% rate, somewhat higher than that seen in the Helzer et al. study, which included both combat veterans and civilians. Women who served in Southeast Asia during the Vietnam War (many of them nurses) had somewhat lower rates. Kulka et al. found an 8.5% PTSD rate for these female veterans, compared to a 0.3% rate for female Vietnam-era veterans.

One important finding of the Kulka et al. study was that significantly higher rates of PTSD were found among members of minority groups. For example, the current prevalence rates for Hispanics was estimated at 27.9%. Among African Americans, 20.6% could be given a current diagnosis of PTSD. These minority figures compare to 13.7% for whites and others. Small samples made it impossible to estimate accurately for other ethnic groups and minorities separately.

In a very important study of 715 monozygotic twin pairs who were discordant for military service in Southeast Asia during the Vietnam conflict, Goldberg, True, Eisen, and Henderson (1990) confirmed the Kulka et al. results. Goldberg et al. found a 16.8% PTSD prevalence rate for the twins that served in the southeast theater compared to 5% for those who did

not see combat. Obviously, this study would also support the notion that with regard to combat-related PTSD at least, pre-Vietnam social-psychological variables and genetic predisposition play only a minor role in the etiology of PTSD when compared to the effects of the trauma itself.

Although prevalence rates vary depending on the design and procedure of the investigation, several other epidemiological studies have found relatively high PTSD rates for Vietnam veterans (Card, 1987; Centers for Disease Control, 1988; Green, Grace, Lindy, Gleser, & Leonard, 1990; Laufer, Brett, & Gallops, 1985; Snow, Stellman, Stellman, & Sommer, 1988). Also, as Goldberg et al. (1990) point out, many of these studies evidenced significant increases in PTSD from base rates among those who experienced high levels of combat as opposed to relatively lower levels, further emphasizing the relative importance of the stressor. Likewise, studies indicate that those who were physically wounded may be at a significantly higher risk for PTSD (Helzer et al., 1987; Kulka et al., 1988; Snow et al., 1988).

Finally, a frequent correlate of the PTSD diagnosis, especially among Vietnam combat veterans, is the tendency for those who are diagnosed with PTSD to also suffer another concurrent psychiatric diagnosis at some time in their lives, especially substance abuse or dependence (Boudewyns, Albrecht, Hyer, & Talbert, 1991; Boudewyns, Woods, Hyer, & Albrecht, 1991; Escobar, Randolph, Puente, Spiwak, Asamen, Hill, & Hough, 1983; Falcon et al., 1991; Faustman & White, 1989; Friedman et al., 1987; Kulka et al., 1988; Sierles, Chen, McFarland, & Taylor, 1983; Sierles, Chen, Messing, Besyner, & Taylor, 1986).

Thus, while estimates vary depending on the sample studied, comorbidity rates tend to be the rule rather than the exception. Kulka et al. (1988) estimated that 75% of their sample of PTSD sufferers would have been diagnosed with alcohol abuse or dependence at some time in their lives. Boudewyns, Albrecht, Hyer, and Talbert (1991) found 91.2% of their inpatient sample to have a similar history and that almost 33% suffered from major depression and 27% had a current diagnosis of schizophrenia as shown on the Diagnostic Interview Schedule (Robins, Helzer, Croughan, & Ratcliff, 1981).

III. Conceptual Models of PTSD and the Sequelae of Trauma

A. Horowitz's Psychodynamic and Information Processing Theory

Several modern psychodynamic theorists have developed models for understanding and treatment of psychological sequelae of trauma (compare with Horowitz, 1973, 1986; Horowitz & Kaltreider, 1980; Lifton, 1967; Lifton & Olson, 1976; Marmar & Freeman, 1988; Titchner, 1986). Perhaps the most notable pre-PTSD writer in this area is Mardi Horowitz, who originally defined the term *stress response syndrome* (Horowitz, 1976). Horowitz's conceptualization, which has interesting similarities to information processing theory (Hyer, 1994), sees the patient's response to stress as vacillating between two phases: the denial phase and the intrusiveness phase. The denial phase is characterized by the victim functioning in a daze, exhibiting selective inattention. In this phase, the person's consciousness is impaired, with complete or partial amnesia for the event or no recollection at all. Ideational processes include, among others, inflexibility, loss of reality appropriateness, and the use of fantasies to counter reality. Symptoms also include emotional numbing, a decrease in physical activity that would bring on somatic responses that could be interpreted as anxiety or panic, and actions that run from frantic overactivity to withdrawal. The denial phase might be seen as a general defense against the anxiety emergent in the intrusiveness phase.

The intrusiveness phase involves hypervigilance and abnormal startle reactions, sleep and dream disturbances, intrusive repetitive thoughts and behaviors, overgeneralization, inability to concentrate, confusion and disorganization, emotional attacks or "pangs" of chronic fight-or-flight readiness, and compulsive efforts to search for lost persons and situations attached to the trauma (Horowitz & Kaltreider, 1980).

Horowitz's brief psychoanalytic-oriented psychotherapy is currently one of the most commonly used treatment modalities for PTSD. He recommends a dose-related approach, whereby the nature and intensity of the treatment is dictated by the phase the patient

is in and the ability of the patient to withstand direct therapeutic exposure and processing of the memory of the trauma.

During the intrusive phase, the patient is encouraged to avoid, as much as possible, engaging in disturbing memories. The patient may be given medications to help control these anxiety-eliciting internal responses and encouraged through reassurance that he or she can learn to control this stress. Relaxation therapy and other stress management techniques, such as suggestions for appropriate structuring of time and activity, as well as support through a strong and positive therapeutic relationship and positive regard, are essential.

During the denial phase when the patient is prone to more avoidant defensive strategies, he or she is encouraged to confront memories with "associations and abreactions." If this strategy is successful in reducing affect, then talk therapy—leading to an integration of the event via the therapist focusing on the relationship of the stress event to the patient's self-concept—will complete the process.

Titchner (1986) has taken Horowitz's ideas one step further and identifies what he terms "posttraumatic decline," which is an excellent description of the chronic aspect of the disorder commonly seen in combat veterans (Boudewyns, Albrecht, et al., 1991). This decline phase is characterized by

> altered attitudes in human relationships consisting of regressive deterioration of trust in others, alternating with unrealistic dependency, and pathetic longings for help from others. This changed sense of the reliability of relationships reflects the sudden cruelty of the catastrophic or traumatic experience causing a drastic change in world view from trust to distrust and failing confidence. (Titchner, 1986 p. 6)

Several authors have reported uncontrolled studies or case evaluations of brief psychoanalytic psychotherapy for PTSD with positive results (for example, Horowitz, Marmar, Weiss, DeWitt, & Rosenbaum, 1984; Lindy, 1986; Lindy, Green, Grace, & Titchener, 1983; Marmar & Freeman, 1988). One multigroup controlled outcome study (Brom, Kleber, & Defares, 1989) found Horowitz's technique to be more effective than a wait-list control and almost as effective as two comparison groups treated with exposure strategies.

B. Conditioning and Learning Models

The theoretical approach with the largest database with regard to PTSD is a learning (conditioning) model, specifically, avoidance learning. Many early behavior therapists, such as John Dollard and Neal Miller (1950), Joseph Wolpe (1958), Andrew Salter (1949/1961), L. J. Reyna (1964), and Thomas Stampfl (Stampfl & Levis, 1967), relied heavily on the largely animal-based learning theories of I. P. Pavlov (1960), Clark Hull (1943), and O. Hobart Mowrer (1947, 1960) to deduce treatment approaches for the reduction of learned anxiety. Of all the macro-learning theories, Mowrer's two-factor theory of learned fear is particularly germane as an analogue to understanding human phobias and trauma-induced anxiety (Boudewyns & Shipley, 1983; Levis & Hare, 1977; Solomon, Kamin, & Wynne, 1953). Several more recent publications have used learning theory to explain the etiology of trauma-induced anxiety or PTSD (compare with Fairbank & Nicholson, 1987; Keane, Fairbank, Caddell, Zimering, & Bender, 1985; Kilpatrick, Veronen, & Best, 1985; Kolb & Mutalipassi, 1982). Keane, Zimering, and Caddell (1985) offer an especially clear and concise explanation of Mowrer's theory as it applies to combat-related PTSD.

Briefly, in Mowrer's model, two learning paradigms are involved—classical conditioning through aversive stimulation and operant learning of avoidance. Fear is acquired through classical conditioning when a neutral stimulus is paired with an aversive unconditioned stimulus. The result of this association is that the originally neutral stimulus becomes a conditioned stimulus eliciting fear. Fear motivates the individual to attempt to escape the aversive unconditioned stimulus and ultimately to learn to avoid those same stimuli by responding with operant avoidance to conditioned stimuli that signal the aversive consequences (that is, the unconditioned stimulus). Successful avoidance then reduces the classically conditioned fear reactions and, thus, negatively reinforces the avoidance behavior through operant conditioning. Highly successful avoidance strategies can ultimately be so effective at avoiding fear that the organism evidences little or no physiological fear responding, even when exposed briefly to the conditioned fear stimulus, as long as avoidance is not hindered. Early experimentation with dogs found that this operant avoidance was remarkably resistant to extinction even after many exposures to nonreinforced conditioned stimuli. Based on these data, Solomon and Wynne (1954) defined their "conservation of anxiety" hypothesis, suggesting that under certain conditions this fear response was not extinguishable and may be irreversible. The analogue to human phobias and to PTSD is obvious.

Stampfl and Levis (1967) presented evidence that did not support the conservation of anxiety hypothesis (Levis & Stampfl, 1972) but have used Mowrer's theory to explain how fear is learned and have included the Pavlovian concepts of higher-order conditioning and stimulus and response generalization to explain how seemingly irrational fears are maintained for many years in humans as neurotic symptoms (Levis & Hare, 1977; Stampfl & Levis, 1967).

In this conception, a "fear gradient" exists across the conditioned stimulus–unconditioned stimulus interval, with those portions of the conditioned stimulus complex temporally closest to the unconditioned stimulus acquiring the most fear. Thus, to a boy who was about to be spanked and who had experienced past spankings, being thrown over his father's knee would elicit more fear than seeing his father's angry face. In attempting to extinguish conditioned fear, it would be best to present the entire conditioned stimulus complex (in the absence of the aversive unconditioned stimulus). However, if only a portion of the conditioned stimulus could be presented, presentation of the portion temporally closest to the aversive unconditioned stimulus should result in the greatest generalization of extinction effects. Boyd and Levis (1976) conditioned rats to avoid a three-component serial conditioned stimulus consisting of (in order) a tone, white noise, and a buzzer. This series of stimuli was followed by a shock. Rats were then given forced exposure to one component of the serial conditioned stimulus complex— either the tone, the white noise, or the buzzer. All animals were then given avoidance or extinction trials using the entire serial conditioned stimulus complex.

As expected, extinction exposure to the buzzer, which was the conditioned stimulus component immediately preceding the shock, resulted in faster extinction of the avoidance responding than did exposure of the conditioned stimulus components more distant in time from the shock. Thus, extinction of fear is facilitated by presenting those stimuli most closely associated in time with the aversive stimulus. Of course, exposure to the entire conditioned stimulus complex remains the most desirable strategy.

The Pavlovian notion of higher-order conditioning, where a conditioned stimulus (for example, the tone in the experiment discussed earlier) can come to be used essentially as an unconditioned stimulus through pairing with another neutral stimulus, may explain how fear can be so resistant to extinction. In humans suffering from PTSD, for example, if one conditioned stimulus becomes a cue to signal the possible occurrence of another conditioned stimulus that is closer to the aversive unconditioned stimulus (as in the buzzer, white noise, and tone paradigm), we would expect that avoidance would occur early in this "serial cue hierarchy" (Stampfl & Levis, 1967). Because of their more superior cognitive abilities, humans have more sophisticated avoidance strategies. It is therefore often difficult to determine just what these cues are. A woman who has experienced rape, for example, may find sexual intercourse with a previously desirable and arousing partner to have become unwelcome and un-exciting at best and even aversive at times. We would expect, however, that over time the problem would be resolved through the woman's repeated sexual encounters with the desired partner. In learning theory terms, the diminished sexual response would be interpreted as the result of stimulus generalization from the rape experience, and the diminution of this generalized response to the previously desired partner as extinction and perhaps discrimination learning. Although this is what usually occurs within about two to three months in most cases of rape (Kilpatrick & Calhoun, 1988), in a significant percentage of cases, irrational fear continues (Foa, Rothbaum, Riggs, & Murdock, 1991), and PTSD may be diagnosed.

Based on the serial cue hierarchy concept, such continuing fear could be explained by the fact that the woman in our example was not exposed to the entire conditioned stimulus complex. How could this happen when she had attempted sex with her partner many times? She might have been able to remain in the situation physically, but because of anxiety, or even feelings of disgust or nausea, she might have continued to be unable to cognitively attend to her partner, thus effectively avoiding experiencing the interaction. As her partner continued his sexual advances, the woman would avoid the aversive feelings through cognitive distractions that could take place at a lower level of awareness (that is, she might have very little awareness of this cognitive avoidance strategy). She might even have tried to remain highly conscious of her partner in an effort to regain her past pleasure. Unfortunately, as any sex therapist knows, making a highly conscious effort to be aware of and attend to one's sexual partner can, in and of itself, interfere with the highly complex sexual response. In such a situation, the woman might learn to control fear and disgust but experience sexual intercourse as nothing more than the physical components (that is, her partner's grunting, groaning, and sweating; and sensations of increased vaginal pressure and genital friction). Such a response, often interpreted as "numbing" of emotions by the victim, is a hallmark symptom of PTSD.

As a result of this numbing experience, efforts to overcome the problem are given up, resulting in lowered self-esteem, diminished pleasure, reduced socialization, and increased isolation. Eventually, advances by men would all be seen as threatening because they could not be responded to in a "normal" fashion. Diminished social and sexual pleasure and lowered self-esteem often result in internalized anger and the resultant depression that we see in many chronic PTSD patients.

Two-factor theory would predict that effective treatment should include exposure to the entire conditioned stimulus complex (Boudewyns & Shipley, 1983; Keane, Zimering, & Caddell, 1985). In vivo or imaginal therapeutic exposure or flooding, shown to be effective with other anxiety disorders such as simple phobias, agoraphobia, and obsessive-compulsive disorders (Barlow & Wolfe, 1981), should also reduce the symptoms of PTSD.

However, several investigators and theorists have suggested that while conditioning theory may account for how an individual contracts and maintains some symptoms of PTSD, other symptoms, especially physiological hyperarousal, are exacerbated and maintained through permanent central or autonomic nervous system changes (compare with Friedman, 1991; Kolb & Mutalipassi, 1982; van der Kolk, Greenberg, Boyd, & Krystal, 1985) that make exposure less effective.

C. Foa's Behavioral-Cognitive Model

In an elegant and thoughtful review of the cognitive and behavioral literature as it pertains to PTSD, Edna Foa and her colleagues (Foa, Steketee, & Rothbaum, 1989) found Mowrer's theory could account for the maintenance of certain fear responses commonly observed in rape victims who suffered PTSD as well as hyperarousal to some generalized stimuli and avoidance of these stimuli. However, Foa et al. concluded that the other symptoms of PTSD were less well explained by conditioning theory. They also found it necessary to postulate what they termed *meaning concepts* to explain some observed behavior in rape victims. Foa et al. observed that stimulus-response theory has difficulty incorporating the observation that "perceived threat is a better predictor of PTSD than actual threat" (or, perhaps more precisely, *experienced* actual threat). Foa et al. referenced Lang's (1977) information processing theory of how fear structures exist in memory to explain this. As an example of why meaning concepts are required to explain PTSD, Foa et al. cited a case of a rape victim who suffered delayed PTSD but did not develop symptoms until after she had learned that the rapist had killed his next victim.

While Foa et al.'s argument for the need to use meaning or cognitive phenomena to explain the development of PTSD is compelling, it is reminiscent of a very old dialogue in theoretical psychology. Early stimulus-response learning theorists had little problem incorporating "meaning" phenomenon into their models by simply making the "conceptual" leap of defining verbal cues (thoughts) as stimuli and responses with the same capacity for motivation and reinforcement (secondary reinforcement/higher-order learning) as external reinforcers. Kimble (1961) notes that:

The fact that thoughts are capable of providing cues means that, theoretically, they can provide the same conditions for the control of behavior as environmental events do. . . . From the same general fact it follows that thoughts can be punishing or rewarding if they have been associated with rewards or punishments in the past. (p. 462)

D. Biological Approaches

Although hypotheses regarding the physiological and neurological basis for the long-term effects of trauma have been in the literature for more than a century (Trimble, 1985), it was not until relatively recently that experimentally controlled investigations of this notion began to appear (Dobbs & Wilson, 1960). In the past several years, there has been a significant increase in the number of studies that have substantiated abnormal functional biological correlates of PTSD.

To date, the most promising physiological indicator of PTSD is the predictable psychophysiological response of PTSD sufferers to stimuli associated with the trauma. For example, several research groups have shown that, compared to controls, combat-related PTSD patients can be very reliably identified by their psychophysiological response (heart rate, skin conductance, electromyographic response) to taped sounds and visual facsimiles of combat (Blanchard, Kolb, Gerardi, Ryan, & Pallmeyer, 1986; Orr et al., 1990; Pitman, Orr, Forgue, de Jong, & Claiborn, 1987). Ornitz and Pynoos (1989) have shown that children who have PTSD resulting from being victims of sniper fire on a playground exhibit startle responses characterized by the eye blink reflex that are significantly different from normal controls. These experimenters speculate that this could be the result of a chronic brain stem dysfunction. Also Boudewyns and Hyer (1990) have shown that these psychophysiological responses in veterans, at least, show little evidence of diminution or habituation even after intensive inpatient treatment using direct therapeutic exposure in combination with more traditional approaches. The Veterans Administration is presently completing a large, multisite study (Keane & Kolb, 1988) of the potential for using this psychophysiological methodology to diagnose combat-related PTSD more accurately.

As shown in Table 7.1, in addition to the characteristic increased psychophysiological arousal, other alterations that correlate with PTSD are found to occur in (1) increased catecholamine levels and reduced

Table 7.1 Biological alterations associated with PTSD

1. Sympathetic nervous system hyperarousal.
   a. Elevated baseline sympathetic physiological indices.
   b. Sympathetic psychophysiological response upon exposure to traumagenic stimuli.
   c. Elevated urinary catecholamine levels.
   d. Reduced platelet MAO activity.
   e. Down-regulation of adrenergic receptors.
2. Hypofunction of hypothalamic-pituitary-adrenocortical axis.
   a. Decreased urinary cortisol levels.
   b. HPA suppression following dexamethasone.
   c. Unique elevation of urinary catecholamine/cortisol ratio.
3. Abnormalities of the endogenous opioid system.
   a. Stress-induced analgesia by traumagenic stimuli.
   b. General lowering of the pain threshold at rest.
4. Sleep abnormalities.
   a. Initiating and maintaining sleep: increased sleep latency, decreased total sleep time, decreased sleep efficiency, increased number of awakenings, increased body movements.
   b. Sleep architecture: changes are controversial.
   c. Traumatic nightmares are unique.

Source: From "Biological Approaches to the Diagnosis and Treatment of Post-Traumatic Stress Disorder," by M. J. Friedman, 1991. *Journal of Traumatic Stress, 4*, p. 70. Copyright © 1992 Plenum Press. Reprinted by permission.

monoamine oxidase (MAO) and adrenergic receptor activity; (2) reduced hypothalamic-pituitary-adrenocortical axis response; (3) significant variations in the production of the endogenous opioid system at various levels of psychophysiological stimulation; and (4) sleep disturbances and sleep EEG activity (Friedman, 1991).

Future research in this exciting area should continue to determine relationships between more basic physiological findings and the reliable psychophysiological and psychological indicators of PTSD. An excellent example of this type of bio-psycho-social research was recently demonstrated by Pitman, van der Kolk, Orr, and Greenberg (1990) in a study in which combat-related PTSD patients showed a 30% decrease in pain response (that is, a 30% increase in pain threshold) after witnessing scenes from the movie *Platoon.* This would appear to indicate that PTSD sufferers have a generally lowered level of endogenous opioids in their system at rest that results in the increase in chronic

pain (Friedman, 1991) and that opioid levels are significantly increased in response to stimuli associated with the trauma. These results might explain why some combat-related PTSD sufferers seek out and even appear to enjoy violent activities (Solursh, 1989).

E. A Comprehensive Model of PTSD

Pointing to the complex nature of PTSD and the emerging literature in epidemiology and etiology, Barlow (1988) and Jones and Barlow (1990) have suggested an inductive "comprehensive" model to explain PTSD that includes biological, psychological, and social factors. As shown in Figure 7.1, this model suggests that only certain biologically predisposed or vulnerable individuals, possibly genetically inherited, are likely to ultimately develop PTSD, but other social and psychological factors play a major role. Negative

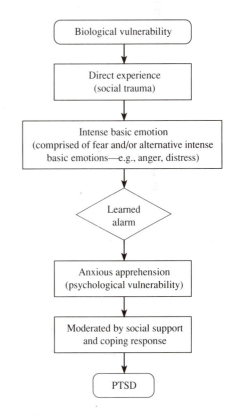

Figure 7.1 A model of the etiology of PTSD
source: *From* Anxiety and Its Disorders: The Nature and Treatment of Anxiety and Panic, *by D. H. Barlow, p. 507. Copyright © 1988 Guilford Press. Reprinted by permission.*

life events can vary in intensity and frequency ("direct experience" in Figure 7.1) and can produce intense basic emotion that motivates the "fight or flight" response. Jones and Barlow point out that this intense emotion can result from a true alarm (that is, a real danger is present) or a false one. In either case, a learned response to the alarm signal will occur. It is not clear at this point just how this learning takes place, although it would seem to necessarily involve some form of conditioning.

Psychological vulnerability as the result of early environmental learning also plays an important role in this inductive model. Jones and Barlow point out that if an individual's early experiences have resulted in learning that the environmental and social events are unpredictable/uncontrollable and threatening, this results in a heightened psychological vulnerability to anxiety. Finally, regardless of an individual's psychological and social vulnerability and the intensity of the stressor, Jones and Barlow suggest that social supports and learned coping responses can have a moderating influence on symptoms.

IV. Treatment Strategies

Early psychological treatment strategies for traumatic neurosis or, to use one of Freud's earlier terms, traumatic hysteria, were strongly influenced by the Belgian psychophysicist J. L. R. Delboeuf and the French clinician-scientists Alfred Binet and, especially, Pierre Janet. In their earliest papers, Freud and Breuer cite these writers as having already developed a therapy similar to the one they proposed (compare with Riviere, 1953; van der Hart, Brown, & van der Kolk, 1989). The "therapy" to which Freud and Breuer were referring was Breuer's use of hypnosis and catharsis, probably with the famous case of Anna O. This treatment could be considered the forerunner of psychoanalytic technique. Freud ultimately determined that hypnotic abreaction did not bring about a permanent cure with most hysterics. But as Nichols and Zax (1977) point out in their book on catharsis, Freud could probably have utilized more effective abreaction. Apparently, unlike Breuer, Freud tended to intervene in the patient's emotional process, sealing it over

and discouraging complete catharsis. In describing Freud and Breuer's treatment, Boudewyns and Shipley (1983) point out the similarities between this technique and their direct therapeutic exposure treatment process.

The French therapists, on the other hand, especially Janet, were much more enthusiastic about an exposure methodology. van der Hart, Brown, and van der Kolk (1989) note that Janet's approach utilized an aggressive form of abreaction under hypnosis, which Janet called "neutralization," as the central intervention.[1] But this was only a part of Janet's multimodal approach to traumatic neurosis. His treatments included many pragmatic behavioral and cognitive interventions that are quite similar to those commonly used today and for which we now have empirical evidence of effectiveness. These techniques included: (1) thought stopping; (2) "substitution," a technique similar to Michenbaum's (1977) "coping imagery" and Ellis's (1962) positive imagery to counter negative thoughts; and (3) reframing.

A. Behavioral Strategies

Exposure therapies, including direct therapeutic exposure as well as more graded approaches, have been used effectively for some symptoms of PTSD, especially combat-related PTSD. Direct therapeutic exposure (compared with flooding, implosive therapy, response prevention), defined as repeated or extended exposure (either in reality or in fantasy) to objectively harmless but feared stimuli for the purpose of reducing negative affect (Boudewyns & Shipley, 1983) and based on Mowrer's two-factor theory (Mowrer, 1960), would appear to be a logical treatment choice for PTSD. For many years now this approach and, to a lesser extent, more graded exposure strategies, such as systematic desensitization, have been considered standard and effective treatment for several other anxiety disorders including simple phobias, agoraphobia, panic disorder with agoraphobia, social phobia, and obsessive-compulsive disorder

---

[1] van der Kolk and van der Hart and colleagues (Putnam, 1989; van der Hart, Brown, & van der Kolk, 1989; van der Hart & Horst, 1989; van der Kolk, Brown, & van der Hart, 1989) offer an excellent and interesting review of Janet's contribution to the conceptualization and treatment of traumatic neurosis and to modern-day PTSD.

(Barlow & Wolfe, 1981). Also, as discussed earlier, many early psychotherapists used similar techniques to treat the psychological sequelae of trauma. Keane and his colleagues pioneered the notion of using therapeutic exposure with PTSD (Keane & Kaloupek, 1982). They have written several conceptual articles describing their technique and the logic of using exposure therapy for PTSD, especially combat-related PTSD (Fairbank & Nicholson, 1987; Keane, Fairbank, Caddell, Zimering, & Bender, 1985; Keane, Zimering, & Caddell, 1985; Lyons & Keane, 1989). Therefore, it is not surprising that most treatment outcome studies of behavior therapy for PTSD have evaluated the effects of exposure therapy. Also, a new (and novel) form of exposure therapy, called eye movement desensitization (EMD) (Shapiro, 1989a), and more recently eye movement desensitization and reprocessing (EMD/R) (Shapiro, 1991), drew the interest of several investigators as a treatment for PTSD and will be reviewed in this section.

Cognitive behavioral approaches, such as stress inoculation training, which include such specific strategies as thought stopping (Wolpe, 1958), cognitive restructuring (Beck & Emery, 1985; Ellis, 1962), guided self-dialogue (Michenbaum, 1977), and modeling, have also been explored as treatment for PTSD, especially with victims of sexual assault (compare with Kilpatrick, Veronen, & Best, 1985).

A few uncontrolled clinical trials have been carried out using more direct stress reduction techniques, such as relaxation therapy and biofeedback, as treatment for PTSD. Finally, several case reports and clinical studies have been carried out with children with PTSD, and these will be reviewed in this section also.

B. Case Demonstrations and Uncontrolled Outcome Studies

Several of the single case designs and uncontrolled clinical trials published over the past ten years have demonstrated how behavior therapy can be used with PTSD brought on by different types of stressors. Although the term *PTSD* was not used in the paper, an early report by Schindler (1980) demonstrated the apparently successful application of a combination of graded exposure, systematic desensitization (Wolpe, 1958), and a self-administered form of that same

technique with a 29-year-old Vietnam veteran "whose chief complaint was a chronic recurring nightmare, a vivid reexperiencing of an extremely traumatic war experience." Black and Keane (1982) found only three sessions of "implosive therapy" to be effective in treating a 55-year-old World War II veteran with PTSD and multiple past hospitalizations. The patient maintained treatment gains at two years. In the first controlled single case design to use exposure, Keane and Kaloupek (1982), using psychophysiological (heart rate) data during 19 sessions of imaginal flooding, reported "empirical, objective evidence of treatment efficacy." A one-year follow-up found that the improvements in general overall adjustment, as well as specific symptoms of nightmares and flashbacks, have been maintained.

For purposes of demonstrating direct therapeutic exposure in clinical practice, Boudewyns and Shipley (1983) offered a very detailed account of the successful use of a combination of exposure techniques (in vivo flooding, imaginal flooding, and implosive therapy) with a Vietnam veteran with PTSD who originally presented as suffering from what the patient called a "thunderstorm phobia." Fairbank, Gross, and Keane (1983) gave a detailed account of the effective use of their particular exposure methodology to treat a wounded Vietnam combat veteran who had watched one of his friends tortured, killed, and mutilated by the enemy during combat. This paper describes the treatment methodology developed by Keane and his colleagues while at the Jackson, Mississippi, VA Medical Center in the early 1980s. This technique is unique in that it consists of exposure therapy (implosive therapy) similar to that described in Levis and Hare (1977) in combination with relaxation therapy, guided positive imagery, and in vivo and imaginal "homework" sessions where appropriate.

Several other case studies have described a variety of exposure methodologies used to treat other than combat-related PTSD. Rychtarik, Silverman, Van Landingham, and Prue (1984) used a controlled single case design and psychophysiological outcome measures to successfully demonstrate the use of implosive therapy with a female victim of sexual abuse. Here again, however, the patient was not specifically diagnosed as suffering from PTSD, even though the diagnosis was officially available and symptoms described would appear to support such a diagnosis. McCaffrey and Fairbank (1985) used the Jackson technique to effectively treat two PTSD sufferers, both of whose trauma events involved transportation accidents (helicopter and automobile).

In a rather unusual methodology, Richards and Rose (1991) had patients imagine and recount their traumatic experiences on audio tape, then listen to the tape "at least four times" between therapy sessions. This technique is similar to a more graded methodology reported by Williams (1976) earlier with a case of "traumatic neurosis." Richards and Rose described the treatment of four cases of PTSD: (1) an engineer who had been burned in the explosion of an electrical panel and suffered "electrical panel phobia"; (2) a policeman who had occupational problems after having been injured in a shoplifting arrest; (3) a female robbery victim with "agoraphobia"; and (4) another policeman who had a fear of crowded places and had been crushed in a crowd control situation. Finally, Rothbaum and Foa (1991) report on an unusual but interesting case of a PTSD rape victim with conversion mutism treated with a combination of in vivo and imaginal exposure therapy.

C. Controlled Outcome Studies

Several studies have been reported recently using controlled multigroup experimental designs to compare the effectiveness of various behavioral treatment strategies. In an interesting and somewhat unusual methodology, Peniston (1986) treated a sample of eight combat veterans each with 45 sessions of "EMG-assisted desensitization" and compared the results to a group of eight untreated controls. The treatment consisted of Wolpe's (1958) systematic desensitization procedure, but used a combination of patient report and EMG microvolt levels to determine whether the patient was experiencing anxiety during exposure. Peniston found that the treated participants had significantly reduced frontalis EMG resting levels compared with controls based on pre- to posttherapy evaluation. Also, a two-year telephone interview follow-up revealed that the treated group reported significantly fewer nightmares and flashbacks than the controls. Also, none of the treated participants had

rehospitalizations to the center in which they had been treated, while five of the eight control participants had "frequent" readmission to the hospital. These results are encouraging given that the sample consisted of long-standing, chronic PTSD patients. Unfortunately, the only comparison group was a nontreated group, while the treated group received an extraordinary number of sessions. Thus, it could be argued that the specific effects of the treatment were not tested and that so many sessions of any treatment might have influenced rehospitalization and nightmare/flashback rates. EMG changes could easily have resulted from the fact that the treated group was much more familiar with the laboratory setting than were the controls. Finally, some patients were receiving pharmacotherapy, but Peniston did not specify the type of medication or group membership by type much less control for this variable. Regardless of these concerns, Peniston's unique exposure methodology group did show significant positive change when compared to controls. Clearly, Peniston's procedure deserves further study.

Keane, Fairbank, Caddell, and Zimering (1989) randomly assigned 24 male combat veterans with PTSD to either a therapy group ($n = 11$) or a wait-list control ($n = 13$). The therapy group received 14 to 16 sessions of implosive therapy/relaxation therapy/in vivo flooding, as previously described. Several standard psychometric measures and therapist ratings were used to evaluate change immediately following therapy, or after appropriate time lapses for controls, and at a six-month follow-up. Results were mixed. Participants in the experimental group evidenced significantly more positive change than controls for some symptoms in the reexperiencing category, while measures that generally reflected numbing and avoidance were largely unchanged for either group. However, the patients' general anxiety and depression levels appear to have been reduced by the exposure treatment. That avoidance was not affected by the treatment while overall anxiety was somewhat surprising since, theoretically at least, one should follow the other. One difficulty with the study design was that a majority (but not all) of the participants in both the treatment and the wait-list control were also receiving psychotropic medications, potentially confounding treatment both within and across the two comparison groups.

In a similar study with a smaller sample, Cooper and Clum (1989) compared two groups of treated combat veterans ($n = 7$ for each). Both groups were offered "standard group treatment and individual treatment that they would ordinarily have been assigned by a VA psychologist" (p. 385). In addition to this standard treatment, the exposure treated group received a maximum of nine sessions of imaginal flooding. As with Keane et al. (1989), a majority of the participants (four in each group) were receiving psychotropic medications, although Cooper and Clum reported data indicating that the groups were evenly matched as to the types of medications prescribed. Treatment outcome was measured immediately following therapy and at a three-month follow-up using standard outcome measures as well as a rather novel behavioral avoidance test (BAT) using a slide tape show of Vietnam with the sound track as the "phobic" stimulus.

Again, results were mixed but were somewhat inconsistent with Keane et al. (1989). Measures of depression and trait anxiety were not affected by flooding, while several symptoms related directly to the trauma and reflecting change in all three classes of symptoms including reexperiencing, avoidance, and increased arousal were positively influenced by the exposure.

In another controlled design, Boudewyns, Hyer, Woods, Harrison, and McCranie (1990) selected 58, medication-free Vietnam combat veterans who had been treated in a special inpatient unit. Twenty-six of these 58 participants had also received direct therapeutic exposure (Boudewyns & Shipley, 1983) while the others had received "conventional therapy." From this larger group of 58, they also identified a group of 15 "successes" and 15 "failures," determined by their scores three months after discharge on the VETs scale (Ellsworth et al., 1979), a reliable outcome measure for veteran mental patients at three months postdischarge. Boudewyns et al. found that a significantly greater number of successes had been treated with direct therapeutic exposure when compared to the failures. The study can be criticized for its retrospective design and the fact that only one outcome measure of overall adjustment was used.

Boudewyns and Hyer (1990) reported on a sample of 38 medication-free Vietnam combat veterans suffering from chronic PTSD and other concurrent disorders, treated on the same inpatient unit as the previous study. Half of their sample were given up to 12 sessions of direct therapeutic exposure in addition to the usual treatment milieu on the special PTSD ward. The other 19, who were given a similar number of sessions of more "conventional" treatment, served as controls. Psychophysiological responses to idiosyncratically designed imaginal flooding (exposure) scenes of combat (including frontalis electromyography, skin conductance, and heart rate) that were all significantly elevated at pretherapy testing did not decline significantly for the direct therapeutic exposure group in comparison with the controls after therapy. Furthermore, only one psychophysiological measure, skin conductance, evidenced significant decline for the sample as a whole from pre- to posttherapy. Boudewyns and Hyer concluded that psychophysiological responding to facsimiles of combat, already shown to be an important diagnostic indicator of PTSD of combat, was not easily affected by even intensive inpatient treatment. Yet, while neither treatment appeared to reduce psychophysiological responding, those individuals who did, for whatever reason, show a decrement in psychophysiological responding at posttherapy testing were significantly more likely to show improvement on the VETs scale at the three-month follow-up. This belated improvement with imaginal exposure therapy has been shown to have occurred elsewhere in controlled experimentation with other types of anxiety disorders (Boudewyns, 1975; Chambless, Foa, Groves, & Goldstein, 1980) as well as with noncombat-related PTSD (Foa, Rothbaum, Riggs, & Murdock, 1991).

In an eight-month averaged follow-up to this study, Boudewyns, Albrecht, and Hyer (1992) reported that the trend in the psychophysiological measures seen immediately following therapy did not continue at follow-up. Instead, subjects continued to show strong psychophysiological responding to the idiosyncratic flooding scenes, regardless of treatment. There was, however, evidence on several standard psychological outcome measures that corroborated the three-month follow-up improvement in overall adjustment of the exposure treated group compared with the more conventionally treated group. These experimenters concluded that the results supported the efficacy of direct therapeutic exposure with these chronic patients in terms of overall adjustment. Also, compared to controls, those individuals who did show a diminution in psychophysiological responding to idiosyncratic exposure scenes at follow-up, regardless of treatment condition, were better adjusted eight months following therapy.

This series of controlled outcome studies by Boudewyns and colleagues treating these chronic, multiply-disordered inpatient veteran PTSD sufferers represents a very rigorous and conservative test of the exposure methodology. In sum, what is evidenced by these trials is that while exposure therapy is effective in contributing to the overall adjustment of these chronic patients, unfortunately there is little evidence that treatment influences the most salient indicator of the disorder—that is, psychophysiological responding to images and memories of the trauma. This would lend support to the earlier findings of Keane et al. (1989). Nevertheless, as already shown by others (Blanchard et al., 1986; Pitman et al., 1987), these findings support the important notion that regardless of the effects of treatment a reduction in psychophysiological responding to trauma memories is consistent with an improvement in adjustment. This latter finding adds considerable support to the hypothesis that psychophysiological responses to facsimiles of the trauma is a valid diagnostic measure of PTSD (Keane & Kolb, 1988).

At least two multigroup controlled outcome studies (Brom et al., 1989; Foa et al., 1991) have compared a form of exposure therapy with other types of behavioral and nonbehavioral treatment using nonveteran samples. Brom et al. sampled 112 participants from the Netherlands who were diagnosed as suffering from PTSD. Trauma events included violent crime victimization ($n = 19$), being involved in a traffic accident ($n = 4$), loss of a loved one as a result of murder/ suicide ($n = 83$), and other ($n = 6$). Three approximately equal treatment groups were formed. Participants in one group were given 15 sessions of an individual imaginal exposure therapy called "trauma desensitization." The second group was offered an average of 14.4 sessions of hypnotherapy, while a third was treated with an average of 18.8 sessions of psychodynamic therapy as described

by Horowitz & Kaltreider (1980). A waiting list group was used as a control. Several standard psychometric measures were taken before, immediately following, and at three months following therapy. Brom et al. reported that all three treatment groups improved significantly more than the controls on almost all measures and that "clinically significant" improvements were evidenced in 60% of the treated patients compared to only 26% of the untreated patients. Also, trauma desensitization individuals appeared to show improvements immediately following therapy and maintained these gains at follow-up, while the psychodynamic individuals were more likely not to evidence significant change until follow-up. These experimenters also concluded that trauma desensitization and hypnotherapy had a stronger influence on the symptoms of intrusion and that psychodynamic therapy had more influence on the symptoms of avoidance. While this study did not find much difference between any of the treated groups, it is important to note that the psychodynamic group participants required several more sessions than did the other two groups. Also, although Brom et al. did not describe the treatment approaches in much detail, it was clear that all three involved the use of exposure to the imagined trauma to some degree as part of the process, and this would appear to confound results. The psychopharmacological medication status was not reported.

In a particularly well-designed and well-controlled study, Foa et al. (1991) treated a sample of female rape victims who suffered from PTSD with one of three types of therapy: stress inoculation training ($n = 14$), supportive counseling ($n = 10$), or prolonged exposure ($n = 11$). A group on a wait list served as controls ($n = 10$). Foa et al. concluded that while stress inoculation training appeared to be the most effective treatment immediately following therapy (followed, in order, by prolonged exposure, supportive counseling, and wait list), prolonged exposure therapy was superior at the three and one-half month follow-up (followed, in order, by stress inoculation, wait list, and supportive counseling).

Finally, Kilpatrick and colleagues at the Medical University of South Carolina (compare with Kilpatrick, Best, et al., 1985; Kilpatrick, Veronen, & Best, 1985) have developed a multimodal cognitive strategy for treating victims of rape that includes coping skills using stress inoculation training (Michenbaum, 1977), relaxation therapy, and thought stopping. Only recently have studies of rape victims included diagnostic verification of PTSD (Foa et al., 1991). In the Foa et al. study previously reviewed, the stress inoculation group treatment was based on the Kilpatrick methodology. A strong argument can be made for the case that the PTSD status of victims of sexual assault should be determined before being inducted as participants into treatment outcome studies since symptoms in rape victims often remit on their own within a few weeks of the event (Kilpatrick & Calhoun, 1988). Also, from a clinical standpoint, sexual assault victims might have a better opportunity for effective treatment if their experience was seen by mental health professionals as one of a class of experiences that can have long-lasting traumatic effects (Burge, 1988).

Two controlled multigroup studies of treatment outcome have used victims of sexual assault as participants. While these participants had not specifically been diagnosed as suffering from PTSD, there is reason to assume that perhaps as many as 86% suffered moderate to severe PTSD symptoms (Burge, 1988). Frank et al. (1988) evaluated the effects of graded exposure (systematic desensitization) compared with a "cognitive behavior therapy" using a sample of rape victims. The design also divided the sample into those who sought treatment immediately following therapy and those who delayed treatment by up to several months. These authors found no difference in effectiveness between the two types of behavior therapy and also reported that behavior therapy was about as effective in reducing symptoms regardless of whether treatment was delayed or immediate. They also noted that although no participant was instructed to do so, 75% of the participants in their study "developed a pattern of following each treatment session with self-directed in vivo exposure to stimuli described in that session." Stewart et al. did not report outcome separately for these self-exposure participants.

Kilpatrick and Calhoun (1988) criticized the Frank et al. (1988) study. Citing evidence, Kilpatrick, Saunders, Veronen, Best, and Von (1987) noted that although about 57% of individuals who have been raped go on to develop PTSD, many appear to overcome emotional problems associated with the rape within the first two months postassault. Kilpatrick and Calhoun therefore concluded that future studies of treatment outcome for those who have experienced rape should include appropriate no-treatment controls if recent rape victims are used as subjects.

At about the same time, Resick, Jordan, Girelli, Hutter, and Marhoefer-Dvorak (1988) reported on a sample of 37 individuals who had been raped, all of whom were at least three months posttherapy. Three types of group therapy were compared: stress inoculation, assertion training, and supportive psychotherapy plus information. Wait-list participants served as controls. Resick et al. reported that all three types of therapy were effective in producing lasting improvements at six-month follow-up, while the wait-list control did not improve. There were no significant differences among the three treatment groups.

A new form of exposure therapy, called eye movement desensitization and reprocessing (EMD/R), is gaining some support in the literature as a treatment for PTSD. This somewhat unusual technique also has support from several very enthusiastic advocates who have had at least immediate success at the clinical level. Shapiro (1989a, 1989b) reports that the treatment is often effective in only a single session.

The EMD/R technique (Shapiro, 1989b) has the patient move his or her eyes in a "saccadic" or rhythmic side-to-side manner while engaging in self-described, free-floating imaginal exposure, or flooding. Except for the eye movements, EMD/R is very similar to another therapy technique called "desensitization therapy using free association," which may also be effective with veteran patients suffering from anxiety and depression (Boudewyns & Wilson, 1972). In their earlier study, Boudewyns and Wilson found both implosive therapy and desensitization using free association to be helpful in reducing the anxiety resulting from traumatic experiences. However, a five-year follow-up of this study (Boudewyns, 1975) found implosive therapy to have more lasting effects when compared to desensitization using free association.

Several clinical-level case reports have demonstrated the EMD/R technique to be of use in reducing negative affect caused by several types of stressors (Lipke & Botkin, in press; Puk, 1991; Shapiro, 1989b;

Wolpe & Abrams, 1991). To date only two researchers have attempted to test the effects of EMD/R (in Shapiro's early publications referred to only as eye movement desensitization or "EMD") using a controlled design (Boudewyns, Stwertka, Hyer, Albrecht, & Sperr, 1991; Shapiro, 1989a). Shapiro (1989a) divided 23 participants with PTSD and several types of traumatic events into a treatment and a placebo control group. The treatment group received EMD, and the placebo group received a "modified" flooding procedure (describing the traumatic event in detail by the participant). Outcome was assessed immediately following therapy and at a three-month follow-up using (1) self-report measures of "subjective units of disturbance" (SUDs) (Wolpe, 1958, 1982); (2) changes in presenting complaint using such verbal descriptors as "eliminated" or "decreased"; (3) several other nonstandard idiosyncratic measures that were specific to the treatment process; and (4) pulse rate. Unfortunately, because Shapiro determined that the EMD-treated participants had benefited from the therapy, she then, "for ethical reasons" treated all the placebo participants with EMD, making follow-up comparisons between the treated and placebo treated groups impossible. Therefore, even though Shapiro reported significant improvement among the EMD-treated participants immediately following therapy, there was no way to determine whether these differences would have been maintained at follow-up. The placebo group might have improved during the interim without active treatment. As noted earlier, belated improvement in exposure treated participants is not uncommon. Nevertheless, the placebo group, which was given delayed treatment with EMD, also appeared to improve at follow-up on all measures.

There are several difficulties with these rather dramatic "one session" results. First, the study was carried out by the originator of the technique who apparently also administered many of the dependent measures. Second, there apparently was no attempt to objectively or formally diagnose the patients (patients were diagnosed by the referring professional as suffering from PTSD), and we therefore have no way of knowing if the technique has relevance for patients

who suffer "full-blown" PTSD. Third, comparative follow-up was not carried out.

A pilot study by Boudewyns, Stwertka, et al. (1991) attempted to confirm Shapiro's results with a group of chronic veteran inpatients with combat-related PTSD. In this trial, SUDs measures similar to Shapiro's methodology were used, and treatment effects were tested with psychophysiological outcome measures (that is, heart rate, skin conductance levels, electromyographical frontalis responding, and hand temperature) in response to flooding scenes of the traumatic memories pre- and posttherapy (Boudewyns & Hyer, 1990). Three groups were formed: the EMD group received two sessions of EMD, the exposure control group received a treatment equivalent in all aspects to EMD except that the patient was not required to produce saccadic eye movements during therapy, and the control group received only the usual treatment milieu of the inpatient ward. Results were consistent with Shapiro's in that SUDs levels dropped significantly for EMD-treated participants in comparison to the exposure control group. However, the psychophysiological measures were unaffected by any treatment and did not confirm patient self-report. No follow-up was attempted in this pilot study.

It should be pointed out that this study by Boudewyns, Stwertka, et al. (1991) represents a very conservative test of EMD. The patient population is multiply-disordered and chronic. Also, as noted in experiments by Boudewyns and his colleagues reviewed earlier, psychophysiological measures appear not to change (Boudewyns & Hyer, 1990; Boudewyns et al., 1992), even when using many sessions of intensive individual therapy. A controlled multigroup study with appropriate follow-up and standard outcome measures carried out by independent experimenters is clearly warranted for this approach.

Finally, with regard to the EMD/R technique, the question arises as to what significance the saccadic eye movements hold for what would otherwise be little more than a rather unstructured desensitization technique. Shapiro (personal communication, August 1990) has no commitment to any particular hypothesis or theory but makes a comparison to the rapid eye movements (REM) observed during some phases of sleep, which also appear to have some stress-reducing capacity. In terms of psychological or learning theory, the presumed effects of the technique could be explained on the basis of interference notions of extinction (Kimble, 1961) or by Hull's elaborate theory of reactive and conditioned inhibition (Hull, 1943). Clearly, if it is hypothesized that eye movements represent a counterconditioning phenomena, assuming EMD/R works, the explanation could lie in Wolpe's (1958) notion of reciprocal inhibition. Perhaps this is why Wolpe has shown such positive inclinations toward EMD (Shapiro, 1989b).

V. PTSD in Children

Although there is relatively less literature on children with PTSD, it is clear that children do suffer from the disorder (Collins, Baum, & Singer, 1983; Klingman & Ben Eli, 1981; Saigh, 1984a, 1984b, 1988, 1989, 1991) and may have unique vulnerabilities (Lyons, 1987). Lyons offers a nice conceptual review addressing some of the central issues regarding PTSD in children. There is now an emerging awareness by educators and others involved in children's services of how traumatic events can affect children. As a result, children who are traumatized in groups and in public, such as when held down by sniper fire on a public playground (Ornitz & Pynoos, 1989), are now usually followed by counselors and therapists after the event to treat and prevent lasting effects. Privately traumatized (abused) children are often not reached in time.

There have been no controlled treatment outcome studies of children suffering from PTSD. Several clinical case-level studies have demonstrated behavior therapy with children. For example, McNeil and Todd (1986) used an operant learning/positive reinforcement and a "stimulus narrowing" technique similar to the common time-out-for-worry procedure and applied it successfully to a 5-year-old girl who had experienced abuse. Also, Philip Saigh has demonstrated what he terms *in vitro flooding*, a direct therapeutic exposure procedure, with several children with

PTSD (Saigh, 1986, 1987a, 1987b). Clearly, considerably more research on understanding and treating children suffering from PTSD would be in order.

VI. Conclusions Regarding Treatment of PTSD

It seems obvious that successful psychological treatment for PTSD should include some form of exposure therapy aimed primarily at extinction or habituation of the specific symptoms of PTSD, including intrusive thoughts, flashbacks, and avoidance behavior. Even nonbehavioral treatments such as those developed by Horowitz and earlier by Janet have a significant exposure component. Early psychoanalytic-oriented treatments used this technique. Also, combat experience groups, offered through VA special treatment programs or Vet Centers for veterans with combat-related PTSD, encourage patients to engage in "cathartic reexperiencing" of the trauma, which involves a great deal of exposure to the traumatic event.

Given this conclusion, it is curious to note that even though the VA has made a significant effort to train its therapists to use direct therapeutic exposure for PTSD (Regional Medical Education Center, 1989), according to one VA report (Fontana, Rosenheck, & Spencer, 1990), exposure therapy is used very infrequently for combat-related PTSD. Fontana et al. found that of the 18 types of therapy being used by professionals who were on the staffs of the (then) 24 specially funded PTSD clinical treatment teams at various VA Medical Centers around the country, "exposure therapy" as such was rated to be the most effective. Yet, in that same report exposure therapy was judged to be among those treatment modalities that were the "least frequently delivered." These writers speculated that the reason for the low usage rate was because exposure therapy was considered to be "specialized interventions that focus on delimited problems." This is a curious conclusion, since intrusive thoughts, dreams, and avoidance behaviors are the "hallmark" symptoms of PTSD—the very symptoms addressed by direct therapeutic exposure.

A more likely reason for this nonuse is therapists' attitudes about direct exposure. Soon after imaginal exposure was first introduced, researchers and clinicians began to object to it, warning that it was dangerous and would produce lasting, undue anxiety and negative side effects (Boudewyns & Shipley, 1983). This concern continues to the present day with clinicians continuing to offer individual case examples of patients who have problems during therapy as "evidence" (Kilpatrick & Best, 1984; Pitman et al., 1991) for this danger. Yet there are still no controlled trials to support the notion that direct therapeutic exposure results in a significant number of negative side effects. In fact, the cost-to-benefit ratio in terms of effectiveness and efficiency is quite good (Boudewyns & Levis, 1975; Boudewyns & Shipley, 1983; Shipley & Boudewyns, 1980, 1988).

VII. A Word about Pharmacotherapy for PTSD

Symptoms of depression and anxiety are part of PTSD. Evidence from one of the few adequately controlled studies on the effectiveness of psychotropic medications for PTSD appears to indicate that amitriptyline was helpful in at least partly alleviating these symptoms, especially depression (Davidson et al., 1990), in some PTSD sufferers. Evidence that medications are effective with the more salient symptoms of PTSD, such as intrusions and avoidance, is mixed (Davidson et al., 1990; Frank et al., 1988). Based on the literature to date, psychotropic medications alone have not been shown to be particularly effective for most of the specific symptoms of PTSD. Medication appears to be helpful primarily in the context of psychotherapy (Friedman, 1991).

From a theoretical perspective at least, we might be particularly concerned about the use of drugs with PTSD sufferers. As has been shown, there is considerable evidence that exposure to facsimiles of the trauma or to the internal and external stimuli that are associated with the original event is an essential element in reducing the conditioned emotional response to the memory of trauma and in effectively reducing other symptoms of PTSD. Presumably, this exposure

could take place through unstructured, everyday posttraumatic experiences of the victim or as a result of structured treatment. In either case, psychotropic medications tend to restrict and diminish perceptions, sensations, and experiences and, thus, reduce the chances of extinction, habituation, or "mastery" of these stimuli. It is only speculation, yet it would be reasonable to conclude that the many traumatized Vietnam veterans who "self-medicated" with abuse of street drugs and alcohol both during combat and after returning home (Boudewyns, Albrecht, et al., 1991; Stephenson, Boudewyns, & Lessing, 1977) may well have reduced their chances for bringing about a "natural extinction" of their emotional response and therefore increased the probabilities that they would become chronic PTSD sufferers.

VIII. Summary and Conclusions

After a long history of both scientific and political debate, the notion that extreme psychological traumatic experiences, in and of themselves, could result in a severe, even malignant, psychiatric disorder is now established. In 1980 posttraumatic stress disorder finally became an officially classified anxiety disorder.

Since then, the few controlled treatment outcome studies that have been carried out appear to indicate that the most effective treatment for PTSD is some form of exposure therapy. This is not surprising in light of the fact that several other types of anxiety disorders respond well to this form of behavioral treatment. However, PTSD may be more complex than the other types of anxiety disorders, especially with regard to the variety of symptoms involved. In its chronic form or in combat-related PTSD, no one type of treatment tested so far has been successful in reducing all the symptoms of the disorder. Psychophysiological overarousal to imaginal facsimiles of the traumatic event is especially difficult to influence with treatment. Identifying techniques that reduce or at least control this arousal will likely be grist for the research mill for many years.

Theoretical and conceptual formulations regarding both the etiology and treatment of the disorder are in early stages of development. It is hoped that these efforts will eventually mature our understanding of the disorder as researchers explore important issues such as (1) predisposing factors; (2) how the nature and intensity of the stressor relates to the severity of the disorder; and (3) how biological, psychological, social, and cultural variables interact to result in PTSD and to either ameliorate or exacerbate its symptoms.

References

AMERICAN Psychiatric Association. (1952). *Diagnostic and statistical manual of mental disorders.* Washington, DC: Author.

AMERICAN Psychiatric Association. (1968). *Diagnostic and statistical manual of mental disorders* (2nd ed.). Washington, DC: Author.

AMERICAN Psychiatric Association. (1980). *Diagnostic and statistical manual of mental disorders* (3rd ed.). Washington, DC: Author.

AMERICAN Psychiatric Association. (1987). *Diagnostic and statistical manual of mental disorders* (3rd ed., rev.). Washington, DC: Author.

BARLOW, D. H. (1988). *Anxiety and its disorders: The nature and treatment of anxiety and panic.* New York: Guilford Press.

BARLOW, D. H., & Wolfe, B. E. (1981). Behavioral approaches to anxiety disorders: A report on the NIMH-SUNY Albany research conference. *Journal of Consulting and Clinical Psychology, 49,* 448–455.

BECK, A. T., & Emery, G. (1985). *Anxiety disorders and phobias: A cognitive perspective.* New York: Basic Books.

BLACK, J. L., & Keane, T. M. (1982). Implosive therapy in the treatment of combat related fears in a World War II veteran. *Journal of Behavior Therapy and Experimental Psychiatry, 13,* 163–165.

BLANCHARD, E. B., Kolb, L. C., Gerardi, R. J., Ryan, P., & Pallmeyer, T. P. (1986). Cardiac response to relevant stimuli as an adjunctive tool for diagnosing post-traumatic stress disorder in Vietnam veterans. *Behavior Therapy, 17,* 592–606.

BOUDEWYNS, P. A. (1975). Implosive therapy and desensitization therapy with inpatients: A five-year follow-up. *Journal of Abnormal Psychology, 84,* 159–160.

BOUDEWYNS, P. A., Albrecht, J. W., & Hyer, L. A. (1992, August). *Long-term effects of direct therapeutic exposure in combat-related PTSD.* Paper presented at the convention of the American Psychological Association, Washington, DC.

BOUDEWYNS, P. A., Albrecht, J. W., Hyer, L., & Talbert, F. S. (1991). Comorbidity and treatment outcome in inpatients with chronic combat-related PTSD. *Hospital and Community Psychiatry, 42,* 847–849.

BOUDEWYNS, P. A., & Hyer., L. (1990). Physiological response to combat memories and preliminary treatment outcome in Vietnam veteran PTSD patients treated with direct therapeutic exposure. *Behavior Therapy, 21,* 63–87.

BOUDEWYNS, P. A., Hyer, L., Woods, M. G., Harrison, W. R., & McCranie, E. (1990). PTSD among Vietnam veterans: An early look at treatment outcome using direct therapeutic exposure. *Journal of Traumatic Stress, 3,* 359–368.

BOUDEWYNS, P. A., & Levis, D. J. (1975). Autonomic reactivity of high and low ego-strength subjects to repeated anxiety eliciting scenes. *Journal of Abnormal Psychology, 84,* 682–692.

BOUDEWYNS, P. A., & Shipley, R. H. (1983). *Flooding and implosive therapy: Direct therapeutic exposure in clinical practice.* New York: Plenum.

BOUDEWYNS, P. A., Stwertka, S. A., Hyer, L. A., Albrecht, J. W., & Sperr, E. V. (1991, August). *Eye movement desensitization for PTSD of combat: A treatment outcome pilot study.* Paper presented at the convention of the American Psychological Association, San Francisco, CA.

BOUDEWYNS, P. A., & Wilson, A. E. (1972). Implosive therapy and desensitization therapy using free association in the treatment of inpatients. *Journal of Abnormal Psychology, 79,* 259–268.

BOUDEWYNS, P. A., Woods, M. G., Hyer, L., & Albrecht, J. W. (1991). Chronic combat-related PTSD and concurrent substance abuse: Implications for treatment of this frequent "dual diagnosis." *Journal of Traumatic Stress, 4,* 549–560.

BOYD, T. L., & Levis, D. J. (1976). The effects of single-component extinction to a three-component serial CS on resistance to extinction of the conditioned avoidance response. *Learning and Motivation, 7,* 517–531.

BROM, D., Kleber, R. J., & Defares, P. B. (1989). Brief psychotherapy for posttraumatic stress disorders. *Journal of Consulting and Clinical Psychology, 57,* 612–617.

BROMET, E. J., Parkinson, D. K., Schulberg, H. C., Dunn, L. O., & Gondek, P. C. (1982). Mental health of residents near the Three Mile Island reactor: A comparative study of selected groups. *Journal of Preventive Psychiatry, 1,* 225–276.

BURGE, S. K. (1988). Post-traumatic stress disorder in victims of rape. *Journal of Traumatic Stress, 2,* 193–210.

CARD, J. J. (1987). Epidemiology of PTSD in a national cohort of Vietnam veterans. *Journal of Clinical Psychology, 43,* 6–17.

CENTERS for Disease Control. (1988). Health status of Vietnam veterans: I. Psychosocial characteristics. *The Journal of the American Medical Association, 259,* 2701–2707.

CHAMBLESS, D. L., Foa, E. B., Groves, G. A., & Goldstein, A. J. (1980, September). *The role of anxiety in flooding with agoraphobics.* Paper presented at the convention of the American Psychological Association, Montreal, Canada.

COLLINS, D. L., Baum, A., & Singer, J. E. (1983). Coping with chronic stress at Three Mile Island: Psychological and biochemical evidence. *Health Psychology, 2*, 149–166.

COOPER, N. A., & Clum, G. A. (1989). Imaginal flooding as a supplementary treatment for PTSD in combat veterans: A controlled study. *Behavior Therapy, 20*, 381–391.

DALY, R. J. (1983). Samuel Pepys and post-traumatic stress disorder. *British Journal of Psychiatry, 143*, 64–68.

DAVIDSON, J., Kudler, H., Smith, R., Mahorney, S. L., Lipper, S., Hammett, E., Saunders, W. B., & Cavenar, J. O. (1990). Treatment of posttraumatic stress disorder with amitriptyline and placebo. *Archives of General Psychiatry, 47*, 259–266.

DOBBS, D., & Wilson, W. P. (1960). Observations on persistence of war neurosis. *Diseases of the Nervous System, 21*, 686–691.

DOLLARD, J., & Miller, N. E. (1950). *Personality and psychotherapy: An analysis in terms of learning thinking and culture.* New York: McGraw-Hill.

ELLIS, A. (1962). *Reason and emotion in psychotherapy.* New York: Lyle Stuart.

ELLSWORTH, R. B., Collins, J. F., Casey, N. A., Schoonover, R. A., Hickey, R. H., Hyer, L., Twemlow, S. W., & Nesselroade, J. R. (1979). Some characteristics of effective psychiatric treatment programs. *Journal of Consulting and Clinical Psychology, 47*, 799–817.

ESCOBAR, J. I., Randolph, E. T., Puente, G., Spiwak, F., Asamen, J. K., Hill, M., & Hough, R. L. (1983). Posttraumatic stress disorder in Hispanic Vietnam veterans. *Journal of Nervous and Mental Disorders, 171*, 585–596.

FAIRBANK, J. A., Gross, R. T., & Keane, T. M. (1983). Treatment of post-traumatic stress disorder: Evaluation of outcome with a behavioral code. *Behavior Modification, 7*, 557–568.

FAIRBANK, J. A., & Nicholson, R. A. (1987). Theoretical and empirical issues in the treatment of post-traumatic stress disorder in Vietnam veterans. *Journal of Clinical Psychology, 43*, 44–55.

FALCON, S. P., Batres, A., Boudewyns, P. A., Friedman, M. J., Furey, J., Gelsomino, J., Gusman, F. G., Harrington, J. L., Petty, S., Podkul, T. B., & Wittlin, B. J. (1991). *Seventh annual report of the Chief Medical Director's Special Committee on Post-Traumatic Stress Disorder.* Washington, DC: Department of Veterans Affairs.

FAUSTMAN, W. O., & White, P. A. (1989). Diagnostic and pharmacological treatment characteristics of 536 inpatients with posttraumatic stress disorder. *Journal of Nervous and Mental Disorders, 177*, 154–159

FOA, E. B., Rothbaum, B. O., Riggs, D. S., & Murdock, T. B. (1991). Treatment of posttraumatic stress disorder in rape victims: A comparison between cognitive-behavioral procedure and counseling. *Journal of Consulting and Clinical Psychology, 59*, 715–723.

FOA, E. B., Steketee, G., & Rothbaum, B. O. (1989). Behavioral/cognitive conceptualizations of post-traumatic stress disorder. *Behavior Therapy, 20*, 155–176.

FONTANA, A., Rosenheck, R., & Spencer, H. (1990). *The long journey home: The first progress report on the Department of Veterans Affairs PTSD clinical teams program.* West Haven, CT: Northeast Program Evaluation Center, Evaluation Division, National Center for PTSD, Department of Veterans Affairs.

FRANK, E., Anderson, B., Stewart, B. D., Dancu, D., Hughes, C., & West, D. (1988). Efficacy of cognitive behavior therapy and systematic desensitization in the treatment of rape trauma. *Behavior Therapy, 19*, 403–420.

FREUD, S. (1953). Four prefaces (A) psycho-analysis and war neuroses. In J. Riviere (Trans.), E. Jones (Ed.), *Sigmund Freud, M.D., LL.D. collected papers* (Vol. 5, pp. 83–87). London: Hogarth Press and Institute of Psycho-Analysis. (Original work published in 1919)

FRIEDMAN, M. J. (1991). Biological approaches to the diagnosis and treatment of post-traumatic stress disorder. *Journal of Traumatic Stress, 4*, 67–91.

FRIEDMAN, M. J., Batres, A., Falcon, S., Furey, J., Gelsomino, J., Gusman, F. G., Keane, T. M., Kolb, L. C., Petty, S., Podkul, T. B., & Smith, J. R. (1987). *Third annual report of the Chief Medical Director's Special Committee on Post-Traumatic Stress Disorder.* Washington, DC: Department of Veterans Affairs.

GOLDBERG, J., True, W. R., Eisen, S. A., & Henderson, S. A. (1990). A twin study of the effects of the Vietnam war on posttraumatic stress disorder. *Journal of the American Medical Association, 263*, 1227–1232.

GREEN, B. L., Grace, M. C., Lindy, J. D., Gleser, G. C., & Leonard, A. (1990). Risk factors for PTSD and other diagnoses in a general sample of Vietnam veterans. *American Journal of Psychiatry, 147*, 729–733.

GREEN, B. L., Grace, M. C., Lindy, J. D., Gleser, G. C., Leonard, A., & Kramer, T. L. (1990). Buffalo Creek survivors in the second decade: Comparison with unexposed and nonlitigant groups. *Journal of Applied Social Psychology, 20*, 1033–1050.

GREEN, B. L., Lindy, J. D., Grace, M. C., Gleser, G. C., Leonard, A., Korol, M., & Winget, C. (1990). Buffalo Creek survivors in the second decade: Stability of stress symptoms. *American Journal of Orthopsychiatry, 60*, 43–54.

GRINKER, R. R., & Spiegel, J. P. (1945). *Men under stress.* Philadelphia: Blackiston.

HELZER, J. E., Robins, L. N., & McEvoy, L. (1987). Posttraumatic stress disorder in the general population: Findings of the epidemiological catchment area survey. *New England Journal of Medicine, 317*, 1630–1634.

HOROWITZ, M. J. (1973). Phase oriented treatment of stress response syndrome. *American Journal of Psychotherapy, 27*, 506–515.

HOROWITZ, M. J. (1976). *Stress response syndrome.* New York: Aronson.

HOROWITZ, M. J. (1986). Stress-response syndromes: A review of posttraumatic and adjustment disorders. *Hospital and Community Psychiatry, 37,* 241–249.

HOROWITZ, M. J., & Kaltreider, N. B. (1980). Brief psychotherapy of stress response syndromes. In T. B. Karasu & L. Bellak (Eds.), *Specialized techniques in individual psychotherapy* (pp. 162–183). New York: Brunner/Mazel.

HOROWITZ, M. J., Marmar, C. R., Weiss, D. S., DeWitt, K. N., & Rosenbaum, R. (1984). Brief psychotherapy of bereavement reactions: The relationship of process to outcome. *Archives of General Psychiatry, 41,* 438–448.

HULL, C. L. (1943). *Principles of behavior.* New York: Appleton-Century-Crofts.

HYER, L. A. (1994). Theoretical perspectives of PTSD. In L. A. Hyer & associates (Eds.), *Trauma victim: Theoretical issues and practical suggestions* (pp. 93–150). New York: Accelerated Development.

JONES, J. C., & Barlow, D. H. (1990). The etiology of posttraumatic stress disorder. *Clinical Psychology Review, 10,* 299–328.

KARDINER, A. (1941). *The traumatic neuroses of war.* New York: Hoeber.

KEANE, T. M., Fairbank, J. A., Caddell, J. M., & Zimering, R. T. (1989). Implosive (flooding) therapy reduces symptoms of PTSD in Vietnam combat veterans. *Behavior Therapy, 20,* 245–260.

KEANE, T. M., Fairbank, J. A., Caddell, J. M., Zimering, R. T., & Bender, M. E. (1985). A behavioral approach to assessing and treating post-traumatic stress disorder in Vietnam veterans. In C. R. Figley (Ed.), *Trauma and its wake* (pp. 257–294). New York: Brunner/Mazel.

KEANE, T. M., & Kaloupek, D. G. (1982). Imaginal flooding in the treatment of a posttraumatic stress disorder. *Journal of Consulting and Clinical Psychology, 50,* 138–140.

KEANE, T. M., & Kolb, L. C. (1988). *A psychophysiological study of chronic post traumatic stress disorder* (Cooperative Study No. 334). Washington, DC: Department of Veterans Affairs.

KEANE, T. M., Zimering, R. T., & Caddell, J. M. (1985). A behavioral formulation of posttraumatic stress disorder in Vietnam veterans. *The Behavior Therapist, 8,* 9–12.

KILPATRICK, D. G., & Best, C. L. (1984). Some cautionary remarks on treating sexual assault victims with implosion. *Behavior Therapy, 15,* 421–423.

KILPATRICK, D. G., Best, C. L., Veronen, L. J., Amick, A. E., Villeponteaux, L. A., & Ruff, G. A. (1985). Mental health correlates of criminal victimization: A random community survey. *Journal of Consulting and Clinical Psychology, 53,* 866–873.

KILPATRICK, D. G., & Calhoun, K. S. (1988). Early behavioral treatment for rape trauma: Efficacy or artifact? *Behavior Therapy, 19,* 421–427.

KILPATRICK, D. G., Saunders, B. E., Veronen, L. J., Best, C. L., & Von, J. M. (1987). Criminal victimization: Lifetime prevalence, reporting to police, and psychological impact. *Crime and Delinquency, 33,* 479–489.

KILPATRICK, D. G., Veronen, L. J., & Best, C. L. (1985). Factors predicting psychological distress among rape victims. In C. R. Figley (Ed.), *Trauma and its wake* (pp. 113–141). New York: Brunner/Mazel.

KIMBLE, G. A. (1961). *Hilgard and Marquis' conditioning and learning.* New York: Appleton-Century-Crofts.

KLINGMAN, A., & Ben Eli, Z. (1981). A school community in disaster: Primary and secondary prevention in situational crisis. *Professional Psychology, 12,* 523–533.

KOLB, L. C., & Mutalipassi, L. R. (1982). The conditioned emotional response: A sub-class of the chronic and delayed post-traumatic stress disorder. *Psychiatric Annals, 12,* 979–987.

KULKA, R. A., Schlenger, W. E., Fairbank, J. A., Hough, R. L., Jordan, B. K., Marmar, C. R., & Weiss, D. S. (1988). *Contractual report of findings from the National Vietnam Veterans Readjustment Study.* Research Triangle Park, NC: Research Triangle Institute.

LANG, P. J. (1977). Imagery in therapy: An information processing analysis of fear. *Behavior Therapy, 8,* 862–886.

LAUFER, R. S., Brett, E., & Gallops, M. S. (1985). Dimensions of posttraumatic stress disorder among Vietnam veterans. *Journal of Nervous and Mental Disease, 173,* 538–545.

LEVIS, D. J., & Hare, N. A. (1977). A review of the theoretical rationale and empirical support for the extinction approach of implosive (flooding) therapy. In M. Hersen, R. Eisler, & P. Miller (Eds.), *Progress in behavior modification* (Vol. 4, pp. 299–374). New York: Academic Press.

LEVIS, D. J., & Stampfl, T. G. (1972). Effects of serial CS presentation on shuttlebox avoidance responding. *Learning and Motivation, 3,* 73–90.

LIFTON, R. J. (1967). *Death in life: Survivors of Hiroshima.* New York: Random House.

LIFTON, R. J., & Olson, E. (1976). The human meaning of total disaster: The Buffalo Creek experience. *Psychiatry, 39,* 1–18.

LINDY, J. D. (1986). An outline for the psychoanalytic psychotherapy of post-traumatic stress disorder. In C. R. Figley (Ed.), *Trauma and its wake* (Vol. 2, pp. 195–212). New York: Brunner/Mazel.

LINDY, J. D., Green, B. L., Grace, M. C., & Titchner, J. L. (1983). Psychotherapy of survivors of the Beverly Hills fire. *American Journal of Psychotherapy, 27,* 593–610.

LIPKE, H. J., & Botkin, A. L. (1992). Brief case studies of eye movement desensitization and reprocessing (EMD/R) with chronic post-traumatic stress disorder. *Psychotherapy, 29,* 591–595.

LYONS, J. A. (1987). Posttraumatic stress disorder in children and adolescents: A review of the literature. *Developmental and Behavioral Pediatrics, 8,* 349–356.

LYONS, J. A., & Keane, T. M. (1989). Implosive therapy for the treatment of combat-related PTSD. *Journal of Traumatic Stress, 2,* 137–152.

MARMAR, C. R., & Freeman, M. (1988). Brief dynamic psychotherapy of post-traumatic stress disorders: Management of narcissistic regression. *Journal of Traumatic Stress, 3,* 323–337.

McCAFFREY, R. J., & Fairbank, J. A. (1985). Behavioral assessment and treatment of accident-related posttraumatic stress disorder: Two case studies. *Behavior Therapy, 16,* 406–416.

McNEIL, J. W., & Todd, F. J. (1986). The operant treatment of excessive verbal ruminations and negative emotional arousal in a case of child molestation. *Child and Family Behavior Therapy, 8,* 61–69.

MICHENBAUM, D. (1977). *Cognitive behavior therapy: An integrative approach.* New York: Plenum.

MOWRER, O. H. (1947). On the dual nature of learning—A reinterpretation of "conditioning" and "problem-solving." *Harvard Educational Review, 17,* 102–148.

MOWRER, O. H. (1960). *Learning theory and behavior.* New York: Wiley.

MURPHY, S. A. (1986). Health and recovery status of victims one and three years following a natural disaster. In C. R. Figley (Ed.), *Trauma and its wake* (Vol. 2, pp. 133–155). New York: Brunner/Mazel.

NICHOLS, M. P., & Zax, M. (1977). *Catharsis in psychotherapy.* New York: Gardner.

ORNITZ, E. M., & Pynoos, R. S. (1989). Startle modulation in children with posttraumatic stress disorder. *American Journal of Psychiatry, 146,* 866–870.

ORR, S. P., Claiborn, J. M., Altman, B., Forgue, D. F., de Jong, J. B., & Pitman, R. K. (1990). Psychometric profile of posttraumatic stress disorder, anxious, and healthy Vietnam veterans: Correlations with psychophysiologic responses. *Journal of Consulting and Clinical Psychology, 58,* 329–335.

PAVLOV, I. P. (1960). *Conditioned reflexes* (G. V. Anrep, Trans. & Ed.). New York: Dover. (Original work published in 1927)

PENISTON, E. G. (1986). EMG biofeedback-assisted desensitization treatment for Vietnam combat veterans' post-traumatic stress disorder. *Clinical Biofeedback and Health, 9,* 35–41.

PITMAN, R. K., Altman, B., Greenwald, E., Longpre, R. E., Macklin, M. L., Poiré, R. E., & Steketee, G. S. (1991). Psychiatric complications during flooding therapy for posttraumatic stress disorder. *Journal of Clinical Psychiatry, 52,* 17–20.

PITMAN, R. K., Orr, S. P., Forgue, D. F., de Jong, J. B., & Claiborn, J. M. (1987). Psychophysiological assessment of post-traumatic stress disorder imagery in Vietnam combat veterans. *Archives of General Psychiatry, 44,* 970–975.

PITMAN, R. K., van der Kolk, B. A., Orr, S. P., & Greenberg, M. S. (1990). Naloxone-reversible analgesic response to combat-related stimuli in posttraumatic stress disorder: A pilot study. *Archives of General Psychiatry, 47,* 541–544.

PUK, G. (1991). Treating traumatic memories: A case report on the eye movement desensitization procedure. *Journal of Behavior Therapy and Experimental Psychiatry, 22,* 149–151.

PUTNAM, F. W. (1989). Pierre Janet and modern views of dissociation. *Journal of Traumatic Stress, 2,* 413–429.

REGIONAL Medical Education Center, Cleveland (Producer), Palcetti, G. (Director), Boudewyns, P. A., Hyer, L., Fairbank, J., & Shurell, R. (Presenters). (1989). *Flooding techniques in the treatment of post traumatic stress disorder.* Washington, DC: Department of Veterans Affairs.

RESICK, P. A., Jordan, C. G., Girelli, S. A., Hutter, C. K., & Marhoefer-Dvorak, S. (1988). A comparative outcome study of behavioral group therapy for sexual assault victims. *Behavior Therapy, 19,* 385–401.

REYNA, L. J. (1964). Conditioning therapies, learning theory, and research. In J. Wolpe (Ed.), *The conditioning therapies* (pp. 169–179). New York: Holt, Rinehart & Winston.

RICHARDS, D. A., & Rose, J. S. (1991). Exposure therapy for post-traumatic stress disorder: Four case studies. *British Journal of Psychiatry, 158,* 836–840.

RIVIERE, J. (Trans.). (1953). *Collected papers of Sigmund Freud* (Vol. 1). E. Jones (Ed.). London: Hogarth.

ROBINS, L. N., Helzer, J. E., Croughan, J., & Ratcliff, K. S. (1981). National Institute of Mental Health diagnostic interview schedule: Its history, characteristics, and validity. *Archives of General Psychiatry, 38,* 381–389.

ROTHBAUM, B. O., & Foa, E. B. (1991). Exposure treatment of PTSD concomitant with conversion mutism: A case study. *Behavior Therapy, 22,* 449–456.

RYCHTARIK, R. G., Silverman, W. K., Van Landingham, W. P., & Prue, D. M. (1984). Treatment of an incest victim with implosive therapy: A case study. *Behavior Therapy, 15,* 410–420.

SAIGH, P. A. (1984a). Pre- and postinvasion anxiety in Lebanon. *Behavior Therapy, 15,* 185–190.

SAIGH, P. A. (1984b). An experimental analysis of delayed posttraumatic stress. *Behaviour Research and Therapy, 22,* 679–682.

SAIGH, P. A. (1986). In vitro flooding in the treatment of a 6-year-old boy's posttraumatic stress disorder. *Behaviour Research and Therapy, 24,* 685–688.

SAIGH, P. A. (1987a). In vitro flooding of childhood posttraumatic stress disorders: A systematic replication. *Professional School Psychology, 2,* 135–146.

SAIGH, P. A. (1987b). In vitro flooding of an adolescent's posttraumatic stress disorder. *Journal of Clinical Child Psychology, 16,* 147–150.

SAIGH, P. A. (1988). Anxiety, depression, and assertion across alternating intervals of stress. *Journal of Abnormal Psychology, 97,* 338–341.

SAIGH, P. A. (1989). The validity of the DSM-III posttraumatic stress disorder classification as applied to children. *Journal of Abnormal Psychology, 98,* 189–192.

SAIGH, P. A. (1991). The development of posttraumatic stress disorder following four different types of traumatization. *Behavior Research and Therapy, 29,* 213–216.

SALTER, A. (1949/1961). *Conditioned reflex therapy.* New York: Farrar/Capricorn Books–Putnam's Sons.

SCHINDLER, F. E. (1980). Treatment by systematic desensitization of a recurring nightmare of a real life trauma. *Journal of Behavior Therapy and Experimental Psychiatry, 11,* 53–54.

SIERLES, F. S., Chen, J. J., McFarland, R. E., & Taylor, M. A. (1983). Posttraumatic stress disorder and concurrent psychiatric illness: A preliminary report. *American Journal of Psychiatry, 140,* 1177–1179.

SIERLES, F. S., Chen, J. J., Messing, M. L., Besyner, J. K., & Taylor, M. A. (1986). Concurrent psychiatric illness in non-Hispanic outpatients diagnosed as having posttraumatic stress disorder. *Journal of Nervous and Mental Disorders, 174,* 171–173.

SHAPIRO, F. (1989a). Efficacy of the eye movement desensitization procedure in the treatment of traumatic memories. *Journal of Traumatic Stress, 2,* 199–223.

SHAPIRO, F. (1989b). Eye movement desensitization: A new treatment for post-traumatic stress disorder. *Journal of Behavior Therapy and Experimental Psychiatry, 20,* 211–217.

SHAPIRO, F. (1991). Eye movement desensitization and reprocessing procedure: From EMD to EMD/R—A new model for anxiety and related traumata. *The Behavior Therapist, 14,* 133–135.

SHIPLEY, R. H., & Boudewyns, P. A. (1980). Flooding and implosive therapy: Are they harmful? *Behavior Therapy, 11,* 503–508.

SHIPLEY, R. H., & Boudewyns, P. A. (1988). The mythical dangers of exposure therapy. *Behavior Therapist, 11,* 8.

SLOAN, P. (1988). Post-traumatic stress in survivors of an airplane crash-landing: A clinical and exploratory research intervention. *Journal of Traumatic Stress, 2,* 211–229.

SNOW, B. R., Stellman, J. M., Stellman, S. D., & Sommer, J. F. (1988). Post-traumatic stress disorder among American Legionnaires in relation to combat experience in Vietnam: Associated and contributing factors. *Environmental Research, 47,* 175–192.

SOLOMON, R. L., Kamin, L. J., & Wynne, L. C. (1953). Traumatic avoidance learning: The outcomes of several extinction procedures with dogs. *Journal of Abnormal and Social Psychology, 48,* 291–302.

SOLOMON, R. L., & Wynne, L. C. (1954). Traumatic avoidance learning: The principles of anxiety conservation and partial irreversibility. *Psychological Review, 61,* 353–385.

SOLURSH, L. P. (1989). Combat addiction: Overview of implications in symptom maintenance and treatment planning. *Journal of Traumatic Stress, 2,* 451–462.

STAMPFL, T. G., & Levis, D. J. (1967). Essentials of implosive therapy: A learning-theory-based psychodynamic behavioral therapy. *Journal of Abnormal Psychology, 72,* 496–503.

STEPHENSON, N. L., Boudewyns, P. A., & Lessing, R. A. (1977). Long-term effects of peer group confrontation therapy used with polydrug abusers. *Journal of Drug Issues, 7,* 135–149.

TITCHNER, J. L. (1986). Post-traumatic decline: A consequence of unresolved destructive drives. In C. R. Figley (Ed.), *Trauma and its wake* (Vol. 2, pp. 5–19). New York: Brunner/Mazel.

TRIMBLE, M. R. (1985). Post-traumatic stress disorder: History of a concept. In C. R. Figley (Ed.), *Trauma and its wake.* New York: Brunner/Mazel.

van der HART, O., Brown, P., & van der Kolk, B. A. (1989). Pierre Janet's treatment of post-traumatic stress. *Journal of Traumatic Stress, 2,* 379–396.

van der HART, O., & Horst, R. (1989). The dissociation theory of Pierre Janet. *Journal of Traumatic Stress, 2,* 397–412.

van der KOLK, B. A., Brown, P., & van der Hart, O. (1989). Pierre Janet on post-traumatic stress. *Journal of Traumatic Stress, 2,* 365–378.

van der KOLK, B. A., Greenberg, M., Boyd, H., & Krystal, J. (1985). Inescapable shock, neurotransmitters and addiction to trauma: Toward a psychobiology of post-traumatic stress. *Biological Psychiatry, 20,* 314–325.

WHITE, R. W. (1948/1956). *The abnormal personality.* New York: Roland.

WILLIAMS, T. (Ed.). (1980). *Post-traumatic stress disorders of the Vietnam veteran.* Cincinnati: Disabled American Veterans.

WILLIAMS, W. (1976). Acute traumatic neurosis treated by brief intensive behavior therapy. *Journal of Behavior Therapy and Experimental Psychiatry, 7,* 43–45.

WINFIELD, I., George, L. K., Swartz, M., & Blazer, D. G. (1990). Sexual assault and psychiatric disorders among a community sample of women. *The American Journal of Psychiatry, 147,* 335–341.

WOLPE, J. (1958). *Psychotherapy by reciprocal inhibition.* Stanford: Stanford University Press.

WOLPE, J. (1982). *The practice of behavior therapy.* New York: Pergamon Press.

WOLPE, J., & Abrams, J. (1991). Post-traumatic stress disorder overcome by eye-movement desensitization: A case report. *Journal of Behavior Therapy and Experimental Psychiatry, 22,* 39–43.

NAME INDEX

Abrams, J., 182
Abramson, L. Y., 36, 104
Adams, H. E., 9
Agras, W. S., 125
Aitken, D., 140, 142
Akiskal, H. S., 37
Albert, I., 152
Albrecht, J. W., 170, 171, 179, 182, 184
Alessi, N., 45
Alexander, J. F., 42
Alicke, M. D., 27
Allen, V., 34
Allgood-Merten, B., 33
Allmon, D., 57
Alstrom, J. E., 86, 88
Altman, B., 174
Amaro, H., 132
American Psychiatric Association (APA), 28, 75, 76, 78, 80, 167
Amick, A. E., 169
Amidei, T., 126
Amies, P. L., 76, 86
Anderson, S., 130
Andreasen, L., 152
Andrews, J., 30, 52, 55, 61
Anshel, M. H., 146
Antonuccio, D. O., 37, 41
APA. *See* American Psychiatric Association
Arconad, M., 107
Arkowitz, H., 85, 102
Armstrong, H. E., 57
Armstrong, M. S., 125
Arnow, B., 81
Aronoff, M. S., 31
Asamen, J. K., 170
Asarnow, J. R., 32, 45, 47
Ashton, R., 142
Atwood, G. E., 100
Augusto, F., 85
Avener, M., 142, 143
Ayers, W. A., 27
Ayllon, T., 7, 8
Azrin, N. H., 7

Badenoch, A., 114
Baker, M., 29
Balassone, M. L., 35, 64
Bale, R. M., 142, 144
Bandura, A., 139, 144
Bangert-Drowns, R. L., 148
Barling, J., 104
Barlow, D. H., 6, 75, 76, 85, 90, 125, 173, 175, 177
Barnett, M. L., 141, 150, 151

Barrnett, R. J., 27, 28
Barton, C., 42
Bass, D., 27, 60, 61
Bass, S. M., 57
Baucom, D. H., 107
Baum, A., 183
Bauserman, S. A. K., 104, 107
Beach, S. R. H., 99, 100, 101, 102, 103, 104, 105, 107, 111, 112, 114, 115, 116, 117
Beardslee, W. R., 34, 58
Beck, A. T., 10, 11, 12, 18, 20, 36, 37, 41, 42, 44, 52, 53, 55, 58, 102, 113, 139, 144, 177
Beck, S., 6
Becker, R. E., 37, 76, 77, 90, 91, 112
Becker, W. C., 7
Beckham, E. E., 37, 38, 63
Bedrosian, R., 39
Beidel, B., 11
Beidel, D. C., 76, 78
Belanger, A., 57
Bell, M., 35, 64
Bellack, A. S., 37, 77, 112
Belsher, G., 52, 59
Bemporad, J., 43, 44
Bender, M. E., 172, 177
Ben Eli, Z., 183
Bennett, J. G., 157
Bergin, A. E., 62, 146, 150
Berkowitz, L., 155
Berman, J. S., 27, 37, 43, 146, 154
Bernstein, G. S., 123, 125, 127, 133, 134
Berzon, B., 132
Best, C. L., 169, 172, 177, 180, 181, 184
Best, L., 40
Besyner, J. K., 170
Biddle, S. J., 141
Biglan, A., 41, 100, 102
Binet, A., 176
Biran, M., 85, 90, 94
Birchler, G. R., 107
Birmaher, B., 55
Black, J. L., 177
Blanchard, E. B., 174, 180
Blaney, P. H., 105
Blaszczynski, A., 125
Blazer, D. G., 169
Blechman, E. A., 128
Blendell, K. A., 93
Blum, T. C., 104
Blumber, S. L., 118
Blumstein, P., 129
Blyth, D., 34
Bögels, S. M., 83
Bonaccorsi, M., 143, 152

Borduin, C. M., 27, 33
Bornstein, M., 45
Bornstein, P. H., 40
Bornstein, R. F., 44
Botkin, A. L., 181
Boudewyns, P. A., 165, 170, 171, 172, 173, 174, 176, 177, 179, 181, 182, 184
Bower, G. H., 102, 105
Boyd, H., 174
Boyd, T. L., 172
Boylan, M., 55
Boyle, M., 30
Bradbury, T. N., 105
Branch, J. D., 35
Branch, M. N., 2
Brandsma, J. M., 10
Brantley, P. J., 6
Brasfield, T. L., 126
Brenner, C., 7
Brent, D., 55, 59
Brett, E., 170
Breuer, J., 176
Broderick, J. E., 106
Brody, R., 35
Brom, D., 171, 180
Bromet, E. J., 101, 169
Brookman, C. S., 45, 46
Brooks, A. E., 99
Brown, C. H., 35
Brown, G. W., 101
Brown, L. A., 128
Brown, P., 176
Browne, M. A., 146
Brownstein, A. J., 3, 20, 21
Bruch, M. A., 77, 93
Bruya, L. D., 141
Bryant, B., 82
Bryant, M., 44
Bunker, L., 146
Burbach, D. J., 33
Burge, S. K., 169, 181
Burgeson, R., 34
Burke, P., 33
Burnett, C. K., 101
Burns, D. D., 92
Burtles, C. J., 125
Burton, D., 141
Busse, T. V., 148
Butler, G., 85, 86, 87, 88, 91, 94, 95
Butler, L., 48, 53

Caddell, J. M., 172, 173, 177, 178
Calhoun, K. S., 173, 181
Calhoun, S. K., 9
Campbell, J. L., 141
Campbell, S. B., 112

Canton-Dutari, A., 125
Cantwell, D. P., 30, 65
Card, J. J., 170
Carlson, G. A., 29, 30, 45, 47
Carlton-Ford, S., 34
Carr, S., 37, 38, 62
Carver, C. S., 145
Casey, R. J., 27, 43
Cashdan, S., 21
Castrone, L., 130
Catania, A. C., 2
Caudill, D., 142, 144, 152
Cautela, J. R., 9
Centers for Disease Control, 130, 170
Chambers, W., 29
Chambless, D. L., 179
Chaney, D. S., 152
Chen, J. J., 170
Cheng, T., 35, 64
Chevron, E., 37, 116
Chomsky, N., 14
Christian, J. L., 103, 110
Ciminero, A. R., 9
Claiborn, J. M., 174
Clarizio, H. F., 38
Clark, E., 54
Clark, J. V., 85
Clark, M. S., 105
Clarke, G. N., 25, 35, 41, 42, 50, 52, 53,
    57, 61, 62
Clarke, J. C., 77, 87
Clarkin, J. F., 31, 117
Cloninger, C. R., 30
Clum, G. A., 56, 179
Coates, T. J., 126
Coats, K. I., 48, 53, 54
Cogswell, K. A., 40
Cohen, J., 148
Cole, E., 53
Colfer, M., 45
Collins, D. L., 183
Committee on Gay and Lesbian Concerns,
    126, 129, 133
Conger, A. J., 9
Conger, J. C., 9
Connell, M. M., 101
Conners, C. K., 44, 45
Conrad, S. R., 125
Cooke, C. J., 140, 142, 152, 157
Cooper, H. M., 27
Cooper, N. A., 179
Copping, W., 44
Corber, S., 34
Corbin, C. B., 139, 142, 146
Corn, R., 31
Cornes, C., 64
Costa, A., 143, 152
Covi, L., 57
Coyne, J. C., 18, 102, 104, 112
Crits-Cristoph, P., 61
Crocker, P., 17
Cronkite, R. C., 100

Croughan, J., 170
Crouse-Novak, M., 30
Crumley, F. E., 55
Csikszentmihalyi, M., 139, 141
Cullen, J., 142
Cullington, A., 86
Curran, J. P., 85
Cuvillier, C., 140

Daly, R. J., 166
Dancu, C. V., 76
Davidson, J., 184
Davies, M., 32, 33
Davison, G. C., 6, 124, 125, 127, 133
Day, W., 2, 8
Decenteceo, E. T., 89
Defares, P. B., 171
de Jong, J. B., 174
Delamater, A., 45
Delboeuf, J. L. R., 176
Dent, J., 112
de Perczel, M., 126
Derogatis, L., 57
Derry, P. A., 102
DeRubeis, R., 6
Devany, J. M., 21
DeVoge, J. T., 6
DeWitt, D. J., 140, 143, 146
DeWitt, K. N., 171
Deykin, E. Y., 30
DiClementi, J. D., 126
Diener, E., 104
Dietz, S. G., 31
DiNardo, P. A., 76
Dinicola, V., 44
Dobbs, D., 167, 174
Dobson, K. S., 113, 115, 147
Dodge, C. S., 76, 77, 90, 92, 93, 94, 95
Dodson, J. D., 143
Dollard, J., 172
Donahue, J. A., 146
Donenberg, G., 28
Donnerstein, E., 155
Donovan, C., 138
Dorenwhend, B. P., 57
Dorwrick, P. W., 54
Dougher, M. J., 9
Dubow, E. F., 34, 35
Duda, J. L., 141
Duehn, W. D., 125, 131
Duncan, S. W., 101
Dunn, L. O., 169
D'Zurilla, T. J., 110

Eardley, D., 11
Earls, F., 35
Egan, G., 109
Egri, G., 57
Eisen, S. A., 170
Eldridge, N. S., 127
Elkin, I., 37, 44

Elkind, D., 34
Elliott, G. R., 45
Ellis, A., 10, 14, 42, 83, 176, 177
Ellis, T. E., 126
Ellsworth, R. B., 179
Emery, G., 10, 12, 36, 37, 39, 58, 102,
    113, 177
Emmelkamp, P. M. G., 83, 84, 87, 88, 89
Engs, R., 140
Epkins, C., 144
Epstein, L. H., 146
Epstein, M. L., 142
Epstein, N., 107
Erbaugh, J. K., 52
Erffmeyer, E. S., 145
Escobar, J. I., 170
Esveldt-Dawson, K., 33
Evans, I. M., 6

Faberow, N., 129
Fairbank, J. A., 172, 177, 178
Falcon, S. P., 170
Falloon, I. R. H., 82, 84
Faustman, W. O., 170
Feely, M., 6
Feiguine, R. J., 44
Feinberg, T., 30
Feinberg-Steinberg, T., 55
Feldman, M. P., 125
Feldman, W., 34
Feltz, D. L., 139, 142, 146, 149, 151, 153,
    154
Fenker, R., 146
Ferguson, H., 44
Ferster, C. B., 8, 20
Fialkov, M. J., 45
Fincham, F. D., 105
Fine, S., 39, 51, 54, 60
Finkelstein, R., 30
Fischer, S. C., 125
Fischetti, M., 85
Fisher, J., 114
Fisher, M., 35
Fisher, S., 44
Fleming, J., 30, 32
Floyd, F. J., 117
Foa, E. B., 9, 173, 174, 178, 179, 180, 181
Foley, S. H., 116, 117
Fontana, A., 183
Forgas, J., 105
Forgue, D. F., 174
Forth, A., 54
Foster, J., 157
Foster, S., 42
Frame, C., 45, 46
Frank, E., 64, 181, 184
Frank, J. D., 7, 38
Franks, V., 127
Freeman, M., 171
Freeman, N., 125
Fremouw, W. J., 126
French, N. H., 33

Freud, S., 7, 166, 176
Friedman, A., 113, 114
Friedman, M. J., 170, 174, 175, 184
Friedman, R., 53
Friedman, R. C., 31
Friedman, S., 125
Frommelt, G. M., 27
Fruzzetti, A. E., 103, 113, 115
Fuchs, C., 37
Fudge, H., 32
Fyer, A. J., 75, 76

Gabriel, T. J., 157
Galassi, J. P., 154
Galassi, M. D., 154
Gallops, M. S., 170
Garamoni, G. L., 93
Garber, J., 36, 39
Garfield, S. L., 155
Garfinkel, B. D., 61
Garfinkle, E. M., 129
Garland, H., 141
Gatsonis, C., 31
Gelder, M. G., 75, 76, 86
Gelernter, C. S., 94
Geller, B., 44
George, L. K., 169
Gerardi, R. J., 174
Gibbon, M., 75
Gilbert, M., 54
Gillis, J. H., 146
Girelli, S. A., 181
Girgus, J. S., 32, 33
Glass, G., 148
Glass, G. V., 26
Glenn, S., 2, 6, 20
Gleser, G. C., 169, 170
Glick, D., 129
Glick, I. D., 117
Goetz, C., 101
Goldberg, J., 170
Goldfinger, K., 91
Goldfried, M. R., 6, 88, 89, 94, 95, 110
Golding, J. M., 157
Goldstein, A. J., 179
Goldston, D., 32
Gondek, P. C., 169
Gonsiorek, J. C., 127, 131, 132
Gordon, A. N., 126
Gordon, R., 129
Gorman, J. M., 76, 78
Gotlib, I. H., 18, 102
Gottesfeld, D., 140, 142
Gottman, J. M., 108
Gould, D., 143, 144, 146, 157
Grace, M. C., 169, 170, 171
Graham, D. L., 44
Grange, R., 139
Grauer, L., 113
Gravel, R., 145, 154
Greben, S. E., 21
Green, B. L., 169, 170, 171

Green, T., 34
Greenberg, M. D., 44
Greenberg, M. S., 174, 175
Greenberg, R. L., 12
Greenberg, R. P., 44
Greenspan, M. J., 146, 149, 153, 154
Greenspoon, J., 20
Greer, H. S., 140
Greist, L. H., 57
Gretter, M. L., 38
Griffith, C. M., 139
Grinker, R. R., 167
Gross, R. T., 177
Grosscup, S. J., 36, 37
Groves, G. A., 125, 179
Guerney, B. G., 117
Guidano, V. F., 10, 12, 13
Guthrie, D. M., 108, 109

Haas, G. L., 117
Hafner, R. J., 114
Hahlweg, K., 102, 117, 118
Hakstian, R., 58
Haley, G., 54
Hall, C., 142, 151
Hall, E. G., 145
Hall, H. K., 141
Halliwell, W., 146, 156, 157
Hamburg, B. A., 33
Hamilton, S. A., 6, 20
Hand, I., 84
Harding, M., 86
Hare, N. A., 172, 177
Harper, R. A., 42
Harpin, R. E., 82
Harrington, R., 32, 45, 59
Harris, D. V., 142
Harris, T., 101
Harrison, E., 132
Harrison, W. R., 179
Harter, S., 34
Hautzinger, M., 37, 102
Hawkins, W. E., 64
Hayes, L. J., 4, 21
Hayes, S. C., 2, 3, 4, 6, 17, 20, 21
Haynes, S. N., 2
Hazelrigg, M. D., 27
Heard, H. L., 57
Hecker, J. E., 143
Heimberg, R. G., 37, 74, 75, 76, 77, 78, 79, 80, 81, 82, 86, 90, 91, 92, 93, 94, 95, 112
Heinecke, C. M., 43
Heishman, M. F., 146
Helzer, J. E., 168, 169, 170
Hemmings, K. A., 38
Henderson, S. A., 170
Herbert, J. D., 77, 78
Herceg-Baron, R. L., 101
Herek, G. M., 132
Herman, S. H., 125
Hersen, M., 9, 112

Heyman, R. E., 108
Hill, J., 32, 34
Hill, M., 170
Himadi, W., 10
Himmelhoch, J. M., 112
Hinchliffe, M., 102
Hisanga, B., 143, 152, 154, 155
Hoberman, H. M., 25, 37, 58, 61, 63, 64
Hoch, J., 35
Hodgson, C., 34
Hoffman, N., 102
Hokanson, J. E., 109
Holder, D., 55
Holliday, S., 102
Hollingsworth, B., 141
Hollon, S. D., 10, 11, 12, 13, 18, 36
Holmbeck, G., 34
Holmes, W. E., 39
Holt, C. S., 74, 76, 77, 78, 79, 80, 81, 93
Holtzbauer, R., 140
Holtzworth-Munroe, A., 110
Honikman, B., 138
Honikman, L., 138
Hood, H. V., 126
Hooker, E., 124
Hooley, J. M., 100, 102, 103, 113
Hooper, D., 102
Hope, D. A., 76, 77, 78, 79, 80, 93
Hops, H., 30, 31, 33, 41, 42, 52, 53, 54, 61, 100
Horn, T., 143
Hornig, C. D., 76
Horowitz, M. J., 171, 180
Hough, R. L., 170
Howard, G. S., 38
Howard, K. I., 7, 34
Howes, P. W., 101
Hull, C. L., 143, 172, 183
Hunter, P., 125, 131
Hurt, S. W., 31
Hutter, C. K., 181
Hutter, M., 102
Hyde, M. L., 132
Hyer, L., 170, 171, 174, 179, 182

Ilfeld, F. W., 101
Ince, L. P., 125

Jackson, A., 141, 142, 143, 144, 145, 151, 153
Jacobson, N. S., 2, 8, 18, 19, 21, 102, 103, 107, 110, 111, 113, 115, 116
James, S., 125
Jamieson, K., 117
Janet, P., 75, 176
Jason, L. A., 134
Jensen, J. B., 61
Jensen, P. S., 44
Jenson, W. R., 54
Jerremalm, A., 83, 89, 94, 95
Johansson, J., 83
Johnson, J., 76
Johnson, M. H., 102

Johnson-O'Conner, E. J., 144
Jones, J. C., 175
Jones, M. C., 7
Jordan, C. G., 181
Jouriles, E. N., 101
Jung, K., 35
Juster, H. R., 74

Kaczor, L. M., 143
Kahn, E. J., 157
Kahn, J., 102
Kahn, J. S., 49, 54
Kaiser, G., 84
Kaloupek, D. G., 177
Kaltreider, N. B., 171, 180
Kamin, L. J., 172
Kandel, D., 32, 33
Kanter, N. J., 88, 94, 95
Kaplan, D. W., 31
Kardiner, A., 167
Kashani, J. H., 29, 30, 31
Kaslow, N. J., 40, 54
Kaufman, P. A., 132
Kausch, D. F., 34
Kazdin, A. E., 8, 27, 28, 33, 39, 45, 60,
    61, 153, 155
Keane, T. M., 10, 172, 173, 174, 177, 178,
    179, 180
Kehle, T. J., 54
Kellam, S. G., 35
Keller, M. B., 29, 30, 31, 34, 35
Kellet, J., 81
Kelloway, E. K., 104
Kelly, J. A., 125, 126, 131
Kelso, E., 125, 131
Kendall, P. C., 11, 61
Kennedy, C. R., 77, 92
Kent, R. N., 42
Keys, D., 76
Kiev, A., 55
Kilgore, H., 126
Kilpatrick, D. G., 169, 172, 173, 177, 180,
    181, 184
Kim, N. S., 8
Kimble, G. A., 174, 183
Kimmel, D. C., 132
King, K., 146
Kipnis, D., 11
Kirk, M., 124
Kirschenbaum, D. S., 140, 142, 143, 144,
    146, 152, 154
Klass, E., 44
Kleber, R. J., 171
Klein, D. F., 10, 76
Klein, M. H., 57
Klein, R., 44
Klerman, G. L., 30, 37, 43, 52
Klingman, A., 183
Klinzing, J., 143
Klosko, J. S., 76
Klotz, M. L., 27
Kohlenberg, B. S., 1, 21

Kohlenberg, R. J., 1, 2, 5, 6, 8, 19, 20, 21
Kolb, L. C., 172, 174, 180
Kolko, D., 55
Kolligian, J., 141
Kolvin, I., 30, 58, 59
Koplewicz, H., 44
Korenblum, M., 29
Korol, M., 169
Kovacs, M., 28, 30, 31, 32, 35, 53, 64
Kowalik, D. L., 102
Kramer, A. D., 44
Kramer, T. L., 169
Krantz, S. E., 11
Krasner, L., 7
Kriss, M. R., 10, 11, 12, 13, 18
Krokoff, L. J., 108
Kroks, G. N., 129
Krystal, J., 174
Kuiper, N. A., 102
Kulka, R. A., 170
Kuno, R., 126
Kupfer, D. J., 64
Kutcher, S. P., 29

Ladouceur, R., 145
Lambert, C., 81
Lambert, M. J., 62, 146, 149, 150, 154
Lamiotte, J., 146
Land, H., 130
Landers, D. M., 139, 142, 143, 146, 149,
    151
Landrine, H., 124
Lang, P. J., 9, 174
Lanning, W., 143, 152, 154, 155
Latham, G. P., 140
Laufer, R. S., 170
Lavori, P. W., 34
Leahy, R. L., 34, 58
Lee, C., 143, 157
Leff, J. P., 101
Lehrer, P. M., 143
Leigland, S., 9
Lemieux, G., 145
Lemke, A., 126
Leonard, A., 169, 170
Lerner, M. S., 56
Lessing, R. A., 184
LeUnes, A. D., 138
Levin, A. P., 76, 78
Levine, F. M., 104
Levis, D. J., 172, 173, 177, 184
Levitt, E. E., 26
Levy, J. C., 30
Lewin, L., 100
Lewin, N., 56
Lewinsohn, P. M., 30, 31, 32, 33, 35, 36,
    37, 38, 41, 42, 50, 52, 53, 54, 55, 57,
    61, 62, 100, 107, 118
Lewis, S., 142
Liddle, B., 50, 53
Liebowitz, M. R., 75, 76, 77, 78, 79, 80,
    94

Lifton, R. J., 171
Liles, L., 142
Lim, L., 85
Linden, M., 102
Lindy, J. D., 169, 170, 171
Linehan, M. M., 21, 56, 57, 59, 63
Liotti, G., 10, 12, 13
Lipke, H. J., 181
Lipman, R., 57
Lips, C., 84
Livingston, R., 40, 53
Lizotte, P., 142
Ljungqvist, C., 86
Lloyd, G. G., 82
Locke, E. A., 140, 141
Loehr, J. E., 157
Lohr, M., 57
LoPiccolo, J., 125
Loulan, J., 131
Lovko, K. R., 34
Loy, J. W., 147
Lubin, G., 113
Lukes, C. A., 130
Lutzker, J., 7
Lynch, M., 34
Lyons, J. A., 177, 183

MacCorquodale, K., 14
MacCulloch, J., 125
MacEwen, K. E., 104
MacPhillamy, D. J., 41
Madsen, H., 124
Magaro, P. A., 102
Magnusson, D., 34
Mahoney, M. J., 138, 140, 142, 143, 144,
    146, 150, 157
Maletzky, B. M., 125
Malizio, J., 35
Mandler, G., 105
Mansfield, R. S., 148
Marans, S., 43
Margolin, G., 102, 107
Marhoefer-Dvorak, S., 181
Markman, H. J., 101, 117, 118
Markowitz, L. M., 128
Marks, A., 35
Marks, I., 82
Marks, I. M., 75
Marlow, L., 34
Marmar, C. R., 171
Marshall, W. L., 125
Marsteller, F. A., 44
Martens, R., 143, 146, 155
Martin, A., 127
Martin, G., 7
Martin, J. D., 104
Marton, P., 29
Marzillier, J. S., 81, 82, 84, 95
Maser, J. D., 30
Mash, E. J., 61
Masters, J. C., 6
Matson, J. L., 45

Mattick, R. P., 77, 87, 88, 91, 94
Maxwell, S. C., 38
Mayadas, N. S., 125, 131
McAuley, E., 140, 141
McCaffrey, R. J., 178
McCandless, B. R., 134
McCauley, E., 33
McConaghy, N., 125
McCrady, R. E., 125
McCranie, E., 179
McCullagh, P., 140
McCullough, J. P., 62
McEachran, A. B., 64
McEvoy, L., 168
McFarland, R. E., 170
McFatter, R. M., 144
McGraw, B., 148
McKinlay, T. K., 125, 131
McKinney, W. T., 37
McKusick, L., 126
McLean, P. D., 37, 38, 58, 62, 113
McMain, S., 17
McNeil, J. W., 183
McNeill, C., Jr., 126
Meacci, W. G., 145, 151
Mees, H. L., 7
Meichenbaum, D., 89, 139, 143, 153
Melancon, S. M., 20
Melton, G. B., 132
Mendels, J., 101
Mendelsohn, F. S., 57
Mendelson, M., 52
Mendoza, D., 142
Merikangas, K. R., 113
Mersch, P. P. A., 83, 84, 87, 90
Messing, M. L., 170
Meyer, R. G., 125
Meyers, A. W., 128, 137, 139, 140, 141,
    142, 143, 144, 145, 146, 147, 152,
    157, 158
Michenbaum, D., 176, 177, 181
Michener, J. A., 138, 140
Miezitis, S., 53
Milberg, S., 105
Miller, J. T., 140, 141
Miller, M. E., 123, 125, 127
Miller, N. E., 172
Miller, S., 117
Miller, T. I., 26
Mischel, W., 139
Mitchell, J., 33
Mock, J. E., 52
Monroe, S. M., 101
Mook, D. G., 155
Moos, R. H., 100
Moreau, D., 43, 52
Morgan, W. P., 139, 158
Morin, S. F., 129
Morris, E. K., 2
Morris, J. B., 44
Morris, R. J., 61
Morris, W., 128

Moss, S., 33
Mott, F. W., 166
Motto, J. A., 55
Mowrer, O. H., 172, 176
Moylan, S., 105
Mueller, G. P., 77
Mufson, L., 43, 52, 59
Mumford, B., 142, 151
Munby, M., 86
Münchau, N., 84
Munoz, R., 38
Murdock, T. B., 173, 179
Murphy, B. C., 127
Murphy, M., 64
Murphy, S. A., 169
Murphy, S. M., 137, 140, 142, 143, 147,
    152, 157
Murray, P., 17
Mutalipassi, L. R., 172, 174
Myer, A., 167
Myers, J. K., 57
Myers, M. F., 125, 131

Nation, J. R., 138
National Bowling Council, 138
National Golf Foundation, 138
National Sporting Goods Association, 138
Neimeyer, R. A., 37
Nelson, G. M., 100, 101, 102, 103, 104,
    105, 107
Nelson, R. O., 6, 21
Nezu, A. M., 110
Nezu, C. M., 110
Nicholls, J. G., 141
Nichols, A., 141
Nichols, M. P., 176
Nicholson, R. A., 154, 172, 177
Nideffer, R. M., 157
Nietzel, M. T., 38
Noel, R. C., 145
Nolen-Hoeksema, S., 32, 33
Nordlund, C. L., 86
Norwood, R. M., 75
Nunally, E. W., 117

O'Brien, W. H., 2
Offer, D., 34
Office of Technology Assessment, 64
Offord, D., 30, 34
Ogilvie, B. C., 139
Ogston, K., 113
O'Hara, M. W., 112
Okwumabua, T. M., 139, 152
O'Leary, K. D., 6, 7, 42, 100, 101, 103,
    104, 106, 107, 110, 111, 112, 114,
    115, 116, 117
Olson, E., 171
Ordman, A. M., 140
Orley, J., 103
Orlick, T., 141, 143, 145, 157
Orlinsky, D. I., 7
Ornitz, E. M., 174, 183

Orr, S. P., 174, 175
Orvaschel, H., 52
Orwin, A., 125
Öst, L. G., 83, 89, 95
Ostrov, E., 34
Otto-Salaj, L., 11
Overholser, J. C., 56
Owen, N., 157

Padesky, C. A., 125, 131
Pagano, B., 3
Pallmeyer, T. P., 174
Paris, A. E., 40
Parkinson, D. K., 169
Parrish, M. W., 142
Parsons, B. V., 42
Partington, J., 157
Patterson, G. R., 106
Patterson, J., 125, 131
Paul, G., 6
Paulauskas, S., 28, 30, 31
Pavlov, I. P., 172
Paykel, E. S., 101
Pencik, E. C., 31
Peniston, E. G., 178
Pepper, S. C., 4
Pepys, S., 166
Perel, J., 44
Perkins, T. S., 157
Perri, M. G., 110
Persons, J. B., 92
Persson, G., 86
Peterfreund, N., 35, 64
Peters, L., 87, 88, 91
Petersen, A. C., 33
Peterson, C. B., 58, 63
Petti, T. A., 39, 45, 54
Phil, M., 44
Phillips, D., 125
Pickles, A., 32
Pietromonaco, P. R., 105
Pilkonis, P. A., 75
Pitman, R. K., 174, 175, 180, 184
Platt, J. R., 84
Popper, C., 45
Porter, K., 157
Powell, G. E., 142
Pozanski, 53
Pravitz, J. E., 157
Price, E. P., 145, 151
Prien, R., 44
Priest, P. N., 125
Prince, D., 54
Prinz, R. J., 42
Prue, D. M., 177
Prusoff, B. A., 101
Puente, G., 170
Puig-Antich, J., 31, 32, 33, 44, 52
Puk, G., 181
Pynoos, R. S., 174, 183

Quattrone, G. A., 11

Quinn, A., 34
Quinton, D., 101
Quitkin, F. M., 78

Radloff, L. S., 57
Rainwater, N., 128
Ramsey, R. W., 8
Ramsey-Klee, D. M., 43
Randolph, E. T., 170
Rapee, R. M., 76, 85
Ratcliff, K. S., 170
Rayner, M., 7
Reese, S. W., 4
Regional Medical Education Center, 183
Rehm, L. P., 36, 37, 62, 112, 125
Reid, J. B., 106
Reisinger, J. J., 8
Renick, M. J., 118
Resick, P. A., 181
Reveis, V., 33
Reyna, L. J., 172
Reynolds, W. M., 40, 48, 53, 54
Richards, C., 31
Richards, D. A., 178
Richardson, A., 139, 142
Ricks, D. F., 58, 59
Riddle, D. I., 133
Riggs, D. S., 173, 179
Riggs, S., 35, 64
Rimm, D. C., 6
Risley, T., 7
Risso, L. P., 112, 115
Riviere, J., 176
Robbins, D., 45, 47
Roberts, F. J., 102
Roberts, G., 146, 156, 157
Roberts, R. E., 30, 33, 57
Robin, A. L., 42
Robins, L., 35
Robins, L. N., 168, 170
Robinson, L. A., 37, 38
Robinson, W. J., 142
Rodgers, A., 27
Roffman, R. E., 126
Rohde, P., 31, 32, 35, 42, 53, 61
Roman, P. M., 104
Rook, K. S., 105
Rose, J. S., 178
Rosenbaum, R., 171
Rosenberg, S. E., 43
Rosenheck, R., 183
Ross, C. P., 55
Ross, J., 105
Rossman, P. G., 43, 44, 58
Roth, S., 127
Rothbaum, B. O., 173, 174, 178, 179
Rotheram-Borus, M., 40, 56, 58
Rounsaville, B., 37
Rounsaville, B. J., 101, 116
Rouse, L. W., 40, 53
Rozensky, R. H., 125
Rude, S. S., 62

Ruff, G. A., 169
Ruscher, S. M., 102
Rush, A., 10, 36, 37
Rush, J. A., 40, 58, 102, 113
Rushall, B., 139
Russell, A., 125
Russell, G., 35
Russell, P. L., 10
Russell, R. L., 7, 27, 28, 38, 43
Rutman, J., 31
Rutter, M., 32, 39, 101
Ryan, D. E., 146
Ryan, N. D., 29, 30, 31, 34, 44
Ryan, P., 174
Rychtarik, R. G., 177

Safran, J. D., 6, 11, 12, 17, 18, 63
Saigh, P. A., 169, 183
Salholz, E., 129
Salovey, P., 10
Salter, A., 172
Salusky, S., 113, 115
Salzman, D. G., 93, 94
Sambrooks, J. E., 125
Sanchez-Lacay, A., 56
Sandeen, E. E., 100, 104, 111, 117
Sandell, J. A., 43
Sanderson, W. C., 76
Sandford, D. A., 125
Sang, B., 133
Saoud, J. B., 76
Saunders, B. E., 181
Saunders, S. M., 25
Schaeffer, E. S., 101
Scheier, M. F., 145
Schiavo, R. S., 42
Schindler, F. E., 177
Schinke, S. P., 126
Schleser, R., 139, 140, 145, 152
Schless, A. P., 101
Schmaling, K. B., 102, 103, 110, 113, 115, 126
Schneider, S. G., 129
Schneier, F. R., 75, 76, 78, 79
Schonert, K. A., 34
Schroeder-Hartwig, K., 84
Schulberg, H. C., 169
Schwartz, L., 101
Schwartz, P., 129
Schwartz, R. M., 93
Scott, R., 10
Scrimali, T., 143, 152
Seabourne, T., 144, 145, 151, 153, 154, 155
Sechrest, L., 153, 154
Seeley, J. R., 30, 31, 32
Segal, E., 124, 127
Segal, Z. V., 6, 12, 17, 18, 63
Seiffge-Krenke, I., 34
Seligman, M. E. P., 32, 33, 36
Sellstrom, E., 40
Shaffer, M., 100
Shapiro, D. A., 62, 146, 150

Shapiro, F., 177, 181, 182, 183
Shapiro, R. W., 29
Sharpe, R. C., 157
Shaw, B., 10
Shaw, B. F., 12, 36, 37, 113
Shaw, P., 82
Shaw, P. M., 76
Shelby, J., 21
Shelton, T. O., 143, 150
Sherick, R. B., 33
Shick, J., 142, 143, 156
Shipley, R. H., 172, 173, 176, 177, 179, 184
Shirk, S. R., 27, 28, 43
Sholomaskas, D., 116
Shrout, P. E., 57
Siegel, T. C., 60
Sierles, F. S., 170
Silva, J. M., 139, 146
Silver, L., 30
Silverman, J., 11
Silverman, J. D., 11
Silverman, W. K., 177
Silverstein, C., 127
Simeon, J., 44
Simmons, R., 34
Simons, J., 146
Singer, J. E., 183
Singh, R., 125
Skinner, B. F., 2, 3, 6, 8, 14, 15, 17, 20
Sloan, P., 169
Smith, B., 154
Smith, D., 142, 143
Smith, J. E., 126
Smith, M., 148
Smith, M. L., 26
Smith, R. E., 140, 143, 146, 153
Smith, R. J., 143
Snow, B. R., 170
Sobotka, K. R., 28
Solomon, R. L., 172
Solursh, L. P., 175
Sommer, J. F., 170
Sonis, W. A., 45
Spence, J. T., 143
Spence, K. W., 143
Spence, S. H., 50, 53
Spencer, H., 183
Sperr, E. V., 182
Spiegel, J. P., 167
Spielberger, C. D., 143
Spigner, C., 64
Spirito, A., 56
Spitzer, R. L., 75, 79
Spiwak, F., 170
Spreeman, J., 143
Stampfl, T. G., 172, 173
Stanicek, J. A., 141, 150, 151
Stanley, S. M., 117
Stark, K. D., 40, 45, 46, 49, 53, 54
Start, K. B., 142
Stattin, H., 34

Steinberg, L., 33, 34
Steinbrueck, S. M., 38
Steiner, S. C., 101
Steinmetz, J. L., 37, 41
Steketee, G., 9, 174
Stellman, J. M., 170
Stellman, S. D., 170
Stephens, R. S., 109
Stephenson, N. L., 184
Sternberg, R. J., 141
Stiffman, A., 35
Stites, D. P., 126
St. Lawrence, J. S., 126
Storaasli, R. D., 101
Stravynski, A., 82, 84, 90, 94
Strickland, B. R., 134
Strupp, H. H., 7, 43
Stuart, R. B., 107
Stwertka, S. A., 182
Suarez, A., 57
Suinn, R. M., 139, 140, 142, 143, 145,
    146, 153, 157
Sullivan, H. S., 7, 17
Sullivan, J. M., 37
Sullivan, L., 31
Swartz, M., 169
Sweet, A. A., 6
Swift, H., 114
Swindle, R. W., 100

Talbert, F. S., 170
Tanner, B. A., 125
Tanner, J., 101
Task Force on DSM-IV (APA), 80
Taylor, C. B., 81
Taylor, M. A., 170
Teasdale, J. D., 36, 100, 103, 112, 113
Teri, L., 37, 41
Thase, M. E., 112
Thompson, N. L., Jr., 134
Thompson, W. C., 57
Tillitski, C. J., 60
Titchner, J. L., 171
Todd, F. J., 183
Tomarken, A. J., 140, 144
Toolan, J., 43
Townsley, R. M., 78
Tramontana, M., 26
Trautman, P. D., 40, 56, 58
Trimble, M. R., 166, 174
Triplett, N., 139
Trower, P., 82, 83, 84, 95
Truax, P., 103
True, W. R., 170
Tsai, M., 1, 2, 5, 6, 8, 19, 20, 21
Tuma, J. M., 28
Turk, D., 10
Turkat, I. D., 6
Turner, R. K., 125

Turner, S. M., 11, 76, 78
Tustin, R. D., 125
Tutko, T. A., 139
Tynes, L. L., 144

Ungerleider, S., 157
Unis, A. S., 33
United States Cycling Federation, 138
United States Masters Swimming, Inc., 138
United States Tennis Association, 138

Vallis, T. M., 12
van der Hart, O., 176
van der Helm, M., 87
van der Kolk, B. A., 174, 175, 176
van der Sleen, J., 83
Van Landingham, W. P., 177
Vaughn, C. E., 101
Vealey, R. S., 141, 142, 146
Vermilyea, J. A., 91
Veronen, L. J., 169, 172, 177, 180, 181
Villeponteaux, L. A., 169
Vissia, E., 87
Vivian, D., 103, 110
Von, J. M., 181

Wachtel, P. L., 8
Wackman, D. B., 117
Waddington, J. L., 125
Wagner, E. F., 64
Wagner, K. D., 39
Wallander, J. L., 85
Ward, C. H., 52
Waring, E. M., 117
Waterhouse, G. J., 43
Watson, J. B., 7
Weinberg, L., 89
Weinberg, R. S., 141, 142, 143, 144, 145,
    146, 151, 152, 153, 155, 157
Weinberg, W. A., 31
Weiss, B., 27, 28
Weiss, D. S., 171
Weiss, M., 157
Weiss, R. L., 107
Weissman, M. M., 37, 43, 52, 100, 101,
    116
Weissman, M. W., 57, 76
Weisz, J. R., 27, 28, 60
Welker, R., 109
Wells, V., 30
Wessells, M. G., 18
Westen, D., 63
Weston, R. E., 126
Whelan, J. P., 137, 138, 140, 141, 144,
    146, 147, 149, 151, 153, 155, 157, 159
Whisman, M. A., 103
Whitaker, A., 30, 34
White, K. D., 142, 151
White, P. A., 170

White, R. W., 167
Whitehead, A. N., 6
Whittrock, D. A., 146
Whybrow, P. C., 37
Wichman, H., 142
Widiger, T. A., 79
Wiggins, D. K., 139
Wilensky, M., 125, 131
Wilkes, T. C. R., 40, 52, 58, 59
Will, G. F., 138
Williams, M. H., 152
Williams, T., 167
Williams, W., 178
Williamson, K., 143
Wilson, A. E., 181
Wilson, G. T., 6, 8, 85, 125, 133
Wilson, T. G., 6
Wilson, W. P., 167, 174
Wincze, J. P., 125
Winfield, I., 169
Wing, R. R., 146
Winget, C., 169
Winkler, R., 125
Winnett, R. L., 40
Withers, L. D., 31
Wittrock, D. A., 144
Wlazlo, Z., 84, 88, 95
Wolberg, L., 7
Wolf, F. M., 147, 148
Wolf, M. M., 7
Wolfe, B. E., 173, 177
Wolman, B., 7
Wolpe, J., 6, 9, 126, 172, 177, 178, 182, 183
Woods, M. G., 170, 179
Woolfolk, R. L., 140, 142, 143, 152
Wraith, S. C., 141
Wright, K. R., 99
Wrisberg, C. A., 146
Wulfert, E., 21
Wunder, J., 34
Wynne, L. C., 172

Yardley, K., 82
Yeaton, W. H., 153
Yerkes, R. M., 143
Yule, W., 82

Zakin, D., 34
Zax, M., 176
Zeiss, A., 38, 58
Zeiss, T., 41
Zettle, R. D., 17
Ziegler, S. G., 143, 152, 153, 155
Zimbardo, P. D., 75
Zimering, R. T., 172, 173, 177, 178
Zollo, L., 77
Zuriff, G., 14

SUBJECT INDEX

AABT. *See* Association for the Advancement of Behavior Therapy
ABC paradigm
  contingency-shaped behavior and, 14
  problems with, 10–12
  thought-behavior relationship and, 18–20
  verbal behavior and, 14–16
Acceptance and commitment therapy (ACT), 20–21
Adolescent Coping With Depression course (CWDA), 26, 41–42, 52, 61, 62
Adolescent depression. *See also* Adolescents; Depression
  case studies on, 45, 46–51
  clinical characteristics of, 30–33
  critique of treatments for, 60–64
  defined, 28–29
  developmental factors in, 33–34, 59, 63
  epidemiology of, 30
  etiological factors in, 38–39, 62, 63
  future of treatments for, 60–64
  mental health services and, 34–35, 64
  models of treatment for, 39–44
  pharmacologic treatment for, 44–45, 63
  phenomenology of, 29–30
  prevention of, 57–58
  psychosocial correlates and antecedents of, 33
  psychotherapy for, 38–44, 45–55
  suicidal behavior and, 55–57
  treatment outcome research on, 44–55
  treatment tactics for, 58–60
Adolescents. *See also* Adolescent depression; Children
  psychotherapy research on, 26–28
  suicidal behavior among, 55–57, 126
Aerobic exercise program, 57
African Americans, 124
Aggressive behavior, 102–103
AIDS, 126, 130
Alcohol abuse. *See* Substance abuse
Alprazolam, 94
Altering attentional focus, 152
American Psychiatric Association, 127, 134, 167
American Psychological Association, 127, 134, 140
Amitriptyline, 44, 184
Anaclitic depression, 43
Analysis of variance (ANOVA), 149
Anhedonia, 35
Animal model, behavior therapy and, 6–7
Antidepressant medications
  for adolescents, 44–45, 63
  for marital-discord depression, 117

Anxiety disorders. *See also* Posttraumatic stress disorder; Social phobia
  adolescent depression and, 31
  cognitive interventions for, 88–94
  exposure treatment and, 85–88
  in lesbians and gay men, 131
  personality disorders and, 79
  situational, 79–80
  social skills training and, 81–85
  sport psychology and, 143–144
Anxiety management training
  social phobia and, 86, 91, 95
  sport psychology and, 143–144, 152, 154
Anxiolytic medications, 86
APD. *See* Avoidant personality disorder
Applied relaxation, 83, 95
Arbitrary reinforcement, defined, 8
Arousal management, 143–144, 145, 152
Assertiveness skills, 125, 131
Association for the Advancement of Applied Sport Psychology (AAASP), 140
Association for the Advancement of Behavior Therapy (AABT), 2, 125, 126, 127, 134, 139
Associative therapy, 86
Athletes, elite, 157–158
Athletic Congress, 138
Athletic performance enhancement. *See* Sport psychology
Athletic personality, 139
Attention-placebo approach, 53, 92–93, 94
Attributions, 33, 36, 105
Australian Journal of Science and Medicine in Sport, The, 147
Automaticity, 139
Automatic negative thoughts (ATs), 92
Aversive therapy, 125, 126, 172
Avoidance strategies, 172–173
Avoidant personality disorder (APD)
  diagnostic criteria for, 76, 78–79
  generalized social phobia and, 78–79

Basal therapy, 86
Battle fatigue, 166
Battle neurosis, 166
Beck Depression Inventory (BDI), 52, 53, 101
Behavior. *See also specific type of behavior*
  beliefs and, 20
  thinking as, 18–20
Behavioral avoidance test (BAT), 179
Behavioral conversion therapy, 125, 126
Behavioral marital therapy (BMT), 100, 114–117

Behavioral premarital intervention (BPI), 117–118
Behavioral problem-solving (BPS), 54
Behavioral reactors, 83–84
Behavior therapy (BT). *See also* Cognitive-behavioral therapy; Cognitive therapy
  for adolescent depression, 39–41
  for adult depression, 36
  functional analysis of, 4–7
  historical contexts of, 7–9
  for lesbians and gay men, 124–127, 131–134
  for marital depression, 105–118
  outpatient treatments in, 9–10
  for posttraumatic stress disorder, 176–177
  therapeutic relationship in, 5–7
Behavior Therapy, 139
Beliefs
  behavior and, 20
  social phobia and, 88–89
Bellevue Index of Depression (BID), 54
Bias in Psychotherapy with Lesbians and Gay Men (Committee on Lesbian and Gay Concerns), 126
Bibliotherapy, 131
Biobehavioral model of depression, 37
Biofeedback training, 143, 152, 177
Biological correlates of posttraumatic stress disorder, 174–175
  exposure therapy and, 179–180, 182, 184
Booster sessions, 111
Boulder Model, 167
BT. *See* Behavior therapy

Canadian Journal of Applied Sport Science, The, 147
Caring gestures, 107–108
Case studies
  on adolescent depression, 45, 46–51
  on posttraumatic stress disorder, 177–183
Catharsis, 176, 183
Cause and effect relations, 2, 15
CBT. *See* Cognitive-behavioral therapy
Ceiling effect, 118
Center for Epidemiological Studies—Depression Scale (CES—D), 57
Center for Stress and Anxiety Disorders, 75
Child custody, sexual orientation and, 133
Children. *See also* Adolescents
  posttraumatic stress disorder in, 174, 183
  psychotherapy research on, 26–28, 65
Children's Depression Inventory (CDI), 53, 54
Children's Depression Rating Scale, 53

Circumscribed social phobia, 76–77
Civil rights movements, 124–125
Classical conditioning, 172
Classroom control approach, 53
Client-therapist relationship. *See* Therapeutic relationship
Clinical syndromes, personality disorders vs., 78
Cognitive-behavioral group therapy (CBGT), 92–94
Cognitive-behavioral therapy (CBT). *See also* Behavior therapy; Cognitive therapy
　for adolescent depression, 39–40, 41–42, 45, 54, 62, 63
　for marital-discord depression, 117–118
　for posttraumatic stress disorder, 177, 181
　for social phobia, 77, 88, 90–94, 95–96
　in sport psychology, 140–146
　for suicidal adolescents, 56
Cognitive manipulation, 19–20
Cognitive products, 12
Cognitive reactors, 83–84, 89–90
Cognitive restructuring (CR)
　for adolescent depression, 53, 58
　for posttraumatic stress disorder, 177
　for social phobia, 85–86, 87–88, 90–92, 94
　in sport psychology, 144, 152
Cognitive self-disclosure, 117
Cognitive self-regulation, 144–145, 152–153
Cognitive structures
　contingency-shaped behavior and, 17–18
　defined, 12
Cognitive therapy (CT). *See also* Behavior therapy; Cognitive-behavioral therapy
　ABC paradigm and, 10–12, 14–16, 18–20
　for adolescent depression, 39–41, 42, 52
　for adult depression, 36
　contingency-shaped behavior and, 13–14, 17–18
　functional analysis of, 10–20
　for lesbians and gay men, 131, 132
　for marital-discord depression, 112–115
　revised formulation of, 12–13
　for social phobia, 82, 87, 88–94, 95
　thought-behavior relationship and, 18–20
　verbal behavior and, 14–16
Cohesion, marital therapy and, 107–108
Combat exhaustion, 166
Coming-out issues, 128
Communication skills training
　adolescent depression and, 42
　marital-depression therapy and, 108–109
Comorbidity
　adolescent depression and, 31, 45, 52, 60
　posttraumatic stress disorder and, 170
　social phobia, 82
Companionship activities, 107
Compensation neurosis, 166

Competitive performance, 138–139, 156
Conditioning models, 172–174, 183
Conduct disorders, 31, 32
Confiding relationship, 101
Context characteristics, 156
Contextualism, 3–4
Contingency-shaped behavior
　cognitive structures and, 17–18
　reinforcement and, 13–14
　verbal behavior and, 14–16
Controlled outcome studies
　on adolescent depression, 52–53
　on posttraumatic stress disorder, 178–183
Conversion therapy, 125, 126
Coping imagery, 143, 176
Counseling, 180
Covert rehearsal, 139
CR. *See* Cognitive restructuring
Crisis intervention therapy (CIT), 55
CT. *See* Cognitive therapy
CWDA. *See* Adolescent Coping With Depression course

DD. *See* Dysthymic disorder
Decline phase, 171
Deep structures, 12
Demoralization, 57
Denial phase, 171
Depersonalization, 85
Depression. *See also* Adolescent depression
　cognitive therapy and, 112–113
　efficacy of psychotherapy for, 37–38
　inpatient outcome work and, 117
　marital discord and, 100–104
　marital therapy for, 105–111
　outcomes of marital interventions for, 113–117
　outpatient outcome work and, 114–117
　posttraumatic stress disorder and, 170, 184
　prevention of, 117–118
　social skills training and, 112
　spousal interaction and, 101–103
　suicidal behavior and, 55–57
　theories and models of treatment for, 36–37
　types of, 28–29
Depression Adjective Checklist, 113
Depression Awareness, Recognition, and Treatment (DART) program, 61
Depressive behavior, 102–103
Desensitization, systematic, 81–82, 84, 94, 95, 178, 181
Desensitization therapy using free association, 181
Developmental issues, depression and, 33–34
Diagnostic and Statistical Manual of Mental Disorders (DSM-III/DSM-III-R)
　on adolescent depression, 28, 52, 53, 55, 57
　on avoidant personality disorder, 76, 78–79

Diagnostic and Statistical Manual of Mental Disorders (continued)
　on posttraumatic stress disorder, 167–168
　on social phobia, 75–76, 78–79, 80–82, 85
Diagnostic Interview Schedule, 170
Dialectical behavior therapy (DBT), 56–57
Differential self-monitoring, 144
Direct behavior training, 112
Disaster victims, 169
Discordance, 102–103
Discrimination, sexual-orientation, 129–130
Dissociation, 85
Divorce, 101
Double depression, 29, 31
Drug abuse. *See* Substance abuse
DSM-III/DSM-III-R. See *Diagnostic and Statistical Manual of Mental Disorders*
Dyadic Adjustment Scale (DAS), 107, 114, 115, 116
Dyadic treatment, 113–114
Dysathesia aethiopica, 124
Dysthymic disorder (DD)
　in adolescents, 29–32, 62
　defined, 29

Ecological validity, 155
Effect-size (ES) analysis, 27, 117–118, 148–153, 155–157
Elite athletes, 157–158
EMG-assisted desensitization, 178
Emotional development, adolescent depression and, 33–34
Empathy skills, 109
Empiricism, 8–9
Epidemiology
　of adolescent depression, 30
　of posttraumatic stress disorder, 168–170
Erotophobia, 131
Etiological factors
　in adolescent depression, 38–39, 62, 63
　in marital-discord depression, 104
　in posttraumatic stress disorder, 170, 175–176, 184–185
Exposure plus anxiety management (EX/AM), 86–87
Exposure therapy
　for posttraumatic stress disorder, 176–181, 183–184
　for social phobia, 85–88, 91–92, 94, 95
　therapist guidance in, 86–87
Expressed emotion (EE) dyads, 102
External homophobia, 128
Extinction, 172–173, 183, 184
Eye movement desensitization (EMD), 177, 182
Eye movement desensitization and reprocessing (EMD/R), 177, 181–183

Face value history, 4
Family therapy
  for adolescent depression, 44, 45, 61
  inpatient family intervention and, 117
  in sport psychology, 158
  for suicidal adolescents, 56
Fear gradient, 172
Fears. *See also* Anxiety disorders; Post-
    traumatic stress disorder; Social phobia
  extinction of, 172–173
Feedback skills, 109
First International Congress of Sport Psy-
    chology, 139
Flooding, imaginal, 82, 173, 177, 178–
    179, 181–182
Flow, in sports, 139
Fluoxetine, 44
Formal analysis, 9–10
Free association therapy, 181
Functional analysis
  alternative approaches to, 8–9
  behavior therapy and, 4–7
  cognitive therapy and, 10–20
  defined, 2–4
  formal analysis and, 9–10
  new types of, 20–21
Functional analytic psychotherapy (FAP),
    20–21

Gay and Lesbian Community Center of
    Colorado, 130
Gay men
  assessment and case formulation for,
    129–131
  cultural and institutional context for,
    128–130
  evolution of behavior therapy for, 132–
    134
  history of behavior therapy with, 124–
    127
  percentage of population as, 124
  social bias against, 124, 126, 127, 128–
    130, 132, 133–134
  treatment for, 131–132
Gender
  adolescent depression and, 30, 33–34,
    63
  sexual-orientation discrimination and,
    129–130, 133–134
Generalizability, of research, 155–157
Generalized social phobia (GSP)
  avoidant personality disorder and, 78–
    79
  defined, 80–81
  described, 76–78
Goal setting
  social phobia and, 92
  in sport psychology, 140–142, 150–151
Government discrimination, 129
Graded exposure. *See* Systematic desensi-
    tization
Group exposure (GE), 84, 88

Group therapy
  for adolescent depression, 39, 45, 63–
    64
  for suicidal adolescents, 55–56
GSP. *See* Generalized social phobia
Guerney's Relationship Enhancement Pro-
    gram, 117
Guided self-dialog, 177

Hate crimes, 130
"Heat," therapeutic, 21
Heterosexuality
  conversion therapy and, 125
  social bias for, 128–129, 132, 133–
    134
HIV-related literature, 125–126
Homophobia, 128, 129, 131
Homosexuals. *See* Gay men; Lesbians
Hypnosis, 152, 176
Hypnotherapy, 180
Hypothesis testing, 40

Imagery-based relaxation, 152
Imagery-induced anxiety, 89, 91
Imaginal exposure therapy, 178
Imaginal flooding, 82, 173, 177, 178–179,
    181–182
Imaginal rehearsal, 142–143, 145, 151–152
Imipramine (IMI), 44
Impact level measurements, 61
Implosive therapy, 177–178, 181
Individual exposure (IE), 84
Individual interpersonal psychotherapy
    (IPT), 116
Information processing theory, 171, 174
Inpatient family intervention (IFI), 117
Inpatient therapies, 117
Integrative model of depression, 37
Interaction anxieties, 80
Internal avoidance, 85
Internalized homophobia, 128, 129, 131,
    132, 134
*International Journal of Sport Psychology,
    The*, 147
Interpersonal psychotherapy (IPT)
  for adolescent depression, 43, 45, 52
  for adult depression, 64
Introjective depression, 43
Intrusiveness phase, 171
In vitro flooding, 183
IPT. *See* Interpersonal psychotherapy
Irrational beliefs, 88–89, 92

Journal of Applied Sport Psychology, 139–140
Journal of Sport and Exercise Psychology,
    139, 147
Journal of Sport Behavior, 147

Laws, sexual-orientation discrimination,
    129, 130
Learning disorders, 31
Learning theories, 172–173, 183

Lesbians
  assessment and case formulation for,
    129–131
  cultural and institutional context for,
    128–130
  evolution of behavior therapy for, 132–
    134
  history of behavior therapy with, 124–
    127
  percentage of population as, 124
  social bias against, 124, 126, 127, 128–
    130, 132, 133–134
  treatment for, 131–132
Levels of treatment approach, 40
Liebowitz Social Anxiety Scale (LSAS),
    79–80
Life Table results, 57, 58
Limited-interactional subtype, 80
Listener skills, 108–109
Little League baseball, 138

Major depressive disorder (MDD)
  in adolescents, 29–32, 62
  defined, 28–29
Manding-to-self, 14–16
Mands
  contingency-shaped behavior and, 14–16
  defined, 13, 14
  rule-governed behavior and, 17
Marital-depression therapy
  eliminating stressors with, 106–108
  enhancing communication with, 108–
    109
  increasing cohesion with, 107–108
  individual approaches to, 111–113
  maintaining gains from, 110–111
  outcomes of, 113–117
  overview of, 105–106
  problem solving through, 110
  studies on, 113–114
Marital discord
  cognitive therapy and, 112–113, 114–
    115
  depression and, 100–104
  marital-depression therapy and, 105–
    111, 114–117
  model of depression overview, 104–
    105
  observational studies of, 101–103
  programs for decreasing, 117–118
  social skills training and, 112
MDD. *See* Major depressive disorder
Meaning concepts, 174
Medications. *See also* Pharmacologic
    treatment
  antidepressant, 44–45, 63, 117
  anxiolytic, 86
  psychotropic, 184
Men at Work (Will), 138
Mental health services, 34–35, 64
Mental rehearsal, 139, 142–143, 151–152
Meta-analysis, 146–148, 159

Minnesota Couples Communication Program, 117
Minority groups, adolescent depression in, 64
Modeling, 177
Monoamine oxidase inhibitors (MAOIs), 45, 78
Multicomponent interventions, 145–146, 153
Multidimensional developmental psychotherapy (MDP), 63

National Association of Social Workers, 134
National Bowling Council, 138
National Golf Foundation, 138
National Sporting Goods Association, 138
National Vietnam Veterans Readjustment Survey (NVVRS), 170
Natural reinforcement, 8
Negative cognitions, 88–89, 92–93
Negative evaluations, 88, 95–96
Negative interactions, 106–107
Negotiation skills training, 42
Neutralization, 176
NIMH Collaborative Study of the Treatment of Depression, 37
NIMH Epidemiologic Catchment Area program database, 168
Nongeneralized social phobia, 77
North American Society for the Psychology of Sport and Physical Activity, 139
Nortriptyline (NTP), 44
Numbing experience, 173, 178

Observational studies, of marital discord, 101–104
Obsessive-compulsive disorder, 31
Olympic Training Center (OTC), 158
Ontario Child Health Study (OCHS), 30
Operant conditioning, 7, 172
Oral sex laws, 129
Oregon Research Institute, 102
Outcome work
    with depressed inpatients, 117
    with depressed outpatients, 114–117
    dyadic treatment and, 113–114
Outpatient therapies
    described, 9–10
    marital depression and, 114–117

Pain threshold, 175
Parasuicidal individuals, 56–57
Parents
    depressed, 58
    disclosure of sexual orientation to, 128, 132
    involvement in CWDA course by, 42
Parents and Friends of Lesbians and Gays, 132
Path analysis, 33

Peer befriender group, 55
Performance anxiety, 78
Performance subtype, 80
Personality disorders. *See also specific type of disorder*
    adolescent depression and, 31
    anxiety disorders and, 79
    clinical syndromes vs., 78
Pharmacologic treatment. *See also* Medications
    for adolescent depression, 44–45
    for posttraumatic stress disorder, 184
    for social phobia, 77, 82–83, 94
Phenelzine, 77, 78, 94
Phenomenology, of adolescent depression, 29–30
Phobias. *See* Social phobia
Physical development, adolescent depression and, 33–34
Physician and Sportmedicine, 147
Physiological reactors, 83, 89–90
Pill-placebo approach, 94
Platoon (film), 175
Pleasant activity training, 41–42
Pleasant events schedule (PES), 41–42
Positive imagery, 176, 177
Posttraumatic stress disorder (PTSD). *See also* Anxiety disorders
    in children, 174, 183
    codiagnoses and, 170
    conceptual models of, 171–176
    defined, 167–168
    early terminology for, 166–167
    epidemiology of, 168–170
    in females, 168–170
    pharmacotherapy for, 184
    treatment strategies for, 176–184
Practice, social skills, 112
Premarital Relationship Enhancement Program (PREP), 117–118
Problem-solving skills
    adolescent depression and, 42, 56
    marital-discord depression and, 103, 110
Problem-solving techniques training, 42, 56
Progressive relaxation, 152
Psychodynamic therapy
    for adolescent depression, 43–44, 61–62, 63
    adolescent psychotherapy research on, 27–28
    for posttraumatic stress disorder, 171, 180
Psychoeducational interventions, 131
Psychological Abstracts, 147
Psychopathology, social biases and, 124, 134
Psychophysiological correlates of posttraumatic stress disorder, 174–175
    exposure therapy and, 179–180, 182, 184

Psychosocial impairment, 31–32
Psychotherapy
    for adolescent depression, 38–44, 45–55, 58–60
    adult depression and, 37–38
    interpersonal, 43
    by reciprocal inhibition, 9
    research on adolescents, 26–28
Psychotropic medications, 184
Psych-up effect, 143–144
PTSD. *See* Posttraumatic stress disorder
Puberty, adolescent depression and, 33–34

Quest, 147

Radical behaviorism, 2, 15
Rape victims. *See* Sexual assault victims
Rapid eye movement (REM), 182–183
Rascality, 124
Rational-emotive therapy (RET), 83–84, 85, 87, 88–89, 94
Rational self-talk, 91
Recurrence. *See* Relapse
Reformulated Learned Helplessness Theory (RLHT), 36
Reframing, 176
Regression analysis, 77
Reinforcement
    animal model of, 7–8
    cognitive structures and, 18
    contingency-shaped behavior and, 13–14
    defined, 3
    functional analysis and, 3–4
    verbal behavior and, 14–16
Rejection sensitivity, 78
Relapse
    of adolescent depression, 32–33, 61
    of marital-discord depression, 103–104, 110
Relaxation therapy
    for adolescent depression, 41, 54
    for posttraumatic stress disorder, 171, 177, 178, 181
    for social phobia, 83, 86, 91, 95
    in sport psychology, 143, 152, 154
Repression, 166
Research Quarterly, 147
Residual functioning, 32
Respondent conditioning, 7
RET. *See* Rational-emotive therapy
Retarded ejaculation, 125
Reynolds Adolescent Depression Scale (RADS), 53–54
Role playing
    adolescent depression and, 40, 53
    marital-depression therapy and, 109
    social phobia and, 83, 87, 91, 92, 95
Rule-governed behavior, 17

Schedule for Affective Disorders and Schizophrenia for School-Aged Children (K-SADS), 29, 30

Schemas, 12
Schizophrenia, 170
School-based clinics, 64
Science, values and, 124
SCT. *See* Self-control therapy
SD. *See* Systematic desensitization
Self-concept, 34
Self-control desensitization (SCD), 89, 95
Self-control therapy (SCT)
    for adolescent depression, 40, 54
    adult depression and, 36–37
Self-evaluation training, 112
Self-instructional training (SIT), 87, 89–
    90, 94, 145, 152
Self-monitoring strategies, 144–145, 152–
    153, 154
Self-reinforcement training, 112
Separation anxiety disorder, 31
Serial cue hierarchy, 173
Sex therapy, 131
Sexual assault victims
    controlled studies of, 180–181
    posttraumatic stress disorder among,
        169, 177, 178, 180–181
Sexual behavior
    high-risk, 126
    of lesbians and gay men, 132
Sexual dysfunction
    marital-discord depression and, 110
    view of homosexuality as, 127
Sexual orientation
    child custody and, 133
    disclosure of, 131
    social bias and, 124, 126, 127, 128–130,
        132, 133–134
Shell shock, 166
Short Marital Adjustment Test (SMAT), 101
Shyness, 75, 77
SIT. *See* Self-instructional training
Situational anxiety, 79–80
Social biases
    against lesbians and gay men, 124, 126,
        127, 128–130, 132, 133–134
    psychopathology and, 124, 134
Social functioning
    adolescent depression and, 31–32
    of lesbians and gay men, 131
    suicidal behavior and, 56
Social Interaction Anxiety Scale (SIAS),
    77
Social perception training, 112
Social phobia. *See also* Anxiety disorders
    adolescent depression and, 31
    avoidant personality disorder and, 78–79
    cognitive interventions for, 88–94
    diagnostic criteria for, 76, 78–79
    exposure treatment and, 85–88
    pharmacotherapeutic treatment for, 77,
        82–83, 94
    situationist perspective on, 79–80
    social skills training and, 81–85
    subtypes of, 76–78, 80–81, 95

Social Phobia Scale (SPS), 77
Social problem-solving therapy, 56
Social skills deficit, 84, 95
Social skills group (SSG), 54–55
Social skills training (SST)
    for adolescent depression, 39, 42, 54–55
    for lesbians and gay men, 131
    for marital-discord depression, 112
    as outpatient therapy, 9–10
    for social phobia, 81–85, 90–91, 92, 94, 95
Socratic method, 20
Sodomy laws, 129
Soldier's heart, 166
Speaker skills, 109
Speaking anxieties, 80
Specifying level measurements, 61
Sport Psychologist, The, 139, 147
Sport psychology
    arousal management and, 143–144, 152
    cognitive self-regulation and, 144–145,
        152–153
    criticism of studies in, 153–155
    effectiveness of, 148–153
    elite athletes and, 157–158
    generalizability of studies in, 155–157
    goal setting strategies and, 140–142,
        150–151
    history of, 138–140
    imagery and mental rehearsal strategies
        and, 142–143, 151–152
    multicomponent interventions and, 145–
        146, 153
    quantitative review of, 146–157
    scope of, 138
SST. *See* Social skills training
Standard deviation (SD), 31
States of Mind (SOM) model, 93
Stereotypes, lesbian and gay, 128, 132
Stimulus narrowing technique, 183
Stress inoculation training, 125, 131, 143,
    153, 177, 180–181
Stress management training, 153, 171
Stressors
    marital depression and, 105, 106–108
    posttraumatic stress disorder and, 185
Stress response syndrome, 171
Subject characteristics, 157
Subjective units of disturbance (SUDs),
    182
Substance abuse
    adolescent depression and, 31
    posttraumatic stress disorder and, 170, 184
Substitution technique, 176
Suicidal behavior
    adolescent depression and, 55–57
    among lesbians and gay men, 126, 129
*Suicide Risk: Assessment and Response Guide-
    lines* (Fremouw, de Perczel, & Ellis), 126
Summarizing skills, 109
Supportive counseling, 180
Supportive therapy (ST), 86
Suppression effect, 102–103

Surface structures, 12
Survivor guilt, 166
Symptom Checklist-90-Revised, 57
Systematic desensitization (SD), 81–82,
    84, 94, 95, 178, 181
Systematic rational restructuring (SRR),
    89, 95

Tacting-to-self, 14–16, 17
Tacts
    contingency-shaped behavior and, 14–16
    defined, 13, 14
    rule-governed behavior and, 17
Talk therapy, 171
Team sports, 155–156
Therapeutic relationship
    adolescent depression and, 59–60
    in behavior therapy, 5–7
    cognitive therapy and, 10–12, 17–20
    "heat" in, 21
    historical contexts of, 7–9
    with lesbian/gay clients, 132–134
    outpatient treatments in, 9–10
    posttraumatic stress disorder and, 171
    social biases and, 124, 133–134
Therapeutic support group (TSG), 54–55
Therapist-directed prolonged exposure
    (EXP), 86–87
Thinking
    as behavior, 18–20
    irrational, 88–89, 92
Thought stopping, 176, 177, 181
Thunderstorm phobia, 177
Time-out-for-worry procedure, 183
Trauma. *See* Posttraumatic stress disorder
Trauma desensitization therapy, 180
Traumatic hysteria, 176
Traumatic neurosis, 166–167, 178
Treatment reception, 154
Tricyclic antidepressants (TCAs), 44–45
Two-factor theory, 172, 173, 176

Uncontrolled outcome studies, 177–178
Unipolar affective disorder, 52, 57, 112
United States Cycling Federation, 138
United States Masters Swimming, Inc., 138
United States Tennis Association, 138

Values, therapy and, 124
Verbal behavior
    contingency-shaped behavior and, 14–16
    rule-governed behavior and, 17
Verbal Behavior (Skinner), 6, 8, 14
VETs scale, 179
Vietnam veterans
    case studies of, 177–179
    posttraumatic stress disorder among,
        168, 169–170, 177–179
Visuo-motor behavior rehearsal (VMBR),
    145–146, 153, 154, 155

War neurosis, 166–167